The Old Testament in Byzantium

Dumbarton Oaks Byzantine Symposia and Colloquia

Series Editor
Margaret Mullett

Editorial Board
John Duffy
John Haldon
Ioli Kalavrezou

Exaltation of David, Paris Psalter, Paris, Bibl. Nat. gr. 139, fol. 7v.

The Old Testament in Byzantium

Edited by Paul Magdalino *and* Robert Nelson

DUMBARTON OAKS RESEARCH LIBRARY AND COLLECTION

Copyright © 2010 by Dumbarton Oaks
Trustees for Harvard University, Washington, D.C.
All rights reserved.
Printed in the United States of America by Sheridan Books, Inc.

Second cloth printing, first paperback printing, 2013.

LIBRARY OF CONGRESS CATALOGING-IN-PUBLICATION DATA

The Old Testament in Byzantium /
edited by Paul Magdalino and Robert S. Nelson.
p. cm. — (Dumbarton Oaks Byzantine Symposia and Colloquia)
Includes bibliographical references and index.
ISBN 978-0-88402-348-7 (cloth : alk. paper)
ISBN 978-0-88402-399-9 (paperback : alk. paper)
1. Bible O.T.—Criticism, interpretation, etc.—Byzantine Empire—Congresses.
2. Theology—Byzantine Empire—Congresses.
I. Magdalino, Paul. II. Nelson, Robert S., 1947–
BS1171.3.043   2010
221.09495'0902—dc22
                                                                    2009020763

Designed and typeset by Barbara Haines

Cover and frontispiece illustration: Exaltation of David,
Paris Psalter, Paris, Bibl. Nat. gr. 139, fol. 7v.

www.doaks.org/publications

CONTENTS

Acknowledgments vii

ONE • Introduction 1
PAUL MAGDALINO *and* ROBERT NELSON

TWO • The Greek Bible Translations of the Byzantine Jews 39
NICHOLAS DE LANGE

THREE • The Prophetologion:
The Old Testament of Byzantine Christianity? 55
JAMES MILLER

FOUR • Psalters and Personal Piety in Byzantium 77
GEORGI R. PARPULOV

FIVE • Illustrated Octateuch Manuscripts:
A Byzantine Phenomenon 107
JOHN LOWDEN

SIX • Old Testament "History" and the Byzantine Chronicle 153
ELIZABETH JEFFREYS

SEVEN • Old Testament Models for Emperors in Early Byzantium 175
CLAUDIA RAPP

EIGHT • The Old Testament and Monasticism 199
DEREK KRUEGER

NINE • New Temples and New Solomons:
The Rhetoric of Byzantine Architecture 223
ROBERT OUSTERHOUT

TEN • Old Testament Models and the State in Early Medieval Bulgaria 255
IVAN BILIARSKY

ELEVEN • Connecting Moses and Muḥammad 279
JANE DAMMEN MCAULIFFE

Abbreviations 299
About the Authors 303
Index 307

ACKNOWLEDGMENTS

The major renovations at Dumbarton Oaks from 2003 to 2008 prompted Alice-Mary Talbot, then Director of Byzantine Studies, to explore other venues and other times for symposia and colloquia. Early in this period plans were afoot to hold a major exhibit of Bible manuscripts at the Freer Gallery of Art, which holds a small but important collection of early Greek Bible manuscripts, seldom seen in public. The planned exhibition inspired Dr. Talbot to form an alliance with the Freer and Sackler Galleries, to hold a concomitant symposium on the Bible. Paul Magdalino and Robert Nelson, Senior Fellows of Dumbarton Oaks, continued the planning of that symposium with Dr. Talbot's help. The Freer's impressive exhibit, "In the Beginning: Bibles Before the Year 1000," displayed more than threescore early manuscripts of the Bible, in many languages, loaned from collections around the world. The Dumbarton Oaks symposium, "The Old Testament in Byzantium," held 1–3 December 2006 in the Meyer Auditorium of the Freer Gallery, shared in the success of that exhibit, and has resulted in this eponymous volume.

As always, Dr. Talbot was gracious and efficient in shepherding the papers delivered at that symposium into the published material that makes up the volume in hand. We are grateful for her aid in this and so many other scholarly endeavors in the past. We also wish to remember the hospitality of the Freer and the Sackler and Dr. Ann Gunter, then the Curator of Ancient Near Eastern Art and Head of Scholarly Publications and Programs at the Galleries, and to thank the staff of the Publications Department at DO for their meticulous care in converting talk into print.

This is the second volume in the series Dumbarton Oaks Byzantine Symposia and Colloquia. The first, published in 2009, was *Becoming Byzantine: Children and Childhood in Byzantium*, edited by Alice-Mary Talbot and Arietta Papaconstantinou. Other volumes in progress include *San Marco, Byzantium, and the Myths of Venice* (edited by Henry Maguire and Robert Nelson), and *Trade and Markets in Byzantium* (edited by Cécile Morrisson).

Paul Magdalino
Robert Nelson

ONE

Introduction

Paul Magdalino *and* Robert Nelson

Μωσέα τὸν μέγαν οὐ λάβεν εἰς τύπον ἄρκιον οὐδείς

Byzantine Christianity has been studied in great depth in all its manifestations, from high theology to the simple, mechanical piety of formulaic prayers inscribed on cheap pectoral crosses. Yet the Bible, the foundation of all Christian belief, has never previously been the focus of any monograph, journal, handbook, volume of collected studies, conference, or exhibition devoted to Byzantium. Such apparent neglect is perhaps not surprising, if we take the view that the importance of the Bible in any Christian culture is self-evident, and that the ubiquity of the Bible in all Christian worship both inhibits meaningful comment and makes the theme very difficult to isolate for coherent historical presentation or discussion. The slightest acquaintance with Byzantium is sufficient to reveal that the Bible was everywhere we would expect it to be. Its exegesis by the Fathers ran to dozens of volumes. Manuscripts containing various divisions of Scripture—Pentateuchs, Octateuchs, Psalters, Prophet books, Gospel books, and Epistles—were to be found in most if not all of the empire's myriad churches and monasteries, and in every household that could afford to own a book or two. No church or chapel could function without lectionaries of Bible readings for the daily offices, the Sunday Eucharists, and the festal calendar of the liturgical year. The Bible was cited in every conceivable milieu, in word and in image. Not only were hymns, prayers, homilies, theological tracts, ecclesiastical records, and religious paintings and inscriptions suffused with biblical

---

Epigraph: "No one has sufficiently taken great Moses into account as a model." John Geometres, *Prayer*, in *Jean Géomètre, poèmes en hexamètres et en distiques élégiaques*, ed. E. M. van Opstall (Leiden, 2008), no. 290, line 51.

allusions; the Bible was also quoted extensively in secular literature, official documents, and government propaganda. What more is there to say?

One answer is that, whereas exactly the same can be said of Western Christendom, we do have a number of books on the Bible in the Western Middle Ages[1] and on early Bibles,[2] but the *Bible in Byzantium* has yet to be written.[3] Another answer is that no two Christian churches use the Bible in exactly the same way, and their different usage is part of what makes them distinctive and worth studying. The authority of a literal, unmediated reading of Holy Scripture was notoriously a major point of contention at the Reformation, and the appropriateness of a literal reading is still a live issue in the debate over the content of the science curriculum taught in schools in some parts of the United States. At a less controversial level, the scriptural canon varies among major Christian traditions, and gains or loses variously in each different translation; each tradition has evolved its own selection and sequence of texts for liturgical reading, and trains its clergy in its own tradition of scriptural exegesis. These are all reasons why students of Byzantine religion can benefit from a sharper focus on the Bible in the Orthodox tradition. Moreover, while there is obviously a lot of common biblical ground that Byzantine Christianity shares with the Western traditions, the familiarity with the Bible text that was second nature to earlier generations of Byzantinists can no longer be taken for granted; thus, a visit to the common scriptural foundations on which Byzantine art and literature based their distinctive evolution is useful for the orientation of Byzantine studies in

---

1 E.g., B. Smalley, *The Study of the Bible in the Middle Ages* (Oxford, 1941); R. E. McNally, *The Bible in the Early Middle Ages* (Atlanta, 1959); W. Lourdaux and D. Verhelst, eds., *The Bible and Medieval Culture* (Leuven, 1979); P. Riché and G. Lobrichon, eds., *Le Moyen Âge et la Bible* (Paris, 1984); B. S. Levy, ed., *The Bible in the Middle Ages: Its Influence on Liturgy and Art* (Binghamton, NY, 1992); R. Gameson, ed., *The Early Medieval Bible: Its Production, Decoration, and Use* (New York, 1994).

2 Our symposium in Washington took place during an important exhibition of early Bibles from many cultures: M. Brown, ed., *In the Beginning: Bibles Before the Year 1000* (Washington, DC, 2006). Early Bibles, of necessity, are discussed in the broader survey edited by W. E. Klingshirn and L. Safran, *The Early Christian Book* (Washington, DC, 2007). A useful survey of illustrated early Bibles is J. Williams, ed., *Imaging the Early Medieval Bible* (University Park, PA, 1999).

3 There will, however, be an important survey of the medieval Bible manuscripts of eastern Christian communities by G. R. Parpulov, "The Bibles of the Christian East," forthcoming in R. Marsden and A. Matter, eds., *The New Cambridge History of the Bible*, vol. 2, *The Middle Ages*. One relevant set of decorated Byzantine Old Testament manuscripts that warrants further study is the so-called Bible of Niketas from the tenth century. First published under this name by H. Belting and G. Cavallo, *Die Bibel des Niketas: Ein Werk der höfischen Buchkunst in Byzanz und sein antikes Vorbild* (Wiesbaden, 1979), these manuscripts have been further considered by J. Lowden, "An Alternative Interpretation of the Manuscripts of Nicetas," *Byzantion* 53 (1983): 559–74.

the twenty-first century. At the same time, modern notions of the Scriptures, derived from printed or digitized editions of the whole Bible, are likely to distort our understanding—even if "we" are Orthodox—of the ways in which medieval Byzantines read, heard, recalled, and applied the sacred text. For believers then and now, the Bible message is timeless and divine, but actual readers are neither.

But where to begin, and how to circumscribe such a potentially vast and amorphous topic as the Bible in Byzantium? The solution adopted by the organizers of the 2006 symposium out of which this volume grew was to limit the topic to the Old Testament. This choice might seem surprising, since the New Testament is not only shorter and therefore more manageable, but also, being by definition exclusively Christian, was more central to Byzantine worship and belief and to the raison d'être of Byzantium as Christ's kingdom on earth. Yet for the culture and society of an earthly kingdom, the Old Testament was richer in tangible historical precedents. The New Testament promises personal salvation through individual belief in a master who transcends all social roles and institutions, as well as the division between humanity and divinity, because his kingdom is not of this world. The Old Testament, by contrast, tells the story and charts the destiny of a chosen people through the social, political, and ritual institutions by which they defined their collective special relationship with God, their exclusive separation from other peoples and empires, and their claim to a promised, holy land. For believers, the Old Testament is God's word—often his only or last word—on a variety of human experiences that God's people must undergo: warfare, inheritance, tyranny, captivity, exile, deliverance, pollution, purification, reward for obedience, and punishment for disobedience and apostasy. It also contains the divinely approved paradigms of the institutions by which God's people organize themselves to worship and obey him: law, charismatic leadership, kingship, priesthood, prophecy, the holy city of Jerusalem, sacred space (the Tabernacle and Temple), and sacred objects (the Ark of the Covenant). In addition to these models of social behavior and experience, the Old Testament provides, in Genesis, a world view and a creation myth; in the Psalms and the Song of Songs, it yields a rich, emotional poetry of penitence, supplication, and praise for individuals as well as groups to use for their private devotions. The New Testament's relations with contemporary society are different, because it was written partly to spiritualize and personalize, and partly to appropriate, the culture of the Old.

Also of particular interest for the cultural historian is the process of the Christianization of the Old Testament, or the ways in which it was appropriated and reconfigured by a Church that sharply diverged from the communities for which it was written and in which it continued to be read and revered for centuries. On the one hand, it originated and remained as the sacred text of the Children of Israel. On a literal and straightforward level, the Old Testament recorded their history and genealogy, laid down their law, and set out God's mandate, voiced through their patriarchs, kings, and prophets, for their ultimate possession of the promised land and the establishment of a Messianic kingdom. On the other hand, it became part one of the Christian Bible, which Christians, starting with the authors of the Gospels and St. Paul, interpreted as a prelude to and prefiguration of the Gospel story. Important persons, situations, literary images, and sacred objects in the Jewish Scriptures were construed as "types" of someone or something in the life of Christ and the mystery of the Incarnation; the Law of Moses was declared to have been made redundant by Christ's teaching, while the visions of the prophets concerning the Jews and the Messiah were all applied to Christ and the Church.[4] Thus, depending on how it was read and by whom, the Old Testament was for all Christian societies the most authoritative source of "native" wisdom and inspiration and, at the same time, the book that defined and enshrined the "otherness" of a distinct religious group that formed a disenfranchised and resented minority.

The tension between these two readings existed long before the foundation of Constantinople, and it affected all branches of the Christian Church, but it was particularly relevant to the Byzantine perception and reception of the Bible. Byzantium had a longer, closer, and more fraught relationship with the Jews than any other Christian community before the eleventh century.[5] The Septuagint, the Greek Old Testament adopted by the Church, had been translated by Jews for Jews in Alexandria before the advent of Christianity, and it continued to circulate in the Byzantine Jewish community along with the Hebrew and Aramaic texts and the other Greek translations, notably that of Akylas.[6] From the fourth century to the seventh, the Roman empire based in Constantinople was

---

4 See the classic discussion by M. Simon, *Verus Israel: Étude sur les relations entre chrétiens et juifs dans l'Empire romain* (Paris, 1948); also R. Ruether, *Faith and Fratricide: The Theological Roots of Anti-Semitism* (New York, 1974), chapters 2–3. For anti-Jewish literature in Byzantium set in the context of its late-antique background, with reference to older literature in German, see A. Külzer, *Disputationes Graecae contra Iudaeos: Untersuchungen zur byzantinischen antijudischen Dialogliteratur und ihrem Judenbild*, Byzantinisches Archiv 18 (Stuttgart–Leipzig, 1999).
5 See in general A. Sharf, *Byzantine Jewry from Justinian to the Fourth Crusade* (London, 1971); the collection of essays and text editions by G. Dagron and V. Déroche in *TM* 11 (1991): 18–380; and Av. Cameron, "Byzantines and Jews: Some Recent Work on Early Byzantium," *BMGS* 20 (1996): 249–74.
6 See Chapter 2, below.

responsible for a series of policies that had permanent and widespread effects on Jewish-Christian relations and entrenched both sides in their divergent interpretations of their common biblical heritage: the repressive legislation that turned Jews into second-class citizens;[7] the transformation of the land of Israel into a Christian holy land;[8] and Heraklios's attempt, in the aftermath of the empire's great war with Persia, to force the Jews to convert.[9]

Byzantine Judaism not only proved resilient to this oppression but also found new confidence in the seventh-century crisis of the Christian empire. The Jews welcomed first the Persian and then the Arab invasions, which on the whole improved the outlook for them.[10] The Islamic conquests deprived the Christian empire of most of its territory, including the Holy Land; they removed the Jews of Syria, Palestine, North Africa, and Spain from Christian domination, and seriously challenged the teleology of Christian universalism, along with the doctrine, on which this ideology was based, of the kingship and divinity of Jesus Christ, the ultimate fulfilment of the Law, the Prophets, and all sacred history. The appearance of a new, expansionist, starkly monotheist faith that advertised itself as the true heir to the Hebrew Bible, planting its own place of worship on the site of Solomon's Temple,[11] compromised Christianity's claim to have superseded Judaism, and created the hope that the outcome would ultimately vindicate the original keepers of the divine covenant.[12] The catastrophic reversals of the Christian Empire cast doubt on Christian interpretations of Old Testament apocalyptic texts, notably the Book of Daniel, and boosted Jewish expectations that these events presaged not the Second Coming of Christ but the first appearance of their own Anointed One.[13] At the same time, the clash of

---

7   *CTh* XVI 8.1, 5–7, 19, 22, 24–25, 27–29; XVI 9; Justinian, *Novel* 146; translations in A. Linder, ed., *The Jews in Roman Imperial Legislation* (Detroit–Jerusalem, 1987). For discussion, see, among others, Simon, *Verus Israel*, 155–62.
8   R. Wilken, *The Land Called Holy* (New Haven–London, 1992), chapters 5–10.
9   Sharf, *Byzantine Jewry*, 43–57; Dagron and Déroche, 28–38.
10 Sharf, *Byzantine Jewry*, 47–77; Wilken, *Land Called Holy*, chapter 10; Dagron and Déroche, 22–28, 38–43, 208–11 (*Doctrina Jacobi nuper baptizati* 5.16), 246–47.
11 See O. Grabar, *The Dome of the Rock* (Cambridge, MA, 2006); G. Fowden, *Empire to Commonwealth: Consequences of Monotheism in Late Antiquity* (Princeton, 1993), 143, 151, 158.
12 V. Déroche, "Polémique anti-judaïque et émergence de l'Islam (7e–8e siècles)," *REB* 57 (1999): 141–61.
13 See in addition W. J. van Bekkum, "Jewish Messianic Expectations in the Age of Heraclius," in *The Reign of Heraclius (610–641): Crisis and Confrontation*, ed. G. Reinink and B. H. Stolte (Leuven, 2002), 98–112; idem, "Four Kingdoms Will Rule: Echoes of Apocalypticism and Political Reality in Late Antiquity and Medieval Judaism," in *Endzeiten: Eschatologie in den monotheistischen Weltreligionen*, ed. W. Brandes and F. Schmieder, Millennium-Studien 16 (New York, 2008), 101–33, esp. 109–15.

empires encouraged the flourishing of heretical communities, some with pronounced judaizing tendencies, in Byzantium's deep frontier zone with Islam.[14] In these conditions, the Jews of the seventh to tenth centuries could argue their interpretation of Scripture with conviction, and the indications are that they did so not unsuccessfully. They continued to engage in debate with Christians,[15] who were sometimes at a loss for arguments, and in 861 they achieved the conversion of the ruling elite of a major steppe kingdom, the Khazars.[16] Eminent Byzantine churchmen, such as Maximos the Confessor,[17] Andrew of Crete,[18] Theodore Stoudites,[19] and the patriarch Photios,[20] wrote about the Jews with a virulence suggestive of more than literary and theological convention. Indeed, the fact that the Byzantine Jewish community endured, and survived, three further attempts at forced conversion—by Leo III in 721–22, by Basil I in 873–74, and by Romanos I in 931–32—demonstrates the continuing relevance of anti-Judaic polemics.[21] All this involved reading and rereading the books of the Old

14   P. Crone, "Islam, Judaeo-Christianity, and Byzantine Iconoclasm," *Jerusalem Studies in Arabic and Islam* 2 (1980): 59–95.

15   See, e.g., St. Constantine-Cyril's famous debate with Jews before the Khazar khagan: *Les légendes de Constantin et de Méthode vues de Byzance*, trans. F. Dvornik (Prague, 1933; 2nd ed. Hattiesburg, MS, 1969), 360–68; English, *The Vita of Constantine and the Vita of Methodius*, trans. M. Kantor and R. S. White (Ann Arbor, 1976), 11–13. See also Theodore Stoudites' letter to an abbot Auxentios, referring him to St. Basil's commentary on Isaiah in order to refute the Jewish interpretation of Is 49.16 (ed. G. Fatouros, *Theodori Studitae epistulae*, CFHB 31, 2 vols. [Berlin–New York, 1992], 2:771–73, no. 518), and Arethas of Caesarea's speech in a public dispute involving other bishops (*Arethae archiepiscopi Caesariensis scripta minora*, ed. L. G. Westerink, 2 vols. [Leipzig, 1968–70], 1:271–78, no. 33).

16   Sharf, 98ff.; C. Zuckerman, "On the Date of the Khazars' Conversion to Judaism and the Chronology of the Kings of the Rus Oleg and Igor," *REB* 53 (1995): 237–70; J. Shepard, "The Khazars' Formal Adoption of Judaism and Byzantium's Northern Policy," *Oxford Slavonic Papers*, n.s., 31 (1998): 11–34.

17   PG 91:533–34; cf. Dagron and Déroche (n. 5 above), 31, 39–40.

18   See especially his second and third homilies on the birth of the Virgin: PG 97:820–61; cf. Ch. Angelidi, Ἀνδρέας Κρήτης: Ὁμιλίες εἰς τὸ γενέθλιον τῆς Θεοτόκου· Μία ἀνάγνωση, Ἐνθύμησις Νικολάου Μ. Παναγιωτάκη, ed. S. Kaklamanis, A. Markopoulos, and G. Mavromatis (Herakleion, 2000), 1–11. For discussion of anti-Judaism as a generic theme in Byzantine preaching, see M. B. Cunningham, "Polemic and Exegesis: Anti-Judaic Invective in Byzantine Homiletics," *Sobornost* 21, no. 2 (1999): 46–68.

19   *Letter* no. 518 (see n. 12 above).

20   *Epistulae*, nos. 30, 76, 125, 132, 219, 256; *Amphilochia*, nos. 15, 26, 36: ed. B. Laourdas and L. G. Westerink, *Photii Patriarchae Constantinopoleos Epistulae et Amphilochia*, 6 vols. (Leipzig, 1983–88).

21   Leo III: Sharf, *Byzantine Jewry* (n. 5 above), 61–66; Dagron and Déroche, 43–45. Basil I: Sharf, *Byzantine Jewry*, 82ff.; Dagron and Déroche, 347–53; F. Ciccolella, "Basil I and the Jews: Two Poems of the Ninth Century," *Medioevo Greco* 0 (2000): 69–94. Romanos I: Sharf, *Byzantine Jewry*, 94–102; Shepard, "Khazars' Adoption of Judaism," 30.

Testament, as the question for whom they were intended and to whom they belonged remained open.

The Old Testament in Byzantium was therefore more than a repository of devotional and doctrinal texts; it was a contested cultural inheritance that deserves to be studied, separately from the New Testament, as an integral component of Byzantine identity. The need for a study is indeed highlighted by pertinent but mainly brief remarks about the Old Testament quality of Byzantine imperial ideology in the seventh and eighth centuries, about Byzantium's self-perceived role as the new Israel, and, more recently, about the Judaic strain in the "exactitude" (*akribeia*) of Orthodox doctrine and ritual.[22] This collection of papers is a first step in these directions. There is much more to do; important areas of the Old Testament and its impact in Byzantium remain untouched. The cosmology of Genesis; the eschatology of the minor prophets; the wisdom literature of Proverbs, Job, and Ecclesiastes; the theodicy of almost every book from Exodus onward: the Byzantine understanding of all these themes still awaits investigation. So too do many obvious examples of Old Testament inspiration in Byzantine art, literature, and religious practice: Byzantine veneration of the holy sites of the Old Testament; the ideological significances of famous illuminated manuscripts such as the Joshua Roll and the Paris Psalter (Frontispiece); the place of Old Testament sacred symbols in the veneration of the Virgin Mary; the use of Old Testament texts and exempla in hagiography, hymnography, and homiletics. Yet in the ground it does cover, the present collection facilitates the approach to these and other important topics by dealing in depth with two major preliminaries. First, it looks at the ways and the forms in which Byzantines, Jews as well as Christians, actually encountered the text of the Old Testament (Chapters 2–5). Secondly, it looks at the most important ways in which Byzantine Christians used the text: to establish the events and chronology of world history (Chapter 6); to find language and inspiration for private devotion (Chapter 4); and as a source of models for comparison and emulation—in political leadership, in the ascetic life, and in the configuration of sacred space as symbolized by the holy building par excellence, the Temple in Jerusalem (Chapters 7–9 respectively).

---

22 P. Alexander, "The Strength of Empire and Capital as Seen through Byzantine Eyes," *Speculum* 37 (1962): 339–357a (repr. in idem, *Religious and Political History and Thought in the Byzantine Empire* [London, 1978]); P. Brown, "A Dark-Age Crisis: Aspects of the Iconoclastic Controversy," *EHR* 88 (1973): 1–34, esp. 24, 25; G. Dagron, *Emperor and Priest: The Imperial Office in Byzantium* (Cambridge, 2003), 47ff., 116ff., 173ff., and passim; S. Averintsev, "Some Constant Characteristics of Byzantine Orthodoxy," in *Byzantine Orthodoxies*, ed. A. Louth and A. Casiday (Aldershot, 2006), 217ff.

Although systematic comparison with other medieval cultures was never an aim of this project—the rich reception of the Old Testament in the Frankish kingdoms, or in the Syriac orient, would require volumes in themselves—the Byzantine experience is not considered in isolation. Rather, the question of the Old Testament contribution to Byzantine style and civilization is further highlighted by setting it in the context of the empire's satellite kingdoms, each of which used this same sacred text to establish an independent political identity and agenda within the common framework of a Christian *oikoumene* (Chapter 10). Finally, the volume concludes with a reminder that Islam, too, included Old Testament figures, notably Moses, in its sacred genealogy of the Prophet Muhammad (Chapter 11).

The appropriation of the Old Testament by Christian Greek culture, through Christian biblical exegesis, began with St. Paul and was completed by the middle of the fifth century. However, the application of Old Testament texts and models to the literature, art, and institutions of the Roman world did not take off until the fourth century, and did not begin to reach full altitude until late in the sixth. The appearance in this period of deluxe illustrated manuscripts of the book of Genesis, the books known as the Vienna Genesis and the Cotton Genesis, is proof of the full acceptance of the Old Testament by aristocratic culture. But these manuscripts are exceptional textually and pictorially and have no successors in later Byzantine art.[23] Both the Vienna and the Cotton Genesis remain isolated, idiosyncratic works, even though scholarship has attempted to read them as normative of early book decoration.[24]

Our volume, however, focuses on the following period, from the seventh to the twelfth centuries, when patterns changed quickly and decisively for later Orthodox culture. During this period, particularly its first half, Byzantine writers, artists, statesmen, and churchmen most explicitly found inspiration and meaning in the language, images, stories, personalities, and values of the Old Testament. The essays that follow discuss how this happened. But why did it happen when it did, and what did it mean? To what extent did Byzantines identify, individually and collectively, with the Old Testament experience? Why did it coincide with a preoccupation with the Old Testament in other, very different Christian societies like Bulgaria, Ireland, Anglo-Saxon England, and

---

23   K. Weitzmann and H. L. Kessler, *The Cotton Genesis: British Library, Codex Cotton Otho B VI* (Princeton, 1986); B. Zimmermann, *Die Wiener Genesis im Rahmen der antiken Buchmalerei: Ikonographie, Darstellung, Illustrationsverfahren und Aussageintention* (Wiesbaden, 2003).
24   See the carefully reasoned essay by J. Lowden, "Concerning the Cotton Genesis and Other Illustrated Manuscripts of Genesis," *Gesta* 31 (1992): 40–53.

Carolingian Francia?²⁵ In what sense did the Old Testament experience lead Byzantines to consider themselves a chosen people and their empire a new Israel? How did it relate to their perception of the old Israel? These are weighty and elusive questions, which could easily fill another volume. Yet some preliminary discussion is in order.

Byzantine literature leaves a strong impression of a literate society completely at home with the Old Testament, a society whose readers were thoroughly steeped in the text—or at least selected texts—of the Septuagint, and writers quoted from it with easy familiarity. This applies as much to the elite, classicizing styles and genres as to more "lowbrow" media such as hagiography, chronicles, and homely advice literature. A perusal of the citation indices of fourteen Byzantine authors from the seventh to the thirteenth centuries published in recent critical editions reveals that all of them quoted from both parts of the Bible; among biblical citations, the proportion of those from the Old Testament was never less than 30 percent, while in the cases of several "high-style" authors from the twelfth century it is consistently higher:

Letters and speeches of Nikephoros Basilakes: ca. 65 percent
Letters of John Tzetzes: ca. 75 percent
Occasional poems of Theodore Prodromos: ca. 75 percent
Orations of Eustathios of Thessalonike: ca. 60 percent
History of Niketas Choniates: ca. 75 percent.²⁶

Monks learned the Psalter by heart, or carried it with them as their constant companion and only possession (Chapter 4). Byzantines commonly applied lines of the Psalms to their own situations, while hagiographers and encomiasts freely interpreted the events they celebrated as fulfilments of Old Testament

---

25 A phenomenon noted briefly but suggestively by P. Brown, *The Rise of Western Christendom*, 2nd ed. (Princeton, 2003), 139–40, 279, 338–39. For Ireland and Francia, see the articles by R. Meens, M. Garrison, and M. de Jong in *The Uses of the Past in the Early Middle Ages*, ed. Y. Hen and M. Innes (Cambridge, 2000); Garrison also includes some consideration of England and Spain.
26 Editions used: A. Garzya, ed., *Nicephori Basilacae orationes et epistolae* (Leipzig, 1984); P. A. M. Leone, ed., *Ioannis Tzetzae epistulae* (Leipzig, 1972); W. Hörandner, ed., *Theodoros Prodromos, historische Gedichte* (Vienna, 1974); P. Wirth, ed., *Eustathii Thessalonicensis opera minora*, CFHB 32 (Berlin–New York, 2000); J.-L. van Dieten, ed., *Nicetae Choniatae historia*, CFHB 11, 2 vols. (Berlin–New York, 1975). In addition to the authors listed here, George of Pisidia, "Genesios," Ignatios the Deacon, Patriarch Nikephoros, Theodore Stoudites, Patriarch Nikolaos Mystikos, Theodore Daphnopates, and Theodosios Diakonos were also surveyed.

prophecies.²⁷ Holy men modeled their predictions on the visions and pronouncements of Old Testament prophets; two southern Italian saints even reenacted the dramatic gestures of Jeremiah. God had commanded the prophet of Jerusalem's destruction to "Go and procure thyself a linen girdle, and put it about thy loins, and let it not be put in water" (Jer. 13:1). St. Elias the Younger accordingly, when prophesying the Arab capture of Taormina, stood in the middle of the town with his habit hitched up to his knee.²⁸ St. Phantinos similarly obeyed God's reported command to "cut off thine hair, and cast it away, and take up a lamentation on thy lips; for the Lord has reprobated and rejected the generation that does these things" (Jer. 7:29).²⁹

These monastic examples from the periphery are perhaps extreme. But the extent to which ordinary Byzantines adopted and replicated the language and mentality of the Old Testament is well illustrated by the fortunes of the words (ὁ) ναὸς (τοῦ) Κυρίου, an expression of unmistakably Septuagint origin meaning "the Temple of the Lord."³⁰ The expression recurs with the same meaning in Jewish and Christian apocrypha, the Fathers, and chronicles.³¹ Then it is used in several middle Byzantine texts to refer to any church. The abbot Euthymios, according to his *Life* in the eleventh-century imperial menologion, "urged [the brethren of his monastery] to keep decent silence ἐν ναῷ Κυρίου."³² According to the ceremonial treatise of Philotheos (899), the investiture of the three highest court dignitaries, the caesar, kouropalates, and nobelissimos, takes place ἐπὶ ναοῦ Κυρίου.³³ The contemporary *Book of the Prefect* (912) specifies that a newly qualified notary is to be invested ἐν ναῷ Κυρίου near his residence, and maintains the biblical flavor by combining two psalm verses (119 [118]:5 and 141 [140]:2).³⁴

---

27 E.g., *Life of Theodore Stoudites*, PG 99:164; *Life of Nicholas Stoudites*, PG 105:876; Theodore Prodromos, ed. Hörandner, no. XVII, pp. 286–300. After the fourth century, both Jews and Christians tended to reinterpret Old Testament prophecies as applying to events that were still to happen: Wilken, *Land Called Holy*, 132ff.
28 G. Rossi-Taibbi, *Vita di Sant'Elia il Giovane: Testo inedito con traduzione italiana* (Palermo, 1962), §50.
29 Recorded in the *Life of St. Neilos the Younger*: Archimandrite Aimilianos, ed., Ὁ Βίος τοῦ Ὁσίου Νείλου τοῦ Νέου (910–1004) (Ormylia, 1991), §24, p. 138.
30 E.g., 1 Sam. (LXX 1 Kgs.) 1:9; 2 Kgs. (LXX 4 Kgs.) 18:16, 23:4, 24:13; 2 Chr. 15:8, 26:16, 27:2, 29:17; Jer. 7:4, 2:1.
31 The references, obtained through a TLG search, are too numerous to list. The best represented texts are the *Protevangelium of James*, the *Testament of Solomon*, the *Homilies* of St. John Chrysostom, and the *Chronicle* of George the Monk.
32 F. Halkin, *Le ménologe impérial de Baltimore*, SubsHag 69 (Brussels, 1985), §17.
33 N. Oikonomides, *Les listes de préséance byzantines des IXe et Xe siècles* (Paris, 1972), 97, 99.
34 *Book of the Prefect* 1.3: *Das Eparchenbuch Leons des Weisen*, ed. J. Koder, CFHB 33 (Vienna, 1991), 76. Only the second of the two psalm quotations is noted in the apparatus.

The near-contemporary book of dream interpretation, the *Oneirocriticon of Achmet*, has an explanation for the dreamer who sees himself standing naked ἐν ναῷ Κυρίου.³⁵ Theodore Stoudites, rejoicing at the news of the murder of the Iconoclast emperor Leo V in the palace church (820), comments, "It was right that he who laid waste the churches should behold the swords bared against him ἐν ναῷ Κυρίου."³⁶ This contemporary remark adds authenticity to a later account of the punishment of Leo's murderers by the emperor Theophilos (829); according to the *Chronicle of Symeon the Logothete*, Theophilos asked the senate, "Of what punishment is he worthy who enters into the Temple of the Lord (εἰς ναὸν Κυρίου) and murders the Lord's anointed?"³⁷ Few Byzantines would have missed the biblical resonance or even the original connotations of these words, and fewer still would have been likely to realize that they were not actually quoted from Scripture. The phrase is consistent with other indications that "Bible-speak" was adopted for solemn effect. Law and legislation in the eighth and ninth centuries imitated the wording of the Pentateuch. The advice literature exemplified by Constantine VII and "Kekaumenos" resonates with echoes of Solomonic wisdom, not all of them genuine quotations.³⁸ The language of the Septuagint, however offensive to "Attic" ears, was beyond reproach.³⁹

To return to the expression ναὸς Κυρίου: in the imperial palace of Constantinople, there was a church dedicated to the Lord, without any other qualification.⁴⁰ Situated as it was in the oldest part of the palace, between the Consistorium and the Scholae, the church—called both ἐκκλησία τοῦ Κυρίου (church of the Lord) and ναὸς τοῦ Κυρίου (temple of the Lord) in the *Book of Ceremonies*—seems to have been one of the earliest buildings in the complex.⁴¹ Its unique dedication, avoiding all specific reference to Christ, would surely

---

35 *Achmetis Oneirocriticon*, ed. F. Drexl (Leipzig, 1925), §118.
36 Ed. Fatouros, *Theodori Studitae epistulae*, no. 417, p. 583.
37 *Symeonis Magistri et Logothetae Chronicon*, §130.6, ed. S. Wahlgren, CFHB 44 (Berlin–New York, 2006), 217.
38 The preface of Constantine Porphyrogenitus's book of advice to his son Romanos is in a patchwork of small quotes from the Psalms and the prophets, and other Septuagint books, as well as Proverbs: *De administrando imperio*, ed. G. Moravcsik, trans. R. J. H. Jenkins (Washington, DC, 1967), 44–47. "Kekaumenos" is still most easily consulted in the old edition by B. Wassiliewsky and B. Jernstedt, *Cecaumeni Strategicon* (1896; repr. Amsterdam, 1965).
39 This sentiment was expressed in a letter of Photios to Leo the Philosopher, ed. Laourdas-Westerink, *Photii epistulae*, no. 208.
40 *De cerimoniis*, ed. J. J. Reiske, I (Bonn, 1829), 11, 32, 85, 98–99, 107, 130, 168–69, 230, 239, 270, 545, 557, 567, 591, 593, 635, 641, 801, 806; book I, ed. A. Vogt (Paris, 1935–40; repr. 1967), 1:7–8, 26, 76, 91, 92, 99, 121, 156–57; 2:38, 46, 76, 78.
41 See E. Bolognesi Recchi-Franceschini and M. Featherstone, "The Boundaries of the Palace: *De cerimoniis* II, 13," *TM* 14 (2002): 37–46, at 37–38.

have called to mind the Temple in Jerusalem. If the allusion was deliberate, the church of the Lord would have functioned like two other objects in the palace that were either relics or, more likely, replicas of famous instruments of power mentioned in the Old Testament: the Rod of Moses and the Throne of Solomon.[42] According to the *Book of Ceremonies*, the Rod of Moses accompanied the emperor as he went in procession, via the church of the Lord, from his palace apartments to Hagia Sophia on major feast days.[43] Today it is a treasured relic of the Topkapı Palace in Istanbul.[44] In a manner that recalls 1 Kings 10:18–25, the emperor sat on the Throne of Solomon in the hall of the Magnaura, when he received foreign ambassadors and preached to the people.[45]

The public use of these Old Testament memorabilia—which were only the most prominent of a large collection of relics divided between the palace and Hagia Sophia[46]—demonstrates that Byzantine imperial ideology sought to sacralize the emperor's power by identifying it with the most powerful symbols of Jewish election. It gave concrete expression to the idea that the Christian Roman Empire was the new Israel and its people the chosen people of the new covenant. This idea of divine election on the Israelite model was not unique to Byzantium; many Christian peoples have embraced it throughout history, either in triumph or in tribulation,[47] because it is built into the New Testament, where

---

42 O. Treitinger, *Die oströmische Kaiser- und Reichsidee nach ihrer Gestaltung im höfischen Zeremoniell* (Jena, 1938), 134–35, notes (9 n. 23) that the Arab observer Harun ibn Yahya records a Table of Solomon as well; A. Pertusi, "Insigne del potere sovrano e delegato a Bisanzio e nei paesi di influenza bizantina," *Simboli e simbologia nell'alto Medioevo* [= *Settimane* 23] (Spoleto, 1996): 515–16.

43 *De cerimoniis*, ed. Reiske, 6, 10, 640; Vogt, 1:4, 7.

44 H. Aydin, et al., *The Sacred Trusts: Pavilion of the Sacred Relics, Topkapı Palace Museum, Istanbul* (Somerset, NJ, 2004), 144–45; McAuliffe, pp. 288–91; I. Kalavrezou, "Helping Hands for the Empire: Imperial Ceremonies and the Cult of Relics at the Byzantine Court," in *Byzantine Court Culture from 829 to 1204*, ed. H. Maguire (Washington, DC, 1997), 79.

45 *De cerimoniis*, ed. Reiske, 566, 567, 570, 583, 593; see G. Dagron, "Trônes pour un empereur," in Βυζάντιο: Κράτος καὶ κοινωνία, ed. A. Avramea, A. Laiou, and E. Chrysos (Athens, 2003), 179–203 at 188–89: "De ce trône de la Magnaure, si parfaitement romain et si parfaitement biblique, l'empereur vaut éblouir les étrangers, mais il veut aussi, comme Salomon, prêcher aux siens la sagesse de Dieu." For an English translation and commentary of the descriptions of the receptions of foreign ambassadors in the *Book of Ceremonies*, see J. M. Featherstone, "Δι' ἔνδειξιν: Display in Court Ceremonial (*De cerimoniis* II, 15)," in *The Material and the Ideal: Essays in Mediaeval Art and Archaeology in Honour of Jean-Michel Spieser*, ed A. Cutler and A. Papaconstantinou (Leiden, 2007), 75–112.

46 Dagron, *Emperor and Priest* (n. 22 above), 98.

47 For a survey that is limited to Western Christendom, see M. Garrison, "Divine Election for Nations: A Difficult Rhetoric for Medieval Scholars?" in *The Making of Christian Myths in the Periphery of Latin Christendom*, ed. L. B. Mortensen (Copenhagen, 2006), 275–314.

God's promise to Israel is transferred to the early Church in words borrowed from Exodus and Deuteronomy: "But you are a chosen race, a royal priesthood, a holy nation, God's own people."[48] Yet the New Testament threw open the election of one people to all nations without discrimination. In contrast, Byzantine and later appropriations of Israelite identity more or less reversed the process and reverted to the exclusiveness of the Jewish model, proclaiming the elect status of one particular group of Christians who identified themselves in political, social, or ethnic terms and reinforced this identity with Old Testament typology. The *verus Israel* of the early Church was a purely spiritual communion, which found unity in religion, whereas the new Israels of the Middle Ages and later based their religious mission on some other form of group identity. The transition from the one source of identity to the other is most easily understood in the cases of newly converted ethnic groups, whose members on the one hand wanted to resist political and cultural absorption into a large imperial polity and on the other hand found that the historical experience of the Jews—their tribal system, nomadic past, and state of constant warfare, not to mention their royal and priestly elites—spoke to their own situation.

The transition is less easy to understand, and to trace, in the case of Byzantium, which was the continuation of the universal Roman Empire that had adopted Christianity in the fourth century without any immediate or conspicuous adoption of Christianity's Jewish cultural heritage and election ideology. It is true that Eusebios hailed Constantine as a new Moses and the Council of Chalcedon acclaimed Marcian as a new David (Chapter 7); it is true also that the Church developed certain basic features of an Old Testament, chosen people mentality, in referring to all non-Christian peoples as "Gentiles," and in regarding all natural disasters and barbarian invasions as punishments for the transgression of God's law.[49] The imperially sponsored development of Palestine as a Christian holy land for elite Christian pilgrimage, with a dense network of monasteries and sacred sites dominated by huge basilicas, can perhaps be seen as the creation of a new promised land for a new Israel.[50] Some of the associations

---

48 1 Peter 2:9: Ὑμεῖς δὲ γένος ἐκλεκτόν, βασίλειον ἱεράτευμα, ἔθνος ἅγιον, λαὸς εἰς περιποίησιν (also Ti. 2:14, where the expression rendered by "God's own people" is λαὸν περιούσιον); cf. Ex. 19: 5–6, Dt. 4:20, 7:6, 10:15, 14:2.
49 See particularly Salvian of Marseilles, *De gubernatione Dei* 5–7, in *Oeuvres*, ed. G. Lagarrigue, SC 220 (Paris 1975).
50 Wilken, *Land Called Holy* (n. 8 above), 143–92.

and attributes of the Temple were transferred to the Holy Sepulchre.[51] But the Christianization of the Holy Land can equally be seen as the final chapter in the Roman suppression of Jewish independence and the Temple cult.

As Christianity came to dominate the urban landscape of late antiquity at the expense of Greco-Roman culture, the Bible gained in importance as a source of inspiration and models. Constantinople was called "a second Jerusalem" ca. 500,[52] and soon afterward a Roman grande dame with imperial pretensions, Anicia Juliana, built a church there that was perhaps the most faithful replica of the Temple ever constructed for Christian worship.[53] Yet Justinian pointedly did not follow this precedent when reputedly outdoing Solomon in the reconstruction of Hagia Sophia, nor when he had a huge basilica, the Nea, erected in Jerusalem on a scale that dwarfed the Temple of Solomon and on a site overlooking the Temple Mount.[54] It was more important to efface than to replicate, to supersede than to appropriate, the Old Testament model. So it was too with the reinterpretation, under Justinian, of Daniel's prophecy of the succession of world empires: the new identification of the Roman Empire not as the perishable fourth, iron kingdom, but as the "fifth monarchy," the kingdom without end, was introduced by the *Christian Topography* attributed to Kosmas Indikopleustes without the comment that this effectively equated the Christian empire with the Messianic restoration of the kingdom of Israel.[55] Similarly, Malalas reproduced verbatim in his chronicle the Old Testament account of Sennacherib's attack on Jerusalem as a "typological and topical" device for averting a Persian capture of Antioch (Chapter 6), but he refrained from explicitly identifying Christian Antioch with Judaic Jerusalem, or the empire of Justinian as the kingdom of Hezekiah. And he "conceived of Solomon as a Byzantine emperor and his kingdom as the empire of the sixth century," perhaps because he wanted to convey the idea "that Greece and Rome had a part in divine revelation and election," implying "that Israel and the Jewish people had never been the sole

---

51 Ibid., 93–100; Chapter 9, below.
52 *Life of Daniel the Stylite*, ed. H. Delehaye, *Les saints stylites* (Brussels, 1923, repr. 1962), 12. On the text and related matters see, P. Guran, "The Byzantine 'New Jerusalem' at the Crossing of Sacred Space and Political Theology," in *New Jerusalems: The Translation of Sacred Spaces in Christian Culture*, ed. A. Lidov (Moscow, 2006), 17–23.
53 On this sentence and the following, see Chapter 9, below, with references.
54 I. Shahîd, "Justinian and the Christianization of Palestine: The *Nea Ecclesia* in Jerusalem," in Κλητόριον εἰς μνήμην Νίκου Οἰκονομίδη, ed. F. Evangelatou-Notara and T. Maniati-Kokkini (Athens–Thessalonike, 2005), 1–13.
55 2.71, 73–75: *Cosmas Indicopleustès, Topographie chrétienne*, ed. W. Wolska-Conus, SC 141 (Paris, 1968), 386–91. For later Byzantine expressions of this theory, see below, n. 116.

repositories of revelation and election."⁵⁶ Israel was thus not the sole or even primary model for Justinian's empire.

Israel assumes greater prominence in the late sixth-century *Life* of the patriarch Eutychios by Eustratios, where, in a text full of Old Testament comparisons, the author describes his hero's triumphant return to Constantinople from Amaseia. On his arrival at Nicomedia, it was not only "the faithful and Christ-loving people, 'the royal priesthood, the holy nation,'" who turned out to welcome Eutychios, but also "the community of the infidel Jews who are outside our fold." The patriarch entered Constantinople in accordance with Isaiah's prophecy of the people bringing priests and Levites into Jerusalem as gifts to the Lord (Is. 66:20–21), "for was it not thus, or even more so, that the faithful people brought their father, pastor, and teacher into the holy city, the New Jerusalem and queen of cities?"⁵⁷

For more sustained comparisons between Israel and the Christian people, Jerusalem and Constantinople, we have to wait for the troubled reign of Herakleios (610–41), when the simultaneous invasions of the Persians and the Avars nearly brought the empire to extinction, and Persian occupation of Syria and Palestine allowed the local Jews to take brief but bloody revenge on their Christian neighbors. The local narrator of events in Palestine, the monk Strategios, resorted to the Old Testament to explain this new Babylonian conquest and enslavement of the true Israel.⁵⁸ The ideology of the new Israel was preached both in Jerusalem itself, after the city was restored to Christian rule and the True Cross that the Persians had carried away was recovered, and in Constantinople, the new Jerusalem that had withstood the onslaught of the raging Gentiles. Sophronios, who became patriarch of Jerusalem after the Persian occupation, made his homily on the Presentation of Christ in the Temple (Hypapante) an extended interpretation of Symeon's canticle (Luke 2:29–32, the *Nunc dimittis*) as a manifesto for "out with the old, in with the new."⁵⁹ "For both the Law and the prophets who came after it had grown old and sought their own dismissal. Until the illuminating manifestation of Christ, the Law held sway and

---

56   J. Beaucamp, "Le passé biblique et l'histoire juive: La version de Jean Malalas," in *Recherches sur la chronique de Jean Malalas*, ed. S. Agusta-Boularot et al. (Paris, 2006), 2:19–33 at 33.
57   *Eustratii Presbyteri Vita Eutychii Patriarchae Constantinopolitani*, ed. C. Laga, CCSG 25 (Turnhout, 1992), 66, 67.
58   See B. Flusin, *Saint Anastase le Perse et l'histoire de la Palestine au début du VIIe siècle* (Paris, 1992), 129–81, esp. 138–40: "le récit du moine Stratègios procède par référence à des précédents bibliques. L'histoire contemporaine, dont il témoigne, est, pour devenir intelligible, projetée sur l'histoire ancienne du peuple d'Israël."
59   H. Usener, ed., *Sophronii de praesentatione domini sermo* (Bonn, 1889).

the prophets prophetically announced Christ's mysteries. But let us in reply confess the amazing prophecies of Christ; let us, who have been transformed from a multitude of Gentiles into a New Israel and constitute God's new people, shout in the words of the psalm, 'Oh sing unto the Lord a new song' (Ps. 97:1) . . . For we have been renewed, made new from old, and we have been ordered to sing a new song unto God who has renewed us through the coming of Christ and revealed us to be his new people."[60] Although Sophronios kept his discourse purely spiritual and avoided topical allusions, his appeal to the Christians of Jerusalem as the New Israel had a special meaning in the light of the violence they had recently suffered at the hands of the children of the old Israel.[61]

No such ambiguity surrounds the remarkable homily that Theodore, the *synkellos* of the Great Church of Constantinople, wrote to celebrate the failure of the joint attack on the city by the overwhelming forces of the Avars and Persians in 626.[62] The homily is devoted largely to demonstrating that certain Old Testament prophecies concerning Jerusalem and Israel found their fulfilment in this event and not in Jewish history. In a discourse stuffed full of Old Testament comparisons, containing several anti-Jewish asides, Theodore argues that the prophets Isaiah (7:1–12, 40:9ff.), Zechariah (8:19), and Ezekiel (38, 39:1–12) are all really foretelling the deliverance of Constantinople, the new Jerusalem, through the miraculous intervention of the Virgin Mary. Most remarkable is his discussion of the prophecy of Ezekiel concerning Gog and Magog. This prophecy was never fulfilled, says Theodore, with respect to the original people of Israel, since the only violent invasion they suffered after the Babylonian captivity was that of Titus, when, far from being destroyed, the Roman invaders had themselves destroyed Jerusalem, the Temple, and much of the Jewish people. Nor can the prophecy ever apply to the Jews in future, since they are scattered all over the world and no longer have a country to call their own. The prophecy surely applies much better to the Avars and the great losses they have suffered in their failure to take Constantinople; indeed, even the topography of Constantinople is more appropriate to Ezekiel's description, which mentions islands and says that the cemetery of Gog was by the sea. "So I am right to interpret Gog as the gathering of nations that the rabid dog [the Avar khagan] mobilized against us, for I have learned from others that the name Gog signifies a multitude and

---

60 Ibid., 14. Unless otherwise indicated, all translations are Magdalino's.
61 For Sophronios's deep attachment to Jerusalem as a Christian city, see Wilken, *Land Called Holy* (n. 8 above), 226–31.
62 Ed. L. Sternbach, "Analecta Avarica," *Rozprawy Akademii Umiejetnosci, Wydial filologiczny*, 2nd scr., 14 (Cracow, 1900), 298–320.

assembly of nations. And rightly have I interpreted the land of Israel to be this city, in which God and the Virgin are piously glorified and all mysteries of pious devotion are performed. For to be a true Israel means to glorify the Lord with a sincere heart and willing soul; and to inhabit a land of Israel without deceit means to offer pure and bloodless sacrifices to God in every place. What else but that is this city, which one would not be wrong to call in its entirety a sanctuary of God?"[63]

The homily of Theodore is an extraordinary, almost indiscreet statement born of extraordinary, apocalyptic circumstances, but there can be no doubt that the author, as a high-ranking member of the patriarch's staff, was expressing an official point of view. It is echoed by contemporary publicity, in the poems of George of Pisidia and in the David Plates, which celebrate the emperor Heraklios through the use of Old Testament types, notably as a new David (Chapter 7); it also corresponds to the emperor's own efforts to sacralize his regime by restoring the Cross to Jerusalem and by adopting a form of imperial title that more explicitly declared his co-kingship (*symbasileia*) with Christ.[64] Moreover, although the issue had been forced by a specific crisis, it did not recede when that crisis passed. The Byzantine Church perpetuated the memory of Constantinople's near escape in annual commemorations, in enhanced devotion to the Virgin, and, probably, in the enrichment of the Lenten liturgical cycle, through the addition of a new "victory" prooimion to the Akathistos hymn, and through the institution of readings from Isaiah that were all selected for their concern with the sins, punishment, and deliverance of Jerusalem from the Assyrians.[65] While the selection spoke to the theme of personal penance during Lent, it also expressed the collective identity of the Byzantines as the new Israelites in the face of their enemies—not just the Avars and Persians, but the Arabs and the Bulgars who replaced them, and then, eventually, the Turks and the Latins.

---

63 Ibid., 316–17.
64 I.e., "faithful *basileus* in Christ" (πιστὸς ἐν Χριστῷ βασιλεὺς): see I. Shahîd, "The Iranian Factor in Byzantium during the Reign of Heraclius," *DOP* 26 (1972): 295–320, esp. 302–5, 307–8. For *symbasileia*, see P. Magdalino, "The Year 1000 in Byzantium," in *Byzantium in the Year 1000*, ed. P. Magdalino (Leiden, 2003), 251–54. To our knowledge, the earliest extant formulation of the concept occurs in the acts of the sixth ecumenical council (680–81): *Concilium universale Constantinopolitanum tertium*, 2 vols., ed. R. Riedinger, *ACO* 2nd ser. (Berlin, 1990–92), 2:120, 816, 854.
65 See A. Kniazeff, "La lecture de l'Ancien et du Nouveau Testament dans le rite byzantin," in *La prière des heures*, ed. Msgr. Cassien and Dom Bernard Botte, Lex orandi 35 (Paris, 1963), 237ff. (following I. Karabinov). For the Akathist hymn, see C. Trypanis, *Fourteen Early Byzantine Cantica* (Vienna, 1968), 19–20, 29–30.

The Old Testament ideology formed in the crisis of the Avar siege thus remained intact in the decades and centuries that followed. It was soon reconfigured to refer to the conquering Arabs—"the abomination of desolation," "the desert Amalek," "the Philistine wolf . . . the Assyrian host"[66]—who were seen as God's scourge for the sins, and especially the heresy, of the Byzantines. This ideology came to the fore again under the last emperor of Heraklios's dynasty, Justinian II (685–695, 705–711). Justinian not only took the propaganda of co-kingship with Christ a stage further by placing the icon of Christ, with the inscription *Rex regnantium*,[67] on the obverse of his gold coinage, but also, at around the same time (691–92) called a reforming church council that gave concrete expression to the idea of the Byzantines as a chosen people by legislating to purify their moral and ritual behavior of all alien—that is, Hellenic and Jewish—adulteration. Though it defined itself as ecumenical, the Council in Trullo or Quinisext,[68] unlike its predecessors, did not discuss theology, but issued only disciplinary canons that concerned the laity as much as, if not more than, the clergy; moreover, it prescribed the usage of the church of Constantinople as normative, condemning as "judaizing" certain ritual practices not only of the Monophysite Armenians, but also of the impeccably orthodox church of Rome. At the same time, the council had to cope with the effects of the Arab and Bulgar invasions that had overrun numerous Christian communities and driven their bishops from their sees. Thus when the assembled prelates, in their opening address, praised the emperor's care for "God's own people (περιούσιος λαός)," "the holy nation, the royal priesthood, on whose behalf Christ died," they were not mouthing an empty formula, or simply repeating the Pauline and Petrine echoes of Exodus and Deuteronomy, for when they referred ambiguously to the πάθη (passions or sufferings) that were tearing the chosen people apart, their ambiguity was deliberate: they meant both the spiritual vices that

---

66 Sophronios of Jerusalem, *Homily on Baptism*, ed. A. Papadopoulos-Kerameus, Ἀνάλεκτα Ἱεροσολυμιτικῆς Σταχυολογίας (Petroupolis, 1891–98), 5:166–67. Anastasios of Sinai, *Sermones duo in constitutionem hominis secundum imaginem Dei necnon Opuscula adversus Monotheletas*, ed. K.-H. Uthemann, CCSG 12 (Turnhout, 1985), 59–60. Andrew of Crete, *Encomium of St. James the Apostle*, ed. Papadopoulos-Kerameus, Ἀνάλεκτα, 1:14.
67 J. D. Breckenridge, *The Numismatic Iconography of Justinian II* (New York, 1959). The inscription is taken from 1 Tim. 6:15 and closely echoes Rev. 17:14, 19:16.
68 Text of the canons in Ralles and Potles, Σύνταγμα τῶν θείων καὶ ἱερέων κανόνων (Athens, 1852), 2:295–554; also edited and translated in *The Council in Trullo Revisited*, ed. G. Nedungatt and M. Featherstone (Rome, 1995), 45–185. On the council, see J. Herrin, *The Formation of Christendom* (Oxford, 1987), 284–87; G. Dagron, "Le christianisme byzantin du VIIe au milieu du XIe siècle," in *Évêques, moines et empereurs (610–1054)*, ed. G. Dagron, P. Riché, and A. Vauchez, Histoire du Christianisme 4 (Paris, 1993), 60–69.

were displeasing to God and the sufferings inflicted by the invaders, who were the instruments of God's wrath—exactly as in the history of Israel.

That Justinian II understood the references to the chosen people in their more restrictive, Old Testament sense is suggested by the information that he gave the name περιούσιος λαός to the army that he sent against the Islamic caliphate in the very same year as the council.[69] According to the source (Theophanes), Justinian's army was composed of captive Slavs, but it is just possible that, as related in book two of the *Miracles of St. Demetrios*, the army included descendants of Christian Greeks who had been taken captive by the Avars and settled in the region of Sirmium ca. 620.[70] According to the anonymous author of the *Miracles*, the community survived and even increased in exile, by keeping their Orthodox faith, "just as the Hebrew people did in Egypt under Pharaoh," until, sixty years later they were led out, "just as it is recorded in the Mosaic book of the Exodus of the Jews." Regardless of the ethnic origins of Justinian II's army, he and the fathers of the council in Trullo used the expression "chosen people" within a general context of reading the Old Testament history of Israel into the contemporary experience of the embattled Christian empire.

Although the failure of Justinian II's "crusade," and the excesses that led to his double downfall discredited his particular style of sacral rulership, including his promotion of the icon of Christ, the basic Old Testament ideology that had informed the council in Trullo was not invalidated. If anything, the conviction was intensified that the chosen people needed to regain God's favor by stricter application of and obedience to divine law. The eighth century saw the promulgation in 741 of a new imperial law code, the *Ecloga* of Leo III and Constantine V, based on the Justinianic corpus but with a more religious and less Roman rationale;[71] it may even have seen an attempt to implement the letter of the law of Moses. It is natural to assume that the Torah had no place in a society founded on antinomian Christianity and Roman jurisprudence. Yet the Christian concept of law was derived from the Old Testament, and this had long been a major source of inspiration for canon law in the West.[72] Several Byzantine manuscripts

---

69   Theophanes, *Chronographia*, ed. C. de Boor, 2 vols. (Leipzig, 1883; repr. Hildesheim, 1980), 1:365–66.

70   2.5: ed. P. Lemerle, *Les plus anciens receuils des miracles de Saint Démétrius et la pénétration des Slaves dans les Balkans* (Paris, 1979), 1:227ff.; see I. Anagnostakis, "Περιούσιος λαός," in *The Dark Centuries of Byzantium (7th–9th c.)* (Athens, 2001), 325–46.

71   *Ecloga: Das Gesetzbuch Leons III und Konstantinos V*, ed. L. Burgmann (Frankfurt am Main, 1983).

72   G. Dagron, "Lawful Society and Legitimate Power: Ἔννομος πολιτεία, ἔννομος ἀρχή," in *Law and Society in Byzantium, Ninth–Twelfth Centuries*, ed. A. E. Laiou and D. Simon (Washington,

preserve a collection of seventy excerpts from the Pentateuch arranged in fifty chapters under the general title *Selection (Ἐκλογὴ) from the Law given by God through Moses to the Israelites*.[73] Since most copies of it are transmitted along with the *Ecloga* of Leo III and Constantine V, and since, moreover, the *Nomos Mosaikos* echoes the *Ecloga* in title and structure, it was natural to assume that both collections were produced at the same time. Andreas Schminck has recently challenged this assumption, and argued that the *Nomos Mosaikos* was produced by the patriarch Photios ca. 865–67 to provide a law code that could be used in place of the *Ecloga* by the newly converted peoples of Eastern Europe.[74]

The argument is compelling but not decisive; it does not offer a better explanation for the manuscript tradition, and it neglects one obvious point. The authors of the *Ecloga*, Leo III and Constantine V, were the emperors who sought to enforce one item of the *Nomos Mosaikos*, namely, the second commandment of the Decalogue, against the making and worshipping of graven images. If there is one thing that students of the ink-intensive issue of Iconoclasm seem to agree on, it is that the imperial reform was basically motivated by a perception that God was punishing his chosen people for the idolatry of icon-worship. The defenders of images consistently accused their opponents of judaizing, which, however unfair, reflects the fact that the veneration of icons and the Cross had been one of the main points of contention between Jews and Christians in the seventh century.[75] An early pro-icon treatise, the *Admonition of the Elder* (*Nouthesia Gerontos*), portrays a venerable iconophile monk in debate with an iconoclast bishop sent by the emperor to preach the abolition of icons in obedience to the law of Moses.[76] The monk objects that Moses and the prophets spoke only for the world before Christ, who had introduced a new law and

---

DC, 1994), 27–51, esp. 35–38; R. Meens, "The Uses of the Old Testament in Early Medieval Canon Law," in Hen and Innes, *Uses of the Past* (n. 25 above), 67–77.

73 L. Burgmann and S. Troianos, eds., "Nomos Mosaikos," *FM* 3 (1979): 126–67.

74 A. Schminck, "Bemerkungen zum sog. *Nomos Mosaikos*," *FM* 11 (2005): 249–68; see also idem, "*Leges* ou *nomoi*? Le choix des princes slaves à l'époque de Photius et les débuts de l'Ἀνακάθαρσις τῶν παλαιῶν νόμων," in *The Eastern Roman Empire and the Birth of the Idea of State in Europe*, ed. S. Flogaitis and A. Pantelis, European Public Law Series 80 (London, 2005), 309–16.

75 V. Déroche, "La polémique anti-juive au VIe et au VIIe siècle: Un memento inédit, les *Képhalaia*," *TM* 11 (1991): 290ff.; Av. Cameron, "The Language of Images: The Rise of Icons and Christian Representation," *Studies in Church History* 28 (1992): 1–42, at 25–26; P. Andrist, "Les *Objections des Hébreux*: un document du premier iconoclasme?" *REB* 57 (1999): 99–140.

76 B. M. Melioranskii, ed., *Georgi Kiprianin i Ioann Ierosalimlianin: Dva maloizvestnikh bortsa za pravoslavie v VIII. Veke*, Zapiski istoriko-filologicheskago fakulteta imperatorskago S. Peterburgskago Universiteta 59 (St. Petersburg, 1901), v–xxxix.

new traditions. The bishop maintains that the prophets uttered their divinely inspired words for all time, and repeatedly insists that, apart from the rules specifically lifted by Christ, "the Law of Moses remains forever," adding that "the holy emperor . . . agrees that the words of the Old Testament are to be observed."

The *Nomos Mosaikos*, like the *Ecloga*, was made redundant by the revival of Roman law in the legislation of the Macedonian emperors after 867. Before that, however, we should not underestimate its impact on Byzantine legal culture of the eighth and ninth centuries.[77] As in prophecy, so in law, the Old Testament provided not only substance but also an authentic style of discourse for an embattled theocratic society. The *Farmer's Law* (*Nomos georgikos*), a rural law code of the eighth or ninth century, besides following the *Ecloga* in its punitive clauses, is heavily influenced by the language and the concepts of the Pentateuch.[78] Traces of this Old Testament tone still persist in the early legislation of the Macedonian emperors, in the prefaces to the *Eisagoge* and the *Procheiros nomos*,[79] and even in chapter 1.3 of the *Book of the Eparch*, which, as we have seen, describes the investment of a notary ἐν ναῷ Κυρίου and ends with quotes from Psalms 118 and 14.

The restoration of icons at the Triumph of Orthodoxy in 843 spelled the end of the attempt to apply the letter of Old Testament law to the reality of Byzantine life. It did not, however, put an end to the Byzantine claim on the identity of the True Israel. That claim in one sense intensified with the production of iconophile propaganda, in word and in image, arguing that the Old Testament had prefigured not merely the Incarnation of Christ but also the images by which he and his mother were depicted.[80] Photios used comparisons with Israel

---

77   See in general P. E. Pieler, "Das Alte Testament im Rechtsdenken der Byzantiner," in *Analecta Atheniensia ad ius byzantinum spectantia*, ed. S. Trioanos (Athens–Komotini, 1997), 1:81–113.
78   W. Ashburner, ed. and trans., "The Farmer's Law," *JHS* 30 (1910): 85–108; 32 (1912), 68–95; see A. Schminck, "Der 'Nomos Georgikos' und die Rechtspraxis," *La réponse des juristes et des experts à la pratique du droit: 59ème Session de la Société internationale Fernand de Visscher pour l'Histoire des Droits de l'Antiquité; Supplementum* (Bochum, 2005), 66–70.
79   See A. Schminck, *Studien zu mittelbyzantinischen Rechtsbüchern* (Frankfurt am Main, 1986).
80   Both in the sacred images that the Jews had employed and in the visions of the prophets, which the *Synodikon of Orthodoxy* endorsed as models of iconography. See J. Gouillard, "Le Synodikon de l'Orthodoxie," *TM* 2 (1967): 51; J.-M. Spieser, "Further Remarks on the Mosaic of Hosios David," in *Urban and Religious Spaces in Late Antiquity and Early Byzantium* (Aldershot, 2001), no. XII, p. 2; L. Brubaker, *Vision and Meaning in Ninth-Century Byzantium: Image as Exegesis in the Homilies of Gregory of Nazianzus* (Cambridge, 1999), 31–33, 281ff.; eadem, "The Christian Topography (Vat. Gr. 699) Revisited: Image, Text and Conflict in Ninth-Century Byzantium," in *Byzantine Style, Religion and Civilization in Honour of Steven Runciman*, ed. E. Jeffreys (Cambridge, 2006), 5–24.

and Jerusalem in his homilies,[81] and Arethas, in debate with the Jews, re-asserted the identity of "us Christians" as the True Israel.[82] The comparison of Christian saints with Old Testament types reached a high point in the panegyrical homilies of Niketas the Paphlagonian in the early tenth century.[83]

The self-image and cultural patronage of the Macedonian emperors were profoundly inspired by Old Testament models. This is most striking in the case of the founder of the dynasty, Basil I (867–86), whose upstart rise to power made him keen to identify himself as a new David and to claim the special protection of the prophet Elijah, to whom he built or rebuilt three churches in Constantinople.[84] They included the magnificent Nea Ekklesia on the edge of the imperial palace, which became a repository for the relics of Old Testament worthies;[85] this church has disappeared without trace, but its ideological significance can be glimpsed in a sumptuous manuscript executed for Basil, perhaps at the initiative of Photios, at around the same time: the copy of the homilies of Gregory of Nazianzos (Par. Gr. 510) that is lavishly illustrated and has a wealth of Old Testament typology.[86]

This concern for Old Testament models of kingship is still to be found in the tenth century. The son of Basil the new David, Leo VI "the Wise" (886–912), posed as a new Solomon through his legislation and learning.[87] When Leo brought the relics of Lazaros to Constantinople, Arethas compared them to the Ark of the Covenant, and the emperor to both Moses and David.[88] The image of the Ark was exploited further by Leo's son, Constantine VII, in regard to the relics that arrived during his personal reign (945–959), both on his own initiative (the body of St. Gregory of Nazianzos), and thanks to his predecessor

---

81 Trans. C. Mango, *The Homilies of Photius, Patriarch of Constantinople* (Cambridge, MA, 1958), 84, 86–87, 90–92.
82 *Scripta minora*, ed. Westerink, 1:277.
83 See, e.g., J. J. Rizzo, *The Encomium of Gregory Nazianzen by Nicetas the Paphlagonian*, SubsHag 58 (Brussels, 1976); F. Halkin, *Saints de Byzance et du Proche-Orient*, Cahiers d'Orientalisme 13 (Geneva, 1986), 109–10, 111–12, 156–57, 166, 168–70.
84 See Dagron, *Emperor and Priest* (n. 22 above), 192–200; P. Magdalino, "Basil I, Leo VI and the Feast of the Prophet Elijah," *JÖB* 38 (1988): 193–96 (= *Studies in the History and Topography of Byzantine Constantinople* [Aldershot, 2007], no. VI).
85 P. Magdalino, "Observations on the Nea Ekklesia of Basil I," *JÖB* 37 (1987): 51–64 (= *Studies*, V); Dagron, *Emperor and Priest*, 207–13.
86 Brubaker, *Vision and Meaning*.
87 S. F. Tougher, "The Wisdom of Leo VI," in *New Constantines: The Rhythm of Imperial Renewal in Byzantium*, ed. P. Magdalino (Aldershot, 1994), 171–79. Dagron, "Trônes pour un empereur" (n. 45 above), n. 47, suggests that the Throne of Solomon in the Magnaura may have been created by Leo VI.
88 Ed. Westerink, *Arethae scripta minora*, 2:12–13, 15.

and father-in-law Romanos I (920–945), who had organized the translation of the Mandylion of Edessa.[89] So powerful and official was this image in the tenth century, with its implication that the emperor was the new David and Constantinople was the new Jerusalem, that it even influenced the perception and portrayal of translations of relics in the past.[90] Thus, the Menologion of Basil II depicts the fifth-century repatriation of the remains of St. John Chrysostom using the imagery of a coffer being carried by bearers, not a casket being transported in a chariot.

Constantine VII, his circle, and successors are associated in other ways with Old Testament images that express political and dynastic concerns. Popular in art of the mid- to late tenth century is the figure of Joshua, Moses' successor, who led the Israelites into the promised land. The famed Joshua Roll and other images of Joshua in ivory have been seen in the context of the Byzantine campaigns in Syria and Palestine in the 960s and 970s.[91] In a Cappadocian church, the portrait of Emperor Nikephoros II Phokas (963–969), who campaigned against the Muslims in Syria, is associated with Joshua.[92] The Byzantine-Arab wars of the ninth and tenth centuries are the general background to the later epic of Digenes Akrites, which mentions the depiction of Joshua, together with other heroes of the Old Testament and Greek mythology, on the gilded mosaic vaults of Digenes' palace.[93]

Perhaps the clearest visual example of the political use of the Old Testament by Macedonian emperors is the large illuminated Psalter in Paris, Bibl. Nat. gr. 139.[94] Through accompanying personifications that "define a contemporary

---

89   Mandylion: E. von Dobschütz, *Christusbilder: Untersuchungen zur christlichen Legende*, TU 18 (Leipzig, 1899), 81**; A.-M. Dubarle, ed., "L'homélie de Grégoire le Référendaire pour la réception de l'image d'Édesse," *REB* 55 (1997): 5–51 at 25. Gregory: B. Flusin, "Le panégyrique de Constantin VII Porphyrogénète pour la translation des reliques de Grégoire le Théologien (*BHG* 728)," *REB* 57 (1999): 5–97, at 63, 65, 73–75.

90   B. Flusin, "Construire une nouvelle Jérusalem: Constantinople et les reliques," in *L'Orient dans l'histoire religieuse de l'Europe: L'invention des origines*, ed. M. A. Amir-Moezzi and J. Scheid (Turnhout, 2001), 51–70, at 42–48.

91   M. Schapiro, "The Place of the Joshua Roll in Byzantine History," *GBA* 35 (1949): 161–76, reprinted in M. Schapiro, *Late Antique, Early Christian and Mediaeval Art* (New York, 1979), 49–66. More recently on the Joshua Roll, see Chapter 5, below, and bibliography cited at 131 n. 57, especially Kresten, "Biblisches Geschehen."

92   A. W. Epstein (A. Wharton), *Tokalı Kilise: Tenth-Century Metropolitan Art in Byzantine Cappadocia* (Washington, DC, 1986), 41–42.

93   *Digenes Akrites*, ed. J. Mavrogordato (Oxford, 1956), 220–23; ed. E. Jeffreys (Cambridge, 1998), 208–9.

94   H. Buchthal, *The Miniatures of the Paris Psalter: A Study in Middle Byzantine Painting* (London, 1938).

meaning," the illustrations of the Paris Psalter create "a self-contained idealized image of the Macedonian Emperor," as Ioli Kalavrezou has explained.⁹⁵ For his part, Hugo Buchthal drew attention to an anomaly in the Paris Psalter's portrait of David, the author of the Psalms, flanked by Sophia on the left holding a book and Prophecy on the right, pointing to David's open book (Frontispiece). Typically, portraits of authors show them writing or displaying their treatise that begins on the facing page. David's book, however, is not inscribed with Psalm 1, but the first verse of Psalm 71 (72), "O God, give thy judgment to the king (τῷ βασιλεῖ), and thy righteousness to the son of the king (τοῦ βασιλέως)."⁹⁶ Since Heraklios, each Byzantine ruler had styled himself as *basileus*, the biblical word for king or emperor. Thus, in the tenth century, this verse would also have been read as asking God for judgment and righteousness for the Byzantine emperor and his son, an association made as well visually.

Here David is crowned and wears the red shoes with pearl ornament of the Byzantine emperor. The patterned silk around his shoulders is of imperial purple and has a large embroidered section in gold with further designs. Buchthal noted that Psalm 71 (72) is quoted several times in the preface to Constantine VII's *De administrando imperio* that was written for the emperor's son, the future Romanos II, and through this analogy, he suggested that the Paris Psalter or its model also might have been created for Romanos.⁹⁷ The action of the figure of Prophecy at the right supports that interpretation. She establishes eye contact with the beholder, points to the book, and visually asserts that the Psalm verse should be read prophetically. That judgment and righteousness have been and will be given to the king is indicated by Wisdom at the left. By her gaze, she catches the attention of the beholder and with the index finger of her left hand she points to David. The white bird above his gilded nimbus resembles the dove of the Holy Spirit at the Baptism of Jesus in the Menologion of Basil II of ca. 1000, and confirms that the subject of the Paris Psalter miniature is sacral kingship.⁹⁸ Further testimony to the interest in David at the time of Constantine VII is provided by a series of epigrams that once served as captions to an extensive David cycle of (mural?) paintings.⁹⁹

---

95 "The Paris Psalter," *Abstracts of Papers: Annual Byzantine Studies Conference* (Chicago, 1982), 50–51, available at http://www.bsana.net/conference/archives/1982/abstracts_1982.pdf, accessed Sept. 23, 2008. These ideas were developed further in Prof. Kalavrezou's paper at our symposium.
96 H. Buchthal, "The Exaltation of David," *JWarb* 37 (1974): 332; reprinted with a postscript in idem, *Art of the Mediterranean World A.D. 100 to 1400* (Washington, DC, 1983), 190.
97 "Exaltation of David," 332.
98 *Il menologio di Basilio II (cod. vaticano greco 1613)* (Turin, 1907), 2: pl. 299.
99 I. Ševčenko, "Captions to a David Cycle in the Tenth-Century Oxford *Auct. D.4.1*," in

Constantine VII, perhaps in unconscious echo of Justinian II, or perhaps in accordance with a continuous tradition of exhortation from the throne, addressed his troops as *periousios laos*.[100] A contemporary homily celebrating the arrival of the Mandylion from Edessa in 944 compares it to the Ark and ends with a prayer to Christ to "strengthen God's own (*periousios*) army against the blasphemers."[101] Other tenth-century texts apply the Old Testament language of election to the whole Byzantine population threatened by Arab raids.[102] In the next century, this identification of the empire and emperor with the kingdom of the Israelites and their king David made possible the illustrated Psalter in the Vatican, gr. 752, whose imagery, it has been argued, functions as a critique of the emperor in the guise of David.[103]

References, explicit or implicit, to Byzantium as the new Israel and to Constantinople as the new Jerusalem recur throughout Byzantine rhetorical literature of the eleventh and twelfth centuries.[104] They reach a crescendo, as one might expect, in the thirteenth, with the conquest of Constantinople by the Fourth Crusade (1204), the "Babylonian exile" of its people, and their repatriation after its liberation from the Latins in 1261.[105] The Latin occupation of

---

Πολύπλευρος Νοῦς: *Miscellanea für Peter Schreiner zu seinem 60. Geburtstag*, ed. C. Scholz and G. Makris (Munich–Leipzig, 2000), 324–41.

100   H. Ahrweiler, "Un discours inédit de Constantin VII Porphyrogénète," *TM* 2 (1967): 393–404, at 398; trans. E. McGeer, "Two Military Orations of Constantine VII," in *Byzantine Authors: Literary Activities and Preoccupations; Texts and Translations Dedicated to the Memory of Nicolas Oikonomides* (Leiden, 2003), 111–35, at 118.

101   Dubarle, "L'homélie de Grégoire le Référendaire" (n. 89 above), 29: τὸν περιούσιον κατὰ τῶν βλασφημούντων δυνάμου στρατόν. The readings for the feast were selected and edited specially to "stress the aspect of the chosen people": see S. G. Engberg, "Romanos Lekapenos and the Mandylion of Edessa," in *Byzance et les reliques du Christ*, ed. J. Durand and B. Flusin (Paris, 2004), 132, 140–42.

102   E.g., the homilies of Peter of Argos, ed. K. Th. Kyriakopoulos, Ἁγίου Πέτρου ἐπισκόπου Ἄργους, Βίος καὶ λόγοι (Athens, 1976), 48, 174; A. Pertusi, "Una acolouthia militare inedita del X secolo," *Aevum* 22–23 (1948–49): 145–68, lines 147–52; T. Detorakis and J. Mossay, "Un office byzantin inédit pour ceux qui sont morts à la guerre, dans le *Cod. Sin. gr. 734–735*," *Le Muséon* 101 (1988): 185–211, lines 105–8.

103   I. Kalavrezou, N. Trahoulia, and S. Sabar, "Critique of the Emperor in the Vatican Psalter gr. 752," *DOP* 47 (1993): 195–219.

104   E.g., *Iohannis Euchaitorum metropolitae quae in Codice Vaticano Graeco 676 supersunt*, ed. P. de Lagarde, AbhGött, Philol.-hist.Kl. 28 (1883; repr. Amsterdam, 1979), 140, 146, 184; Theodore Prodromos, *Historische Gedichte*, ed. Hörandner, I.104 (p. 180); 17.121, 271 (pp. 290, 295); *Eustathii Thessalonicensis opera minora*, ed. Wirth, 73, 158, 222, 268; Gregory Antiochos, *Grégoire Antiochos, Éloge du patriarche Basile Kamatèros*, ed. and trans. M. Loukaki (Paris, 1996), 47; George Tornikes, *Discours annuels en l'honneur du patriarche Georges Xiphilin*, ed. M. Loukaki, trans. C. Jouanno (Paris, 2005), 95, 109, 131.

105   Niketas Choniates, *Nicetae Choniatae orationes et epistulae*, ed. J.-L. van Dieten, CFHB 3 (Berlin–New York, 1972), 124–28, 145–47, 160, 175; Sergios the Deacon, ed. M. Loukaki,

Constantinople proved, according to a contemporary commentary on the *Great Canon* of Andrew of Crete, that the prophecies of Isaiah about the captivity and ruination of Jerusalem "unambiguously concern this new Jerusalem and new Rome."[106] One should not underrate the value of these references, which undoubtedly express the genuine conviction of the Byzantines that they were special—that they had the right religion, that their city was the eye and navel of the world,[107] that their empire was sanctioned by God, and that all other peoples, including other Christians, were Gentiles. This was a period when Byzantium, now under threat from the West as well as from Islam, became increasingly defensive of its ritual and doctrinal purity, and correspondingly assertive of the exclusive, elect status of its traditions and its sacred space. The Byzantines resembled the children of Israel not only in their experience of suffering and exile, but also in their lack of missionary fervor, which differentiated them from both Muslims and Western Christians.[108] The rhetorical texts that reflect this sense of passive superiority in biblical terms often show an impressive familiarity with the Septuagint text, as well as skill in selecting the symbol, the comparison, or the quotation that casts the subject in the right Old Testament role. Yet the lasting impression is one of rhetoricity, of a masked ball in which no disguise can deceive. It is doubtful whether these typological gymnastics added any new dimension or depth to the conception of Byzantium as the new Israel and the Byzantines as the chosen people. The accumulation, repetition, and variation of Old Testament parallels were not systematic or progressive. The words and symbols remained in a world of their own, without closing the gap between the world that had created and the world that received them. This was partly because they had to compete with symbols from the other cultures to which Byzantium was heir: as always, Rome, and, increasingly from the eleventh century, ancient Greece.[109] But mainly it was, it may be suggested, because a literal reading and

---

"Première didascalie de Serge le Diacre: Éloge du patriarche Michel Autôreianos," *REB* 52 (1994): 151–73, at 164–69; Iakobos, Archbishop of Bulgaria, *Oration in Praise of John III Vatatzes*, ed. S. G. Mercati, *Collectanea Bizantina* (Bari, 1970), 1:84, 85–86; Manuel Holobolos, *Manuelis Holoboli orationes*, ed. M. Treu (Potsdam, 1906–7), 39, 41–44, 57, 66, 71, 82–83, 86, 87.

106 *Die beiden byzantinischen Kommentare zum Großen Kanon des Andreas von Kreta*, ed. A. Giannouli, WByzSt 26 (Vienna, 2007), 382, referring to Is. 5:5–6.

107 Cf. P. Magdalino, "Ο οφθαλμός της οικουμένης και ο ομφαλός της γης: Η Κωνσταντινούπολη ως οικουμενική πρωτεύουσα," in *Το Βυζάντιο ως οικουμένη* (Athens, 2005), 107–23.

108 Fowden, *Empire to Commonwealth* (n. 11 above), 65–72; S. Ivanov, "Mission Impossible: Ups and Downs in Byzantine Missionary Activity from the Eleventh to the Fifteenth Century," in *The Expansion of Orthodox Europe*, ed. J. Shepard (Aldershot, 2007), 251–65.

109 See now A. Kaldellis, *Hellenism in Byzantium: The Transformation of Greek Identity and the Reception of the Classical Tradition* (Cambridge, 2007).

imitation of the Old Testament was blocked. Every attempt to use Old Testament typology as a prescription for the new Israel had proved a dead end. The idea of concretizing the reality of Constantinople as the new Jerusalem with a church built according to the specifications of the Temple was tried in St. Polyeuktos, but rejected in Justinian's Hagia Sophia and in the middle-Byzantine domed cross-in-square model. The relevance of Old Testament prophecy to the Byzantine situation was never denied, but Theodore Synkellos took it as far as it could safely or credibly go in the extraordinary circumstances of the Avar siege. As for the partial revival of the law of Moses, this could never compete with the existing corpus of Roman and canon law, and it was in any case irretrievably discredited by iconoclasm, the failed attempt to condemn a traditional devotional practice as idolatry.

To read the Old Testament literally was to read it as a text written by Jews, about Jews, and for Jews, and thus to incur the charge of judaizing, or conversion to Judaism.[110] Judaizing and hellenizing (lapsing into paganism) were the ultimate apostasies to which deviations from Orthodoxy were compared. In this sense, the place of the Old Testament in Byzantine culture bore some resemblance to that of the pagan classics: it was dangerous if taken neat. The perils of intoxication are vividly dramatized in a tenth-century saint's life, the *Life of Basil the Younger*, which contains one of the longest apocalyptic narratives in the whole of Byzantine literature.[111] In this, the probably fictitious saint arranges for Gregory the narrator to be shown an extended preview of the Last Judgment, all because Gregory had had kind thoughts about the Jews, based on his thorough reading of the Old Testament. Contemplating in his cell one day, he had had "the strange and loathsome notion, namely that the Jews piously believe and by their reverence do right by the Creator." He had reflected on the virtues and godliness of all the Old Testament worthies, from Abraham to the prophets, and he had asked himself, "How is their faith evil and ours good? Their faith is surely good, since they do not place faith in idols, but in God who created heaven and earth."[112] Gregory goes off to confess his troublesome thoughts to the holy man, though not without stopping off en route to watch a race at the Hippodrome. When he arrives, he does not need to mention either his thoughts or the Hippodrome: Basil knows and is not amused.[113] He delivers

---

110   See in general G. Dagron, "Judaïser," in *TM* 11 (1991): 359–80.
111   BHG 263: ed. A. N. Veselovskij, in *Sbornik Otdela russkogo jazyka I slovestniosti Imperatorskoj akademii nauk* 53 (St. Petersburg, 1891), 6 suppl. 3–174.
112   Ibid., 3–4.
113   Ibid., 5–7.

a stern lecture on the perdition of the Jews, and brings on the vision of the Last Judgment as a practical demonstration. Of course, Gregory witnesses the damnation of many other groups, including corrupt and sinful clergy. However, the climax of the drama is the moment of truth for the Jews, when they finally realize that the divine judge, Christ, is none other than the man they condemned to death.[114] The moral of the story is that the good Jews of the Old Testament were not really Jews at all, but proto-Christians, and the Old Testament was not really Jewish history.

The concepts of new Israel and chosen people corresponded to two beliefs that the Byzantines held about the place of their society in the world and in history. One was their sense of Orthodoxy, by which they meant not only right belief but also, increasingly from the seventh century, right practice in ritual and worship. The other was their theory of theocracy: the divine institution of the Christian empire, and the Christ-loving emperor's co-kingship with Christ. Both Byzantine Orthodoxy and Byzantine theocracy were fundamentally incompatible with Judaism. At the base of the orthodoxy defined by the early Church councils were the doctrines of the Trinity, and the Virgin Birth, Crucifixion, and Resurrection of Christ as the incarnate God; Orthodoxy also came to embrace the cult of the Virgin Mary, the veneration of icons, and reverence for the monastic life. All these features of Christianity were strenuously rejected by the Jews, as by Islam. Byzantine theocracy was based on the principle that the Christian empire was the earthly manifestation and anticipation of the kingdom of Christ, which superseded all other terrestrial realms; in other words, it was the messianic kingdom announced by the Old Testament prophets and awaited by the Jews along with the true Anointed of God.[115] It is thus not surprising that the three most forceful medieval expressions of the theocratic argument that the Christian empire is not the fourth, iron kingdom of Daniel's prophecy, but the eternal "fifth monarchy," all occur in the context of refutations of the Jews.[116] The need to refute Jewish messianic expectations based on

---

114   Ibid., 126–43.
115   The messianic element in Byzantine imperial eschatology was recognized by P. Alexander, *The Byzantine Apocalyptic Tradition* (Berkeley–Los Angeles–London, 1985), 151–84, though with reference to the Last Roman Emperor rather than to the Christian Roman Empire as a whole.
116   These are: (1) St. Constantine-Cyril's dispute with the Jews before the Khazar khagan, recorded in his Slavonic *Vita* (see above, n. 13); (2) an anti-Jewish tract attributed to Anastasios of Sinai (PG 89:1204–25, at 1210, 1212); (3) a commentary on Daniel by Basil, metropolitan of Neopatras, written in the late tenth century and still unpublished, in Cod. Patmiacus 31 (see Magdalino, "Year 1000" [n. 64 above], 252, 268).

the Bible also helps to explain why Byzantine apocalyptic texts foresee such a negative role for the Jews in the Last Things, as the supporters of Antichrist (i.e., their "false Messiah"),[117] and as the obdurate Christ-killers who refuse to recognize the Supreme Judge until it is too late.[118]

In the final analysis, Byzantine citation of the Old Testament was subordinated and peripheral to the New, and the identity of the new Israel was assumed to the detriment of the old. The emperors who most identified with Old Testament figures—Heraklios the new David, Leo III who enforced the second Commandment and took on the mantle of Melchisedek, and Basil I, another new David, who venerated Elijah—were also the most energetic in pressuring the Jews to convert. Basil I's New Church with its Old Testament relics was on the edge of the palace, while at its center stood the Pharos church that housed the relics of Christ's Passion and death at the hands of the Jews,[119] as Christians were dramatically reminded in the hymns and readings of the Good Friday vigil. Justinian II, the emperor who called his army *periousios laos*, was also the emperor who put the icon of Christ on his coins. For all the interest in Joshua that accompanied the Byzantine offensive against Islam in the tenth century, troops fought under the sign of the Cross and were blessed by contact with the Passion relics and fortified by the prayers of holy ascetics.[120] The triumph of David is displayed on plates, stamped with the hallmarks of Heraklios, but this is private art. When the same emperor sailed from Carthage to Constantinople, the ship's sails bore the public images of the Virgin.[121] Later Byzantines and their emperor went into battle accompanied by icons of the Virgin and relics of the True Cross,[122] and from the time of Constantine, Byzantine crosses, even

---

117 See especially K. Berger, *Die griechische Daniel-Diegese: Eine altkirchliche Apokalypse* (Leiden, 1976), 15.

118 In addition to the vision of the Last Judgment in the *Life of Basil the Younger* (n. 111 above), see the text published by R. Maisano, *L'Apocalisse apocrifa di Leone di Costantinopoli* (Naples, 1975), 106–9. Here the instruments of Christ's Passion are produced as incriminating evidence, and Pontius Pilate speaks as a witness for the prosecution: "the wretched Jews and the other nations behold that the Christians are the nation of the elect (ἐκλεκτὸν ἔθνος)."

119 See in general *Byzance et les reliques du Christ*, ed. J. Durand and B. Flusin (Paris, 2004); in this volume, for the Pharos church see especially P. Magdalino, "L'église du Phare et les reliques de la Passion à Constantinople (VIIe/VIIIe–XIIIe s.)," 15–30.

120 Harangue of Constantine VII, ed. R. Vári, "Zum historischen Exzerptenwerk des Konstantinos Porphyrogennetos," *BZ* 17 (1908): 75–85 at 80, 83, 85; trans. McGeer, "Two Military Orations" (n. 100 above), 118, 129, 132–33.

121 Av. Cameron, "The Theotokos in Sixth-Century Constantinople," *JTS*, n.s., 29 (1978): 97.

122 On icons of Mary and war, see B. V. Pentcheva, *Icons and Power: The Mother of God in Byzantium* (University Park, PA, 2006), 61–103. On recent studies about relics of the True Cross, see

for monastic use, had a triumphal, militaristic character, especially during the Macedonian period.[123]

It would be premature to assert that the Old Testament became more marginal to Byzantine Christianity than to the Christianity of other medieval societies, especially when further research in Byzantine religion and culture may lead to other conclusions and the centrality or marginality of a phenomenon as diffuse as the Old Testament involves an investigation of the entire social, economic, and political structure of a society. An Orthodox scholar has written that "the ultra-traditionalist orientation of Byzantine spirituality helped to preserve ... some themes typical of the religious culture of ancient Israel which were lost in the Occident,"[124] and a Catholic scholar has concluded from a study of the Theodore Psalter that, "important and influential Byzantine Christians were keen to see the common roots between their religion and that of the Jews, in the Old Testament, in apocryphal narrative, and through an interest in liturgical customs."[125] But even at the height of the Old Testament "craze" in the eighth and ninth centuries, one has the impression that the typology was less painstakingly and systematically applied in Byzantium than in the other Christian empire, that of Carolingian Francia—just as the process has been more thoroughly studied by Western medievalists than by Byzantinists.[126] The Orthodox dropped Old Testament readings from the Divine Liturgy after the seventh century, and they did not name their children after Old Testament figures, even though they might take prophetic names on entering the monastic life. Finally, one should not forget that it was Byzantine accusations of judaizing, through the use of azymes (unleavened bread), that sparked the schism with the Latin West in 1054.[127]

After Iconoclasm, Byzantine churches mainly had centralized plans and decoration largely confined to New Testament scenes and images of saints. Thus middle and late Byzantine churches do not have long naves decorated with cycles

---

A. Eastmond, "Byzantine Identity and Relics of the True Cross in the Thirteenth Century," in *Eastern Christian Relics*, ed. A. Lidov (Moscow, 2003), 208 with further references.

123 A. Grabar, "La précieuse crois de la Lavra Saint-Athanase au Mont-Athos," *CahArch* 19 (1969): 99–125; Pentcheva, *Icons and Power*, 69–74.

124 Averintsev, "Constant Characteristics" (n. 22 above), 219.

125 B. Crostini, "Christianity and Judaism in Eleventh-Century Constantinople," in Εὐκοσμία: *Studi miscellanei per il 75° di Vincenzo Poggi S.J.*, ed. V. Ruggieri and L. Pieralli (Soveria Mannelli [Catanzaro], 2003), 169–87 at 187.

126 See M. Garrison and M. de Jong in Hen and Innes, *Uses of the Past* (n. 25 above).

127 Leo of Ochrid, who fired the opening shots, is very explicit in his letters to the pope: E. Buttner, ed., *Erzbischof Leon von Ohrid (1037–1056): Leben und Werk (mit den Texten seiner bisher unedierten asketischen Schrift und seiner drei Briefe an den Papst)* (Bamberg, 2007), 180–282.

of Old Testament narratives as in Italian basilicas, and they never embraced the fashion for stained glass and panels of Old Testament images that are favored in churches north of the Alps. Frontal images of Jesus, Mary, and the saints are preferred to narrative cycles, which reappear only in later centuries. The theology and devotional practices of the icon come to rival if not prevail over the cult of relics. As a result, the many architectural accommodations that medieval western churches made for relic pilgrims find few counterparts in the East. Until 1204, Constantinople possessed the greatest collection of Passion relics in the Christian world, but, sequestered in the palace, those relics were not the objects of mass pilgrimage. In the West, by contrast, even after miraculous icons were imported from Byzantium, relics remained more important there than religious pictures. These larger differences inform the differing use and significance of Old Testament imagery in Greek and Latin Christianity.

From the twelfth century, Old Testament representation and exegesis played an ever more important role in Western Europe.[128] When King Louis IX received the great Passion relics from Constantinople, he had constructed that masterpiece of Gothic architecture, the Ste. Chapelle (Fig. 1), dedicated in 1248. The new setting, it has been remarked, was "very similar in concept to that of the Byzantine palace church of the Pharos,"[129] and indeed both churches were embedded within palaces that stood not far from the cathedrals of both cities. Because the two palatine chapels are so similar, the differences in their pictorial decoration are telling. The mosaics of the ninth-century Pharos chapel, though destroyed, are known from a homily of Patriarch Photios. In the dome Christ presided as overseer. Below in concave segments were angels, in the apse, the Virgin with arms outstretched, and elsewhere, apostles, martyrs, prophets, and patriarchs.

Of the latter, only David and Jacob at the Pharos chapel can be identified through the texts they presented. Though silent, according to Photios, the prophets cry out their "sayings of yore."[130] By the pictorial economy of holy images, this communication most likely consisted of frontal figures, who were available and accessible to beholders, as in later Byzantine churches (Fig. 2). These holy figures displayed texts, and since reading then was predominately oral, not silent, these "sayings" were indeed audible, when voiced by literate viewers/readers. The Ste. Chapelle, in contrast, has rows of tall stained glass windows filled with dense

128   H. Stahl, *Picturing Kingship: History and Painting in the Psalter of Saint Louis* (University Park, PA, 2008), 154–67. We have benefited from A. Kumler's review of the book in *ArtB* 91, no. 1 (2009): 113–17.
129   Kalavrezou, "Helping Hands" (n. 44 above), 57.
130   Mango, *Homilies of Photius* (n. 81 above), 187–88.

FIGURE 1 Ste. Chapelle, Paris, Upper Chapel, view to altar. Photograph Sumner McKnight Crosby. Visual Resources Collection, Yale University Library.

FIGURE 2 Parekklesion, Church of the Chora, Istanbul, view to altar. Photograph Dumbarton Oaks.

imagery. It is an architecture enlivened not by the reflected light of gold mosaics, lit by candles and lamps, but by direct illumination passing through webs of pictorial narratives. Some are so distant that individual figures cannot be deciphered, at least with the visual skills that most have today, and accompanying inscriptions are absent.[131] Following tradition, the north and south sides of the church are devoted to the Old Testament, visually narrated in such a way as to articulate "the foremost components of French medieval monarchic rule and the specifically Capetian claims to sacral kingship." In so doing they "fuse biblical past and historical present in the figure of Louis IX," thereby including him and his people among the chosen people of the Bible.[132]

Contemporary Parisian illuminated manuscripts emphasized Old Testament narratives to an extent that would be astounding in Byzantium. It has been estimated that while the Ste. Chapelle has 650 Old Testament images, the contemporary Bibles moralisées each have 1800, the Medieval Picture Bible in the Morgan Library 350, and the famed Psalter of St. Louis, 130 scenes.[133] The Morgan manuscript (Fig. 3), in particular, makes explicit the connection with contemporary France, because its biblical heroes are dressed as knights, who wage war with the full panoply of available technology.[134] Nowhere in evidence is the visual distinction between past and present of the tenth-century Joshua Roll and its subtle political allegory. Now the Old Testament is appropriated, directly and fully, and one almost wants to say, crudely, in the service of a different ruler and army that aspired to conquer the Holy Land.

Looking for parallel representations in Byzantium, one can point to the later thirteenth-century Vatopedi Octateuch that reproduces the iconography of the Joshua Roll and might have some connection with the imperial family,[135] a subject treated in John Lowden's chapter in this volume, but at no moment does it narrate the conquest of the Holy Land as graphically and realistically as the Morgan Picture Bible. Early Palaeologan Psalters repeat images from the tenth-

---

131 A. A. Jordan, *Visualizing Kingship in the Windows of the Sainte-Chapelle* (Turnhout, 2002), 2–3, 10–14.
132 Ibid., 3, 73.
133 In general, on Old Testament imagery in thirteenth-century France, see D. H. Weiss, *Art and Crusade in the Age of Saint Louis* (New York, 1998), 47 and passim; and idem, "The Old Testament Image and the Rise of Crusader Culture in France," in *France and the Holy Land: Frankish Culture at the End of the Crusades*, ed. D. H. Weiss and L. Mahoney (Baltimore, 2004), 3–21.
134 W. Noel and D. Weiss, eds., *The Book of Kings: Art, War, and the Morgan Library's Medieval Picture Bible* (Baltimore, 2002).
135 J. Lowden, *The Octateuchs: A Study in Byzantine Manuscript Illustration* (University Park, PA, 1992), 32–33.

FIGURE 3   Samuel Anointing Saul and Sacrificing. New York, The Morgan Library and Museum, MS 638, fol. 23v.

century Paris Psalter (Frontispiece) or a sister manuscript,[136] but without the latter's ideology of imperial power and succession.[137] Thus, while the Macedonian manuscript was likely made for the son of Constantine VII, to date no Palaeologan Psalter has been found to have a history to match the Psalter of St. Louis that, it has been speculated, might have been created for the son of Louis IX.[138] The multivolume Leo Bible from the mid-tenth century (Rome, Vat. Reg. gr. 1) has illustrated frontispieces to books of the Old Testament, but has no successors, and in general the Bible in Byzantium was packaged in multiple textual units, unlike the pandects of late antiquity,[139] the Italian Giant Bibles of the

136   K. Weitzmann, "Eine Pariser-Psalter-Kopie des 13. Jahrhunderts auf dem Sinai," *JÖBG* 6 (1957): 125–43; H. Belting, "Zum Palatina-Psalter des 13. Jahrhunderts: Aus der Werkstattpraxis eines byzantinischen Malers," *JÖB* 21 (1972): 17–38; G. Parpulov, in *Byzantium: Faith and Power (1261–1557)*, ed. H. C. Evans (New York, 2004), 273–74.
137   While one copy in St. Petersburg, Publ. Lib. cod. gr. 269, represents David with the same verse as the Paris Psalter, another in Rome, Vat. Palat. gr. 381, inscribes only the first half of the verse, thus omitting the reference to the king's son. See A. Cutler, *The Aristocratic Psalters in Byzantium* (Paris, 1984), 44, 83.
138   Stahl, *Picturing Kingship* (n. 128 above), 211.
139   T. F. Mathews, "The Epigrams of Leo Sacellarios and an Exegetical Approach to the Miniatures of Vat. Reg. Gr. 1," *OCP* 43 (1977): 94–134; Parpulov, "Bibles of the Christian East" (n. 3 above). On the epigrams accompanying the miniatures in the Leo Bible, see M. D. Lauxtermann,

Romanesque period, or the standardized single volume Bibles associated with thirteenth-century Paris.[140]

Since the imperial palace at Blachernae was pillaged at the end of the empire, Constantinople today lacks a royal chapel to compare to that of Louis IX, but the church of the Chora offers an approximate analogy (Figs. 2 and 4). Redecorated by the prime minister of Andronikos II, Theodore Metochites, it is the finest aristocratic church of its day and was located near the imperial palace.[141] In the narthex, as one of us has argued, the Chora has narrative scenes of the biblical past that, like the Ste. Chapelle, legitimate the present by means of the New, not the Old, Testament.[142] Indirect reference is made to the reigning emperor Andronikos II through an unprecedented emphasis on the otherwise obscure St. Andronikos, who looks toward the politically salient mosaic of Joseph and Mary enrolling for taxation in Bethlehem.[143] The isolated Old Testament scenes on the side walls of the nearby parekklesion (Fig. 2) do not narrate the story of the chosen people, but serve as antitypes of the Virgin, largely drawn from Marian liturgies.[144] Similarly, the fancifully dressed warriors below (Fig. 4) are military saints, not crusading Israelites, as in the Morgan manuscript (Fig. 3).[145] These near-life-size figures and the saintly clergy at the east end of the parekklesion are positioned close to beholders and encourage veneration by those visiting the tombs here. These icons support and visually dominate the narrative scenes above (Fig. 2).

During the later Middle Ages, the East and the West had different "aristocratic practices of the sign" and "conditions of representation [that] are both determined and mediated by [them]."[146] In the twelfth and thirteenth centuries, Capetian rulers subscribed to a secular typology and a "virtually causal"

Byzantine Poetry from Pisides to Geometres, Texts and Contexts, WByzSt 24, no. 1 (Vienna, 2003), 1:191–96, 348 (where a projected volume on the manuscript is announced).

140 W. Cahn, *Romanesque Bible Illumination* (Ithaca, 1982), 101–7; C. de Hamel, *A History of Illuminated Manuscripts* (Boston, 1986), 113–20.

141 P. A. Underwood, *The Kariye Djami* (New York, 1966 [vols. 1–3]; Princeton, 1975 [vol. 4]).

142 R. S. Nelson, "Taxation with Representation: Visual Narrative and the Political Field of the Kariye Camii," *Art History* 22 (1999): 56–82.

143 R. S. Nelson, "Heavenly Allies at the Chora," *Gesta* 43 (2004): 31–40.

144 S. Der Nersessian, "Program and Iconography of the Frescoes of the Parecclesion," in Underwood, *Kariye Djami*, 4:316–18.

145 Underwood, *Kariye Djami*, 1:252–58. On military saints, see C. Walter, *The Warrior Saints in Byzantine Art and Tradition* (Burlington, VT, 2003)

146 R. H. Bloch, *Etymologies and Genealogies: A Literary Anthropology of the French Middle Ages* (Chicago, 1983), 28.

FIGURE 4   St. George, Parekklesion, Church of the Chora, Istanbul. Photograph Dumbarton Oaks.

relationship between biblical heroes and the French king.[147] They accorded ever greater significance to Old Testament narratives that are visible signs of a hierarchical social structure and the vertical integration of the past and present.[148] Byzantine Macedonian emperors of the ninth and tenth centuries promoted the Old Testament for political and dynastic reasons (Frontispiece) and encouraged an identification with the biblical chosen people, especially when going on the offensive in the direction of the Holy Land. Consequently, our volume focuses on the period up to the end of the twelfth century.

Matters changed, however, in the Palaeologan period. When the first Palaeologan emperor Michael VIII was excommunicated and his successor Andronikos II overthrown by his grandson Andronikos III, it was not the moment to extol dynasty and genealogy through the Old Testament. Instead, emperor, aristocracy, and the rest were ever more faithful to icons. The program of the Chora associated the aristocracy with Christian saints, not Old Testament figures, as befits a society that, compared to the West, had looser interpersonal ties and a more horizontal social structure.[149] In the last days of the empire, when Ottoman cannon were pounding the land walls of Constantinople, its defenders put their faith less in relics or imagery of Old Testament heroes than in the icon of the Virgin Hodegetria that had long been the wonder-working palladium of the city. In the prior Ottoman siege of 1422, the icon had been brought to the Chora, and once that siege ended, it was taken back to its own monastery, an event that was sermonized by means of Old and New Testament allusions.[150] Three decades later, when the city was attacked and the situation was graver, the Hodegetria again came to the Chora. After the Turks had breached the walls, the Greek historian Ducas reported that the Janissaries rushed to the church, hacked the icon into four pieces, and cast lots for the fragments. Whether true or not, this last detail makes reference to the soldiers who vied for Jesus' garments at the Crucifixion, and thereby rhetorically deepens the tragedy through reference now to only the New Testament.[151]

University of St. Andrews
Yale University

147   G. M. Spiegel, "Political Utility in Medieval Historiography," *History and Theory* 14 (1975): 321–22.
148   Bloch, *Etymologies*, 64–91.
149   Nelson, "Heavenly Allies," 31–40; A. Kazhdan and G. Constable, *People and Power in Byzantium: An Introduction to Modern Byzantine Studies* (Washington, DC, 1982), 23–36.
150   Pentcheva, *Icons and Power* (n. 122 above), 142–43.
151   Ducas, *Historia byzantina* (Bonn, 1834), 272, 288; H. J. Magoulias, *Decline and Fall of Byzantium to the Ottoman Turks by Doukas* (Detroit, 1975), 215, 225.

TWO

The Greek Bible Translations of the Byzantine Jews

NICHOLAS DE LANGE

THE VERY SUGGESTION THAT Byzantine Jews used Greek Bible translations may well come as a surprise. Those Byzantinists who pay any attention to the Jewish minority tend to assume that their language, for most or all purposes, was Hebrew. The aim of the present study is to correct this too sweeping generalization, at least so far as the Bible is concerned, and to clear up certain misconceptions, in the light of the manuscript evidence, an important part of which has become available only recently.[1]

Byzantine Judaism: General Remarks

Despite having to endure a regime of discriminatory legislation, the Jewish communities of the Byzantine empire maintained a continuous existence for as long as the empire itself endured. Occupying a central geographical position in the Jewish world, these communities kept up a high level of scholarship and played an important role in the transmission of Jewish texts and ideas. Byzantine Jewish scholarship is characterized by a high regard for tradition coupled with an openness to new ideas.

Our main source of information for Byzantine Judaism is its manuscripts. We have hundreds of Hebrew manuscripts copied in Byzantine lands; although

---

1 The study is based on research currently being carried out in a project titled "The Greek Bible in Byzantine Judaism," funded by the British Arts and Humanities Research Council (AHRC). The main aim of the project is to make the manuscript evidence for the translations available both online and in print. I am grateful to my research associates on the project, Cameron Boyd-Taylor and Julia Krivoruchko, for helpful advice in the preparation of this article.

dated examples do not become common until the fourteenth century, earlier ones are now coming to light. Particularly important in this context are the mainly very fragmentary Cairo Genizah manuscripts, retrieved from a synagogue in Old Cairo (Fustat). Most of these manuscripts were taken to Cambridge by Solomon Schechter in 1896–97.[2] There are many tens of thousands of fragments, and they come from or relate to many different parts of the world. Among them are quite a number that are connected with Byzantium; most of these were written in the tenth to early thirteenth centuries: this is important, because the other Byzantine Hebrew manuscripts we have date from the later Byzantine period (after the Latin Conquest). Among all these manuscripts, copies of Bibles, as well as biblical commentaries, figure prominently.

The primary language of all these writings is Hebrew, but they freely use Aramaic and Greek as well. (There are also occasional indications of a knowledge of Arabic.) For Byzantine Jews, Hebrew and Aramaic were written languages only: their usual spoken language was Greek. During the Middle Ages, Jews normally used the Hebrew alphabet for writing all these languages; only very rarely do we find the Greek alphabet used.

Byzantine Judaism was not entirely homogeneous; in fact, it was split by a number of schisms. The most important schism, which began in the eleventh century, divided Karaites, adherents of a kind of *sola scriptura* position, from Rabbanites, who accorded authority to the Talmud as well as to the biblical writings. For the Karaites, divine revelation was contained in the written Scriptures only and was accessible to humans through the exercise of reason. They rejected the notion that what the Rabbanites called "oral Torah," the rabbinic teachings embodied in the Talmud, had any divine status. Because the Bible was so important to the Karaite–Rabbanite schism, biblical studies inevitably occupied a central position in Byzantine Jewish scholarship and polemics.[3]

Although relations between the Jewish minority and the Orthodox Christian majority were not free from tensions and pressures, there is no reason to

---

2 See S. C. Reif, *A Jewish Archive from Old Cairo: The History of Cambridge University's Genizah Collection* (Richmond, Surrey, 2000).
3 On the schism see N. de Lange, "Can We Speak of Jewish Orthodoxy in Byzantium?" in *Byzantine Orthodoxies: Papers from the Thirty-Sixth Spring Symposium of Byzantine Studies, University of Durham, 23–25 March 2002*, ed. A. Louth and A. Casiday (Aldershot, 2006), 167–78. The key work on the subject remains Z. Ankori, *Karaites in Byzantium: The Formative Years, 970–1100* (New York–Jerusalem, 1959). See also D. Frank, "Karaite Exegetical and Halakhic Literature in Byzantium and Turkey," in *Karaite Judaism: A Guide to Its History and Literary Sources*, ed. M. Polliack (Leiden, 2003), 528–58.

think of them as living completely separate lives. There were personal contacts, as well as formal meetings (including theological disputations), and some conversions of Jews to Christianity are attested.[4]

The Bible in Medieval Judaism

The Hebrew Bible played a central part in Jewish worship, and consequently in medieval Jewish education. At the heart of public worship was a reading from the Torah (the Pentateuch). Because, following ancient custom, the Hebrew text used for this purpose was written on a single parchment scroll, by specially trained scribes, without vowel signs or any annotations, in a careful book hand, the reading of such a text also required special training. The reading of the Torah was followed by a reading from the prophetic books. The pentateuchal readings were accompanied by a translation into Aramaic, a targum. The targum was preserved in written texts, though it may have been delivered orally on occasion.

Passages from the Bible were also incorporated in the prayers, and the Psalms were recited in private and public worship. On certain days in the liturgical calendar the five small scrolls (Esther, Song of Songs, Ruth, Lamentations, and Ecclesiastes) were read.

For purposes of study, the biblical books were copied in codex form; in these codices the texts were equipped with vowel signs and punctuation marks to assist the reading and with a textual apparatus known as the masorah. This form of biblical manuscript was developed by the so-called masoretes, specialist scholars who established the text of the Hebrew Bible and its apparatus between the eighth and tenth centuries. The codex format was used for Hebrew books from around the eighth century; the earliest extant masoretic Bibles were written in Muslim lands in the tenth century.[5]

Biblical study featured at every level of Jewish education. Education was divided into three levels similar to those familiar to us today. At the elementary level boys underwent preparation to chant the prayers and the biblical readings in synagogue. At the secondary level they acquired a deeper knowledge of Hebrew and were introduced to other traditional writings, notably the Mishnah and Talmud, but also midrash and biblical commentaries. The highest level

---

4   See N. de Lange, "Jews and Christians in the Byzantine Empire: Problems and Prospects," in *Christianity and Judaism*, ed. D. Wood (Oxford, 1992), 15–32.
5   See further C. Sirat, *Hebrew Manuscripts of the Middle Ages* (Cambridge, 2002), especially 35, 38–55.

of education, involving notably more profound study of the legal sources, was reserved for rabbis and other communal functionaries.[6]

Midrash, a distinctively Byzantine genre that originated in Byzantine Palestine and spread gradually to other parts of the Jewish world, appears to be closely connected to synagogue preaching, although it also has clear links to the classroom or lecture hall. Midrashic works, which are generally but not always presented in the form of a commentary on a single biblical book, expand on biblical narratives and teachings, and often collect comments ascribed to different teachers, in a manner reminiscent of Christian catenae.[7]

Commentaries proper emerge in Judaism only in the tenth century. Among the Byzantine Jewish writings are many commentaries on biblical books, including some early examples of the genre. These commentaries reveal strong connections with non-Byzantine centers of Jewish scholarship but often betray specifically Byzantine interests. The rift between Karaites and Rabbanites gave a boost to biblical scholarship; many of the Byzantine Bible commentaries are by Karaite scholars.[8]

The synagogal liturgy in Byzantium (as elsewhere) was adorned with hymns (piyyutim) that are full of biblical allusions, relying on a rich tradition of exegesis.[9] In addition, the biblical books were prominent in polemic and debate between Jews and Christians. Some commentaries include explicit reference to matters of controversy, with a view to preparing Jews for debate with Christians.

Hebrew and Greek Bibles in Byzantium

It is clear from epigraphical and other sources that in late antiquity the normal language of Jewish worship in Egypt, Asia Minor, and Europe was Greek.[10] It is equally clear that by the tenth century Hebrew had replaced Greek for this purpose, and that public readings from the Bible throughout the Jewish world were conducted in Hebrew. We do not know when or why or how the Hebrew Bible

---

6 See N. de Lange, "Jewish Education in the Byzantine Empire in the Twelfth Century," in *Jewish Education and Learning*, ed. G. Abramson and T. Parfitt (Chur, Switzerland, 1994), 115–28.
7 See N. de Lange, "A Thousand Years of Hebrew in Byzantium," in *Hebrew Study from Ezra to Ben-Yehuda*, ed. W. Horbury (Edinburgh, 1999), 147–61 (here 148–49).
8 See D. Frank, "Karaite Exegesis," in *Hebrew Bible/Old Testament: The History of Its Interpretation*, ed. M. Sæbø (Göttingen, 1996–), 1.2:110–28 (here 126–28).
9 On these see L. J. Weinberger, *Jewish Hymnography: A Literary History* (London, 1998), especially chap. 4, "Synagogue Poets in Balkan Byzantium."
10 See V. Colorni, "L'uso del greco nella liturgia del giudaismo ellenistico e la Novella 146 di Giustiniano," *Annali di storia del diritto* 8 (1964): 1–69.

acquired its preeminent position, but an interesting clue is provided by a decree of emperor Justinian I dated 8 February 553, which depicts a Jewish community seriously divided on this issue. It states in the preamble: "We have learnt from their [i.e., the Hebrews'] petitions [*proseleuseis*], which they have addressed to us, that while some maintain the Hebrew language only and want to use it in reading the Holy Books others consider it right to admit Greek as well, and they have already been quarrelling among themselves about this for a long time."[11] Commentators have disagreed about where this quarrel took place (was it in Constantinople or in the land of Israel?) and which side was promoting change and which side defending the status quo. Another question relates to the position of the Hellenists: did they want a reading only in Greek, or did they want a Greek reading in addition to a Hebrew reading? My own view is that the dispute did not take place in Israel but in Constantinople and perhaps in other places in the empire, and that it arose from efforts by the Hebraist party to impose a reading in Hebrew on congregations that had traditionally read the Bible in Greek. There is no evidence for the use of Hebrew by Jews in Europe in more than a symbolic way before the end of the eighth century (the evidence in general for European Judaism in the seventh and eighth centuries is admittedly very thin). The dominant language in this earlier period is clearly Greek, although occasional Hebrew words and phrases occur in inscriptions from the fifth century onward. After the year 800 there is increasing evidence for the use of Hebrew, and it is clear that by the turn of the millennium the primary language of written culture and worship for Jews in Byzantium and elsewhere in Europe was Hebrew, a language that has come to be identified uniquely with the Jews. Consequently I interpret the mid-sixth-century quarrel as an early attempt by Hebraists to have Hebrew replace Greek in the synagogue.[12]

---

11   Justinian, *Novel* 146; translation in *The Jews in Roman Imperial Legislation*, ed. A. Linder (Detroit–Jerusalem, 1987), 408.
12   See N. de Lange, "The Hebrew Language in the European Diaspora," in *Studies on the Jewish Diaspora in the Hellenistic and Roman Periods*, ed. B. Isaac and A. Oppenheimer (Tel Aviv, 1996), 111–37; D. Noy, "'Peace Upon Israel': Hebrew Formulae and Names in Jewish Inscriptions from the Western Roman Empire," in *Hebrew Study from Ezra to Ben-Yehuda*, ed. W. Horbury (Edinburgh, 1999), 135–46. For a full discussion of Justinian's novel see A. M. Rabello, *Giustiniano, Ebrei e Samaritani alla luce delle fonti storico-letterarie, ecclesiastiche e giuridiche* (Milan, 1987–88), 2:814–28. For more recent studies see G. Veltri, "Die Novelle 146 Περὶ Ἑβραίων: Das Verbot des Targumsvortrags in Justinians Politik," in *Die Septuaginta zwischen Judentum und Christentum*, ed. M. Hengel and A. M. Schwemer (Tübingen, 1994), 116–30; E. Klingenberg, "Justinians Novellen zur Judengesetzgebung," *Aschkenas* 8 (1998): 7–27; L. V. Rutgers, "Justinian's Novella 146 between Jews and Christians," in *Jewish Culture and Society under the Christian Roman Empire*, ed. R. Kalmin and S. Schwartz (Leuven, 2003), 385–407.

Justinian, in his novel, comes down firmly on the Hellenist side. He allows Jews to read the Scriptures in synagogue, or anywhere else, in Greek or in any other language that those present can understand, the key point being that they can understand the teachings and put them into practice in their lives. And, although he expresses a strong preference for the Septuagint version (the Old Testament of the Church), he adds that "we permit also the use of the translation of Akylas, although he was a gentile and in some readings differs not a little from the Septuagint."

In making this concession the emperor recognizes a preference among Jews for the translation by Akylas (also known by the Latinized form of his name, Aquila), thought to have been made in the early second century and written in a very distinctive Greek style that clings deliberately to the wording of the Hebrew original. Origen, more than three centuries before Justinian wrote his novel, had contrasted this "Jewish" version with the "Christian" versions, those of the Septuagint and Theodotion. In a letter to Julius Africanus written around 248, Origen states that Akylas "is preferred by those Jews who know Hebrew, as being the most successful translator of all."[13] In permitting the use of Akylas Justinian may also be offering a consolation prize to the defeated Hebraist faction, because Akylas was much closer to the Hebrew text than the Septuagint was.

Nowadays the consensus among specialists is that all these Greek translations of the Old Testament—the Septuagint, Akylas, and Theodotion, as well as another version, attributed to Symmachos—are of Jewish, not Christian, origin. Origen included all four, along with some other versions, in his great synoptic compilation, the *Hexapla*, along with the Hebrew text twice, in Hebrew letters and in Greek letters. Of the *Hexapla* only fragments survive. The versions, or perhaps we should call them revisions, of Akylas, Theodotion, and Symmachos (collectively called by Origen "the Three"), survive mainly through these fragments. All of them are thought to have circulated among Jews in the second and third centuries. Thus in the later Roman period Jews used a diversity of Greek Bible texts: there was no single authorized version, even if there was a preference in some circles for Akylas.

When later texts, Jewish and Christian, mention the Jews' Greek Bible, they always refer to it as Akylas. This is the case in the Talmud and Midrash, where

---

13 *Epistula ad Africanum* 4, ed. N. de Lange in *Origène, Sur les écritures: Philocalie, 1–20, et la Lettre à Africanus sur l'Histoire de Suzanne*, ed. M. Harl and N. de Lange, SC 302 (Paris, 1983), 526. For the dating, see ibid., 498–501.

some fragments of Akylas are quoted.[14] A Christian example is the Slavonic *Life of Constantine* [i.e., Cyril]: recording the Byzantine missionary's debate with Jews in Khazaria, it gives a biblical quotation that is said to come from Akylas.[15] These testimonies to the continuing use of the translation of Akylas are confirmed by fragments recovered from the Cairo Genizah, and by some other Jewish sources. In what follows we shall take a closer look at this evidence, and consider what it tells us about the use of Greek Bible translations in the medieval synagogue.

Greek Bible Translations in Byzantine Judaism: Manuscript Evidence

No Jewish source refers unambiguously to the use of Greek biblical versions by Jews in Byzantium, and we have no Jewish manuscripts of the entire Bible in Greek, or even of the Pentateuch. We do, however, have some continuous texts in manuscripts, as well as a printed version of the Pentateuch, to which we shall return below. The absence of more extensive manuscripts does not necessarily mean that these never existed: we should bear in mind the enormous losses of manuscripts in Byzantium. It is clear from booklists and stray leaves of otherwise unknown works that many texts, even ones that were once quite widely distributed, have disappeared.

With rare exceptions, the manuscript evidence that points to a continuing tradition of Greek Bible translation by Jews is highly fragmentary, and consists largely of stray pages surviving in the Cairo Genizah.

The earliest Genizah manuscripts are palimpsests, i.e., parchments that have been reused for writing a second text over the first. Some fragments of reused biblical manuscripts in majuscule Greek writing, containing a version identified as that of Akylas, were among the first Genizah fragments to be published. They contain parts of the books of Kings and Psalms, and have been dated by the Greek script to the sixth century.[16]

---

14 The citations are set out and discussed in G. Veltri, *Libraries, Translations, and "Canonic" Texts: The Septuagint, Aquila, and Ben Sira in the Jewish and Christian Traditions* (Leiden, 2006), 176–85.
15 *The Vita of Constantine and The Vita of Methodius*, trans. M. Kantor and R. S. White (Ann Arbor, 1976), 27.
16 F. C. Burkitt, *Fragments of the Books of Kings according to the Translation of Aquila* (Cambridge, 1897); C. Taylor, *Hebrew–Greek Cairo Genizah Palimpsests* (Cambridge, 1900). See also M. Sokolov and J. Yahalom, "Christian Palimpsests from the Genizah," *Revue d'Histoire des Textes* 8 (1978): 107–32. For the latest discussion of the dating, see N. Tchernetska, "Greek-Oriental

While it cannot be proved conclusively that these were Jewish rather than Christian copies, several factors combine to make it more likely that they were. The wording of Justinian's novel cited above (with which they are roughly contemporary) provides a plausible Jewish context for them. They are carefully executed. They may have come from one or more synagogue libraries, or they may have been kept in a synagogue for public reading. If so, they confirm that Akylas's translation was still being read publicly in the sixth century and maybe much later. (They were reused as palimpsests in the tenth or eleventh century.)

Another palimpsest contains part of a biblical glossary arranged in parallel columns presenting Hebrew words with their Greek equivalents. The Greek script, a distinctive type of majuscule, is much less carefully executed than that of the Akylas fragments. The manuscript has been dated to the ninth century. The glosses are closely related to Akylas, although the orthography is nonstandard and the forms of the words are often closer to spoken than to written Greek.[17]

This discovery, fragmentary as it is, is of extraordinary significance, not only as a testimony to the beginnings of biblical lexicography and the Masoretic text of the Hebrew Bible, but as a witness to Bible study in Greek by Jews at a time for which any evidence of Greek-speaking Jewish culture is sparse. The continuing presence of much earlier translations, particularly Akylas, is significant, as is the use of Greek script at a time when, among Jews, Hebrew writing was taking over from Greek. With very few exceptions, all subsequent Jewish Greek manuscripts, including Greek words and phrases embedded within Hebrew manuscripts, are written in Hebrew script.

The only book of Scripture preserved in its entirety in Greek in medieval manuscript is Jonah, which figures as the prophetic reading (*haftarah*) in the afternoon service for the Day of Atonement. It was the custom in at least some congregations to read the book in Greek, and the text is preserved in two fourteenth/fifteenth-century prayer books. The language is essentially medieval Greek, but with a number of striking archaic features, and the translation

---

Palimpsests in Cambridge: Problems and Prospects," in *Literacy, Education and Manuscript Transmission in Byzantium and Beyond*, ed. C. Holmes and J. Waring (Leiden, 2002), 243–56.

17 N. Tchernetska, J. Olszowy-Schlanger, and N. de Lange, "An Early Hebrew–Greek Biblical Glossary from the Cairo Genizah," *Revue des Études Juives* 166 (2007): 91–128; N. de Lange, "An Early Hebrew–Greek Bible Glossary from the Cairo Genizah and Its Significance for the Study of Jewish Bible Translations into Greek," in *Studies in Hebrew Literature and Culture Presented to Albert van der Heide on the Occasion of His Sixty-Fifth Birthday*, ed. M. F. J. Baasten and R. Munk (Dordrecht, 2007), 31–39.

adheres very closely to the diction of the Hebrew. The text was transcribed into Greek letters and published by the Hellenist D. C. Hesseling in 1901.[18]

Among the Genizah fragments the only continuous translation is a fragment of the book of Ecclesiastes in Greek. The translation clings very closely to the word order and syntax of the Hebrew, and each verse in Greek is preceded by its opening word in Hebrew. It is possible, though by no means certain, that it comes, like the Jonah version, from a prayer book, in this case for the festival of Tabernacles, for which Ecclesiastes is a prescribed reading. It shares some characteristics of the ancient Greek version, which purely for convenience we shall here call LXX (this is the version found in Christian Bibles today). LXX Ecclesiastes adheres very closely to the word order and grammar of the Hebrew. It is generally thought to have been made in Palestine in the early second century CE, and some have maintained that it was made by Akylas himself. The Genizah translation is, however, not simply a variant text of the ancient version.[19]

Any two translations that adopt a strict word-for-word approach to translating the same original are bound to have some similarities, but in the present case the similarities go beyond the bounds of mere coincidence. This is most clearly visible in the use of the Greek word *syn* (in ancient Greek a preposition meaning "with") to render the Hebrew particle *et*, which marks the definite direct object. This usage is a solecism commonly associated with Akylas; it is present in LXX Ecclesiastes. The Genizah fragment from Ecclesiastes uses *syn* less systematically than LXX does. This is a startling usage in a medieval text, as *syn* is not used at all in ordinary medieval Greek, and outside the synagogue it is never found in Greek of any period except as a preposition governing the dative case.

The vocabulary and syntax of our version belong somewhere between that of the ancient version and modern Greek. Examples of late vocabulary are *lesmono*, "to forget" (first attested in the fifth century) and *mertikon*, "a share" (not found before the sixth century). Prepositions are generally constructed with the accusative and rarely with the genitive, but never with the dative, indicating that the language of our fragment is essentially medieval, not ancient, Greek. These characteristics of our version confirm that the fragment, though not an actual copy of an ancient version, stands in a tradition that derives ultimately from the ancient version preserved in the Christian Church and shares its approach to translation.

18   Oxford, Bodelian Library, Opp. Add. 8vo 19, fols. 220r–227v; Bologna, University Library, 3574, fols. 249v–252r. See D. C. Hesseling, "Le livre de Jonas," *BZ* 10 (1901): 208–17.
19   Cambridge, University Library, T-S Misc. 28.74. See N. de Lange, *Greek Jewish Texts from the Cairo Genizah* (Tübingen, 1996), 71–78.

The other Genizah fragments come from glossaries, scholia, and commentaries—in other words, from the apparatus of biblical study. The dividing lines between these three genres are not always easy to draw. One clear example of a glossary is a fragment that lists difficult Hebrew words from the books of Malachi and Job with their Greek translations. Unlike the palimpsest glossary mentioned above, the Greek words are written in Hebrew characters. The manuscript dates probably from the tenth or eleventh century.[20] Once again, the glosses show striking agreements with the fragments of Akylas, who is very consistent in the Greek equivalents he uses for specific Hebrew words. Examples of his vocabulary in the fragment are *dolieuomai* (to defraud), *dokimazo* (to try or test), *motono* (to dress a wound), *onucha* (onyx), and *kataluo* (to destroy). Some words are built according to the distinctive method developed by Akylas, who created new Greek compounds very freely, often employing his own theory of semantics, e.g., *gennematizo* (to beget), *aposkolopizo* (to remove a stumbling block or paling), and *spiloma* (fine gold). On the other hand, one of the telltale signs of Akylas's version—*syn* rendering *et*—is absent, and there are some late words, such as *sapounin* for soap. We may infer that this glossary, like the other texts under consideration, is based directly not on Akylas but on a much later translation deriving from it.

A more developed form of glossary combines Hebrew lemmata, Greek translations, and occasional short Hebrew comments.[21] Sometimes two alternative translations are given. Similar glossaries, known from northern France, have glosses in Old French. Close study has led to the discovery that these glosses are derived from actual Old French Bible translations made by Jews, and are not (as some had supposed), extempore, ad hoc translations of the Hebrew words.[22]

From these more developed glossaries it is only a short step to scholia—short comments on the Hebrew which employ Greek glosses.[23] Philological exposition is characteristic of the scholia. The scholia in their turn are a step toward the commentary, which is usually fuller in its coverage and may well display a unity of exegetical style, an overarching concern (for example, relating a biblical book

---

20   Cambridge, University Library, T-S NS 309.9. See de Lange, *Greek Jewish Texts*, 79–84.
21   A good example is Cambridge, University Library, T-S K24.14. See de Lange, *Greek Jewish Texts*, 155–63.
22   See M. Banitt, "L'étude des glossaires bibliques des Juifs de France au moyen âge," *Proceedings of the Israel Academy of Sciences and Humanities* 2, no. 10 (Jerusalem, 1967).
23   For an example, see the scholia on Genesis and Exodus in Cambridge, University Library, T-S C6.117 and Cambridge, Westminster College, Talmudica I.110 (two parts of the same manuscript), edited in de Lange, *Greek Jewish Texts*, 85–116.

to specific historical events), or a technique of interpretation beyond philological exposition—for instance, a homiletical or allegorical interpretation.

An early example of a commentary is a large Genizah fragment of a commentary on Ezekiel and the Minor Prophets written on a rotulus (a vertical scroll) and datable, on codicological grounds, to not later than the end of the tenth century. This commentary, whose author seems to have been an otherwise unknown scholar named Reuel, has a large number of Greek glosses.[24] It is actually quite common for Byzantine biblical commentaries written in Hebrew, by both Rabbanites and Karaites, to contain Greek glosses. Once we recognize that the Greek glosses are not ad hoc translations of individual words but are related to a tradition of translation, they become an important source; unfortunately many commentaries were copied by scribes who did not know Greek and made many mistakes in transmitting the Greek words. One of the great advantages of the Genizah fragments is that they were mostly written by writers for whom Greek was a living language.

The term "gloss" is also commonly applied to marginal and interlinear annotations in the vernacular. These are found written in biblical texts and also in scholia or commentaries. We have examples of both from the Genizah, but the most spectacular example found to date comes from outside the Genizah. It is a copy of the Former Prophets with masorah, now in the Fitzwilliam Museum, Cambridge, written in the eleventh or twelfth century in the Byzantine cultural sphere. In the year 1643, when it was already damaged and incomplete, it was taken from Canea, in Western Crete, to Negroponte (Chalkis), and dedicated in the synagogue there. The manuscript has 123 glosses written in the margins, mostly in Greek (in Hebrew letters); a few glosses are in Hebrew. They were written by four different hands, one of which is very similar to that of the scribe who wrote the masorah, which shows that the annotations began around the time the manuscript was written.[25]

The numerous marginal annotations in Greek in the Fitzwilliam Museum manuscript share some of the characteristics we have already noted. They are written in medieval Greek, mostly of a colloquial type. The presence of an unusually large number of Latin loanwords may point to the place of writing

---

24 Jerusalem, JNUL Heb. 4° 577.7/1 with Cambridge, University Library, T-S C2.87 and other fragments, edited in de Lange, *Greek Jewish Texts*, 165–294.
25 Cambridge, Fitzwilliam Museum 364*. See J. Olszowy-Schlanger, "An Early Hebrew Manuscript from Byzantium," in *Zutot 2002*, ed. S. Berger, M. Brocke, and I. Zwiep (Dordrecht, 2003), 148–55; N. de Lange, "The Greek Glosses of the Fitzwilliam Museum Bible," in ibid., 138–47.

(Venetian Crete?); some of the Greek words are nowhere otherwise attested. In some cases we have two alternative Greek translations of one Hebrew word. This feature, shared with some of the Genizah fragments, seems to point to a situation where several more or less different versions are in current use. Sometimes glosses are repeated: the same Hebrew word in two or more places is translated by the same Greek word. This striking consistency of translation can be found in the Genizah materials, and it confirms the view that we are dealing with a tradition of translation, and not just ad hoc renderings. In some cases the renderings are identical or close to those of Akylas and the other ancient versions; some glosses seem to be corruptions or revisions of glosses from Akylas.

Before turning from our discussion of the extant manuscripts of the Greek biblical tradition in Byzantine Judaism, we should take note of a printed book that may well be a witness to a medieval version. In 1547 an Italian Jewish printer, Eliezer Soncino, printed in Constantinople a Pentateuch containing the Hebrew text, the Aramaic targum, Rashi's Hebrew commentary, and two further translations, one into Spanish and one into Greek, the whole being printed in Hebrew characters. It is a very interesting question whether the Greek translation was prepared for this publication, or whether it represents a traditional Greek text. So far no conclusive evidence has been mustered either way, but the Greek is strikingly free of the Turkish vocabulary we might expect in the language of Jews in Constantinople a century after the Ottoman conquest. It is at least possible, then, that this printed Greek Pentateuch is a precious relic of the medieval Greek-speaking synagogue; if so, it is by far the most substantial and most important such survival, and it cries out for further study. The translation was transcribed into Greek letters and published in 1897 by Hesseling,[26] who realized its importance for Greek historical linguistics. It has attracted some interest from other Greek linguists since then, but it has not received the attention it deserves from the point of view of biblical or Jewish studies.

Medieval Remains and Ancient Versions

Thus, when Byzantine Jews studied the Hebrew Bible, whether as children or as adults, they not only studied in Greek but referred to preexisting Greek translations. They may have been familiar with these translations from hearing

---

26 D. C. Hesseling, *Les cinq livres de la Loi (Le Pentateuque)* (Leiden–Leipzig, 1897). See also N. Fernández Marcos, "El Pentateuco griego de Constantinopla," *Erytheia* 6 (1985): 185–203; idem, *Introducción a las versiones griegas de la Biblia*, 2nd ed. (Madrid, 1998), 187–92.

them recited aloud in synagogue, as we can deduce from the surviving translations of Jonah and Ecclesiastes and perhaps from the Constantinople Pentateuch, which shows some signs of having been designed to accompany the Hebrew readings of the weekly Torah portions. These translations employed many words or forms that no longer existed in the spoken Greek language of the later Byzantine era. When we bear in mind that Jews had no formal education in Greek, we must suppose that they were taught to understand the Greek of the traditional Bible versions. In Jewish education, the study of Hebrew was the main object, but the Greek versions played a key role. This was true both of Karaites and of Rabbanites.

Did they learn a Greek translation by heart? If so, that explains in part the facility with which annotators and commentators quote it. It also helps to explain why we find so few manuscripts of the Greek versions, as opposed to fragmentary quotations. If Byzantine Jews learned the Greek by heart as children, they would not need written copies. To posit this memorization is to claim the existence of a real oral tradition. There is also another synthesis that accounts for the evidence: rather than committing a Greek translation to memory, boys may have been taught to translate the Hebrew reading into Greek, using the characteristic words and phrases of the traditional versions, but extemporizing to some extent, which would explain the medieval vocabulary and grammar in the medieval manuscripts.

A striking feature of these medieval texts is their relationship to the ancient versions, particularly that of Akylas. This translation was based (unlike the Septuagint) on an early form of the Masoretic text, and it was made by an excellent Hellenist with very strong and unusual ideas about translation. He tried to conserve as far as possible in Greek all the characteristics of the Hebrew text: the grammar, the semantic relationships between the words and their roots, tiny and seemingly trivial details that could be significant in exegesis, and even at times the sounds of the words. Akylas's approach differed radically from that of other translators mentioned earlier. It would probably be mistaken, however, to think of the medieval versions as being derived solely from Akylas. The distinctive features of Akylas's translation do not appear consistently in the medieval versions, and we have also noted some hints of a plurality of versions circulating side by side.[27]

27   Given the evident influence of the ancient versions on the medieval Jewish materials, the question arises how these materials can best be exploited by scholars working on the text of these ancient Greek versions. The question was briefly discussed by the late Joseph Ziegler, who accepted some of the Genizah glosses as representing genuine readings of Akylas in Job; see J. Ziegler, ed.,

Jewish and Christian Bibles

A final point to consider here is the possible influence of this Jewish Greek Bible tradition on that of the Church. The Ambrosian Library in Milan contains an early witness to the text of the Greek Bible, a copy of the Octateuch, now incomplete, written in majuscule letters in the fifth century. The editors refer to this manuscript as F. A number of much later, cursive hands, designated collectively by the siglum F^b, have inserted numerous variants in the margins. At one point a variant is attributed to *to Ioud[aïkón]*, "the Jewish (text)." A comparison of the readings of F^b with the Jewish evidence—for example, the Constantinople Pentateuch or the Fitzwilliam Museum glosses—reveals striking similarities.[28] Furthermore, this is not the only Christian manuscript to contain such glosses. A similar phenomenon is found in at least two others (designated M and i).

How did these Jewish renderings make their way into a Christian manuscript? The use of the term *to Ioudaïkón* suggests that reference is being made to a written text, probably one written in Greek letters. Such a text is likely in principle to have been very old, since we do not find any continuous texts written by Jews in Greek letters after the sixth century, and even occasional use of Greek letters by Jews is very rare after that. On the other hand it cannot go back to the time of Akylas, because the glosses, like the Jewish glosses discussed earlier, use later vocabulary and morphological forms.[29]

The consequence of the citation of Jewish translations in the margins of manuscripts kept and studied by Christians was that the Jewish tradition of Bible study directly influenced the Christian one. How this happened and the implications for Christian Bible study in Byzantium still have to be explored.

Conclusions

I have argued on the basis of the evidence of the manuscripts that Byzantine Jewish men, from an early age, learned to read the Hebrew Bible not only through

---

Iob (Göttingen, 1982), 160. But there is room for a good deal more examination of this complex question.

28 See Fernández Marcos, *Introducción*, 182–83 and 189–90, where he takes up a suggestion first made by D. S. Blondheim in "Échos du judéo-hellénisme: Étude sur l'influence de la Septante et d'Aquila sur les versions néo-grecques des Juifs," *Revue des Études Juives* 78–79 (1924): 1–14.

29 See also the discussion in A. Salvesen, "The Relationship of LXX and the Three in Exodus 1–24 to the Readings of F^b," in *Jewish Reception of Greek Bible Versions*, ed. N. de Lange, J. G. Krivoruchko, and C. Boyd-Taylor (Tubingen, 2009), 103–27, esp. 126–27.

the medium of Greek language (which I take to be uncontroversial) but with the help of translations into Greek that were largely based on the second-century CE translation of Akylas, with its totally distinctive Greek vocabulary and approach to translation. Their education prepared them to stand up in synagogue and read from the Hebrew text, and then to recite a Greek translation, probably verse by verse. In my view this is the only way to account for the phenomena found in the manuscripts, which, although not very numerous, are of several distinct types. Some preserve actual texts of biblical books that were used liturgically (Jonah, Ecclesiastes, and, if we add the printed text, the Pentateuch too); others contain teachers' or pupils' Greek notes added to Hebrew texts, or Greek glosses embedded within scholia or commentaries written mainly in Hebrew.

As I remarked above, I am unable to determine to what extent this was an oral tradition. Clearly, Greek translations were written down, as we have some surviving copies. It is possible, however, that sometimes, and perhaps commonly, students learned translations by heart and/or translated extempore or from memory in synagogue.

One may speculate further. The sixth-century copies of Akylas in Greek majuscules preserved in palimpsests (which do not contain annotations) may have continued in use either in the classroom or in the synagogue for several centuries before they were eventually reused as palimpsests in the tenth or eleventh century. They may thus serve as concrete examples of the kind of text that were used by Byzantine Jews. In time such old manuscripts ceased to be usable, and gradually the Hebrew alphabet replaced the Greek alphabet in Jewish use. However, we do find glosses written in Greek characters long after the introduction of Hebrew writing, and these characters are crudely formed majuscules, not the minuscule Greek writing Christians used at this time. One plausible explanation of this phenomenon is that the writers of the glosses were imitating the old majuscule writing they knew from the Greek biblical texts they had used at school.

The relationship between the medieval translations and the ancient version of Akylas becomes noticeably weaker over time. The palimpsest fragments, although copied some four centuries after Akylas made his translation, are virtually identical with the text of Akylas as we know it from fragments of Origen's *Hexapla*. Some four or five centuries later again, the Genizah fragments still bear the recognizable stamp of Akylas, but their freer renderings display features of medieval Greek. By the time we reach the translations of Jonah, toward the end of the Middle Ages, not to mention the Constantinople Pentateuch, the influence of Akylas is much fainter.

Finally, I have mentioned the presence of similar glosses in the margins of Christian manuscripts. I do not know the background to these borrowings: are they the work of a Jewish convert to Christianity or the result of a chance discovery by Christians of a Jewish manuscript written in Greek script? At any rate, they are an interesting indication that, in this way as in others, the Jewish minority did not live in a tightly sealed compartment, but interacted with its environment.

University of Cambridge

THREE

The Prophetologion
The Old Testament of Byzantine Christianity?

JAMES MILLER

THIS CHAPTER WILL RAISE, then answer, some questions about the basic premise of this volume. More specifically it will be asked whether a modern phenomenon is being projected into the Byzantine era under the guise of a work called the "Old Testament." To be sure, many moderns readily understand the import of this phrase. The concept is now familiar. But was it familiar in the Byzantine era? We begin our discussion with a quotation from a leading twentieth-century authority on the Prophetologion, Günther Zuntz:

> There is no need to waste words over the fundamental significance of the Bible for Byzantine spiritual life. It is less well known, however, that the "Holy Scripture," which defined the life and thought of the populace, was represented, apart from the Psalter, by the lectionary—and not by the Bible as a whole. Segments of the Old and New Testaments, which were recited at divine worship, are contained in the lectionaries; and here, through the reading and through the subsequent preaching, the common man (and not only he) secured and confirmed his life's relation to the Bible. Indeed, there are catenae on the text of the lectionary: indication that scholarly exegesis was expended on it and perhaps, virtually as a sermon, would be read after the lection.[1]

---

1 "Über die grundlegende Bedeutung der Bibel für das byzantinische Geistesleben braucht man keine Worte zu verlieren. Weniger bekannt ist es aber wohl, das die 'Heilige Schrift,' welche das Leben und Denken des Volkes bestimmte, neben dem Psalter wesentlich durch die Lektionare repraesentiert wird—und nicht durch die Bibel als ganzes. In den Lektionaren sind die Abschnitte des Alten und Neuen Testaments enthalten, die im Gottesdienst rezitiert wurden;

The Bible was significant for Byzantine spiritual life, Zuntz tells us, but not the Bible as a whole. Only segments of that book, so familiar and ubiquitous today, played a major role in Byzantine spiritual life. Those formational portions, Zuntz tells us, were the ones included in a set of texts called lectionaries—the plural being used here since there were three main lectionary traditions: the Gospel lectionaries, the epistle lectionaries, and the Old Testament lectionaries. The last of these, called in scholarly literature the Prophetologion, will be the focus of this chapter.

We should note at the outset that the object of Zuntz's remarks is the populace and the common man in Byzantium. Zuntz is thus characterizing, not smaller circles in which more specialized and detailed knowledge about the Bible is likely to have obtained, that is, the upper echelons of church or government.[2] Rather, he speaks to the understanding of these matters held at broader social levels, by the bulk of the population. In this chapter we will likewise be addressing primarily the understanding of the common man.

It is possible to infer from what Zuntz says that the Bible, or what he also refers to as the "Bible as a whole," was a largely unknown entity in Byzantium. The referent Zuntz appears to have in view when he uses this phrase is the modern ponderous tome that now occupies space on so many bookshelves the world over, whether in educational institutions, in public libraries, or in people's homes. Zuntz must intimate the unexpected: a poorly known fact though it is today, this sort of tome would not have played a key role in society's spiritual formation in that age. Instead, he informs us, that role would have been played by what to modern sensibilities would be secondary texts, works containing but excerpts from the larger tome well known to moderns—the lectionaries.

We will argue in this chapter that what Zuntz tells us is true for the whole, that is, for the whole Bible known to many moderns in its two main divisions, the Old and New Testaments, is true also for the parts. That is to say, not only was the Bible as a whole a largely unknown entity in Byzantium, but likewise the parts—

---

und dort, durch die Lesungen und durch anschliessende Predigten, gewann und bestärkte der gemeine Mann (und nicht nur er) seine Lebensbeziehung zur Bibel. Ja, es gibt sogar Katenen zu Lektionar-texten: ein Zeichen, dass gelehrte Exegese auf sie angewandt und vielleicht, *quasi* als Predigt, nach der *lectio* verlesen wurde." G. Zuntz, "Das byzantinische Septuaginta-Lektionar ('Prophetologion')," *Classica et Mediaevalia: Revue danoise de philologie et d'histoire* 17 (1956): 183.

2   Were Zuntz discussing a prominent ecclesiastical figure from the Byzantine period—say Patriarch Photios of Constantinople—instead of the Byzantine common man, he would undoubtedly be saying something quite different regarding how a life's relation to the Bible was gained. To anticipate arguments soon to be offered, Photios was a highly learned man who, because of his office, had access to a large variety of literature—including entire Bibles.

especially the Old Testament—were largely unknown entities as well. If we wish to speak of the Old Testament in Byzantium therefore, we will do well first to identify a text dating to that era that, in some important respects, corresponds to the work we have in mind. A good candidate for that text is the Prophetologion.

Before explaining in greater detail what the Prophetologion is and what makes it a suitable candidate for the Old Testament of Byzantine Christianity, we should consider more carefully why the Bible as a whole, or even the Old Testament, was so poorly known in the Byzantine period. We should also reflect at greater length on what the Old Testament represents to modernity. Doing so will prepare us to judge whether the Prophetologion adequately answers to the role we propose for it.

The Bible and the Old Testament, Then and Now

Undoubtedly the key to understanding the relative obscurity of the whole Bible, or of the Old Testament, that Zuntz hints was characteristic of the Byzantine age, is the rise and proliferation of printing technology. With respect to the Bible, history divides at the development of the printing press. Prior to the advent of this technology, book production was a tedious, expensive, and highly specialized enterprise. Afterward, book production became increasingly efficient and inexpensive. We should bear in mind that precisely the book under discussion—the Bible—was the object of so many early modern printing efforts.

Prior to the development of printing technology, production of a book the size of a Bible or an Old Testament was a monumental undertaking. The manuscript record reflects this reality, there being exceedingly few manuscripts of such scope dated prior to the sixteenth century.[3] After the sixteenth century, copies of the whole Bible become progressively more common.

---

3   Assertions here about biblical manuscripts dating to the Byzantine era are based mainly on the old and new editions of Rahlfs's *Verzeichnis*—a comprehensive listing of extant Septuagint manuscripts that provides such information as their content, condition, probable era of production, and current location (A. Rahlfs, ed., *Verzeichnis der griechischen Handschriften des Alten Testaments: Für das Septuaginta-Unternehmen* [Berlin, 1914]; A. Rahlfs and D. Fraenkel, eds., *Verzeichnis der griechischen Handschriften des Alten Testaments: Die Überlieferung bis zum VIII. Jahrhundert* [Göttingen, 2004]. The revised edition, recently republished, is as yet incomplete, only the first of two proposed volumes having been printed).

How many extant manuscripts contain, or may have at one time contained, the full Old Testament? This researcher is unaware of any studies that classify Septuagint manuscripts according to their scope; in fact, extant manuscript evidence is often so fragmentary that the scope of the original manuscripts probably cannot be determined. Present evidence tells neither for nor

Relatively low literacy rates went hand in hand with the dearth of reading material.[4] There was little to be read and therefore the ability to read was, for most people, either very rudimentary or simply nonexistent.[5] What would be the need for a book the size of a Bible or Old Testament in this setting?

Despite the fact that very few whole Bibles or Old Testaments appear to have been in existence at any given time during the Byzantine period, and notwithstanding the fact that the bulk of the population lacked the ability to read existing texts, the Bible did continue to have an influence on society and on the spiritual life of the common man. How? One key manner in which the Bible nonetheless had an impact on social life during this period was through the reading aloud of biblical passages—also called lections—at public worship services.

How the structure and extent of biblical readings at public worship was determined is a subject treated under the rubric of the history of liturgy. A resolution of that question lies far beyond the scope of this chapter, but suffice it to say that for what were probably largely practical reasons, the biblical text came to be transmitted in large part in the form of lectionaries during the Byzantine period. These texts contained just the portions of the Bible that were appointed for reading during worship. The content was often arranged according to the way the excerpts were used throughout the liturgical year.

---

against the prevalence of the full Old Testament in the Byzantine era. Such inferences about scope as can be drawn from data presented in the *Verzeichnis* should be considered quite tentative. This writer infers from the old (but complete) *Verzeichnis* that, as a generous estimate, seventeen manuscripts either now contain, or stand a chance of at one time having contained, the full Old Testament—this out of a total of some fifteen hundred manuscripts catalogued.

4   Holmes and Waring summarize the current state of knowledge on Byzantine literacy: "There is no monograph treatment of Byzantine literacy; very few publications are concerned with Byzantine education; only rarely is Byzantine manuscript transmission considered in the context of either literacy or education. We do not expect this volume to fill all or any of these gaps. Instead we offer a collection of very different, innovative perspectives designed to provoke further discussion among Byzantinists and Medievalists" (*Literacy, Education and Manuscript Transmission in Byzantium and Beyond* [Leiden, 2002], vii).

5   An authoritative study on ancient literacy that proposes tentative percentages for some areas in the Mediterranean basin holds that the literacy rate was adversely affected by the rise and spread of Christianity and argues that literacy was in general decline in the early part of the Byzantine period (W. V. Harris, *Ancient Literacy* [Cambridge, MA, 1989], 285–322). Within Constantinople, the administrative seat of the empire, as Harris indicates, literacy undoubtedly continued to be on par with earlier, higher, rates (313). See also R. Browning, "Literacy in the Byzantine World," *Byzantine and Modern Greek Studies: Essays Presented to Sir Steven Runciman* (Oxford, 1978), 39–54; E. Patlagean, "Discours écrit, discours parlé: Niveaux de culture à Byzance aux VIIe–XIe siècles," *AnnalesESC* 34 (1979): 264–78; N. Oikonomides, "Mount Athos: Levels of Literacy," *DOP* 42 (1988): 167–78; H. Y. Gamble, *Books and Readers in the Early Church: A History of Early Christian Texts* (New Haven, 1995); and M. E. Mullett, *Letters, Literacy, and Literature in Byzantium* (Burlington, VT, 2007). None of these authors propose definite figures for literacy rates in Byzantium.

To summarize, evidence indicates that very few manuscripts of the whole Bible or of the Old Testament were produced during the Byzantine period. For the few that were, free circulation certainly was not the norm. Instead, the biblical text was most commonly encountered in the form of lectionaries, and the text was transmitted primarily in this form. The common man, possessing at best a rudimentary degree of literacy, gained some familiarity of the content of the Bible through listening to the reading of lections at public worship services.

The Prophetologion as Counterpart to Modernity's Old Testament

If the Old Testament was as rarely encountered in Byzantium as we are suggesting, then with what warrant can we speak of the Old Testament in Byzantium? We will seek a resolution to this question before turning to a more detailed description of the Prophetologion.

When speaking of the Old Testament in Byzantium, it will be wise to have in mind some actual text that dates to the Byzantine period and that answers in important respects to the conception we moderns have in view when we use this phrase. We will now enumerate some of the ways in which the Prophetologion corresponds to our modern Old Testament.

Most obviously, the Prophetologion corresponds to the Old Testament in that it contains excerpts drawn primarily from within that corpus.[6] It contains only a very small percentage of the whole Old Testament, but it does contain segments of text from many of the books found therein. Relatedly, the selection of texts found in the Prophetologion was obviously made in conscious recognition of one of the defining characteristics of the Old Testament as understood both historically and currently, that is, in recognition of the limitations implied in the concept of canon.[7]

---

6 We say primarily because it does contain a limited amount of New Testament material, as well as some non-scriptural, rubrical material. More will be said presently about the content of the Prophetologion.

7 The issue of the Old Testament canon was an important one in early Christianity and certainly there were those during the Byzantine era who were familiar with authoritative Christian writings on the topic. Again, our position is that those with better education, higher social status, and/or ecclesiastical training were likely cognizant of this issue and its particulars, while the common man would have been largely ignorant of it. Among those early ecclesiastical figures whose writings on the biblical canon remain extant are Melito of Sardis, Origen (both authors are pre-Byzantine), Athanasios of Alexandria, Gregory of Nazianzos, Cyril of Jerusalem, Epiphanios of Salamis, Hilary of Poitiers, Jerome, and Augustine of Hippo. See L. M. McDonald, *The Biblical Canon: Its Origin, Transmission, and Authority*, 3rd ed. (Peabody, MA, 2007), 198–206, and A. C. Sundberg, *The Old Testament of the Early Church* (Cambridge, MA, 1964), 133–69. The

Perhaps just as importantly, the Prophetologion would have been one of the more familiar books in the Byzantine era, just as the Old Testament, as a component of the Bible, is to moderns. At each service at which lections were read, the general public would have had at least some exposure to this book. So, just as the Old Testament of today is a familiar and accessible book, so the Prophetologion would have been in the Byzantine era—far more accessible to the common man than would have been any of the complete Old Testaments that were in existence in the period. It is primarily for these reasons that we are suggesting the Prophetologion be considered the Old Testament of Byzantine Christianity.

The Prophetologion: Description, Modern Research, History

Prophetologion is the designation adopted by modern scholars for a Byzantine manuscript tradition that flourished from roughly the ninth through the sixteenth centuries.[8] The manuscripts representing the tradition contain lections, that is, relatively brief excerpts from the Bible meant for public reading—in the case of the Prophetologion, lections to be recited during the worship ceremonies of the annual liturgical cycle of Byzantine Christianity. Since nearly all lections of the Prophetologion are drawn from the Old Testament, the Prophetologion can be adequately characterized as an Old Testament lectionary manuscript tradition.[9]

Interest in the Prophetologion among modern scholars began in conjunction with interest in the text of the Septuagint. The earliest study devoted to the Prophetologion and some of its representative manuscripts was published by the great Septuagint scholar Alfred Rahlfs at the beginning of the twentieth century.[10] Rahlfs's motivation for undertaking his study of the Prophetologion manuscript tradition was undoubtedly a desire to survey and classify

---

tables on pages 58 and 59 of the latter work provide a concise overview of the various canon lists discussed by these authors.

8   S. G. Engberg indicates that the term *Prophetologion* is the invention of a nineteenth-century scholar or librarian ("Prophetologion Manuscripts in the 'New Finds' of St. Catherine's at Sinai," *Scriptorium* 57 [2003]: 94). The lections, regardless of the part of the Old Testament from which they are excerpted, perform a prophetic function, viz., they are read as prophetic or typologically significant of Christ, of events or persons associated with his life, or of the Church.

9   Though the bulk of text in the Prophetologion consists in the lections, rubrical directions and some hymnography form a not insignificant portion. A good deal of the hymnography, e.g., the prokeimenon, is drawn directly from the biblical text as well.

10   *Die alttestamentlichen Lektionen der griechischen Kirche*, Mitteilungen des Septuaginta-Unternehmens 1, pt. 5 (Göttingen, 1915).

this not inconsiderable proportion of manuscript evidence for the text of the Septuagint.[11] This survey was, in its turn, one of the preparatory phases for the grand project for which Rahlfs is best known—the critical edition of the Septuagint published under the auspices of the Göttingen Unternehmen.[12]

Subsequent studies of the Prophetologion focused in yet greater detail on the manuscripts, examining and classifying the bulk of those still in existence. Chief among the more recent scholars deserving credit for deepening scholarly understanding of the manuscript tradition are Carsten Høeg and Günther Zuntz. These two scholars gathered and collated many extant Prophetologion manuscripts, producing from them a critical text, complete with neumes, which was published under the title *Prophetologium* in the series *Monumenta Musicae Byzantinae*.[13] In addition to the critical text, these authors produced several articles on the Prophetologion and its relation to the Septuagint, demonstrating its relevance to the concerns of scholars involved in Septuagint studies.[14]

---

11   In the original *Verzeichnis* (440–44; n. 3 above), Rahlfs classified 150 manuscripts as lectionaries.

12   *Septuaginta: Vetus Testamentum graecum* (Göttingen, 1931–). Publication of volumes in the series, begun in 1931, is still under way, more than 75 years later. At least one volume, that is, the Genesis volume, has already been republished in a new edition. The next volumes due out cover the books of Kingdoms (i.e., 1 and 2 Samuel and 1 and 2 Kings in most English translations of the Bible).

13   Neumes, also referred to as ekphonetic notation, are cantillation markings inserted into the text that indicate to the reader the pitch and stress levels at which various parts of the lection are to be recited. As Engberg has pointed out, the exact value of the markings remains poorly understood (S. Engberg, "Ekphonetic Chant—the Oral Tradition and the Manuscripts," *Jahrbuch der Österreichischen Byzantinistik*, 32, no. 7 [1983]: 41–47).

The full critical text is published as S. Engberg, C. Høeg, and G. Zuntz, eds., *Prophetologium* (vol. 1 of *Monumenta Musicae Byzantinae: Lectionaria* [Copenhagen, 1939–81]). This publication is a volume in a series; the volume is subdivided into two parts, and the two parts are divided into fascicles, six fascicles in part one and two in part two. Since the pagination is continuous in each part—despite the further division into fascicles—where we refer to reference pages from the *Prophetologium*, we will give the title, then the part number, then the page number. All quotations of Greek text from the *Prophetologium* in this article will be taken verbatim from the source, which, though including neumes, does not utilize any diacritical markings.

14   A list of Høeg's and Zuntz's other articles touching on the Prophetologion includes the following entries: C. Høeg, "Sur le Prophétologium" (a paper presented at the fifth international congress of Byzantine studies, Rome, 1936), 46–47; C. Høeg, "L'Ancien Testament dans l'Église grecque: quelques aspects de la question" (paper presented at the sixth international congress of Byzantine studies, Algiers, 1937): 107–9; C. Høeg and G. Zuntz, "Remarks on the Prophetologion," in *Quantulacumque: Studies Presented to Kirsopp Lake by Pupils, Colleagues and Friends*, ed. R. P. Casey et al. (London, 1937): 189–226; G. Zuntz, "Der Antinoe Papyrus der Proverbia und das Prophetologion," *Zeitschrift für die alttestamentliche Wissenschaft* 68 (1956): 124–84; G. Zuntz, "Das Byzantinische Septuaginta-Lektionar (Prophetologion): Memoria Istanbulensis," *Classica et Mediaevalia* 17 (1956): 183–98.

The current leading authority on the Prophetologion is Sysse Gudrun Engberg. She served as editor for the final two fascicles of the *Prophetologium*, the last of which was published more than forty years after the first fascicle appeared in print. In addition, she has written several articles over the past two decades that provide further details about the text, its character, its place in Byzantine history, and its use in modern Eastern Orthodox worship.[15]

Today there are one hundred seventy-four extant manuscripts of the Prophetologion.[16] The oldest of these manuscripts date to the ninth century. Høeg and Zuntz argued that the manuscript tradition originated in the eighth century.[17] This position has not been universally accepted; Engberg has argued that the lectionary tradition enshrined in the Prophetologion did not arise so abruptly. In her view, the development of the lection tradition stretches back to an at-present-indeterminate point certainly not later than the fourth century.[18] In any case, no

---

15 The lectionary tradition represented in the Prophetologion is still actively used in modern Orthodox worship (see below). A fairly thorough listing of Engberg's publications on the subject of the Prophetologion includes the following items: "The *Prophetologion* and the Triple-Lection Theory—the Genesis of a Liturgical Book," *Bollettino della Badia greca di Grottaferrata*, 3rd ser., 3 (2006): 67–91; "Les lectionnaires grecs," *Les manuscrits liturgiques, cycle thématique 2003–2004 de l'IRHT*, O. Legendre et J.-B. Lebigue, dir., Paris, IRHT, 2005 (Ædilis, Actes, 9), n.p. [accessed 23 Oct. 2009] http://aedilis.irht.cnrs.fr/liturgie/05_1.htm; "Romanos Lekapenos and the Mandilion of Edessa," in *Byzance et les reliques du Christ*, ed. J. Durand and B. Flusin (Paris, 2004), 123–42; "'New Finds'" (n. 8 above), 94–109; "Greek Literacy and Liturgical Books: Manolis Glynzouinis' Edition of the 'profetie,' Venice 1595/96," *Epsilon 2* (1988): 31–41; "The Greek Old Testament Lectionary as a Liturgical Book," *Cahiers de l'Institut du Moyen-Âge Grec et Latin* 54 (1987): 39–48; and "An Unnoticed Printed Edition of the Old Testament Lectionary in Greek (Venice 1545)," *Epsilon 1* (1987): 57–67.
16 The original *Verzeichnis* put the number of lectionary manuscripts at 150, but Engberg has since disqualified some of those items and added others (Engberg, "Greek Old Testament Lectionary" [n. 15 above], 39).
17 Høeg and Zuntz, "Remarks" (n. 14 above), 221–23.
18 Engberg, "Triple-Lection," 89–91. She offers in this article a brief but persuasive argument questioning the standard presumption that the older eucharistic service had three lections—one of which was drawn from the Old Testament. In her view, the Byzantine liturgy likely never contained any Old Testament lection; rather, Old Testament lections were restricted to non-eucharistic worship services. Thus, the Prophetologion tradition is not indicative of a liturgical reform movement that, among other changes, moved the Old Testament lection from the divine liturgy to another worship service. It is instead consonant with earlier customs wherein there was likewise no Old Testament lection connected with the eucharistic service. She seems to hold that this more ancient lection tradition is contiguous with a continuous-reading practice involving the book of Genesis, such as is witnessed to in some sermons of John Chrysostom (85, 90). Engberg's proposals concerning the development of the Old Testament lection tradition seem quite congenial to Rahlfs's older thesis, which likewise envisioned a more gradual evolution ("Alttestamentlichen Lektionen" [n. 10 above], 216–17 [122–23]).

records recounting the inception of the tradition or its rationale are known to exist, so the reasons for its appearance and dissemination must remain subject to some speculation.[19]

Høeg and Zuntz concluded provisionally that the Prophetologion manuscript tradition originated as a systematizing effort that stemmed from the heart of the Byzantine empire—the imperial capital at Constantinople. According to this understanding, a need for reform and uniformity in liturgical practice throughout the empire arose. Høeg and Zuntz place the acute perception of this need in the late stages of the Iconoclast controversy. They posit that one element of reform was the establishment of a set of texts that carefully defined the scope and calendrical placement of the Old Testament lections. This set of texts was intended for dissemination throughout the empire. The Prophetologion urtext, these authors argued, is very likely to have been created at the Stoudios monastery. From there, Høeg and Zuntz maintain, copies were probably sent out to many leading churches of the empire, and these copies, in their turn, became the parent texts of later copies as the manuscript tradition flourished and spread.[20]

From the ninth through the sixteenth centuries, the Prophetologion manuscript tradition presents, in its stability, a contrast to the Septuagint manuscript tradition that forms the larger background.[21] Prophetologion manuscripts show comparatively few textual variations over the centuries, though some variations in structure are evident. The manuscript tradition seems to have been quite conservative; some copies even faithfully reproduce patriarchal rubrics, although the patriarch is unlikely ever to have presided at liturgical celebrations in the locations where those manuscripts were copied and used.[22] Over the time span in question, the manuscripts evidence a consistent, stable textual tradition—

---

19 Rahlfs offered some speculations on the prehistory of the tradition ("Alttestamentlichen Lektionen," 165–219 [71–125]). In brief, he holds that the Lenten lection system is a gradual expansion of the Old Testament lections read at the primitive Easter vigil. Høeg and Zuntz likewise allude to earlier lection traditions: "the creators of the new Prophetologion were bound to retain a certain number of lessons familiar to the faithful ... any attempt to introduce new readings was destined to be overcome by the conscious and unconscious resistance of tradition" ("Remarks," 222).
20 "Remarks," 222. Although Engberg has criticized their thesis, it is consistent with the manuscript evidence: no known Prophetologion manuscript is dated earlier than the ninth century.
21 The meaning of the term "Septuagint" is the subject of some debate in the scholarly community. As used in this article it will signify the range of books included in Rahlfs's hand edition.
22 The presence and widespread distribution of these rubrics in part led Høeg and Zuntz to conclude that the tradition originated in the capital and was extended from there into the provinces ("Remarks," 192).

another factor from which Høeg and Zuntz infer a centralized origin and sustenance of the tradition.[23]

When it flourished, the Prophetologion tradition was appropriated in various lands under Byzantine hegemony or influence and the work was translated into other languages. In Slavic-speaking regions, the resulting text became known as the *Parimijnik*.[24] Other lands within the Byzantine orbit likely had their translations as well, though, to date, no study of the tradition in non-Slavic translations seems to have been undertaken.

The Prophetologion tradition did not survive in its original form into the era of modern printing technology, there being only one truncated version known to have been printed.[25] In about the sixteenth century, scribes ceased copying Prophetologion manuscripts, though of course recitation of the Old Testament lections at worship did not cease. On the contrary, up to the present day the lections once contained in the Prophetologion are read in connection with various

---

23 Their thinking on this matter can be summarized as follows: since the Prophetologion manuscript tradition, in its stability and uniformity over the course of several centuries, presents a contrast to the larger Septuagint manuscript tradition for the same period, some powerful stabilizing force must have influenced the tradition over the course of its existence. An obvious candidate for this force in the Byzantine era is the administration in Constantinople (Høeg and Zuntz, "Remarks," 193, 220–21, 223).

24 A transliteration of the Greek word παροιμίαι—incidentally also the title of the Septuagint translation of the book of Proverbs—forms the root of this word. The stock Slavic suffix *nik* connotes, in this instance, a collection (of lessons). As A. Alekseev (*Tekstologia Slavianskoj Biblii* [St. Petersburg, 1999], 23) notes, various spellings of the transliterated term are to be be found in manuscripts, e.g., *parimejnik*, *paremijnik*, and *paremejnik*.

25 We refer to printed editions in Greek. The edition in question is a sixteenth-century publication that contains, in addition to a New Testament lectionary, Old Testament readings for Christmas, Epiphany, and Easter (Høeg and Zuntz, "Remarks," 109, n. 4; Engberg, "Unnoticed" [n. 15 above], 57–67). It is thus only a partial Prophetologion. A commemorative edition of the Prophetologion in Slavonic was printed in Russia as recently as the late nineteenth century (*Parimijnik: siest' sobranie parimii na vse leto* [Saint Petersburg, 1894]). While this article was in preparation it was brought to the author's attention that in the same year R. F. Brandt began publishing in Russia another *Parimijnik*, a multivolume edition whose main text was supplied from a twelfth/thirteenth century Slavic manuscript: *Grigorovichev parimejnik: v slichenii s drugimi parimejnikami* (Moscow, 1894–1904). The Brandt edition was recently republished in Macedonia with some enhancements (*Grigoricev parimejnik: tekst so kriticki aparat*, ed. Z. Hauptova and Z. Ribarova [Skopje, 1998]). Also, a version in a related Slavic language—modern Bulgarian—was printed as recently as 1935 (*Parimejnik* [Sofia, 1935]). This Sofia edition is apparently still in use in Bulgarian Orthodox churches. Thus, the demise of the Prophetologion tradition which occurred in Byzantium and in other Orthodox lands such as Russia may not have signaled its dissolution in the Bulgarian, and perhaps in other, regions. The author is indebted to a friend and former classmate at St. Vladimir's Orthodox Theological Seminary, now a priest of the Bulgarian Eastern Orthodox Diocese of the USA, Canada, and Australia, Fr. Michael Arbanas, for confirming some details regarding the existence and place of this edition in current Bulgarian worship.

celebrations of the annual liturgical cycle at Orthodox worship services according to essentially the same schedule and directives as they were in the Byzantine era. Since the book itself does not survive, it might be asked, whence are the readings supplied?[26] Around the sixteenth century the readings and rubrical material that once made up the text of the Prophetologion were transferred from the discrete Old Testament lectionary volume they had once constituted into other liturgical books used in Byzantine worship: the Old Testament lections for Lent were transferred into the *Triodion*, those slated for reading during the season of Pentecost into the *Pentecostarion*, and those assigned to celebrations during the remainder of the annual liturgical cycle into the *Menaion*. The demise of the Prophetologion text tradition was therefore actually a transmigration.

Reasons for the transmigration of the tradition are difficult to pinpoint. The advent and proliferation of printing technology may have played some role. Why this would dictate transferral of the readings into other books as opposed to simply continuing their reproduction in a dedicated, discrete volume, is not entirely clear. Among other possible causes for the manuscript tradition's disappearance may have been some shifts in liturgical praxis governing how and when the lections were read, as Engberg has suggested.[27] Also, the momentous events connected with the fall of Constantinople and their aftermath cannot be ruled out as factors contributing to the disappearance of the Prophetologion manuscript tradition.[28] In any case, the sixteenth century marks the effective end of the Byzantine manuscript tradition.

---

26 In some current Orthodox worship settings, the Prophetologion has been effectively—though unknowingly—recreated: pages containing the Old Testament readings are placed in three-ring binders from which the reader then recites the lections. The present author discovered just such a volume in use at St. Tikhon's Orthodox Theological Seminary in South Canaan, PA, where he taught Scripture for one year.

27 "Greek Old Testament Lectionary" (n. 15 above), 44–45. Some might argue that a "plenarization" of liturgical books, that is, the gathering together in a single book of all texts for the rites performed by a single celebrant, came about through the displacement of the complex cathedral worship by simpler monastic forms at around this time, and that this development played a key role in the disappearance of the Prophetologion manuscript tradition. It should be noted, though, that while cathedral worship has remained moribund, the Prophetologion nonetheless either persists (in Bulgarian use, see above) or is being recreated (in modern worship settings, see above) in some quarters. In light of these considerations the plenarization theory loses some of its appeal.

28 A connection suggested by Engberg in "Lectionnaires" (n. 15 above), n.p.: "After the conquest of Constantinople by the Ottoman Turks in 1453, the production of manuscripts changed and adapted to new, more difficult, conditions. Production of manuscripts of the Prophetologion gradually ceases while the Old Testament pericopes enter into liturgical books. . . ." (Après la conquête de Constantinople par les Turcs ottomans en 1453 la production de manuscrits a changé et s'est adaptée aux conditions nouvelles, plus difficiles. La production de manuscrits du *prophetologion* s'arrête peu à peu, tandis que les péricopes de l'Ancien Testament entrent dans les livres liturgiques).

Content and Use of the Prophetologion

The Prophetologion contains only a small portion of the Old Testament.[29] Though more than half of the Old Testament books have at least one lection excerpted from them, some books are not represented at all in the Prophetologion.[30] Moreover, the Old Testament lections punctuate the annual liturgical cycle quite sporadically for much of the year. For example, more than two weeks might pass during the summer months without any Old Testament lections being scheduled for reading during worship services.[31] At other times during the cycle, however, Old Testament lections occur with much greater frequency and in more concentrated fashion.

As those familiar with Byzantine worship are aware, there were two interlocking cycles in the Byzantine liturgical year.[32] One cycle formed the overarching framework, and the superstructure of this cycle was the Julian calendar year of 365 days, with one leap day added every four years. This calendar tracked, to the most accurate degree attainable at the time, the length of the solar year. The second cycle is essentially a lunar-based interlude that centers on the spring season of the Julian year, floating somewhat freely around it. The two cycles converge on a solar event, the vernal equinox. The relation of the full moon to the vernal equinox is the major factor in the determination of the date when Pascha will be celebrated each year. Several liturgical occasions that occur some weeks prior to, and some weeks after, Pascha, are contingent on it and move with it.

---

29 Fifteen percent is an approximate but generous estimate. This figure was obtained by calculating the total number of chapters in a canon roughly the size of the one found in Rahlfs's hand edition of the Septuagint (A. Rahlfs, ed., *Septuaginta, id est, Vetus Testamentum graece iuxta LXX interpretes* [Stuttgart, 1935]), counting each lection that covers some part of a chapter of an Old Testament book as though it covers the entire chapter, and dividing the total of the latter into the former. The book of Psalms was excluded from the calculation since the readings and hymns from it that occurred at virtually every worship service of Byzantine Christianity represent an alternate, non-lectionary use of the material.

30 In the Prophetologion no excerpts appear from Ruth, 1 and 2 Kingdoms (1 and 2 Samuel in most English-language Bibles), 1 and 2 Chronicles, 1 and 2 Esdras (Ezra and Nehemiah in most English-language Bibles), Esther, Judith, Tobit, 1–4 Maccabees, Ecclesiastes, Song of Songs, Hosea, Obadiah, Nahum, Habakkuk, Haggai, and Lamentations.

31 Since Byzantine worship comprises a good deal of allusion to or quotation from the Old Testament, worship services were not completely devoid of Old Testament material during these portions of the liturgical year. The Old Testament entered into Byzantine worship in at least two basic forms: (1) as lections and (2) as elements in, or as the basis of, hymnody and liturgical poetry. This study, which focuses on the first, can do little to advance understanding of the second, beyond pointing out that the Old Testament was also incorporated into Byzantine worship in this alternate fashion.

32 The description also applies, in many of its details, to Christian calendar systems of the West.

The two cycles are usually distinguished by liturgists as fixed and movable: the overarching Julian solar year that begins and ends on September first is referred to as the fixed cycle, while the lunar interlude is called the movable cycle.

In concert with the Byzantine liturgical year, the Prophetologion divides into two parts: one part contains the Old Testament lections relating to Pascha and associated occasions from the movable cycle; the other part contains Old Testament lections linked to liturgical occasions of the fixed cycle. Not all Prophetologion manuscripts divide so neatly into these two categories, but enough do to justify speaking of a twofold manuscript tradition.[33]

Most of the Old Testament lections are concentrated within the movable cycle. During this cycle, lections are appointed to be read on every weekday of Lent.[34] The lections constitute a nearly continuous reading from three Old Testament books: Genesis, Proverbs, and Isaiah.[35] In the week immediately prior to Pascha, referred to in contemporary English-speaking Orthodox circles as "Holy Week" and in some Prophetologion manuscripts as ἡ μεγάλη ἑβδομάς, the near-continuous reading from Isaiah, Genesis, and Proverbs of the preceding weeks is replaced by readings from scattered loci throughout the Old Testament.

During the period from Pascha to Pentecost, the post-paschal part of the movable cycle, Old Testament lections are appointed for only a few commemorations.[36] There are far fewer lections in this part of the movable cycle than there are for the period of Lent. Like the daily readings for the week immediately before Pascha—and unlike the daily readings for most of Lent—the Old Testament lections for the period from Pascha to Pentecost are excerpted from discrete locations throughout the Old Testament. They exhibit neither an ordering principle derived from the canon or from a book's internal structure, nor a

---

33 See Engberg, "Greek Old Testament Lectionary," 42–44, for an overview of the differing layouts found in certain manuscripts. Rahlfs's detailed description of the content of five Prophetologion manuscripts is also informative ("Alttestamentlichen Lektionen" [n. 10 above], 124–46 [30–52]).

34 Lent occupies approximately the first half of the total number of days encompassed by the movable cycle. No Old Testament lections are appointed for weekends during the Lenten period with the exception of the Saturday immediately preceding Pascha.

35 The order in which these books are listed here is the order in which they are to be read on most of the weekdays of Lent. Genesis and Proverbs are read in the evening at Vespers—the beginning of the liturgical day—while Isaiah is read at the office of Third/Sixth Hour. Some sections of each book are skipped: as a general rule, as the end of Lent approaches, more material is passed over.

36 Seven commemorations, to be precise: Mid-Pentecost, Ascension, the Holy Fathers in Nicaea, the Saturday of Pentecost (eve of Pentecost), Sunday of the Saints (Pentecost Sunday), the Earthquake, and the Commemoration of all Saints.

continuous reading pattern. In this, the lections of the post-paschal period are much like those of the fixed cycle to be discussed below.

The section of the Prophetologion containing Old Testament lections for the fixed cycle is somewhat smaller than the section containing readings connected with the paschal season. Nothing like a continuous reading schedule involving Old Testament books is found here. Instead, like the post-paschal part of the movable cycle, one finds here groupings of lections excerpted from a variety of Old Testament books. The sequence of these lections is not canonical, that is, it is neither the order in which the books of the Old Testament occur in canon lists or manuscripts nor—for lections from the same book—the order of the narrative. The ordering principle, rather, is thematic: readings for particular celebrations during the fixed cycle were selected from throughout the Old Testament, in accordance with their relevance to the theological theme of the commemoration assigned to the particular date.[37] These lections occur typically in groups of three. Let us look at some examples.

The founding of Constantinople,[38] which was celebrated annually on 11 May, provides an example of some festal readings from the fixed cycle; the occasion, incidentally, overlaps with the range of dates covered by the movable cycle. For the festal commemoration that falls on this calendar date, the Prophetologion appoints three Old Testament lections to be read at Vespers, each from the book of Isaiah: one comes from chapter 54; another from chapters 61 and 62; and the third from chapter 65.[39]

---

37 Intervening verses, which were apparently deemed less relevant to the theological theme of the commemoration, are sometimes skipped over in these lections. Less prevalent are instances of composite readings, that is, lections made up of verses excerpted from more than one biblical book. For example, a lection for the commemoration of the Prophet Elijah (July twentieth) comprises excerpts from 3 and 4 Kingdoms (1 and 2 Kings in most English-language Bibles).

38 The celebration is titled τη παραμονη του γενεθλιου τησ πολεωσ (*sic*) in the *Prophetologium* (2:101–8). To reiterate a point touched on earlier, lection appointments for the movable and fixed cycles are not exclusive of one another but intersperse during periods when the cycles overlap. Thus, at certain junctures of the Byzantine liturgical year, lections from both subsections of the Prophetologion may occur in close proximity. For example, the lections for Ascension (movable cycle) might be read only a few days apart from those for the commemoration of the founding of Constantinople (fixed cycle).

39 The first lection begins, "*Thus says the Lord to the holy city*: From the water at the time of Noe, this is my oath: Just as I swore to him at that time that I would no more be angry at the earth because of you, nor as a threat to you would I remove the mountains, nor would the hills be shifted, so neither shall the mercy that comes from me to you fail, nor shall the covenant of your peace be removed, for the Lord said he would be merciful to you" (NETS translation with this author's adaptations [in italic]). The import of the lesson is the promise of divine sustenance for the "holy city." The holy city within the biblical text would be Jerusalem but, in the liturgical context, the import of the passage would be shifted to the new holy city, Constantinople. Note that

Another example of a fixed cycle celebration for which the Prophetologion appoints Old Testament lections, but one that does not overlap with commemorations of the movable cycle, is the feast of the Transfiguration of Christ, which is celebrated on 6 August, near the end of the Byzantine annual liturgical cycle.[40] Two of the three lections appointed in the Prophetologion for this commemoration are from the book of Exodus (from chapters 24, 33, and 34) and one is from 3 Kingdoms (1 Kings in most English language Bibles; from chapter 19).[41]

Lections from the movable cycle differ from those of the fixed cycle in two principal matters. As we have mentioned, many lections from the movable cycle exhibit continuity from one day's reading to the next, whereas lections from the fixed cycle are ordered thematically to suit the celebration of the particular feast. Further, the manner in which lections were recited within the movable cycle differs from that within the fixed cycle. Let us look now in detail at two further occasions for which lections are provided in the Prophetologion, our first example being taken from the movable cycle, the second from the fixed.

Under the heading for Monday of the second week of Lent—as for most of the weekdays of Lent—the first reading is preceded by rubrical and hymnic material. The first rubrical directive indicates the worship service at which the reading is to occur: at the Third/Sixth Hour.[42] Following this, the hymns that are to precede the lection—the *troparion* and *prokeimenon*—and the tones in which they are to be sung, are given.[43] After the introductory hymns, the reader recites the lection—Isaiah 4:2–5:7. The Prophetologion concludes the Third/Sixth hour lection with a second prokeimenon.[44]

"Thus says the Lord" is a stock *incipit* added to lections to make them better fit the liturgical context, but in this case "to the holy city" has been prepended as well. Although Jerusalem is not mentioned in chapter 54 of Isaiah, this hymn is clearly, in its original context, addressed to it.

40 Titled τη παραμονη τησ μεταμορφωσεωσ του κυριου ημων ιησου χριστου (*sic*) in the *Prophetologion* (2:137).

41 Exodus 24 contains the account of Moses's ascent of Mount Sinai to receive the Law and recounts his vision there of the Lord's glory. The lection thus prefigures Jesus' ascent of the mountain and his appearance in glory there to his disciples, as commemorated at the Transfiguration service. This mountain has been called Mount Tabor in Christian tradition, but the name of the mountain is not given in the New Testament accounts.

42 ΕΙΣ ΤΗΝ ΤΡΙΤΟΕΚΤΗΝ in the *Prophetologium* (e.g., 1:109). This is a part of the daily office associated with midday. In modern Orthodox practice it is often grouped with other services, and the lection is heard in the morning.

43 The troparion is a hymn of several verses that, during the course of Lent, forms a sort of poetic meditation on repentance. The prokeimenon is simply a verse extracted from Psalms that is sung and interspersed with two or three verses from the same psalm chanted in responsorial fashion.

44 During Lent there is an obvious attempt by the Prophetologion's framers to have the entirety of the book of Psalms covered by drawing a representative prokeimenon, in order, from each of the

The next entry for Monday in the second week of Lent indicates that the following set of readings is to occur in conjunction with the Vespers service of that day.⁴⁵ Hymns likewise precede the lections read at Vespers, though only the prokeimenon, and not the troparion, is used for this set of readings. As was the case for the Third/Sixth Hour, the tone in which the prokeimenon is to be sung is given among the liturgical directives. After the prokeimenon, the first lection (Genesis 3:21–4:7) is recited. It is followed by a second prokeimenon, after which ensues the second lection (Proverbs 3:34–4:22). This closes the entry for Monday in the second week of Lent.

A suitable example for consideration from the fixed cycle is the celebration of the Nativity of St. John the Baptist, occurring on 24 June. Three lections are assigned to this date, just as three lections are typically encountered on each day of the Lenten portion of the movable cycle: a reading composed of excerpts from chapters 17, 18, and 21 of Genesis; another made up of excerpts from chapter 13 of Judges; and the third a pastiche of verses from chapters 40, 41, 45, 48, and 54 of Isaiah.⁴⁶

One noteworthy difference between the readings appointed for this celebration in the fixed cycle and those encountered for Monday of the second week of Lent is the fixed cycle's lack of accompanying rubrical material. No troparion or prokeimenon precedes the lections, the only introductory rubric being an indicator that the lections are to be read at Vespers. The fixed cycle readings differ from those of Lent in this respect as well: the three lections are not divided among different parts of the daily office. Rather, as for most commemorations of the fixed cycle—as well as for those that occur during the post-paschal season of the movable cycle—the lections are to be read only during the service of Vespers. Although the Prophetologion entry for this date lacks a troparion as well as a prokeimenon, it does conclude with an indication that a troparion is to be sung at some point after the lections have been read.

Like most other artifacts of antiquity, the Prophetologion does not fit neatly into categories entirely amenable to modern scholarly analysis, and the division of lections into movable and fixed cycles is by no means entirely consistent.

---

150 Psalms. Two prokeimena are prescribed for this midday service so that the desired total will have been completed by the conclusion of Lent.

45   ΕΣΠΕΡΑΣ in the *Prophetologium* (e.g., 1:521).

46   It would appear to modern sensibilities that the Prophetologion's architects sometimes took liberties with the biblical text. As can be seen from the readings for this celebration, the lections sometimes skip over not just phrases or verses but entire chapters. Apparently the intervening material was deemed not sufficiently to the theological point of the commemoration.

Many manuscripts, for example, include among readings for the movable cycle lections dedicated to the celebration of the feasts of Christmas and Theophany, which are fixed commemorations.[47] Many decades ago Rahlfs pointed out that these celebrations are modeled after the celebration of Pascha, the central celebration of the Byzantine Christian liturgical year.[48] Attractive and plausible as that explanation appears, it still remains true that the neat division of lections into those of the movable and fixed cycles is more a product of the analytical thinking modern scholars bring to this ancient tradition than one endemic to the tradition.

His assertion that the Lenten lectionary is an extrapolation from and expansion of the primitive Paschal Vigil is undoubtedly sound. The logic of the primitive Paschal Vigil is that a new age dawned with the appearance, death, and resurrection of Christ. In preparation for the annual commemoration of that cosmic event, the liturgy revisited the pre-incarnational age through a rereading of key Old Testament passages that prefigure events of Christ's incarnation. As Rahlfs rightly divined, this pattern of commemorating the event by preceding it with Old Testament readings was established early on and expanded over the centuries into a period of several weeks, during which readings from the Old Testament became an important element of daily worship. Then, at the commemoration of the event itself, there were no lections from the Old Testament, readings being taken instead from the New Testament.[49]

Rahlfs's insights concerning the modeling of the commemorations of Christmas and Epiphany after the celebration of Pascha are likewise germane. Those celebrations of the fixed cycle are clearly patterned after Pascha in more than just their choice of Old Testament lections: the entire services are permeated with resurrectional language and imagery. Like Christmas and Epiphany, all other commemorations of the Byzantine Christian liturgical year were modeled after the central occasion of the annual liturgical cycle—Pascha. Byzantine

---

47 In fact the critical edition itself is set up in just this way. Part one of the *Prophetologium* otherwise contains lections for the movable cycle, while part two contains lections for the fixed cycle. But the first fascicle of the first part holds the lections for the celebrations of Christmas and Epiphany, feasts of the fixed cycle (*Prophetologium* 1:35–94).

48 "Alttestamentlichen Lektionen" (n. 10 above) 168–71 (74–77).

49 This cannot, of course, be true of the most primitive celebrations of Pascha, since there would have been no New Testament writings in existence in the very earliest decades of the Christian movement. To engage in a bit of speculation on this point, the earliest celebrations of Pascha may well have consisted in a participation in Jewish Passover celebrations, rituals, and lections, and then a later, separate celebration focusing on Christ's resurrection. In any case, the pattern of Old Testament lections preceding the commemoration of the resurrection could apply in this earliest period as well.

Christianity was simply continuing the legacy inherited from the primitive church in using the celebration of Pascha as a sort of template for other commemorations of the liturgical cycle.

If Rahlfs's explanation for the development of the Lenten portion of the Prophetologion is essentially sound, then an assertion made by Engberg that the ancient eucharistic service was never accompanied by Old Testament lections has implications for the development of the lections of the fixed cycle. She convincingly contests the notion that several ancient authors allude to an Old Testament lection in conjunction with the ancient Eucharist.[50] If her position is correct, a certain harmony becomes apparent between the fixed cycle lections and what Rahlfs has proposed about the Lenten lections: Old Testament readings are to precede the commemoration of Christ's death and resurrection, and each celebration of the liturgical cycle is in some sense a celebration of the death and resurrection of Christ as commemorated at the central feast of Pascha. On this understanding, each celebration of the fixed cycle can be seen as a sort of para-Pascha, each being preceded by a Lent in miniature, complete with preparatory Old Testament lections (at Vespers of the eve). Only New Testament readings are slated for the day itself, as is the case with the festival of Pascha after which these celebrations are modeled.

The Prophetologion and Old Testament Traditions in Byzantine Christianity

We argued at the beginning of this chapter that the Old Testament as moderns understand it would have been unknown to the common man of Byzantium. The difficulties attending manuscript production ensured that few exemplars of such scope were produced in antiquity. Low literacy rates precluded the bulk of the populace from engagement with such copies of the Bible or Old Testament as were in existence. This state of affairs led us to propose that an alternate text dating to the Byzantine era, one that corresponds in some important ways to our modern Old Testament—the Prophetologion—should be considered a candidate for the Old Testament of Byzantine Christianity. A summary of the ways in which the Prophetologion corresponds to the Old Testament we moderns know will now be offered.

One of the factors that makes the Prophetologion a suitable candidate for the Old Testament of Byzantine Christianity is its content. The great majority of readings contained in the Prophetologion come from within the range of books

---

50 "Triple-Lection" (n. 15 above), 70–87.

classically conceived of as making up the Old Testament canon. The readings contained in the Prophetologion may be understood, in fact, as a compendium of all parts from that larger corpus that the church deemed crucial to practicing and sustaining the Christian faith. In its day it may even have been viewed, by those more knowledgeable about the issue of canon, as a sort of abridged Old Testament.

Another factor favoring our thesis is the familiarity and accessibility of the work. In our modern understanding, the Old Testament is viewed as a supremely accessible text—at least as far as its physical availability is concerned. Any modern who does not already own an Old Testament can easily acquire one—even without cost. The situation of the Byzantine era differed substantially in terms of the general availability of textual material. The amount of written text in circulation was far lower and longer works, accordingly, did not circulate freely. Such material as existed, increasing in value in proportion to the length of the work, is bound to have been largely inaccessible to the illiterate public.

The Prophetologion, on the other hand, is a book intended for use during public worship services. The church-going segment of the population must have seen it being utilized during worship with some regularity. It would therefore have been a far more familiar volume to a wider portion of the population than were such fuller Old Testament manuscripts as existed during that era.

The accessibility of the text was further heightened through the agency of the reader. Encountered in conjunction with nearly every lection are the key Greek terms ἀνάγνωσμα and ἀναγνώστης—reading and reader. The Prophetologion achieved the level of familiarity it held in Byzantium in part through the office of the reader, who, through his ability to decipher the texts and to convey his understanding through reading aloud with comprehension, made this work familiar to his hearers. In short, the reader was an equalizing force in a largely illiterate society. While the text of the Old Testament can be known to the common man of modernity—usually through private reading—the text of the Old Testament became familiar to the common man of Byzantium through listening.[51]

The root of the terms under discussion is, of course γνῶσις—typically translated into English as "knowledge." In a very real sense, the office of reader involved mediating knowledge, in this case the knowledge contained in the Old Testament texts of the Prophetologion, thus making that knowledge the

---

51 On the development of the reader's office and the importance of the function, see Gamble, *Books and Readers* (n. 5 above), 218–24.

property of the hearers as well.⁵² In addition, the homilist (as Zuntz intimated in the paragraph at the opening of this article) played an equally crucial role on those occasions when a sermon accompanied the reading.

For these reasons we argue that there is commensurability between the Prophetologion within its context and the Old Testament as it is understood today. On the score of familiarity and accessibility, we submit that the Prophetologion is a suitable candidate for the Old Testament of Byzantine Christianity.

Our supposition in arguing the thesis that the Prophetologion was the Old Testament of Byzantine Christianity has been that the Old Testament is reducible to a strictly textual core. Perhaps Zuntz himself, whose words set the tone for this chapter, held a similar supposition. This supposition has proven, during the course of our research and argumentation, to be a modern notion foisted upon the Byzantine era. In attempting to avoid a pitfall we suspected others were stumbling into, we found ourselves faltering on the same obstacle.

We may take as an example the figure of Solomon. Those familiar with the content of the Prophetologion will know that this important biblical figure can scarcely be found among its readings.⁵³ Yet knowledge about, and interest in, Solomon was apparently active and widespread in Byzantium. Some remnants of this interest, for example an amulet depicting Solomon as a horseman, may indicate a knowledge of details about Solomon's life contained in the Old Testament but not found in the Prophetologion.⁵⁴ Byzantine awareness of this important Old Testament figure obviously was not mediated exclusively by the Prophetologion.

The *Testament of Solomon*, a text containing highly imaginative details about Solomon's life that go far beyond what is found within canonical Old Testament texts, appears to have had its influence in the Byzantine era as well.⁵⁵ This text, in turn, is representative of a large and varied stock of lore shared in antiquity by

---

52   Speaking, of course, in idealized terms. Then, as now, the knowledge gotten from publicly read texts hinges on the hearer's attentiveness.

53   Solomon appears in the lections of the Prophetologion only in the opening lines of Proverbs, as their author, and in an excerpt from the eighth and ninth chapters of 3 Kingdoms, in a brief episode that connects him with the Ark of the Covenant and the building of the Temple (*Prophetologium*, 2, 16, 65, and 151). Other, more colorful stories about Solomon that are found in the historical books of the Old Testament are not included among the Prophetologion's lections.

54   H. Maguire, "Magic and the Christian Image," in *Byzantine Magic* (Washington, DC, 1995), 57. These amulets may display an awareness of Solomon's biblical reputation for accumulating vast herds and building an enormous stable complex (1 Kings 4:26; 2 Chronicles 9:24–25).

55   The date of composition of this work remains under dispute, but a majority of scholars now seem persuaded that it originated in the early centuries CE.

Jewish, Christian, and Islamic cultures alike.[56] Textual sources for extra-biblical information about Solomon suggest, in turn, the existence of a complex of oral tradition that undoubtedly circulated for some time before being committed to writing.

Mediation of knowledge about the Old Testament, whether more strictly or more loosely cognizant of the canonical texts, thus clearly followed nontextual channels in the form of oral tradition. But there were yet other vehicles that mediated knowledge about the Old Testament in Byzantium, namely the visual arts—most notably iconography. The symbols and symbolic representations employed in religious artworks and the degree of sophistication that went into their formulation and production made of them repositories of knowledge concerning Old Testament persons and episodes fully on a par with texts of the era.[57] In fact, it seems perfectly reasonable to assume that they were as much an equalizing factor in enabling the illiterate to obtain the knowledge ensconced in the Old Testament text as was the reader who recited the lections at public worship.

Taking adequate account of the fact that both oral tradition and the visual arts served as vehicles for transmitting knowledge about the content of the Old Testament in Byzantium, thus making familiar to the general public a wider compass of the subject matter found there than was available within the Prophetologion's lections, will help to place the thesis argued in this article into proper perspective. It would appear, given these factors, that the Prophetologion, along with the larger Old Testament canon, was a component part of a larger complex of tradition representing the venerable heritage the Byzantines saw as devolving upon themselves. The textual token of that heritage was the Old Testament, with the more familiar literary expression of it being those portions included in the Prophetologion. Iconography and the visual arts mediated the content of both works pictorially, further embellishing it with features drawn from oral tradition and popular imagination.[58] Finally, oral tradition both informed popular

---

56   Another ancient Christian-influenced text embodying various Solomonic traditions is the *Palaia*, a condensed compilation of Old Testament history that circulated much later in the Byzantine period. Rabbinic literature such as *haggadah* likewise contains extrabiblical traditions concerning Solomon. A convenient compilation of rabbinic lore about Solomon can be found in volume four of Louis Ginzburg's *Legends of the Jews*, trans. H. Szold (Philadelphia, 1909–38).

57   J. Lowden ("The Transmission of 'Visual Knowledge' in Byzantium through Illuminated Manuscripts," in *Literacy, Education and Manuscript Transmission in Byzantium and Beyond*, ed. C. Holmes and J. Waring [Leiden, 2002], 59–80) has recently offered a study that follows these lines of inquiry.

58   An apposite juxtaposition of literary, visual-artistic, and oral traditions can be seen on some of the pages of a fifth- or sixth-century illuminated manuscript containing much of the book of Genesis. Here, episodes from the book of Genesis are illustrated but are embellished with

reception of the content of the literature—often augmenting it with imaginative elaborations—and was formed by it.

In retrospect it becomes apparent that the Old Testament of Byzantine Christianity was not limited to a textual corpus. Knowledge at the popular level about Old Testament figures and episodes went beyond the content of the Prophetologion's lections and included information found in the larger Old Testament corpus as defined in the canon lists or as manifested in the pages of full Old Testament exemplars. The range of knowledge did not halt at even these relatively more expansive borders, however, but extended beyond. Much less, then, could it be expected to coincide precisely with what is found between the two covers of a book—whether that book be a liturgical work such as the Prophetologion, or a more weighty tome such as a full Old Testament.

Identifying the Old Testament of Byzantine Christianity—recovering an artifact that, in a very real sense, has been lost through the passage of time and the development of culture and technology—has proven to be no simple task. The story of Lazarus and the poor man may provide here an apt figure: "And besides all this, between us and you a great chasm has been fixed, in order that those who would pass from here to you may not be able, and none may cross from there to us" (Luke 16:26, RSV). The gulf in the present case has been opened by the development of printing technology and pervasion of literacy. We have attempted to traverse that gulf and argued that the Prophetologion is the text most suited to be called the Old Testament of Byzantine Christianity.

---

elements not found in the corresponding biblical text. Some of the elements appear to have been borrowed from Jewish lore, while others are clearly Christian, e.g., the appearance of a church building in the background of one of the scenes depicting events in the life of the patriarch Joseph. See K. Weitzmann, *Late Antique and Early Christian Book Illumination* (New York, 1977), 76–87. Illuminated manuscripts as a class offer fertile ground for investigations of the nexus between oral, visual, and written vehicles for transmitting tradition, as is apparent throughout Weitzmann's many publications.

FOUR

Psalters and Personal Piety in Byzantium

GEORGI R. PARPULOV

Even dead, he is seen here gathering round himself those who are still living. He has just expired. Men as if half-dead (alive but extremely emaciated) are approaching from various directions to perform the funeral rites for the deceased.... Do not be surprised by their multitude. In those times the desert resembled a city: you can see small dwellings all over the rocks with some of the hermits showing from within, perhaps unable to descend the precipices or waiting for those who will carry them. The one who has lowered from his tower a basket in which to pull up food is surely unable to come down, having settled so far from everything. And the one who is sitting in meditation (ἐπὶ συννοίας) and has just stopped writing seems to be lamenting and chanting on the occasion [of the funeral].[1]

I thank Prof. Robert S. Nelson for his invitation to participate in the Dumbarton Oaks symposium on "The Old Testament in Byzantium"; the staffs of the Walters Art Museum library, of the Knott Library at Saint Mary's Seminary and University, and of the Dumbarton Oaks Research Library for their helpfulness; Dr. Audrey Scanlan-Teller and Prof. Alice-Mary Talbot for critically reading this article; the National Library of Greece, the Biblioteca Reale di Torino, and the Bibliothèque nationale de France for allowing me to publish images of manuscripts they own.

1 Καὶ νεκρόν ἐστιν ἐνταῦθα ἰδεῖν τοὺς ἔτι ζῶντας ἐφ᾿ ἑαυτὸν συγκινοῦντα. ἄρτι μὲν ἐπέλιπε τούτῳ τὸ ζῆν. οἱ δ᾿ ἡμιθνῆτες οἱ πλείους καὶ τοῦ βίου λείψανα, φοιτῶσιν ἄλλοθεν ἄλλοι, τῷ κειμένῳ τελέσοντες τὴν ὁσίαν ... τὸ δὲ πλῆθος αὐτῶν, μὴ θαυμάσῃς. πόλιν γὰρ ἡ ἔρημος ὑπεκρίνετο τὰ εἰς ἐκείνους τοὺς χρόνους καὶ οἰκίδια πανταχῇ τῶν πετρῶν ὁρᾶν ἔχεις καὶ τῶν ἀπολειφθέντων ἐνίους ὑπερκύπτοντας τῶν μυχῶν ἤπου τυχὸν οὐ δυναμένους κατιέναι τῶν ἀποτόμων, ἢ προσδεχομένους τοὺς οἴσοντας. ὁ δὲ ἀπὸ τοῦ πύργου καθεὶς τὸν τάλαρον οὗτος, ἐφ᾿ ᾧ τὴν τροφὴν ἀνιμήσασθαι, μαρτύρεται δήπουθεν, ὡς ἀδύνατά ἐστιν αὐτῷ κατελθεῖν, οὕτω πανταχόθεν ἀνῳκοδομημένῳ. καὶ ὁ ἐπὶ συννοίας οὑτοσὶ καθήμενος, ἄρτι τοῦ γράφειν ἀνενεγκών, ὀλοφύρεσθαι ἔοικε καὶ ᾠδὴν ποιεῖσθαι τὴν συμφοράν. John (actually Mark) Eugenikos, *Ekphrasis* 3; ed. C. L. Kayser, *Philostrati libri de gymnastica quae supersunt: Accedunt Marci Eugenici imagines et epistolae nondum editae* (Heidelberg, 1840), 142–44; cf. A. Muñoz, "Le ἐκφράσεις nella letteratura bizantina e i loro rapporti con l'arte figurata,"

The image of Saint Ephraem's Dormition which Mark Eugenikos (d. 1445) describes could not have differed much from the several uniform representations of this scene that survive from the fifteenth century.[2] Nonetheless, although Eugenikos is at pains to emphasize that even those hermits not present at the funeral are participating in it from a distance, in the actual paintings they hardly seem aware of the event. While the novice standing next to the saint's bier is intoning a funerary *sticheron*,[3] the young monk in the cave above has just penned the first words of a Psalter, Psalm 1:1. One might have assumed that the text is being dictated to him, had the elder anchorite seated opposite not had his volume open to a different passage, Psalm 6:1 or 38 (37):1. Just like the inhabitants of the other rock dwellings around them, the two recluses are absorbed in their solitary pursuits. The paintings' background presents, in fact, a panorama of a hermit's daily routine: some monks are seen working with their hands (carving wooden spoons, weaving baskets, copying books), others are engaged in psalmody and prayer. It is recluses like these that John of Gaza (fl. ca. 530) advises:

> [D]o not bind yourself with strict rules, but do whatever the Lord gives you the strength to do. And do not neglect your reading and prayer; little by little, you will gradually spend the day pleasing God. For our perfect fathers were not limited by any particular rule. Indeed, their daily rule included singing Psalms a little, repeating by heart (ἀποστηθίζειν) a little, examining their thoughts a little, working for a living (σχολάζειν περὶ τὴν τροφὴν) a little, and [all] this with fear of God. For it is said: "Whatever you do, do everything for the glory of God."[4]

---

in *Recueil d'études, dédiées à la mémoire de N. P. Kondakov* (Prague, 1926), 139–42, esp. 140. Translations, unless otherwise noted, are my own.
2 See the color illustrations in: K. Weitzmann et al., *The Icon* (New York, 1982), 320; H. Evans, ed., *Byzantium: Faith and Power, 1261–1557* (New York, 2004), 158; *Le Mont Athos et l'Empire byzantin: Trésors de la Sainte Montagne* (Paris, 2009), 214–15. On the scene's iconography: J. R. Martin, "The *Death of Ephraim* in Byzantine and Early Italian Painting," *ArtB* 33 (1951): 217–25; M. Chatzidakis, "Les débuts de l'école crétoise et la question de l'école dite italogrecque," in *In memoria di Sofia Antoniadis* (Venice, 1974), 169–211, pls. 7–34, esp. 189–94, pls. 22–25; repr. in *Études sur la peinture postbyzantine* (London, 1976), no. iv; M. Acheimastou-Potamianou, "Ἡ Κοίμηση τοῦ Ὁσίου Ἐφραίμ τοῦ Σύρου σὲ μία πρώιμη κρητικὴ εἰκόνα τοῦ Βυζαντινοῦ Μουσείου Ἀθηνῶν," in *Εὐφρόσυνον: Ἀφιέρωμα στὸν Μανόλη Χατζηδάκη*, ed. E. Kyprianou, 2 vols. (Athens, 1991–92), 1:41–56, pls. A, 1–8.
3 Δεῦτε τελευταῖον ἀσπασμὸν δῶμεν, ἀδελφοί, τῷ θανόντι, εὐχαριστοῦντες Θεῷ, etc.: E. Follieri, *Initia hymnorum ecclesiae graecae*, 5 vols., ST 211–15 (Vatican City, 1960–66), 1:296, with bibl.; trans. I. F. Hapgood, *Service Book of the Holy Orthodox-Catholic Apostolic Church*, 2nd rev. ed. (New York, 1922), 389, 420.
4 *CPG* 7350, Barsanouphios and John, *Questions and Answers* 85 (ed. F. Neyt and P. de Angelis-Noah, SC 427:374); trans. (here slightly modified) J. Chryssavgis, *Barsanuphius and John: Letters*,

Eight centuries later, at the time of Gregory of Sinai (d. 1346?), this simple regimen has hardly changed: "The solitary (ἡσυχάζων) should first of all have as the basis of his activity (ἐργασία) these five virtues: silence, temperance, vigilance, humility, patient endurance; and his God-pleasing activities should be three: psalmody, prayer, reading, plus (if he is weak) handiwork."[5] Gregory's disciple Philotheos Kokkinos (d. ca. 1376) explains private psalmody in greater detail:

> For a zealous person, the true service to God (I mean psalmody, prayer, and reading the divine Scriptures) is not limited by rules or hours. "I will bless the Lord at all times," says [David]. . . . If you are accustomed to chanting the Hours not in church but in the cell, say the usual initial prayer and chant Terce and Sext with the Typika plus (in winter, because the day then is short) one *kathisma* from the Psalter or (when the days are longer) two *kathismata*. For I want you to recite the [whole] Psalter in your cell once every week at all times, be it Lent or not. For this reason, when you say one kathisma in the morning (because, as explained, of the shortness of the day), say two in the evening at Compline (because the night is long), and in the other season, when the proportion of day to night changes, do the reverse. When you happen to chant the Hours in church, then in the cell immediately after the initial prayer and the "O come, let us worship"[6] say Psalm 50 and start the recitation of the Psalter. . . .[7]

In 1946, a Benedictine visitor to the Lavra of Saint Sabas near Jerusalem reports: "As for private prayer, it consists primarily of reading the Psalter. Each monk ought to recite, in addition to the psalms read in church, at least one *kathisma* a day. This form of devotion is highly recommended and practiced more widely than daily reading of the complete Psalter."[8]

---

2 vols. (Washington, DC, 2006), 1:107f. Further examples from early monastic sources: A. Davril, "La psalmodie chez les pères du désert," *Collectanea cisterciensia* 49 (1987): 132–39. L. Dysinger, *Psalmody and Prayer in the Writings of Evagrius Ponticus* (Oxford, 2005), 48–61.
5 Gregory of Sinai, *Most Beneficial Chapters in Acrostic* 99 (PG 150:1272).
6 *The Great Horologion or Book of Hours*, trans. Holy Transfiguration Monastery (Boston, 1997), 22 et passim.
7 Philotheos Kokkinos, Πρός τινα τῶν σπουδαίων ἀδελφῶν αἰτήσαντα πῶς δεῖ διάγειν ἐν τῷ κελλίῳ, Oxford, Bodleian Library, MS Auct. T.4.4, s. XV, fols. 398r–405v, esp. 399r, 401r–v, ed. G. R. Parpulov, "Toward a History of Byzantine Psalters" (PhD diss., University of Chicago, 2004), 495–505, esp. 496, 499f; Italian trans. (from Vatic. gr. 663, fols. 223r–229v) A. Rigo, *L'amore della quiete (ho tes hesychias eros): L'esicasmo bizantino tra il XIII e il XIV secolo* (Magnano, 1993), 175–80.
8 E. Mercenier, "Le monastère du Mar Saba," *Irénikon* 20 (1947): 283–97, esp. 293. I owe this reference to Dr. Stig R. Frøyshov.

Psalmody, then, is part and parcel of the ascetic life and belongs to the meditation (σύννοια) of hermits. And not only monks practice it in Byzantium. Philotheos Kokkinos recounts how even as a child the future saint Germanos (d. ca. 1336) would secretly imitate the pious observances of his father, a tax collector, and "in solitude (ἡσυχία) talk solely to God, holding in [his] hands the sacred book of Psalms."[9] In the eleventh century the retired general Kekaumenos advised his son, "If you can, pray also at midnight by saying at least one psalm, for at this hour one can speak to God without distraction."[10] Emperor Nikephoros Phokas (d. 969) regularly "spent the whole night without sleep, in prayer and psalmody, holding the Psalter and reading [from it]."[11]

Originally composed in Hebrew as hymns and prayers and generally recognized as inspired by the Holy Spirit,[12] the Psalms form the backbone of personal devotions. "In effect," Paul Bradshaw concludes, "the hymn book of the secular church became the prayer book of monasticism."[13] "O Lord, rebuke me not in thy wrath" reads the verse in the monk's open volume on icons of the Dormition of Saint Ephraem, expressing in the psalmist's words the old man's own contrition. "My son," confides the Egyptian *abba* Philemon, "God has impressed the power of the psalms on my poor soul as He did on the soul of the prophet David."[14] A distich in a ninth-century Psalter succinctly identifies this intimate bond between reader and text: "This book is proper to every devout human being, and the divine David speaks in common for all of mankind."[15] Athanasios of Alexandria makes the point at length:

---

9   BHG 2164, Philotheos Kokkinos, *Life of St. Germanos Maroules* 6, ed. P. Ioannou, "Vie de St. Germain l'Hagiorite par son contemporain le Patriarche Philothée de Constantinople," *AB* 70 (1952): 35–115, esp. 59.
10   Kekaumenos, *Strategikon* 36; ed. G. G. Litavrin, *Sovety i rasskazy: Pouchenie vizatiiskogo polkovodtsa XI veka* (Saint Petersburg, 2003), 210.
11   [Continuator of] George the Monk, *Chronicle* 6 (PG 110:1208D).
12   E.g., *CPG* 2093, Athanasios of Alexandria, *Orations against the Arians* 2.50 (PG 26:253B): τὸ πνεῦμα τὸ ἅγιον, διὰ τῶν ψαλμῶν λέγον.
13   P. F. Bradshaw, *Daily Prayer in the Early Church* (New York, 1982), 94.
14   BHG 2368, ed. Makarios of Corinth and Nikodemos Hagiorites, Φιλοκαλία τῶν ἱερῶν νηπτικῶν, 5 vols., 3rd ed. (Athens, 1957–63), 2:244; trans. G. E. H. Palmer, P. Sherrard, and K. Ware, *The Philokalia: The Complete Text*, 5 vols. (London, 1979–), 2:347.
15   Saint Petersburg, National Library of Russia, MS gr. 216, fol. 347r, reproduced lithographically in V. K. Ernshtedt, "Iz Porfirievskoi Psaltiri 862 goda," *ZhMNP* 236 (1884): 23–35, esp. 34bis with fig. 2: Ἑκάστου ἀνδρὸς εὐσεβοῦς ἴδιον τὸ βιβλίον / Καὶ στόμα κοινὸν τῆς ἀνθρωπότητος ὁ θεῖος Δαυΐδ. Cf. also the four poems printed and translated in E. T. De Wald, *The Illustrations in the Manuscripts of the Septuagint*, vol. 3, *Psalms and Odes*, part 2, *Vaticanus Graecus 752* (Princeton, 1942), xii (where the word ἄλλα in line 12 is a title, not part of the verse!). For a florilegium of Byzantine Psalter epigrams see Parpulov, "Byzantine Psalters" (n. 7 above), 361–95.

But the marvel with reference to the Psalms is this: beyond the prophecies concerning the Savior and the nations, the one saying the other things is speaking as in his own words, and each person sings them as if written concerning himself and relates them not as if another were speaking and not as if they signified another.... I think that these words become like a mirror to the singer for him to be able to understand in them the emotions of his own soul and thus perceiving them to explain them.[16]

Athanasios's text, complete or in excerpts, is found as a preface in a number of Greek Psalters.[17] Either he or an author writing under his name advises an anonymous nun: "Night or day, the word of God should never be absent from your mouth. Your work should be continuous reciting (μελέτη) of the sacred Scriptures.[18] Have a Psalter and learn the Psalms. Let the book be seen in your hands at sunrise."[19]

By contrast with public worship, which is structured according to established rules and based on special liturgical books, private psalmody is "not limited by rules or hours."[20] Byzantine manuscripts of the Psalter are the physical remains of such pious observances. Very few of the medieval Psalters now preserved appear to have been read in church.[21] One clearly meant for liturgical use is mentioned in the late eleventh-century inventory of the Monastery of Christ the All-Merciful in Constantinople: "Another book, containing a *Kontakarion* and Psalter, as well as the verses preceded by Alleluias."[22] Three Psalters, one of them with a decorated binding, appear among the liturgical volumes in a list of the books owned in 1200 by the Monastery of Saint John on Patmos.[23] In a Sinai manuscript, the

16   CPG 2097, Athanasios of Alexandria, *Letter to Marcellinus* 11–12 (PG 27:24); trans. E. Ferguson, "Athanasius, *Epistula ad Marcellinum in interpretationem Psalmorum*," Ἐκκ.Φάρ. 60 (1978): 378–403, esp. 380f. See also John Cassian, *Collationes patrum* 10.11.
17   R. Sinkewicz, *Manuscript Listings for the Authors of the Patristic and Byzantine Periods* (Toronto, 1992), DTMPTR001:I18–K18.
18   On the meaning of μελέτη/*meditatio* in early monastic texts, see H. Bacht, *Das Vermächtnis des Ursprungs: Studien zum frühen Mönchtum*, 2 vols. (Würzburg, 1972–83), 1:244–64.
19   CPG 2248, Athanasios of Alexandria, *De virginitate* 12 (PG 28:265A; ed. E. von der Goltz, TU 29.2a, 46).
20   Philoth. Kokkinos (n. 7 above).
21   This and the following general observations about Byzantine Psalters are based on the 589 parchment manuscripts listed in Parpulov, "Byzantine Psalters," appendix B1. I have not systematically studied Psalters written on paper.
22   P. Gautier, "La diataxis de Michel Attaleiate," *REB* 39 (1981): 5–143, esp. 97; trans. A.-M. Talbot, in *BMFD* 1:359.
23   C. Astruc, "L'inventaire—dressé en septembre 1200—du Trésor et de la Bibliotheque de Patmos: Édition diplomatique," *TM* 8 (1981): 15–30, esp. 23: ψαλτήριον ἔχον εἰς τὸ ἓν μέρος ἀμυγδάλια δ', εἰς τὸ ἕτερον μέρος ἀμυγδάλια δ', βούλλας ϛ', καὶ κομβοθηλύκα δ', τὰ ἀμφότερα ἀργυρᾶ—ψαλτήρια στιχολογίας β'.

Psalter forms a liturgical collection together with an *Oktoechos*, a *Menaion*, and a *Triodion*. In a codex in the Athonite Lavra, it is followed by a Triodion and a Menaion; in one in Vatopedi, by a Triodion and a *Parakletike*; in one in Istanbul, by a Menaion; in one in Paris, by a Parakletike and a Menaion; and finally, in one in Saint Petersburg it is preceded by a Triodion.[24] The text in all these manuscripts is densely written on large pages in two columns of small characters. None contains musical notation. Out of some six hundred books studied, these six are the only Psalters that can be properly called "liturgical." Service books, because of their constant use, do not stand a good chance of survival, which probably explains their slight representation among extant Psalters. It is also likely that many lectors knew the Psalms by heart and did not need a written text to recite them. In short, although the Psalms have always been widely employed in communal, ecclesiastic worship, practically all surviving Byzantine Psalters were copied for personal rather than liturgical use.

Regarding prayer with the Psalms, a further distinction is to be made, that is, between reading aimed at comprehending the theological meaning of the Psalms and their devotional recitation as an act of prayer. These two approaches to the text correspond to two types of books, those in which the Psalms are accompanied by commentary, and those in which they are copied on their own. Psalters with various types of commentary, including *catenae* and short *scholia*, make up 35 percent of the total of surviving manuscripts.[25] The distinction between the two groups is not absolute. On the one hand, many plain-text Psalters contain exegetical prefaces derived from complete commentaries on the Psalms.[26] On the other, volumes that have a limited amount of gloss in the margin (where it does not interfere with viewing the biblical text)[27] can easily be used for devotion. Psalters with more extensive commentary, however, are bulky and correspondingly expensive; they are thus more likely to have belonged to institutional rather than personal libraries. Two mighty twin Psalters now in Paris and Venice that have the same marginal *catena* and, page by page, the same layout, were certainly imperial commissions, although their original owners are unknown (in the early fifteenth century, the Venice copy belonged to a Monastery of the Virgin

---

24 Sinai, MS gr. 550, s. XIV ineunte; Athos, MS Lavra Δ 45, s. XII; ibid., MS Vatopedi 625, s. XII; Istanbul, Ecumenical Patriarchate, MS Kamariotissa 3, s. XII exeunte; Paris, Bibliothèque nationale, MS gr. 13, s. XII–XIII; Saint Petersburg, National Library of Russia, MS gr. 229, s. XIII ineunte.

25 I.e., 210 out of the 589 MSS listed by Parpulov (n. 21 above).

26 For a catalogue of Greek Psalter prefaces see Parpulov, "Byzantine Psalters," 256–99.

27 As opposed to manuscripts where Scripture and commentary alternate in a single block of text.

Peribleptos).²⁸ One of the first books that Saint Athanasios's disciple John copied for the newly founded Athonite Lavra was a large catena Psalter.²⁹ The Patmos inventory lists six Psalters with commentary as opposed to just two "booklets" (one βιβλιδόπουλον and one βιβλιδάριον) with plain Psalms text.³⁰

The two monks in the background of Saint Ephraem's Dormition hold similar small volumes—the "prayer book of monasticism" rather than "the hymn book of the secular church."³¹ Such Psalters are clearly meant not for studying the text but for praying with it. "As for prayer and chanting the Psalms, it should be done not only with the intellect but also with one's lips. For the prophet David says: 'Lord, you shall open my lips, and my mouth shall declare your praise,'" advises John of Gaza.³² Indeed, Peter Damaskenos (fl. ca. 1156) conceives of psalmody in markedly somatic terms: "The fourth form of discipline [after stillness, fasting, and vigils] consists in the recital of psalms—that is to say, in prayer expressed in a bodily way through psalms and prostrations. This is in order to gall the body and humble the soul."³³ By way of such recitation the divinely inspired verses affect the innermost center of one's being: "When through continuous prayer the words of the psalms are brought down into the heart, then the heart like good soil begins to produce by itself various flowers...."³⁴ It is for

---

28 Paris, Bibliothèque nationale, MS grec 139 (the "Paris Psalter"), s. X medio: R. Cormack and M. Vassilaki, eds., *Byzantium 330–1453* (London, 2009), 395: cat. 60 (with bibl.). Venice, Biblioteca Marciana, MS gr. 17 (the "Psalter of Basil II"), s. X exeunte–XI ineunte: S. Gentile, ed. *Oriente cristiano e santità: Figure e storie di santi tra Bisanzio e l'Occidente* (Milan, 1998), 156–58: cat. 7, with bibl.

29 Athos, MS Lavra Δ 70, a. 984: J. Irigoin, "Pour une étude des centres de copie byzantins (2)," *Scriptorium* 13 (1959): 177–209, esp. 196–200; E. Lamberz, "Die Handschriftenproduktion in den Athosklöstern bis 1453," in *Scritture, libri e testi nelle aree provinciali di Bisanzio: Atti del seminario di Erice*, ed. G. Cavallo, G. di Gregorio, and M. Maniaci, 2 vols. (Spoleto, 1991), 1:25–78, pls. i–xix, esp. 30–35, pls. i–iv. Description: Alexandros E. Lauriotes, "Ἀναγραφὴ τοῦ περιεχομένου χειρογράφου τῆς Ἱερᾶς Μονῆς Μεγίστης Λαύρας ἐν Ἄθῳ," *Ἐκκ. Ἀλήθ.*, n.s., 2 (1886): 453–57, 504–7.

30 Astruc, "L'inventaire" (n. 23 above), 23f., 26, 29: ἄλλο βιβλίον, ἑρμηνεία τοῦ αὐτοῦ [τοῦ Χρυσοστόμου] ψαλτηρίου (probably the present-day Patmiacus 159)—βιβλίον ἕτερον, ψαλτῆρος ἐξήγησις ἀκριβεστάτη, ἑρμηνείας ἔχουσα πολλῶν πατέρων (Patm. 65?)—ἄλλο βιβλίον, ψαλτηρίου ἑρμηνείαν ἔχοντος τοῦ ἁγίου Βασιλείου, τοῦ ἁγίου Ἰωάννου τοῦ Χρυσοστόμου, Φωτίου πατριάρχου καὶ ἑτέρων (Patm. 66?)—ἄλλο βιβλίον, ἑρμηνεία τοῦ ψαλτῆρος—ἕτερον, ψαλτήριον ἔχον τὰς ἑρμηνείας διὰ σχολίων—ἕτερον, τοῦ ἁγίου Ἀθανασίου περὶ τῆς βίβλου τῶν ρν´ ψαλμῶν—ἕτερον, βιβλιδόπουλον ψαλτήριον—ἕτερον, βιβλιδάριον ψαλτήριον.

31 Bradshaw, *Daily Prayer* (n. 13 above).

32 Barsanouphios and John, *Questions and Answers* 165 (SC 427:564); trans. Chryssavgis, *Letters* (n. 4 above), 1:182.

33 Trans. Palmer, Sherrard, and Ware, *Philokalia*, 3:91; Greek text: Φιλοκαλία, 3:18 (both n. 14 above).

34 Elias Ekdikos (fl. ca. 1100), *Gnomic Anthology* 78 (PG 127:1164A–B); trans. Palmer, Sherrard, and Ware, *Philokalia*, 3:57.

this reason that the monastic fathers disapprove of singing: "My child, your saying the Psalms with melody (μετὰ ἤχου) is utmost arrogance and presumption. It means: 'I recite Psalms, my brother does not.' For singing makes the heart hard and insensate and does not let the soul attain contrition."[35]

Vocal psalmody need not be excessively long to produce its effects: "As for vespers, the Scetiotes recite twelve Psalms, at the end of each Psalm saying Alleluia instead of the doxology, and simply repeating one prayer. The same also happens at night: they recite twelve Psalms, but after these Psalms they sit down to their handiwork."[36] A list of the twenty-four psalms is preserved in several Psalters (Fig. 1).[37] A late eleventh-century manuscript in Paris contains their full text with troparia and a prayer after each.[38] Three more special Books of Hours of this kind, evidently recited by particularly zealous monks in their cells, survive from the Komnenian period.[39] The Patmian inventory lists among the

---

35   BHG 1450f (PO 8:180). See also BHG 2329b, ed. P. Wessely, "Die Musikanschauung des Abtes Pambo," AnzWien 89 (1952): 50–53 (from the Psalter Vienna, Österreichische Nationalbibliothek, MS theol. gr. 177, s. XII med.), and BHG 1445n (see below, Appendix: no. 3, pp. 459–60). On musical performance of the Psalms in the Byzantine liturgy: C. Troelsgård, "Psalm: III. Byzantine Psalmody," in The New Grove Dictionary of Music and Musicians, ed. S. Sadie, 2nd ed., 29 vols. (New York, 2000–2001), 20:463–66, with bibl.

36   Barsanouphios and John, Questions and Answers 143 (SC 427:520–22); trans. Chryssavgis, Letters, 1:167. On the twelve Psalms see also Palladios, Lausiac History 32, ed. F. Halkin, "L'Histoire Lausiaque et les Vies grecques de S. Pachôme," AB 48 (1930): 257–301, esp. 284, 291; Cassian, De institutis coenobiorum 2.4–6; with detailed discussion in S. R. Frøyshov, "L'Horologe 'géorgien' du Sinaiticus ibericus 34" (PhD diss., Université de Paris-Sorbonne—Institut Catholique de Paris—Institut de théologie orthodoxe Saint-Serge, 2003), 551–609. I thank Dr. Frøyshov for sending me a copy of his thesis.

37   Listed in Parpulov, "Byzantine Psalters" (n. 7 above), appendix C5; see also S. R. Frøyshov, "The Cathedral–Monastic Distinction Revisited: Part I: Was Egyptian Desert Liturgy a Pure Monastic Office?" Studia Liturgica 37 (2007), 198–216, esp. 208–13; idem, "Dvenadtsati Psalmov chin," in Pravoslavnaiia entsiklopediia (Moscow, 2000–), 14:232–34.

38   Paris, Bibliothèque nationale, MS gr. 331, s. XI ex.; description: H.-L. Bordier, Description des peintures et des autres ornements contenus dans les manuscrits grecs de la Bibliothèque nationale (Paris, 1883), 184: cat. 62; text (with the troparia changed) in Εἰκοσιτετράωρον Ὡρολόγιον, ed. I. M. Phountoules, Κείμενα λειτουργικῆς 16 (Thessalonike, 1977).

39   Sinai, MS gr. 869, s. XII in. (originally appended to the Psalter Sinait. gr. 51); Athens, National Library, MS 15, s. XII in. (hours intercalated with the kathismata of a Psalter); Lesbos, Leimonos Monastery, MS 295, s. XII ex. On the Athens MS: R. S. Nelson, "Text and Image in a Byzantine Gospel Book in Istanbul, Ecumenical Patriarchate, Cod. 3" (PhD diss., New York University, 1978), 98–122, figs. 85–101; E. C. Constantinides, "The Tetraevangelion, Manuscript 93 of the Athens National Library," ΔXAE, ser. 4, 9 (1977–79): 185–215, pls. 61–86; repr. in Images from the Byzantine Periphery: Studies in Iconography and Style (Leiden, 2007), 1–39. On the Leimonos MS: P. L. Vocotopoulos, "I manoscritti bizantini illustrati della Moni Limonos di Lesbo," in Bisanzio, la Grecia e l'Italia: Atti della giornata di studi sulla civiltà artistica bizantina in onore di Mara Bonfioli, ed. A. Iacobini (Rome, 2003), 33–44, esp. 36f., 42–44. On both: I. M. Phountoules, Ἡ εἰκοσιτετράωρος ἀκοίμητος δοξολογία (Athens, 1963), 69–116, 123–30. Phountoules argues

parchment volumes one "twelve-hour *Horologion*."[40] It is unclear whether this was a modified version of the longer twenty-four-hour devotional *cursus* or a regular Book of Hours comprising Matins, Vespers, Compline, and Nocturns plus Prime, Terce, Sext, and None with their Mid-Hours (*mesoria*). Although the latter canonical hours belong to public ecclesiastic worship, Philotheos Kokkinos's letter indicates that they could also be recited in private.[41] Another patriarch of Constantinople, Luke Chrysoberges (d. 1170), advises an anonymous solitary monk: "Observe the same order of prayer as [ordinary] Christians do, namely, Nocturns, Matins, the Hours, Vespers, and Compline."[42] To a great extent these daily services consist of selected psalms.[43] Because of this, a number of manuscript Psalters are followed by a Horologion[44] and almost all (some commentary ones excepted) contain the Odes (Canticles) that together with the Psalms form the scriptural nucleus of the liturgy of Hours (e.g., Appendix, nos. 1–3).[45] Finally, a few manuscripts give the following prescription (Fig. 2): "The Psalms said as prayers are the following: Against despondent thoughts—Psalm 54, 53. Against lewd thoughts—Psalm 34, 37. Against rancorous thoughts—Psalm 30. Against captive thoughts—Psalm 12, 16. Against thoughts of forsakenness—Psalm 70, 72.

---

that these Books of Hours correspond to the liturgical rule of the Monastery of the Sleepless Monks (Ἀκοίμητοι) in Constantinople.

40   Astruc, "L'inventaire" (n. 23 above), 28: βιβλίον ἄλλο τὸ δωδεκάωρον ὡρολόγιον.

41   N. 7 above.

42   Luke Chrysoberges, Πῶς ὀφείλει διάγειν ὁ μοναχὸς εἰς τὸ κελλίον αὐτοῦ, ed. Parpulov, "Byzantine Psalters" (n. 7 above), 494: Ἀκολουθίαν, ἣν ἔχουσιν οἱ χριστιανοί, ἔχε καὶ ἐσύ· ἢ μεσονυκτικόν, ὄρθρον, ὥρας, ἑσπερινὸν καὶ ἀπόδειπνον. French summary: V. Grumel and J. Darrouzès, *Les regestes des actes du Patriarcat de Constantinople*, vol. 1, *Les actes des patriarches*, 2nd rev. ed., 7 fascs. (Paris, 1972–), 2–3:536f.: no. 1106. See also Athanasios, *De virginitate* 12 (PG 28:265A–B; ed. Goltz, TU 29.2a, 46).

43   Listed in *The Psalter According to the Seventy of St. David, the Prophet and King: Together with the Nine Odes and an Interpretation How the Psalter Should Be Recited through the Whole Year*, trans. Holy Transfiguration Monastery (Boston, 1974), 295; cf. *Great Horologion* (n. 6 above), 21–234. On the origins and history of the Horologion: E. P. Diakovskii, *Posledovanie chasov i izobrazitel'nykh* (Kiev, 1913); N. Egender, "Introduction," in *La prière des Églises de rite byzantin: La prière des heures (Hōrologion)*, 2nd ed. (Chevetogne, 1975), 11–90, with bibl.; C. Lutzka, *Die Kleinen Horen des byzantinischen Stundengebets und ihre geschichtliche Entwicklung* (Münster, 2007).

44   The earliest example is Turin, Biblioteca Universitaria, MS B.VII.30, s. IX, fols. 139v–142v: S. Parenti, "Nota sul Salterio: Horologion del IX secolo Torino, Biblioteca Universitaria B. VII. 30," *BollGrott*, ser. 3, 4 (2007): 275–87; see also no. 3 in the Appendix below.

45   For a full list of these canticles, which are composed of biblical excerpts or centos plus the matutinal Great Doxology (Δόξα ἐν ὑψίστοις Θεῷ, etc.) and the ancient vesperinal hymn Φῶς ἱλαρόν, see J. Mearns, *The Canticles of the Christian Church Eastern and Western in Early and Medieval Times* (Cambridge, 1914), 7–16; cf. *Great Horologion*, 78–94, 101–4, 188, 192, 204f., 212, 215f. *Psalter According to the Seventy*, 262–87. See also H. Schneider, "Die biblischen Oden seit dem sechsten Jahrhundert," *Biblica* 30 (1949): 239–72; A. S. Korakides, *Ἀρχαῖοι ὕμνοι*, 2 vols. (Athens, 1979).

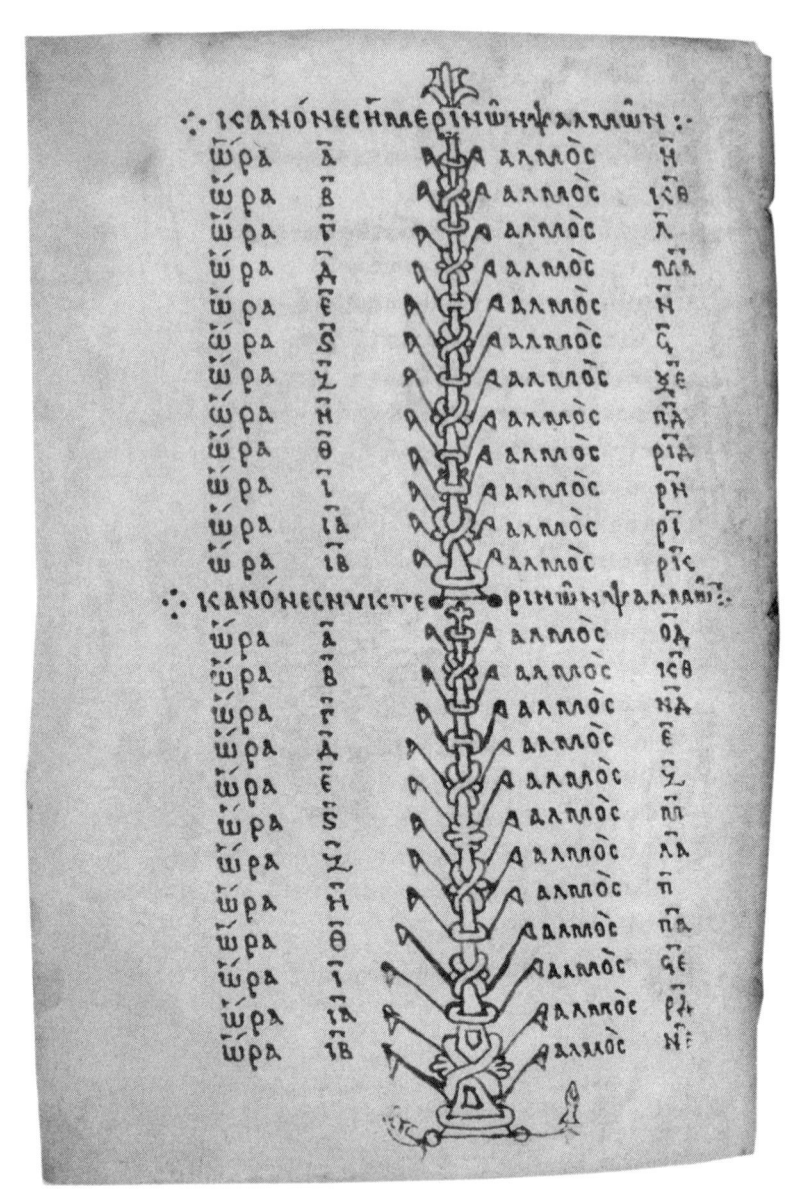

FIGURE 1 Milan, Biblioteca Ambrosiana, MS + 24 sup., ca. 900–950 CE, fol. 6v (Copyright Biblioteca Ambrosiana Auth. No. F 19/08)

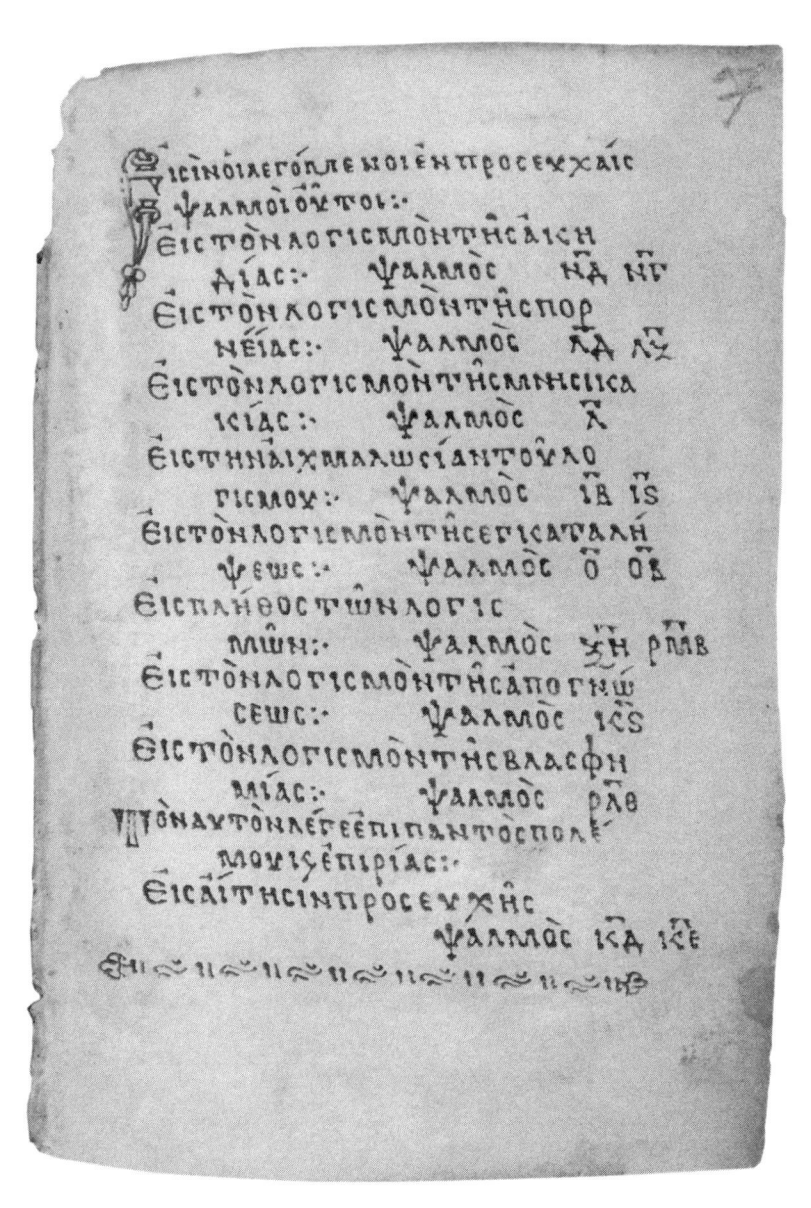

FIGURE 2 Milan, Biblioteca Ambrosiana, MS + 24 sup., ca. 900–950 CE, fol. 7r (Copyright Biblioteca Ambrosiana Auth. No. F 19/08)

Against multitudinous thoughts—Psalm 68, 142. Against thoughts of despair—Psalm 26. Against blasphemous thoughts—Psalm 139. Say the same Psalm [also] against any torment and difficulty (ἀπορία?). In want of prayer—Psalm 24, 25."[46] This belief in the beneficial power of psalms may also take a superstitious form: in the late eleventh century, some Psalters (e.g., Appendix, no. 2) start to be supplied with divinatory sentences, one for each psalm, that can be consulted by opening the volume at random.[47]

As opposed to such selective use of the Psalms, it is common, especially among monks, to recite them in their entirety. This is described, for example, in the story about Abba Serapion and the prostitute:

> One day Abba Serapion passed through an Egyptian village and there he saw a courtesan who stayed at her own cell. The old man said to her, "Expect me this evening, for I should like to come and spend the night with you." She replied, "Very well, abba." She got ready and made the bed. When evening came, the old man came to see her and entered her cell and said to her, "Have you got the bed ready?" She said, "Yes, abba." Then he closed the door and said to her, "Wait a bit, for we have a rule of prayer (νόμον ἔχομεν) and I must fulfill that first." So the old man began his prayers. He took the Psalter and at each Psalm he said a prayer for the courtesan, begging God that she might be converted and saved, and God heard him.... When he had completed the Psalter (ὡς ἐτέλεσεν ὁ γέρων ὅλον τὸ ψαλτήριον), the woman fell to the ground.[48]

Saying the 151 Psalms aloud takes about four hours. The text in most Byzantine Psalters is organized in accordance with such complete reading. It is divided into verses for easier recitation but never accompanied by any musical signs.[49] In manuscripts from the ninth to eleventh centuries, each verse forms a separate

---

46 Parpulov, "Byzantine Psalters" (n. 7 above), 268f. See Derek Krueger's further comments on this text in Chapter 8 of the present volume.

47 The earliest Psalter with such sentences is Paris, Bibliothèque nationale, Ms gr. 164, a. 1070. See in general P. Canart, "Un système byzantin de divination basé sur le Psautier: Sa diffusion dans les aires périphériques de l'oikoumènè et sa traduction slave," *Godishnik na Sofiiskiia universitet, Tsentur za slaviano-vizantiiski prouchvaniia "Ivan Duichev,"* in press. I thank Prof. Canart for sending me a draft of his paper.

48 *BHG* 1618b (PG 65:416A; cf. ed. J.-C. Guy, SC 498:34); trans. B. Ward, *The Sayings of the Desert Fathers: The Alphabetical Collection* (Kalamazoo, 1979), 226; commentary: V. M. Lur'e, "Iz istorii chinoposledovaniia psalmopeniia: polnaia Psaltir' v ezhednevnom pravile (v sviazi s istoriei egipetskogo monashestva)," *VizVrem* 56 (1995): 228–37, esp. 229–34.

49 On the musical notation in Byzantine Gospel lectionaries: S. G. Engberg, "Ekphonetic Notation," in *New Grove Dictionary of Music*, 2nd ed., 8:47–51, with bibl.

paragraph (Fig. 3). Certain psalms are separated by the note "glory" (*doxa*); every third *doxa* is marked "session" (*kathisma*).[50] This rubrication is almost universally present (only Psalters with commentary are sometimes devoid of it) and is identical in all manuscripts, starting with the *Psalterium aureum Turicense*.[51] Unlike chapters, the twenty *kathismata* are numbered at their end (Fig. 3), since the reason for marking the division is not to help one find a passage but to measure the amount of text read.[52] *Doxai* are the ultimate punctuation marks, showing at which point one should pause in reciting psalms and say a doxology.[53] The earliest witness to this practice is John Cassian (d. ca. 435): "In the East [not every psalm but] only the antiphon[54] ends, as a rule, with this glorification of the Trinity ['gloria Patri, et Filio, et Spiritui sancto']."[55] Peter Damaskenos describes such serial recitation:

> After praying in this way [with a long penitential prayer] you should immediately address your own thoughts and say three times: "O come, let us worship and fall down before God our King." Then you should begin the psalms, reciting the *Trisagion* after each subsection of the Psalter (ἀντίφωνον), and enclosing your intellect within the words you are saying. After the Trisagion say "Lord, have mercy" forty times, and then make a prostration and say once within yourself, "I have sinned, Lord, forgive me."

---

50 The earliest reference to this grouping of the Psalms is found in the seventh-century *Miracles* of St. Artemios, *BHG* 173, ed. A. Papadopoulos-Kerameus, *Varia graeca sacra* (Saint Petersburg, 1909), 50: τῆς πνευματικῆς παννυχίδος ἐπιτελουμένης καὶ γενομένου τοῦ καθίσματος μετὰ τὰ τρία ἀντίφωνα τὰ ἑσπερινά (on *antiphons* see n. 54 below). Ps. 119 (118), the longest in the Psalter, is divided into three parts by the rubric στάσις (sometimes accompanied by δόξα). The third *stasis* is a *kathisma*. Cf. C. Du Cange, *Glossarium ad scriptores mediae et infimae graecitatis* (Lyon, 1688; repr. Graz, 1958), 1429, s.v. στάσεις; *BHG* 1438w, ed. A. Longo, "Il testo integrale della 'Narrazione degli abati Giovanni e Sofronio' attraverso le Ἑρμηνεῖαι di Nicone," *RSBN*, n.s., 2–3 (1965–66): 223–67, esp. 251f. (where, exceptionally, not Ps. 119 [118] but the entire Psalter is described as comprising three στάσεις).
51 E. Crisci, C. Eggenberger, R. Fuchs, and D. Oltrogge, "Il Salterio purpureo Zentralbibliothek Zürich, RP 1," *Segno e testo* 5 (2007): 31–98, with fols. 63v *infra*, 123v, 138v, 163v, 168r, 171v, 175v, 179v, 185v, 191r, 195v, 200v, 204r, 207v in the accompanying digital facsimile. The rubrics δόξ(α) and κάθ(ισμα) are in black ink and are not written in the principal scribe's hand. They must have been added before the 780s, when the manuscript was brought to Reichenau from Rome: ibid., p. 69.
52 Only in later manuscripts (after ca. 1300) do the kathismata come to be numbered at their beginning, and this later usage becomes a norm for all printed editions of the Greek Psalter.
53 *Psalter According to the Seventy* (n. 43 above), 293.
54 The rubric ἀντ(ίφωνον) is found in place of δόξ(α) in several ninth-century Greek Psalters, e.g., Sinait. gr. 30 (below, Appendix, no. 1). See also Lampe, s.v. ἀντίφωνος.
55 John Cassian, *De institutis coenobiorum* 2.8 (ed. M. Petschenig, CSEL 17:24; SC 109:72); trans. B. Ramsey, *John Cassian: The Institutes* (New York, 2000), 42.

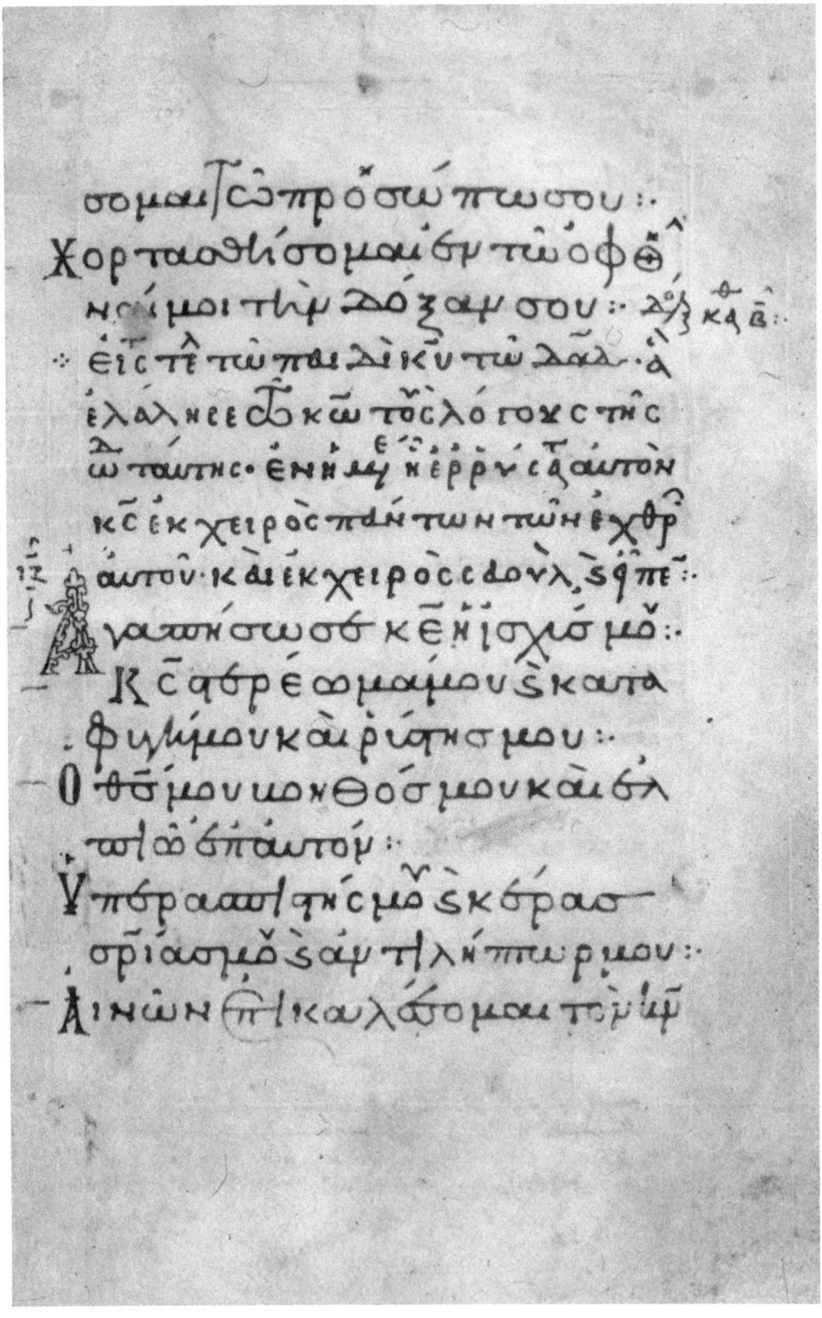

FIGURE 3 Athens, National Library of Greece, MS 3, ca. 1050–1100 CE, fol. 24r
(photo Kostas Manolis, published with permission of the National Library of Greece)

On standing, you should stretch out your arms and say once, "God, be merciful to me a sinner." After praying in this way, you should say once more, "O come, let us worship . . ." three times, and then another sub-section of the Psalter in the same way.[56]

Symeon the New Theologian (d. 1022) advises a monk alone in his cell at night to "stand for prayer, quietly recite psalms and pray to God as one who is heard by no one else. Stand with boldness and collect your thoughts and do not allow them to roam elsewhere; join your hands, place your feet evenly together, and stand in one place without moving."[57] Standing for psalmody was common practice,[58] so the rubric "kathisma" marks points at which one may momentarily sit down and pause for prostrations and prayer.[59] Thus, Saint Athanasia of Aegina "would keep solitary vigils and recite the Psalms of David, making a prayer with the greatest attentiveness at each one of the kathismata."[60] Prayers for the kathismata, doubtless transmitted orally among monks and on occasion probably improvised (like Abba Serapion's), first appear recorded in Greek manuscripts around the year 1100,[61] thus forming an extended Ψαλτήριον σὺν Θεῷ μετὰ τροπαρίων καὶ εὐχῶν τῆς ἡμέρας καὶ τῆς νυκτός (Psalter, with God, Including Troparia and Prayers for the Day and the Night).[62] In the thirteenth century a certain Sabas, perhaps the

---

56 Peter Damaskenos, *Admonition Addressed to His Own Soul* (Φιλοκαλία, 3:41); trans. Palmer, Sherrard, and Ware, *Philokalia*, 3:118f. (both n. 14 above)
57 Symeon the New Theologian, *Discourses* 26.12 (ed. B. Krivochéine, SC 113:92), trans. (here slightly modified) C. J. de Catanzaro, *Symeon the New Theologian: The Discourses* (New York, 1980), 282.
58 See e.g., Gregory of Sinai, *On Stillness* 4, 9; *On Prayer* 5 (Φιλοκαλία, 4:73, 75f., 82), trans. Palmer, Sherrard, and Ware, *Philokalia*, 4:266, 269f., 278.
59 This alternation of psalmody and prayer has been practiced since at least the fourth century CE: A. de Vogüé, "Le psaume et l'oraison: Nouveau Florilège," *Ecclesia Orans* 12 (1995): 325–49; Dysinger, *Psalmody* (n. 4 above), 70–103.
60 *BHG* 180 (ed. F. Halkin, SubsHag 174:183): Ἠγρύπνει δὲ καθ' ἑαυτὴν καὶ δαυϊτικοὺς ἐμελέτα ψαλμούς, καθ' ἕνα τῶν καθισμάτων εὐχὴν μετὰ μεγίστης ποιουμένη τῆς νήψεως. Trans. (here modified) L. F. Sherry, in *Holy Women of Byzantium: Ten Saints' Lives in English Translation*, ed. A.-M. Talbot (Washington, DC, 1996), 146.
61 The earliest witnesses are three closely related Psalters: Cambridge, MA, Houghton Library, MS gr. 3, a. 1105; Athos, MS Pantokratoros 43, s. XI ex.; ibid., MS Iveron 22, s. XI ex.; see further: Parpulov, "Byzantine Psalters" (n. 7 above), 118–24. Most of the prayers in these manuscripts are the same as those published from Paris. gr. 331 in Phountoules's Εἰκοσιτετράωρον Ὡρολόγιον (n. 38 above), whence some are translated in *Voices in the Wilderness: An Anthology of Patristic Prayers*, ed. N. S. Hatzinikolaou (Brookline, MA, 1988), 3, 15, 37, 70–73, 87, 159–60. The text of the Houghton manuscript will be published with translation and commentary in the series OCA: J. C. Anderson and S. Parenti, *Byzantine Monastic Hours in the Early Twelfth Century* (Rome, in press), non vidi.
62 This is the title (fol. 1r) of the Psalter Sinai, MS gr. 40, s. XII. This, to my knowledge, is the only manuscript where the presence of troparia and prayers for the kathismata is noted in the title.

archbishop of Serbia (d. 1235), translated such a Psalter into Slavic and explained its use in a short preface:

> Our God-bearing and most blessed fathers, the lights of the entire world, terrestrial angels, celestial men, those who were first accustomed by the Holy Spirit to the tradition of asceticism ... established for us the God-delivered rule of their psalmody, for it was by tender chants that they propitiated the Lord. Some of them sang the Hours with Mid-Hours and prayers, put together select Psalms and prayers, and named this book the Book of Hours. Others recited only the Psalter, without prayers. Yet others, being more zealous, chanted the Psalter together with prayers, penitential *stichera* and the Trisagion with prostrations. The present Psalter is of this kind.[63]

Since hardly any two surviving Psalters of this kind have the same sets of supplementary texts,[64] each manuscript must have been tailored to its owner's individual needs or preferences.[65] In a few, the prayers are formulated in the feminine.[66]

Even before such texts start to be inserted at the kathismata, prayers for general daily use appear at the end of Psalters (e.g., Appendix, no. 2).[67] One also finds there prayers to be said in private before and after communion,[68] penitential

---

63 The earliest witness of this text is the Bulgarian "Radomir Psalter," Athos, MS Zographou slav. I.д.13, s. XIII, fols. 2r–5v, whence it is edited in *Radomirov Psaltir*, ed. L. Makarijoska (Skopje, 1997), 153; later versions from Russian MSS: B. St. Angelov, "Skazanie o psaltiri," in *Iz starata bulgarska, ruska i srubska literatura*, 3 vols. (Sofia, 1958–78), 3:38–60, esp. 53, 57; commentary: V. M. Lur'e, "Slavianskoe 'Skazanie o Psaltiri' i ego istoriko-liturgicheskoe znachenie," *BSl* 57 (1996): 140–55; on Sabas's authorship: F. J. Thomson, "Medieval Bulgarian and Serbian Theological Literature: An Essential Vademecum," *BZ* 98 (2005): 503–49, esp. 527.
64 There are 316 different prayers in the 36 Psalters I have studied; (incomplete) list and table in Parpulov, "Byzantine Psalters," 306–58, appendix C3.
65 The typographic press brought uniformity to these texts: all three printed Greek Psalters known to me to contain additions for the kathismata (publ. Snagov, 1700; Leipzig, 1761; Venice, 1780) have the same set of troparia and prayers, which in 1906 were reprinted from the Venice edition as Σύντομοι κατανυκτικαὶ προσευχαί (nos. κ′–λθ′) in *Μέγα προσευχητάριον περιέχον ἱερὰς προσευχὰς ἐν πάσῃ περιστάσει καὶ ῥήματα ἱερά*, ed. A. D. Simonof, new ed. (Thessalonike, 2001), 511–37. The exact same troparia and prayers are also found in the Psalter MS Sinait. gr. 2132, s. XV ex. The three printed Psalters are listed in Th. I. Papadopoulos, *Ἑλληνικὴ βιβλιογραφία (1466 ci.–1800)*, 2 vols., Πραγματεῖαι τῆς Ἀκαδημίας Ἀθηνῶν 48 (Athens, 1984–86), nos. 1269, 1290, 1304.
66 E.g., Oxford, Bodleian Library, MS Laud. gr. 2, a. 1336; ibid., MS Holkham gr. 1, s. XIV in.
67 The earliest Psalter with such prayers at the end is Oxford, Bodleian Library, MS Auct. D.4.1, a. 950, fols. 315v–318v, ed. Parpulov, "Byzantine Psalters," 516–22.
68 Some of these personal communion prayers are now printed in the Book of Hours as part of the Ἀκολουθία τῆς θείας μεταλήψεως: *Great Horologion* (n. 6 above), 787–813. Their earliest witness in Psalters is Jerusalem, MS Taphou 53, a. 1053 (sic), fols. 224r–227r, 231r–v with Saint Petersburg, National Library of Russia, MS gr. 266, f. 4r–v. See further Parpulov, "Byzantine Psalters,"

poems,[69] and from the thirteenth century on (e.g., Appendix: no. 3), various hymnographic canons,[70] including the Service of the Akathistos (comprising the eponymous hymn and a special canon).[71] Devout supplications of this kind, in prose or verse, are addressed primarily to Christ or the Mother of God and find their counterpart in a few Byzantine Psalter miniatures. These miniatures are exceptional in that their subject matter does not correspond to the contents of the Psalms but rather reflects the devotional use of the Psalter as a whole. By contrast, the vast majority of Psalter illustrations were intended to divide, embellish, or explain the text and are, thus, linked to the book's contents rather than to its function.[72] The numerous miniatures of the Theodore Psalter (dated 1066), for example, serve primarily as pictorial glosses to the Psalms and just a single one among them, at the very end of the volume, reflects its use.[73] It shows Abbot Michael Stoudites, the book's commissioner and first owner, facing an image of Christ and speaking in dodecasyllables: "I praise you, Savior, having finished the book of your prophet and wise king [David]."[74] Michael has completed the twenty kathismata with the nine matutinal Odes and now says the final doxology.

The simplest form of Psalter illustration is an image of the prophet and wise king David writing, singing, or simply displaying the Book of Psalms (Fig. 4).[75] Such miniatures do not basically differ from author portraits in other Byzantine manuscripts.[76] They are a pictorial equivalent of the book's title (most often Psalter of David [Ψαλτήριον τῷ/τοῦ Δαυΐδ] or some variation

---

17f., 300–305, appendix C2; S. Alexopoulos and A. van den Hoek, "The Endicott Scroll and Its Place in the History of Private Communion Prayers," *DOP* 60 (2006): 146–88.
69 E.g., Sinai, MS gr. 2123, a. 1242, f. 131v: Κατ' ἀλφάβητον στίχοι τοῦ λογοθέ[του Συμεών] (PG 114:132f.); see also n. 86 below.
70 Parpulov, "Byzantine Psalters," 16f., 359f.; see also no. 3 in the Appendix below.
71 *Great Horologion* (n. 6 above), 733–52.
72 On Byzantine Psalter illustration in general: K. Corrigan, "Salterio: Area bizantina," in *Enciclopedia dell'arte medievale*, 12 vols. (Rome, 1991–2002), 10:289–96, with bibl.
73 London, British Library, Add. ms 19,352, a. 1066, fol. 207v; miniature reproduced and described in S. Der Nersessian, *L'illustration des Psautiers grecs du Moyen Age*, vol. 2, *Londres, Add. 19.352* (Paris, 1970), 62, pl. 116 with fig. 325; C. Barber, *Theodore Psalter: Electronic Facsimile* (Champaign, IL, 2000), ad loco (cf. B. Crostini, "Navigando per il Salterio: Riflessioni intorno all'edizione elettronica del Manoscritto Londra, British Library, Addit. 19.352," *BollGrott*, n.s., 56 [2002–3]: 133–209, esp. 191f.); C. Barber, "In the Presence of the Text: A Note on Writing, Speaking and Performing in the Theodore Psalter," in *Art and Text in Byzantine Culture*, ed. L. James (Cambridge, 2007), 83–99, esp. 88f.
74 Αἰνῶ σε, Σῶτερ, τερματήσας τὴν βίβλον / τοῦ σοῦ προφήτου καὶ σοφοῦ βασιλέως.
75 Numerous examples in A. Cutler, *The Aristocratic Psalters in Byzantium* (Paris, 1984).
76 On Byzantine evangelist portraits: H. Hunger, "Evangelisten: A. Evangelistenbilder in Handschriften," *RBK* 2:452–84, 505–7.

FIGURE 4 Paris, Bibliothèque nationale de France, MS grec 169, ca. 1280–1300 CE, fol. 12v (published courtesy of the BnF)

thereupon)[77] and of certain verse epigrams in praise of David.[78] But even such generic imagery is at times affected by the needs of private devotion. There is a unique Psalter frontispiece (dated 1105) in Oxford where the Old Testament king appears anachronistically standing before an icon of the Virgin and chanting, just as the volume's owner once did, from an open Psalter.[79] David is thus depicted not only as author of the book but also as role model for the person actually reading it, who is to utter the Psalms "not as if they were composed by the prophet but as if they were his own utterances and his own prayer."[80] The Oxford manuscript contains at its end a short treatise on the Jesus Prayer, further confirming the book's devotional use.[81]

The inclusion of the viewer/reader is even more explicit in the opening miniature of a Psalter at Harvard (precisely contemporary with the Oxford one).[82] Here, the standard author portrait is reduced to a marginal figure of David as additional intercessor in a Deesis.[83] The book's first owner is shown prostrate to the right of Christ and touching his foot, just as a petitioner at court would touch the emperor's shoe. The miniature thus becomes at once part of the act of prayer (it is Christ's image through which prayers are addressed to Christ himself) and

---

77   For a list of the titles found in Greek Psalter manuscripts see Parpulov, "Byzantine Psalters" (n. 7 above) 253–55.
78   E.g., the poems that accompany the David portraits in the "Leo Bible" (Vatic. Reg. gr. 1, s. X) and the "Barberini Psalter" (Vatic. Barber. gr. 372, s. XI), reprinted and translated respectively in A. Kartsonis, *Anastasis: The Making of an Image* (Princeton, 1986), 197f. and P. Finlay, "A Feast for the Senses," in *Metaphrastes, or, Gained in Translation: Essays and Translations in Honour of Robert H. Jordan*, ed. M. Mullett (Belfast, 2004), 248.
79   Oxford, Bodleian Library, MS Barocci 15, a. 1105, fol. 39v; miniature described and reproduced in Cutler, *Aristocratic Psalters*, 58, 194 with fig. 226; I. Hutter, *Corpus der byzantinischen Miniaturenhandschriften: Oxford, Bodleian Library*, 3 vols. (Stuttgart, 1977–82), 1:55, 179 with fig. 204; 3.1:332.
80   John Cassian, *Collationes patrum* 10.11.4 (ed. M. Petschenig, CSEL 13:304; SC 54:92); trans. B. Ramsey, *John Cassian: The Conferences* (New York, 1997), 384.
81   Cod. Barocci 15, fols. 391v–392v, 394r–v: Ἑρμηνεία εἰς τὸ Κύριε Ἰησοῦ Χριστὲ ὁ Θεὸς ἡμῶν ἐλέησον ἡμᾶς, ed. R. Sinkewicz, "An Early Byzantine Commentary on the Jesus Prayer: Introduction and Edition," *MedSt* 49 (1987): 208–20, esp. 213, 217–19. On the Jesus Prayer and psalmody: Barsanouphios and John, *Questions and Answers* 175; Gregory of Sinai, *On Prayer* 5.
82   Cambridge, MA, Houghton Library, MS gr. 3, a. 1105, fol. 8v; miniature described and reproduced in Cutler, *Aristocratic Psalters*, 35, 160 with fig. 110; I. Spatharakis, *The Portrait in Byzantine Illuminated Manuscripts* (Leiden, 1976), 44, fig. 15; L. Nees, "An Illuminated Byzantine Psalter at Harvard University," *DOP* 29 (1975): 205–24, esp. 209–16 with fig. 1; G. Vikan, ed. *Illuminated Greek Manuscripts from American Collections: An Exhibition in Honor of Kurt Weitzmann* (Princeton, 1973), 128–29 with fig. 56.
83   On the Deesis: I. Zervou Tognazzi, "Deesis. Interpretazione del termine e sua presenza nell'iconografia bizantina," in *Costantinopoli e l'arte delle province orientali*, ed. F. de' Maffei, C. Barsanti, and G. Guidobaldi (Rome, 1990), 391–420; L. A. Shchennikova, "Deisus v vizantiiskom mire. Istoriograficheskii obzor," *Voprosy iskusstvoznaniia* 2–3 (1994): 132–63, with bibl.

a representation of this act. Donor portraits are not found in Psalters alone, but there, in direct proximity to devotional texts, their personal significance is especially marked.[84] The Harvard codex is the first dated manuscript with troparia and prayers for the kathismata.[85] At the end of its Psalter are inserted verses that a certain monk Gregory borrowed, for the most part, from a penitential poem by Symeon the Metaphrast (d. ca. 1000).[86]

Similar use of poetic excerpts is made in an early twelfth-century Psalter now in the Dionysiou Monastery on Athos.[87] There, it is the Metaphrast's contemporary Nikephoros Ouranos (d. after 1007) whose verses are quoted in the margin next to a series of scenes depicting the death and posthumous fate of a monk, evidently the Sabas who is named on folio 244r–v as the manuscript's owner.[88]

---

84   On donor portraits in Byzantine manuscript illumination: Spatharakis, *Portrait* (n. 82 above), passim.

85   See n. 61 above.

86   Cambridge, MA, MS Houghton gr. 3, f. 232v (after Ode 9): Τοῦ μακαριωτάτου μοναχοῦ κὺρ Γρηγορίου στίχοι· Ὦ Πάτερ, Υἱέ, Πνεῦμα, Τριὰς ἁγία, / Ὅταν καθίσῃς εἰς ἐπηρμένον θρόνον / Ὅταν κρίνῃς με τὸν κατακεκριμένον, / Πάντων ὁρώντων καὶ τρόμῳ πεφρικότων / Μὴ διανοίξῃς βιβλίον συνειδήτον / Μὴ στηλιτεύσῃς τὰς ἐμὰς ἀσωτίας / Μή τοῖς ἐρίφοις τοῖς κεκατηραμένοις, / Ἐμὲ συνάψῃς τὸν κεκατηραμένον, / Ἀλλὰ προβάτοις τοῖς μεμακαρισμένοις, / Αἰῶνι τῷ μέλλοντι τῷ σωτηρίῳ. (Verses, by the Most Blessed Monk Sir Gregory: Holy God, the Father, Son, and Spirit, / When you sit on your throne exalted / And my turn for judgment comes before you / (All things looking on in fear and trembling), / Do not open the book of my conscience / And do not announce my grave transgressions, / Do not make me one of the condemned goats [Matt. 25:32], / Sinful that I am and full of error; / Join me to the sheep redeemed and blessed / In the age to come, in your salvation.) The Metaphrast's verses are marked in italics; the full text of his poem is reprinted in Simonof's *Μέγα προσευχητάριον* (n. 65 above), 425–35 (no. λς'), esp. 433, from Nikodemos Hagiorites, ed. *Ἀπάνθισμα διαφόρων κατανυκτικῶν εὐχῶν* (Constantinople, 1799, repr. Thera, 2000), 157–63.

87   Athos, MS Dionysiou 65, s. XII in., fols. 11r–12r; miniatures reproduced and described in S. M. Pelekanidis et al., *The Treasures of Mount Athos: Illuminated Manuscripts*, 4 vols. (Athens, 1974–91), 1:116–17 with color figs. 118–22, 419–20; Cutler, *Aristocratic Psalters* (n. 75 above), 103–6, 236–37 with figs. 361–63; G. R. Parpulov, "Miniatiura 'Rai' iz sobraniia Nauchnoi biblioteki Moskovskogo universiteta," in *Deianiia i Poslaniia apostolov: Grecheskaia illiuminovannaia rukopis' 1072 goda*, ed. E. N. Dobrynina (Moscow, 2004), 104–14, esp. 108–11; Ch. Mauropoulou-Tsioume, "Οἱ μικρογραφίες τοῦ Ψαλτηρίου ἀρ. 65 τῆς Μονῆς Διονυσίου," *Κληρονομία* 7 (1975): 131–71; R. Stichel, *Studien zum Verhältnis von Text und Bild spät- und nachbyzantinischer Vergänglichkeitsdarstellungen* (Vienna, 1971), 70–75, pl. 3.

88   A. Papadopoulos-Kerameus, ed., "Βυζαντινὰ ἀνάλεκτα· Ἀλφάβητος Οὐρανοῦ μαγίστρου," *BZ* 8 (1899): 66–70; emendations: E. Kurtz, "Das paranetische Alphabet des Nikephoros Ouranos," *BZ* 25 (1925): 18; commentary: M. Lauxtermann, *The Spring of Rhythm: An Essay on the Political Verse and Other Byzantine Metres* (Vienna, 1999), 31–35. The excerpts are as follows: (11r, right margin) [Ἰδεῖν οὐκ ἄξιος] εἰμί, [δέσ]π[οτα, πρό]σωπ(όν) σου, ἀλλ[ὰ ζο]φώ[δεις ἄθλιος] ὄψ[ομαι]—φευ—ἰδέας, αἴ μ[οι καὶ] συν[αν]τήσ[ονται καὶ παρα]λήψ[ον]τ[αί με], (11r, lower margin) Μηδ(εὶς) ἐξαπ(α)τ(ά)τ(ω) σε, μηδ(εὶς) π(αρα)μυθήτω, ψυχή· τὸ πῦρ οὐ σβ[έννυ]ται, ὁ σκ(ώ)ληξ οὐ κοιμᾶται, τ(ὴν) σ(ὴν) ἀπεκδεχόμ(εν)α πικρ[ὰν] ἐ[πι]δ[η]μ[ίαν], (11v, left margin) [Κο]λάσ(εις) [τ]ὰς μ[ενο]ύσ(ας) [σε],

The miniatures are mirrored at the end of the book by a long penitential prayer that dwells on death and judgment.[89] Since Ouranos's verses are composed in the first person, the reader/viewer can identify with the person depicted and, through contemplation of death, strive to attain the beatific state illustrated in the last scene and explained by the cryptographic (written from right to left) sentence in the margin below it: "the oil of redemption in the name of the Father, and of the Son, and of the Holy Spirit."[90] On the following page (folio 12v) Sabas appears prostrate before the Virgin and the infant Christ.[91]

In other Psalter miniatures the book's praying owner is left, literally, out of the picture and is instead presented with a devotional image for direct contemplation. Whereas Christ in the Dionysiou manuscript turns toward Sabas and blesses him, the Virgin and Child in the small pictorial frontispieces of two Psalters now in Vienna (dated 1076) and Venice (datable ca. 1130) squarely face the viewer.[92] The Venice miniature follows upon a long penitential prayer addressed

---

ψυχ(ή), [προ]οα[να]τύπ(ου), [εἰ β]ούλ(ει) [με]τὰ [θάν]ατ(ον) [εὐ]ρεῖ(ν) [μετ]ρι[ωτ]έρ(ας), (11v, lower margin) [Ὅταν] ἐμ(ῶν) εἰς πέλαγο(ς) πονηρῶν ἔργων βλέ(ψω), ἄβυσσος χρη[στότητος τῆς σῆς] ψυχαγωγεῖ με, (12r, right margin) Χειρ(ῶν) εἰμι σῶν ποίημα κ(αὶ) χαρ(α)κτήρ μορφῆ(ς) σου, (12r, left margin) [Υἱόν με σὺ κατέστησας,] υἱὸ[ν καὶ] κληρο[νό]μον, [ἐγὼ] (δὲ) δ[οῦλος] γέγο[να], πον[ηρός ἀ]ποσ[τάτης], κ(αὶ) δ[όξη]ς ἧς [ἐξέ]πεσ[α, νῦν] ἔγνω[ν τὴν] ζημ[ίαν]. (I am unworthy, O my Lord, to see your face in full light, / So I shall only get, alas, murky ideas of it / That will confront and overwhelm my sinful self completely.) (Let no one, O my soul, delude and let no one console you: / The fire cannot be put out, the worm is never dormant [Mark 9:48] / And bitter are the punishments that lie in store for you, soul.) (Envision in advance, O soul, the trials that await you, / If you desire, after death, to get a moderate treatment.) (Whenever I cast eyes upon the sea of my transgressions / The infiniteness of your mercy, O God, gives me succor.) (I am the work of your hands and likeness of your image.) (You once appointed me your son and heir of your riches / But I became, instead, a slave, a renegade most wicked / And now I am too well aware what glory I forfeited.)

89 CPG 4688 (PG 63:923–28), MS Dionysiou 65, fols. 227r–230r, inc. Κύριε ὁ Θεός μου, ὁ μέγας καὶ φοβερὸς καὶ ἔνδοξος, ὁ πάσης ὁρωμένης καὶ νοουμένης κτίσεως δημιουργὸς καὶ δεσπότης, ὁ φυλάσσων τὴν διαθήκην καὶ τὸ ἔλεος σου τοῖς ἀγαπῶσι σε, des. καὶ πάντων τῶν ἀπ' αἰῶνος εὐαρεστησάντων σοι ἁγίων. Ἀμήν. (Lord my God, great, formidable and glorious one, maker and master of all creation visible and invisible, you who keep your covenant and have mercy for those who love you . . . and of all saints who for ages have been well pleasing to you. Amen.)

90 ἔλεον (sic) ἀπολυτρώσεως εἰς τὸ ὄνομα [τοῦ Πατρὸς] κα(ὶ) τοῦ Υἱοῦ κα(ὶ) τοῦ ἁγίου Πνεύματος.

91 Spatharakis, *Portrait* (n. 76 above), 49–51, fig. 18; see also n. 87 above.

92 Vienna, Österreichische Nationalbibliothek, MS theol. gr. 336, a. 1076, fol. 16v; miniature described and reproduced in Cutler, *Aristocratic Psalters* (n. 75 above), 89f., 222 with fig. 314, and P. Buberl and H. Gerstinger, *Die Illuminierten Handschriften und Inkunabeln der Nationalbibliothek in Wien*, part 4, *Die byzantinischen Handschriften*, 2 vols. (Leipzig, 1937–38), 2:37, pl. xii.2; color reproduction: O. Mazal, *Byzanz und das Abendland: Ausstellung der Handschriften- und Inkunabelsammlung der Österreichischen Nationalbibliothek* (Graz, 1981), fig. 22. Venice, Biblioteca Marciana, MS gr. II.113 (coll. 565), s. XII, f. 307; miniature described and reproduced in

to the Mother of God through an icon.[93] The Vienna image replaced the text of the Lord's Prayer that the scribe, probably unaware at first that the volume would be illustrated, initially copied on the page and later erased.

Similar devotional images occasionally precede Psalm 78 (77), which opens the eleventh kathisma and thus occupies the middle of the Psalter. Although most painters (or their patrons) choose to illustrate the Psalm with narrative scenes prompted by its first verse "Give ear, O my people, to my law..." some preface it with a frontal bust of Christ who is personally, as it were, urging the reader/viewer to follow his commandments (Fig. 5).[94] In the twelfth century the Savior's image also appears in headpieces above Psalm 1.[95] Such images must have formed a visual focus at the initial moment of concentration before reciting the Psalter, when the reader "should immediately address [his] own thoughts and say three

---

Cutler, *Aristocratic Psalters*, 88, 221 with fig. 307, and M. Bonicatti, "Un salterio greco miniato del periodo comneno," *Bollettino dell'Archivio paleografico italiano*, n.s., 2–3 (1956–57): 117–28, pls. i–xviii, esp. 117f., pl. i; see also *Oriente cristiano e santità: Figure e storie di santi tra Bisanzio e l'Occidente*, ed. S. Gentile (Venice, 1998), 199–201: cat. 27.

93 Εὐχὴ Λέοντος δεσπότου, MS Marcian. gr. II.113, f. 43r–48v, inc. Παρθένε Δέσποινα Θεοτόκε, ἡ τὸν Θεὸν τὸν Λόγον κατὰ σάρκα γεννήσασα, οἶδα μέν, οἶδα ὅτι οὐκ ἔστιν εὐπρεπὲς οὐδὲ ἄξιον ἐμὲ τὸν οὕτω πανάσωτον, εἰκόνα καθαρὰν σοῦ τῆς ἁγνῆς, σοῦ τῆς ἀειπαρθένου, σοῦ τῆς σῶμα καὶ ψυχὴν ἐχούσης καθαρὰ καὶ ἀμόλυντα, [ὀφθαλμοῖς μεμολυσμένοις ὁρᾶν καὶ χείλεσιν ἀκαθάρτοις καὶ βεβήλοις περιπτύσσεσθαι ἢ παρακαλεῖν (omit. MS)], des. ἀξιοῦσα με ἐν τῷ παρόντι αἰῶνι ἀκατακρίτως μετασχεῖν τοῦ παναγίου καὶ ἀχράντου σώματος καὶ αἵματος τοῦ Υἱοῦ καὶ Θεοῦ σου, ἐν δὲ τῷ μέλλοντι, τοῦ οὐρανίου δείπνου τῆς τρυφῆς τοῦ παραδείσου καὶ τῆς βασιλείας τῶν οὐρανῶν, ἔνθα πάντων ἐστὶν εὐφραινομένων ἡ κατοικία. Ἀμήν. (Prayer of Emperor Leo: Virgin Lady Mother of God who gave birth to the incarnate Word, I know, I know well that it is neither decent nor right for me, who is so utterly prodigal, to see with polluted eyes and to venerate or implore with unclean and profane lips a pure image of you, the chaste ever-virgin pure and undefiled in body and soul... deeming me worthy to partake without condemnation in the present age of the most holy and undefiled body and blood of your Son and God and in the age to come, of the celestial supper [prepared] in Paradise and in the Kingdom of Heaven, where the habitation of all who rejoice is. Amen.) The text is almost identical with the one reprinted in Simonof's *Μέγα προσευχητάριον*, new ed., 451–54 (no. λζ′.8) from St. Nikodemos's *Ἀπάνθισμα* (n. 86 above), 96–99 (trans. *Voices in the Wilderness* [n. 61 above], 187–91), and with K. G. Phrantzolas, ed., *Ὁσίου Ἐφραὶμ τοῦ Σύρου ἔργα*, 7 vols. (Thessalonike, 1988–98), 6:405–10. A shorter version of this prayer is ascribed to St. Mary of Egypt in her vita, *BHG* 1042 (PG 87:3713C, trans. M. Kouli, in *Holy Women* [n. 60 above], 83).

94 Detailed discussion of such illustrations to Ps. 77: R. S. Nelson, "The Discourse of Icons: Then and Now," *Art History* 12 (1989): 144–57.

95 Cutler, *Aristocratic Psalters* (n. 75 above), figs. 47, 89, 137, 267, 300, 340; color reproductions: P. L. Vocotopoulos, *Byzantine Illuminated Manuscripts in Jerusalem* (Athens and Jerusalem, 2003), 71 with fig. 30; H. Evans, ed. *Byzantium: Faith and Power 1261–1557* (New York, 2004), 413: cat. 255.

FIGURE 5 Christ in the Synagogue (John 7:14–24), frontispiece to Psalm 77, Turin, Biblioteca Reale, cod. Var. 484, ca. 1400–1450 CE, fol. 59r (published su concessione del Ministero per i Beni e le Attività Culturali)

times: 'O come, let us worship and fall down before God our King.'"⁹⁶ In the earliest known miniature of this kind, Christ speaks the words Moses once heard from the bush that burned but was not consumed: "I am who I am" (Exodus 3:14).⁹⁷ Devotional images in Psalters thus prepare the faithful for the higher contemplation that can be described only with the metaphorical language of mysticism: "When through continuous prayer the words of the psalms are brought down into the heart, then the heart like good soil begins to produce by itself various flowers: roses, the vision of incorporeal realities; lilies, the luminosity of corporeal realities; and violets, the many judgments of God, hard to understand."⁹⁸

APPENDIX

The Contents of Three Byzantine Psalters

Although they all contain the Psalms and Odes (Canticles), there is considerable variety in content among Byzantine Psalter manuscripts. The ones described below are reasonably typical. Number 1 represents a small and uniform group that also includes the famous "Uspensky Psalter" and originates from ninth-century Palestine.⁹⁹ The note "καθὼς ψάλλομεν ἐν τῇ ἁγίᾳ Χριστοῦ τοῦ Θεοῦ ἡμῶν Ἀναστάσει" (fol. 368r) shows that the Psalter conforms to Jerusalem usage, but was *not* used in the Church of the Holy Sepulcher itself. Number 2 is among the first witnesses to the set of prognostic sentences associated with the Psalms (fols. 2r–3r). The predictions these sentences contain point to a courtly milieu and thus to a probably Constantinopolitan origin for the manuscript. The *Typika*

---

96 Peter Damaskenos (n. 33 above).
97 New York, NYPL, MS Spencer gr. 1, s. XII ineunte (sic), fol. 2r: Ἐγὼ [εἰ]μὴ (sic) ὁ ὤν. Miniature reproduced and described in Cutler, *Aristocratic Psalters*, 56, 188 with fig. 206 and idem, "The Spencer Psalter: A Thirteenth-Century Byzantine Manuscript in the New York Public Library," *CahArch* 23 (1974): 129–59, esp. 130f.; repr. (with an addendum) in Cutler, *Imagery and Ideology in Byzantine Art* (Brookfield, 1992), no. i. Cutler identifies the text as Jn 8:12. Description of the MS: N. F. Kavrus-Hoffmann, "Catalogue of Greek Medieval and Renaissance Manuscripts in the Collections of the United States of America. Part II: New York Public Library," *Manuscripta* 50 (2006): 21–76, esp. 51–55.
98 Elias Ekdikos (n. 34 above).
99 Saint Petersburg, National Library of Russia, MS gr. 216, a. 878: Amfilokhii, "Opisanie Grecheskoi Psaltiri 862 goda iz sobraniia rukopisei Preosv. Porfiriia," *Chteniia v Obshchetsvie liubitelei dukhovnago prosvieshcheniia* (1873): 1–8 with pls. 1–2; repr. in id., *Paleograficheskoe opisanie grecheskikh rukopisei opredelennykh let*, 4 vols. (Moscow, 1879–80), 1:9–11; *Paleograficheskie snimki s nekotorykh grecheskikh, latinskikh i slavianskikh rukopisei Imperatorskoi Publichnoi biblioteki* (Saint Petersburg, 1914), 3, with bibl. On the MS's date: D. A. Morozov, "Aleksandriiskaia era v Ierusalime IX v.: K datirovke Porfir'evskoi psaltyri," *Montfaucon* 1 (2007), 89–93, esp. 92. See also Parpulov, "Byzantine Psalters" (n. 7 above), 56–64.

(fols. 83v–84v), texts recited or sung by the people during the Holy Liturgy, were, until circa 1100, often appended to Psalters.[100] The inelegant script and poor-quality parchment characterize number 3 as a provincial product. Made for a monk, it represents the hymnography often appended to Psalters in the Palaeologan period. Canonical Hours, *canons*, the Service of the Akathistos, and New Testament readings like the ones found in this manuscript, together with the Psalter and the Jesus Prayer, form the personal devotional *cursus* described by Philotheos Kokkinos.[101]

---

1. Mount Sinai, Monastery of Saint Catherine, MS gr. 30, Palestine, s. IX, parchment, 431 fols. (fols. 1–48 and 404ff added), 180 × 123 mm, linn. 20:[102]

(49r–50v) **Τὸ σύμβολον τῆς ζωοποιοῦ ὀρθοδοξίας ἐκ πν(εύματο)ς τοῦ παναγίου·** Πιστεύω εἰς ἕνα Θ(εό)ν, etc. (50v) Verses: Τῶν τεττάρων πέφυκε τοῦτο σύμβολον· Ἄθροισμα τῶν θείων τε καὶ θεηγόρων· Τοῖς ὀρθοδόξοις εὐαγῶς βεβλυσμένον.[103] (50v–51r) **Προσευχὴ διδασκάλημα τοῦ κ(υρίο)υ ἡμῶν Ἰ(ησο)ῦ Χ(ριστο)ῦ·** Πάτερ ἡμῶν, etc. (51r) Verses: Προσευκτικὸν δίδαγμα τοῦ Θ(εο)ῦ λόγου· Ὁ τοὺς μαθητὰς ἐκπεπαίδευκε φίλους· Περιττότη τῶν ἀστάτων ὑπέρτατον· Πολυπλόκων λόγων τε βαττολεξίας· Ἐν ᾧ κέκρυπται μυστικῶν διαγμάτων· Ἄπαν νόημα καὶ θεουργίας λόγος· Ζωῆς παρούσης καὶ χρόνων αἰωνίων. (52r–54r) **Παμφίλου ὑπόθεσις εἰς τὸ ψαλτήριον·** Τῆς βίβλου τῶν ψαλμῶν ἤδη [*sic*] ἂν εἴη ἡ διαίρεσις … οὐ μὴν δηλοῦσιν τίνος εἰσίν· ἀνεπίγραφοι ιθ', ἐπιγεγραμμένοι ρλα', ὁμοῦ ψαλμοὶ ρν' καὶ ἰδιόγραφος α' [PG 23:66C–68A]. (54r–55r) Τοῦ ἁγίου Ἰω(άννου) τ(οῦ) Χρυσοστόμ(ου) ἐκ τ(οῦ) λόγ(ου) τοῦ περὶ ὑπομονῆ(ς) καὶ εἰς τὴν τ(ῶν) γραφῶν μελέτ(ην)· Ἀγαπητέ, ὅταν ἀναγινώσκεις ἐπιμελῶς ἀναγίνωσκε … καὶ δηλώσῃ σου τῇ δυνάμει τῶν λόγων αὐτοῦ, ὅτι αὐτῷ πρέπει δόξα εἰς τοὺς αἰῶνας. Ἀμήν [PG 63:940].[104] (55r) Ἴαμβοι· Θείου νοητοὺς ἄνθρακα [*sic*] πυρὸς φέρω· … Ψαλμῶν γὰρ εἰμὶ βίβλος οἷς κεχρημένος.[105]

---

100   Ibid., 17f., 400, appendix C1.
101   Ibid., 495–505; Rigo, *L'amore della quiete* (n. 7 above), 175–80.
102   Washington, DC, Library of Congress, microfilm 5010/30; see also K. Weitzmann and G. Galavaris, *The Monastery of Saint Catherine at Mount Sinai: The Illuminated Greek Manuscripts*, 2 vols. (Princeton, 1990–), 1:15f., pl. x.; M. P. Brown, ed., *In the Beginning: Bibles before the Year 1000* (Washington, DC, 2006), 194–95, 285–86: cat. 47.
103   These and the following verses are listed with bibl. in I. Vassis, *Initia carminum byzantinorum* (Berlin–New York, 2005).
104   This excerpt from *CPG* 4693 consists mainly of a prayer to be said before reading (or listening to someone read) from Scripture: Κύριε Ἰησοῦ Χριστέ, ἄνοιξον τὰ ὦτα καὶ τοὺς ὀφθαλμοὺς τῆς καρδίας μου τοῦ ἀκοῦσαί με τὸν λόγον σου, καὶ συνιέναι, καὶ ποιῆσαι τὸ θέλημά σου, etc.
105   Our scribe copied this poem without its last verse; see the full text in A. Ludwich, "Ein neuer Beitrag zur Charakteristik des Jakob Diassorinos," *BZ* 1 (1894): 293–302, esp. 298.

55v is blank. (56r–367v) **Ψαλτήριον·** Psalms 1–150. (367v) Verses: Ἐνταῦθα μέχρις ἐστὶ τὸ ψαλτήριο(ν)· Ἀλλ' εὐλογεῖτο πᾶσα σὰρξ τὸν κ(ύριο)ν· Τὸν ἐνπνέοντα τοῖς προφήταις τὴ(ν) χάρι(ν). (367v–368r) Stichometric note: Ἔχουσι νοῦν οἱ ρν' ψαλμοὶ καθὼς ὑποτέκται στί(χους) ͵δψπ' οὗτος [sic]· ... ὡς πρόκειται στί(χοι) ͵δψπ', καθὼς ψάλλομεν ἐν τῇ ἁγίᾳ Χ(ριστο)ῦ τοῦ Θ(εο)ῦ ἡμῶν Ἀναστ(άσει). (368r–369r) **Οὗτος ὁ ψαλμὸς ἰδιόγραφος ἐστὶν τοῦ Δα(υΐ)δ κ(αὶ) ἔξοθεν τοῦ ἀριθμοῦ·** Psalm 151. (369v–395v) Odes 1–9.[106] (395v–396r) **[Εὐχ]ὴ Συμεὼν τ(οῦ) δικαίου·** Luke 2:29–32. (396r) Stichometric note: Τῶν ὕμνων καὶ τ(ῶν) ᾠδῶν στίχ(οι) σιη'· ᾠδῶν στίχ(οι) ρνδ', ὕμνων στίχ(οι) νδ',[107] ὡς εἶναι τοὺς πάντ(ας) στίχ(οι) ͵ε. (396r–v) **Ὕμνος ἑσπερινός·** Φῶς ἱλαρὸν, etc. (396v–398r) **Ὕμνος ἑωθινός·** Δόξα ἐν ὑψίστοις, etc. (398r–399r) **Ἐκ τοῦ κατὰ Ματθαῖο(ν) ἁγίου εὐαγγελίου·** Matt. 5:3–12. (399r–400v) **Προφητ(εία) Ἡσαίου·** Μεθ' ἡμῶν ὁ Θ(εό)ς, etc.[108] (400v–403v) **Εὐχὴ Μανάσση·** Κ(ύρι)ε παντοκράτωρ, etc.

---

2. Washington DC, Dumbarton Oaks Museum, MS 3, Constantinople, a. 1083, parchment, 364 fols. (fols. 4, 78, 86–87, 187, 187bis, 254 removed; fols. 341–62 added), 162 × 109 mm, linn. 36:[109]

(2r) **Ἀποκάλυψις ἀληθὴς ἐνθυμήσεων ἐὰν μετὰ πίστεως πράττηται·** Ἐὰν ἔννοιαν ἔχῃς τὴν οἱανοῦν ἐν τῇ καρδίᾳ σου εἰ ὀφείλεις πρᾶγμα ἐπιχειρῆσαι, νήστις ἀνάπτυσσε τὸ ψαλτήριον ... κ(αὶ) εἴ τι γράφει ἔχε αὐτὸ ἐν πληροφορίᾳ, μόνον ἐκ πίστεως προσέρχου.[110] (2r–3r) **Ἑρμ(ηνεῖαι) εἰς τοὺς ψαλμοὺς·** α' Ὡς Ἰωσὴφ ἠξιώθης χάριτος διὰ τῆς ὑπομονῆς ... ρν' Πρᾶγμα μετ' ὀλίγον πληρούμενον.[111] (3v) Paschal table: Ἔτ(ος) ͵ςφ϶β' τ(ῆς) ζ' ἰνδ(ικτιῶνος), κύ(κλοι) (ἡλίου) ιβ', κύ(κλοι) (σελήνης) ιη', ἡ ἀπόκ(ρεως) φε(βρουαρίου) δ', νο(μικὸν) π(ά)σχ(α) μ(α)ρτ(ίου) κε' ἡμέ(ρα) ε', χριστιανὸν [sic] πάσχα μαρτίου λα'. Etc. (4r–5v) Miniatures. (6r–71r) **Δαυῒδ τὸ πρῶτον ᾆσμα τ(ῶ)ν ψαλμ(ῶν) βάσις·** Psalms 1–151. (72r–81r) Odes 1–9. (81v–82r)

---

106 The Odes are numbered α'–ι' in the manuscript, since Ode 9 is divided into its two constituent parts, Lk 1:47–55 and Lk 1:68–79. Cf. A. Rahlfs, ed., *Psalmi cum Odis*, 2nd ed. (Göttingen, 1967), 341–59, or any printed edition of the Greek Horologion.
107 Either I misread the digits from the microfilm or the arithmetic here is faulty.
108 See Compline in any printed Greek *Horologion*.
109 See also S. P. Lambros, *Κατάλογος τῶν ἐν ταῖς βιβλιοθήκαις τοῦ Ἁγίου Ὄρους ἑλληνικῶν κοδίκων*, 2 vols. (Cambridge, 1895–1900), 98: cat. 1083; S. Der Nersessian, "A Psalter and New Testament Manuscript at Dumbarton Oaks," *DOP* 19 (1965): 153–83; Cutler, *Aristocratic Psalters* (n. 75 above), 91–98, 224–30; N. Kavrus-Hoffmann, "Greek Manuscripts at Dumbarton Oaks: Codicological and Paleographic Description and Analysis," *DOP* 50 (1996): 289–307, esp. 296–302.
110 Parpulov, ed., "Byzantine Psalters" (n. 7 above), 508.
111 Ibid., 508–15. See also n. 47 above.

Τὸν Ἐζεκίαν εὐλογοῦντά μοι σκόπει· Isa. 38:10–20. (82v–83v) Σωθεὶς Μαν(άσ)ση τὸν Θ(εὸ)ν μεγαλύνει· Κ(ύρι)ε παντοκράτορ, etc. (83v) Ὕμνος ἑωθινός· Δόξα ἐν ὑψίστοις, etc. **Τυπικὰ τῆς ἁγίας καθολικῆς καὶ ἀποστολικῆς ἐκκλησίας**· Ὁ μονογενὴς υἱὸς κ(αὶ) λόγος τοῦ Θ(εο)ῦ, etc. (83v–84r) Ὁ μυστικὸς ὕμνος· Οἱ τὰ χερουβίμ, etc. (84r) Πληρωθήτω τὸ στόμα ἡμῶν, etc. Ἔκθεσις πίστεως τῶν τιη´ ἁγίων π(ατέ)ρων τ(ῆς) ἐν Νικαίᾳ· Πιστεύω εἰς ἕνα Θ(εό)ν, etc. (84v) **Διδασκαλία τοῦ κ(υρίο)υ ἡμ(ῶν) Ἰ(ησο)ῦ Χ(ριστο)ῦ περὶ προσευχῆς ἐκ τοῦ κατὰ Ματθαῖον εὐαγγελίου**· Π(άτ)ερ ἡμῶν, etc. Εἰς τὰ προηγιασμένα· Νῦν αἱ δυνάμεις, etc. Ἀντὶ τοῦ *Πληρωθήτω*· Εὐχαριστοῦμέν σοι, Χ(ριστ)ὲ ὁ Θ(εὸ)ς ἡμῶν, ὅτι ἠξίωσας, etc. Ὕμνος λυχνικὸς ὁ κατὰ συνήθειαν· Φῶς ἱλαρόν, etc. Προσευχὴ Συμεὼν τοῦ πρεσβύτου· Luke 2:29–32. (84v–85r) Μακαρισμοὶ ἐκ τοῦ κατὰ Ματθαῖον εὐαγγέλιον· Matt. 5:3–12.[112] (85v) Εὐχαὶ λεγομέναι εἰς καθ᾽ ἑκάστην ὥραν τ(ῆς) νυκτὸ(ς) κ(αὶ) τ(ῆς) ἡμέ(ρας)· α´ Κ(ύρι)ε, μὴ ὑστερήσῃς με τῶν ἐπου(ρα)νίων σου ἀγαθῶν.... ιβ´ Κ(ύρι)ε ὁ Θ(εὸ)ς τοῦ οὐ(ρα)νοῦ καὶ τῆς γῆς, μνήσθητί μου τοῦ ἁμαρτωλοῦ ὅτ᾽ ἂν ἔλθῃς ἐν τῇ βασιλείᾳ σου, πρεσβείαις τῆς ὑπεραγίας δεσποίνης ἡμῶν Θ(εοτό)κου, τῶν ἁγίων καὶ νοερῶν σου δυνάμεων, τοῦ τιμίου προδρόμου καὶ βαπτιστοῦ Ἰωάννου, τῶν ἁγίων καὶ πανευφήμων ἀποστόλων, καὶ πάντων τῶν ἁγίων τῶν ἀπ᾽ αἰῶνος εὐαρεστησάντων, ὅτι εὐλογητὸς εἶ εἰς τοὺς αἰῶνας τῶν αἰώνων. Ἀμήν.[113] **Εὐχὴ τοῦ ἁγίου Ἐφραίμ**· Δόξα τῷ Π(ατ)ρὶ τῷ ποιήσαντι ἡμᾶς, καὶ δόξα τ(ῷ) Υἱῷ τῷ σώσαντι ἡμᾶς, καὶ δόξα τῷ ἀνακαινίσαντι ἡμᾶς παναγίῳ Πν(εύματ)ι εἰς τοὺς συμπάντα [sic] αἰώνας. Ἀμήν.[114]

---

3. Ohrid, Naroden muzej, MS gr. 20, Eastern Mediterranean, s. XIII ex.–XIV in., 232 fols. (paginated), 230 × 150 mm, linn. 23–36:[115]

(1–225) Δα(υῒ)δ προφή(του) κ(αὶ) βασιλέ(ως) μέλο(ς)· Psalms 1–151. (225–48) Odes 1–9. (249–91) Ἀκολουθ(ία) τ(οῦ) Ἀκαθίστου.[116] (292–311) Ἀρχ(ὴ) σὺν

---

112 Fols. 84v–85r are reproduced in *The Glory of Byzantium: Art and Culture of the Middle Byzantine Era*, ed. W. D. Wixom and H. C. Evans (New York, 1997), 190.
113 Nos. 1–11 are edited in Saint Nikodemos's *Ἀπάνθισμα* (n. 86 above), 185; reprinted in Phountoules, *Εἰκοσιτετράωρον Ὡρολόγιον* (n. 38 above), 93f.
114 From *CPG* 3909, Ephraem the Syrian, *Ascetic Sermon*, ed. Phrantzolas, *Ἐφραὶμ τοῦ Σύρου ἔργα* (n. 93 above), 1:184.
115 See also V. Mošin, "Les manuscrits du Musée national d'Ochrida," in *Ohrid: Recueil de travaux*, ed. D. Koco (Ohrid, 1961), 163–243, esp. 198f. I was not shown the manuscript in Ohrid and sincerely thank Prof. George Mitrevski of Auburn University for sending me a digitized microfilm thereof.
116 See any printed edition of the Greek Horologion.

Θ(ε)ῷ τοῦ Ὡρολογίου· Nocturns, Matins, Prime, Terce, Sext (with the respective Mid-Hours), Τυπικά, None (with Mid-Hour), Vespers, and Compline. The Mid-Hours are to be sung in the cell, e.g., p. 279: ἐν τοῖς κελί(οις) [sic] ψάλλομεν τῆς α' ὥρας τὸ με(σώ)ρ(ιον). (311–15) **Κα(νὼν) εἰς τ(ὴν) ὑπ(ερα)γ(ίαν) Θ(εοτό)κον·** Πολλοῖς συνεχόμενος, etc.[117] (316–67) **Ἀρχ(ὴ) σὺν Θ(ε)ῷ, τὸ μηνολόγ(ιον) τοῦ ὅλ(ου) ἐνιαυτοῦ·** list of the fixed church feasts with their propers. (367–72) Propers for the Sundays of the movable cycle. (373–401) **Ἀρχ(ὴ) τ(ῶν) μακαρισμ(ῶν) τ(ῶν) η' ἤχ(ων)·** Διὰ βρώσεως ἐξήγαγεν, etc.[118] (401–4) **Τῇ κυρ(ιακῇ) ἑσπ(έρας)·** stichera Ἀσώματοι ἄγγελοι, etc.; kanon Θρόνῳ παριστάμενοι φαιδρῶς, etc. (404–7) **Τῇ β' ἑσπ(έρας)·** stichera Τὴν ἀμαυρωθεῖσαν μου ψυχήν, etc.; kanon Βαπτιστὰ καὶ πρόδρομ(ε) Χ(ριστο)ῦ, etc. (407–11) **Τῇ γ' ἑσπ(έρας)·** stichera Ἀνάστηθι καὶ πρόφθασον, etc.; kanon Πῶς μου θρηνήσω τὸν βίον τὸν ῥυπαρ(όν), etc. (411–19) **Τῇ δ' ἑσπ(έρας)·** stichera Στερωτάτῳ [sic] φρονήματι, etc.; kanon Διηνεκῶς τῷ θείῳ θρόνῳ, etc. (419–23) **Τῇ ε' ἑσπέρ(ας)·** stichera Στ(αυ)ρ(ὸ)ς ἀνυψούμενο(ς), etc.; kanon Στ(αυ)ρῷ διεπέτασας, etc. (423–27) **Τῇ παρα(σκευ)ῇ ἑσπ(έρας)·** stichera Ὄντως φοβερώτατον, etc.; kanon Φαιδρύνεται ἀεὶ ἡ Χ(ριστο)ῦ ἐκκλησία, etc. (427–35) **Τῷ σα(ββάτῳ) ἑσπ(έρας)·** stichera Ἑσπεριν(ὸν) ὕμνον (καὶ) λογικ(ὴν) λατρείαν, etc.; kanon Τὴν παντοδύναμον, etc. (435–42) **Ἀποστ(ο)λ(ο)ευα(γγέλια) τ(ῆς) ἐυδ(ομάδος). Τῇ κυριακῇ·** 2 Cor. 6:16–7:1, Lk. 5:1–11, **Τῇ β' τ(ῶν) ἀσωμ(ά)τ(ων)·** Heb. 2:2–10, Lk. 10:16–21, **Τῇ γ' τοῦ Προδρ(όμου)·** Acts 19:1–8, John 1:29–34, **Τῇ δ' εἰς τ(ὴν) ὑπ(ερα)γ(ίαν) Θ(εοτό)κον·** Phil. 2:5–11, Lk. 10:38–42, **Τῇ ε' τ(ῶν) ἁγί(ων) ἀπο(στόλων)·** 1 Cor. 4:9–16, Matt. 10:1–8, **Τῇ παρα(σκευ)ῇ στ(αυ)ρώ(σι)μο(ς)·** Gal. 6:11–18, John 19:25–35, **Τῷ σα(ββάτῳ) εἰς κοιμηθέντ(ας)·** 1 Thess. 4:13–17, John 6:35–39. (442–44) **Κα(νὼν) κ(α)τ(α)νυκ(τικ)ὸ(ς) ψαλλόμ(εν)ο(ς) καθ' ἑσπέραν.** *Τὴν ἐνεστῶσαν ἡμέραν, etc. (444–47) **Ἕτε(ρος) κα(νὼν) τ(ῆς) ὑπ(ερα)γ(ίας) Θ(εοτό)κου ψαλλόμ(ενος) ἐν συμφορᾷ κ(αὶ) θλίψει κ(αὶ) πειρασμῷ κ(αὶ) κινδύνῳ.** *Προσδέχου τ(ὴν) ἐκ ψυχῆς παράκλησ(ιν), etc. (447–50) **Καν(ὼν) εἰς τ(ὸν) κ(ύριο)ν ἡμ(ῶν) Ἰ(ησοῦ)ν Χ(ριστὸ)ν περὶ νήψε(ως)·** Ἰ(ησο)ῦ γλυκύτατε Χ(ριστ)έ, etc. (450–53) **Καν(ὼν) εἰς τ(ὸν) κ(ύριο)ν ἡμ(ῶν) Ἰ(ησοῦ)ν Χ(ριστὸ)ν κ(αὶ) εἰς τ(ὴν) ὑπ(ερα)γ(ίαν) Θ(εοτό)κον κ(αὶ) εἰς τ(ὸν) ἅγιον Νικόλ(αον) καὶ εἰς πάντας τοὺς ἁγίους.** Μὴ ἀπόσει με, etc. (453–59) **Τοῦ ὁσ(ίου) π(ατ)ρ(ὸ)ς ἡμ(ῶν) Συμεὼν μ(ητ)ροπολί(του) Εὐχαΐτων ἐπιστολ(ὴ) πρὸ(ς) Ἰω(άννην) μοναχὸν καὶ ἔγκλειστον, αὕτη (δὲ) ἁρμόζει παντὶ μοναχῷ κελιώτῃ [sic]·** Ἐδεξάμην σου,

---

117   This hymn and all the following ones (except those marked with an asterisk) are listed with bibliography in Follieri's *Initia hymnorum* (n. 3 above).

118   Fifty-six sets (eight musical modes for each of the seven days of the week) of eight troparia each: see any printed edition of the Greek Parakletike.

πάτερ πνευματικέ, τὴν θεοφιλεῖ ταύτην γραφὴν καὶ ἀποδεξάμην τὴν κατὰ Θεόν σου ταπείνωσιν . . . καὶ ἐνισχύσει σε εἰς τὸ θέλημα αὐτοῦ. Ἀμήν.[119] (459–62) **Ἀπὸ τὸ Γεροντικ(ὸν) ἀποφθέγματα·** Διηγήσατο ἡμῖν ὁ ἀββᾶς Παῦλος ὁ Καππαδόξ, etc. [BHG 1445n].[120] Διηγήσατο ἡμῖν ὁ ἀββᾶς Θεόδωρο(ς) ὁ Βυζαντεῦς, etc. [BHG 1445nb].

University of Oxford

---

119 K. Mitsakis, ed., "Symeon Metropolitan of Euchaita and the Byzantine Ascetic Ideals in the Eleventh Century," *Βυζαντινά* 2 (1970): 301–34, esp. 319–32; cf. M. Grünbart, *Epistularum byzantinarum initia* (Hildesheim, 2001), 65.

120 Cf. the partial English trans. in R. Taft, "Cathedral vs. Monastic Liturgy in the Christian East: Vindicating a Distinction," *BollGrott* 3rd ser., 2 (2005): 173–219, esp. 190–92. It is strange to find this text, which censures singing as spiritually harmful (μακρὰν οὖν ὀφείλει εἶναι τὸ ᾆσμα ἀπὸ τοῦ μοναχοῦ τοῦ θέλοντος σωθῆναι), next to numerous pieces of hymnography.

FIVE

Illustrated Octateuch Manuscripts
A Byzantine Phenomenon

JOHN LOWDEN

The first recorded use of the word Ὀκτάτευχος (literally "eight books") was by Prokopios of Gaza (d. 538), who called a volume of his biblical commentary *Exegeses of the Octateuch* (Εἰς τὴν Ὀκτάτευχον ἐξηγήσεις).[1] The term is derived from the more commonly encountered term "Pentateuch." The Octateuch is a unit commencing with the five books of Moses, generally known to both hellenized Jews and Greek-speaking Christians as the Law (ὁ Νόμος [Torah])—that is, Genesis, Exodus, Leviticus, Numbers, and Deuteronomy. To the Pentateuch were added the historical books of Joshua and Judges, which continue the narrative of Deuteronomy, and the short book of Ruth, which is set in the period of Judges (Ruth 1:1).[2] Although no manuscript of a complete single-volume Greek Octateuch survives from earlier than the tenth century,[3] the special status of these

---

I am particularly grateful to Robert S. Nelson and Alice-Mary Talbot for their support and advice, and to an anonymous reader.

1 B. Atsalos, *La terminologie du livre-manuscrit à l'époque byzantine* (Thessalonike, 1971), 128; A. Iacobini, "'Lettera di Aristea': Un prologo illustrato al ciclo degli Ottateuchi mediobizantini," *Arte medievale* 7 (1993): 92 n. 6; J. Lowden, *The Octateuchs* (University Park, 1992), 1; K. Weitzmann and M. Bernabò, *The Byzantine Octateuchs*, Illustrations in the Manuscripts of the Septuagint 2 (Princeton, 1999), 7. Prokopios's text was referred to by Photios, *Bibliothèque*, ed. R. Henry, 9 vols. (Paris, 1959–91), 3:104 as ἐξηγητικαὶ σχολαὶ εἴς τε τὴν Ὀκτάτευχον.

2 See the useful lists in H. B. Swete, *An Introduction to the Old Testament in Greek* (Cambridge, 1900), 197–214.

3 See A. Rahlfs, *Verzeichnis der griechischen Handschriften des Alten Testaments* (Berlin, 1914), 374–82. It was misleading for Weitzmann and Bernabò, *Byzantine Octateuchs*, 299, to claim that "in the Early Christian tradition the Octateuch seems to have been more popular than the Pentateuch." This assertion was based on a selective use of the lists in Rahlfs: fragments of any of the books from Genesis to Ruth were assumed to originate from Octateuchs, whereas only those manuscripts actually containing the Pentateuch were acknowledged as Pentateuchs.

biblical books in the Greek world is already implied in the fifth century.[4] Theodoret of Cyrrhus (died ca. 466) wrote a commentary on the first eight books of the Old Testament, although he did not, as it happens, use the term Octateuch.[5] Nevertheless, we can say with some confidence that the Octateuch as a distinct codex was an innovation of the fifth or sixth century, even though no examples from that era now survive.

If we look widely at the book production of late antiquity we find remarkably little evidence for the circulation of Octateuchs.[6] Although the evidence for Pentateuchs is plentiful, we search in vain for an Octateuch in a Syriac, Coptic, Gothic, Armenian, Georgian, Arabic, or Slavonic version.[7] Only in Ethiopic do we find a number of (unillustrated) Octateuchs, but these are much more recent, the earliest surviving manuscript being from the thirteenth century.[8] In a Latin milieu, however, there is this positive evidence: Cassiodorus, writing in the mid-sixth century, in his discussion of his multivolume Latin Bible, the *Codex grandior*, stated plainly that "Primus scripturarum diuinarum codex est Octateuchus" (the Octateuch is the first volume of the Holy Scriptures).[9] Also, the prefatory image in the Codex Amiatinus, the one-volume Bible made at Monkwearmouth/Jarrow in Northumbria around the year 700, shows the priest Ezra (Esdras) at work in front of a cupboard in which is a Bible in nine

---

4   Ruth is annotated ὁμοῦ βιβλία η′ ("together eight books") in the table of contents of the fifth-century Bible known as the Codex Alexandrinus (London, British Library [BL], MS Royal I.D.v–viii, fol. 4r). But it is not clear how much weight to allow this reference, for 2 Paralipomena was marked in a similar way as "together six books" (that is, implying a separate unit for 1–2 Samuel, 1–2 Kings, and 1–2 Chronicles [Paralipomena]), but this "division" was not referred to elsewhere as a Hexateuch. In general on the manuscript see S. McKendrick, "The Codex Alexandrinus, or the Dangers of Being a Named Manuscript," in *The Bible as Book: The Transmission of the Greek Text*, ed. S. McKendrick and O. O'Sullivan (London, 2003), 1–16.

5   Theodoret prefers ἡ θεία γραφή. In general, see N. Fernández Marcos and A. Sáenz-Badillos, *Theodoreti Cyrensis Quaestiones in Octateuchum* (Madrid, 1979). His volume of "Quaestiones" is referred to by Photios, *Bibliothèque*, 3:103 as ἐξηγήσεις εἰς τὴν Ὀκτάτευχον. For a recent text and translation, see Theodoret of Cyrus, *The Questions on the Octateuch*, trans. R. C. Hill, 2 vols. (Washington, DC, 2007).

6   Compare, for example, the entries in the index of *In the Beginning: Bibles before the Year 1000*, ed. M. P. Brown, exhibition catalogue (Washington, DC, 2006): "Pentateuch"–20 entries; "Hexateuch"–2 entries; "Octateuch"–no entry. McKendrick and O'Sullivan, *Bible as Book*, also makes no mention of "Octateuch."

7   S. Jellicoe, *The Septuagint and Modern Study* (Oxford, 1968), 243–68.

8   For Ethiopic manuscripts see London, British Library, MS Or. 480; Paris, Bibliothèque nationale de France, MS Abbadie 22, MS éthiop. 3: cited in H. Buchthal and O. Kurz, *Handlist of Illuminated East Christian Manuscripts* (London, 1942); see also *The Christian Orient*, British Library exhibition catalogue (London, 1978), no. 63. On the Ethiopian tradition of commentary on the Octateuch see R. W. Cowley, *Ethiopian Biblical Interpretation* (Cambridge, 1988), 116–17.

9   *Cassiodori Senatoris Institutiones*, ed. R. Mynors (Oxford, 1937), I.i [p. 11 line 7].

volumes. The first of these is titled on the spine "OCT.LIB.LEG" (Eight Books of Law[s], or perhaps Octateuch Book of Law[s]).[10] This material apart, however, there is scarcely any evidence for the circulation of Octateuch manuscripts in the West, and this is surprising.[11] In our conclusion we return briefly to the absence of comparative material for the Byzantine Octateuchs.

The special relevance of the Octateuch in the Byzantine world lies not merely in issues concerning the transmission, study, and use of this part of the Septuagint text. Byzantine interest in the Octateuch inspired the production of six illustrated manuscripts (five of them each containing hundreds of images) from the period ca. 1050–1300. These richly informative manuscripts ("the Octateuchs"), among the most profusely illustrated books from the Byzantine world, are considered in detail here, together with some examples of other types of artwork dependent to some extent on Octateuch themes or narratives.

The topic of Octateuch illustration also has a wider significance, as defined and elaborated in numerous studies by Kurt Weitzmann (d. 1993), and more recently by his collaborator Massimo Bernabò.[12] According to Weitzmann, the illustrated Byzantine Octateuch manuscripts are significant primarily for what they reveal about the origins and early history of Old Testament iconography. He traced the illustration of the Old Testament back from the Octateuchs through various lost models as far as the mid-third century, and thereby located the origins of Octateuch illustration in a pre-Byzantine context.[13] His influential hypothesis, which makes the Octateuchs of exceptional importance in the development and transmission of narrative art, is considered later in this chapter. My conclusion, however, is that the illustrated Octateuch manuscripts are not a late-antique, even less a pre-Constantinian, product, but a middle and late Byzantine phenomenon.

The five profusely illustrated Octateuch manuscripts mentioned above are all closely related. The sixth manuscript, which is very different, has only a few

---

10   *La Bibbia Amiatina*, ed. G. Ricci, CD-ROM publication (Florence, 2000). The other titles are formulated differently, e.g., HIST. LIB. VII, EVANG. LIB. IIII (Seven books of Histories, Four books of Gospels).

11   To confirm the paucity of evidence see, for example, the three volumes of the *Mittelalterliche Bibliothekskataloge Deutschlands und der Schweiz* (Munich, 1918–39); there is just one Octateuch ("Octoteuchus"), at Bamberg Cathedral (3:343 lines 31–32 and 3:345 lines 24–25). In the eleven volumes of the *Corpus of British Medieval Library Catalogues* published to date (2006) there is not one mention of an Octateuch.

12   Further references and discussion in Weitzmann and Bernabò, *Byzantine Octateuchs* (n. 1 above). See also the reviews by I. Hutter, *BZ* 94 (2001): 359–65; G. Parpulov, *JÖB* 52 (2002): 424–29; B. Zimmermann, *JbAChr* 44 (2001): 252–59.

13   Weitzmann and Bernabò, *Byzantine Octateuchs*, 299–311.

miniatures and is in various ways problematic.[14] The family of five is as follows: Rome, Biblioteca Apostolica Vaticana [BAV], MS Vat. gr. 747 (ca. 1050–75); Izmir (Smyrna—but presumed destroyed in 1922) Evangelical School, MS A.1 (ca. 1125–55); Istanbul, Topkapı Sarayı, MS gr. 8 (ca. 1125–55); BAV MS Vat. gr. 746 (ca. 1125–55); Mount Athos, Monastery of Vatopedi, MS 602 (ca. 1270–1300). All five are very closely related textually, sharing a standard set of prefaces and epilogues as well as the biblical text and marginal catena in a variant textual form.[15] The catena—a "chain" of excerpts from various named and anonymous commentators—in these manuscripts is laid out in the margins of the pages, flanking the Septuagint. The sixth Octateuch is Florence, Biblioteca Medicea-Laurenziana [Laur.] MS plut. 5.38; there has long been agreement in dating it to the eleventh century (ca. 1050–75?), but recently it has been redated by some palaeographers to ca. 1275–1300.[16] This manuscript does not include the marginal catena, prefaces, or epilogues of the other Octateuchs, and it looks quite different from them.

To explore what the illustrated Octateuchs can reveal when studied as a Byzantine phenomenon, it is appropriate to trace what are the usual and what the unusual features of the production and use of these manuscripts, both

---

14 In general see Weitzmann and Bernabò, *Byzantine Octateuchs*; Lowden, *Octateuchs* (n. 1 above), both with discussion and further bibliography.
15 The biblical text in all five represents a subgroup (cI) of the type termed "C" for "Catena group" (the manuscripts have the following sigla: Vat. gr. 747 = 57, Vat. gr. 746 = 73, Topkapı gr. 8 = 413, Vatopedi 602 = 320). The C text is characteristic of catena manuscripts, and is described as "a late mixed text" by J. Wevers, *Text History of the Greek Genesis* (Göttingen, 1974), 82 and 89–90 on "cI" subgroup. The Octateuch catena is built around the commentary of Theodoret (*Quaestiones in Octateuchum* is the modern title), and its origins are found to be contemporary with and linked in some way to the "Exegesis of the Octateuch" of Prokopios of Gaza, hence of the first half of the 6th century. Its editors have defined the illuminated Octateuchs as belonging to "Type III," a secondary tradition characterized by a limited choice of texts, important omissions, and the frequent abbreviation of the excerpts: G. Karo and H. Lietzmann, *Catenarum Graecarum Catalogus* (Berlin, 1902), 7–17; Fernández Marcos and Sáenz-Badillos, *Quaestiones in Octateuchum* (n. 5 above), xxv–xxvi; F. Petit, *Catenae Graecae in Genesim et Exodum*, vol. 2, *Collectio Coisliniana in Genesim*, CCSG 15 (Louvain, 1986), lxxvi–xcv, and stemma on p. cxiii; F. Petit, *La Chaîne sur la Genèse, édition intégrale* (Louvain, 1991), xxii–xxiv. Because the Septuagint and catena texts characteristic of the illuminated Octateuchs both represent late and subsidiary types, they are likely to descend from a model significantly later than the mid-6th century (the earliest possible date).
16 L. Perria and A. Iacobini, "Gli Ottateuchi in età paleologa: Problemi di scrittura e illustrazione; Il caso del Laur. Plut. 5.38," in *L'arte di Bisanzio e l'Italia al tempo dei Paleologi 1261–1453*, ed. A. Iacobini and M. della Valle (Rome, 1999), 69–111.

individually and as a group. This is a large topic (witness the scale of Weitzmann and Bernabò's two-volume study of 1999), and hence it is possible only to sketch out the arguments here and to present a small portion of the supporting evidence.

A large and costly book like an illustrated Octateuch, the production of which was time consuming, was certainly made in response to a special commission, rather than in speculation of a potential future purchase. From whom did the demand come, and what purpose was such a book intended to serve? Among the illustrated Octateuchs, we are fortunate to have one manuscript that appears to reveal for whom it was made. This is the Topkapı (or Seraglio) Octateuch. It begins with a unique text, a lengthy paraphrase of the prefatory *Letter of Aristeas*, which gives an account of the first translation of the Law/Torah from Hebrew into Greek.[17] The worn and damaged title attributes the authorship of this paraphrase to a *porphyrogennetos*, son of the emperor Alexios I Komnenos (d. 1118; Fig. 1). This must be Isaak, the younger brother of Emperor John II Komnenos (ruled 1118–43). (Uspenskij, followed by all later commentators, reconstructed the text to include the name "Lord Isaak," but this is impossible as there is no space for these words.)[18] Isaak's motivation in composing the paraphrase is explicit in the title: "[Finding] the preface to the Old [Testament], which Aristeas expounded to Philokrates, prolix and confused, the Porphyrogennetos, son of the Great King Lord Alexios Komnenos, refashioned it with conciseness and clarity."[19] In addition to his other literary endeavors, which are

---

17   The paraphrase is published with a Russian translation in T. Uspenskij, *L'Octateuque de la bibliothèque du Sérail à Constantinople*, IRAIK 12 (Sofia, 1907), 1–14. See most recently the discussion in Weitzmann and Bernabò, *Byzantine Octateuchs* (n. 1 above), 335–36. For an up-to-date treatment of the *Letter of Aristeas*—one, however, that does not consider the manuscript tradition—see A. Wasserstein and D. Wasserstein, *The Legend of the Septuagint: From Classical Antiquity to Today* (Cambridge, 2006).

18   The preface reads as follows (abbreviations expanded in round brackets; missing passages supplied in square brackets): Τὸ τῆς παλαιᾶς προοίμι(ον) ὅπ(ερ) ὁ Ἀ[ριστέ/ας] πρὸς τὸν Φιλοκράτ(ην) ἐκτέθεικ(εν) μακ[ρη/γορίᾳ] καὶ ἀσαφείᾳ ὁ δὲ πορφυρογ[έννη/ητος] καὶ υἱὸς τοῦ μεγάλ(ου) β(ασιλέως) κ(ὺρ) Ἀλε[ξίου] / τοῦ Κομνην(οῦ) εἰς συντομί(αν) μετερύθμι/σε καὶ σαφήνει(αν).

Transcribed to show the spacing of the text it is clear there is no room for the words Κὺρ Ἰσαάκιος between πορφυρογέννητος and καὶ υἱός:

ΤΟΤΗΣΠΑΛΑΙΑΣΠΡΟΟΙΜΙΟΠΟΑ[ΡΙΣΤΕ
ΑΣ]ΠΡΟΣΤΟΝΦΙΛΟΚΡΑΤΕΚΤΕΘΕΙΚΜΑΚ[ΡΗ
ΓΟΡΙΑ]ΚΑΙΑΣΑΦΕΙΑΟΔΕΠΟΡΦΥΡΟΓ[ΕΝΝ
ΗΤΟΣ]ΚΑΙΥΙΟΣΤΟΥΜΕΓΑΛΒΚΑΛΕ[ΞΙΟΥ
ΤΟΥΚΟΜΝΗΝΕΙΣΣΥΝΤΟΜΙΜΕΤΕΡΥΘΜΙ
ΣΕΚΑΙΣΑΦΗΝΕΙ

19   I have modified the translation found in J. C. Anderson, "The Seraglio Octateuch and the Kokkinobaphos Master," *DOP* 36 (1982): 84 and n. 10.

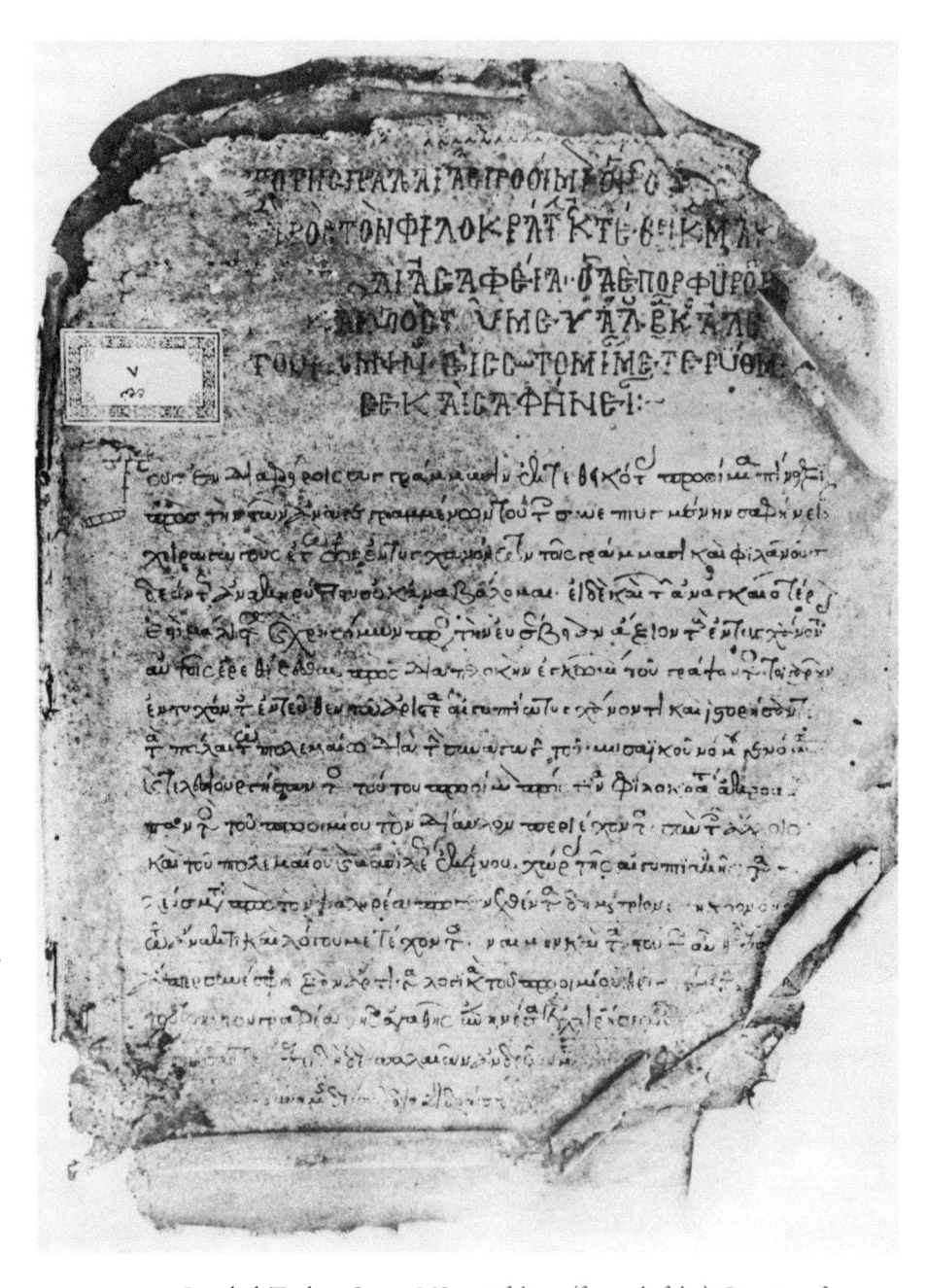

FIGURE 1 Istanbul, Topkapı Sarayı, MS gr. 8, folio 3r (formerly fol. 1). Opening of paraphrase of *Letter of Aristeas*; condition ca. 1905 (photo: after Uspenskij, *L'Octateuque du Sérail*)

referred to by Theodore Prodromos,[20] Isaak was an important patron of art and architecture: he was seemingly the restorer of the Constantinopolitan monastery of the Savior in Chora (Kariye Camii), and he was certainly the founder of the monastery of the Theotokos Kosmosoteira in Thrace (1152), where he lived in forced retirement.[21]

Isaak's paraphrase is on two short quires (folios 3–6 [4] and 7–9 [2+1]), codicologically distinct from the rest of the book, and was written by a different scribe in a larger script. Unfortunately, no quire numbers survive to confirm beyond question what the original number and order of the quires was. But a codicological anomaly is revealing: the paraphrase was written on alternate lines of the ruling pattern used throughout the rest of the book. This indicates that the paraphrase was made at the same time as the Octateuch, and for its present context. (Were the paraphrase a later addition it would have made no sense for the scribe to have ruled double the number of lines necessary.) It is also significant that the scribe of the paraphrase left spaces for miniatures that correspond, in their size and location, to spaces left for miniatures in the *Letter of Aristeas* itself, so a similar illustrative cycle was intended for both.[22] The most likely explanation for the presence of the paraphrase in this one Octateuch is that Isaak was not only the paraphrase's author but the one who commissioned the entire volume. That it was made in Constantinople is borne out by the presence later in the volume of miniatures by an outstanding artist, sometimes known as the Kokkinobaphos Master in recognition of his work on two illustrated copies

---

20 W. Hörandner, *Theodoros Prodromos, Historische Gedichte*, WByzSt, 11 (Vienna, 1974), poem 42, p. 397. See also how Theodore identifies Isaak Komnenos simply as "porphyrogennetos" in the title of poem 40, p. 391.

21 Lowden, *Octateuchs*, 24–25; Weitzmann and Bernabò, *Byzantine Octateuchs*, 336–37 (both n. 1 above).

22 Lowden, *Octateuchs*, 25; Iacobini, "'Lettera di Aristea'" (n. 1 above), 94 n. 61. The text has been considered to be Isaak's autograph (Uspenskij, *L'Octateuque* (n. 17 above), 1; and see Anderson, "Seraglio Octateuch," 84–85). This is most unlikely. The mid-12th-century date has been maintained by some scholars: L. Perria, "La scrittura degli Ottateuchi fra tradizione e innovazione," in *Bisanzio e l'Occidente: arte, archeologia, storia; Studi in onore di Fernanda de' Maffei* (Rome, 1986), 220–21; Perria and Iacobini, "Ottateuchi" (n. 16 above), 71. Yet for others the paraphrase is a 13th-century addition to the Octateuch: *Lettre d'Aristée à Philocrate*, ed. A. Pelletier, SC 89 (Paris, 1962), 11; O. Kresten, "Oktateuch-Probleme: Bemerkungen zu einer Neuerscheinung," *BZ* 84–85 (1991–92): 509–10; I. Hutter, review of Weitzmann and Bernabò, *Byzantine Octateuchs*, in *BZ* 94 (2001): 362. But note that Pelletier, *Lettre*, 11, thought that the transcription of the *Letter of Aristeas* was made in the second half of the 13th century, and that the script of the paraphrase was somewhat earlier in date. The problems with a late date for the paraphrase are considerable. There is no evidence that the manuscript had been rebound before the 1930s. The motive for inserting the unique text, if not at the behest of Isaak, is obscure. The presence of spaces for miniatures in both the *Letter* and its paraphrase strongly imply a similar history for both.

of homilies of the monk James of Kokkinobaphos.²³ The Kokkinobaphos Master worked for other members of the ruling family.

Unfortunately Isaak did not explain in his preface *why* he wanted an illustrated Octateuch catena manuscript. His connection with the Topkapı Octateuch, though, may indicate a broader pattern—that illuminated Octateuchs tended to be produced under the patronage of Constantinopolitan aristocrats. The Vatopedi Octateuch, for example, was at a later date owned by an obscure member of the Asan Palaiologos family, and hence might have been passed down from a more prominent member of the imperial family.²⁴ There are, moreover, illustrated Old Testament manuscripts with marginal catenae that were definitely made for aristocratic lay patrons: the constituent volumes of the so-called "Bible" of the courtier Niketas, for example,²⁵ and both the Paris Psalter, often thought to be imperial, and its close textual relative, the Psalter of Emperor Basil II in the Marciana Library.²⁶ These books are among the high points of Byzantine manuscript production. At the same time we should contrast to these catena books the one illustrated Octateuch manscript without a marginal catena, namely, Laur. 5.38. It is also the only illustrated Octateuch to contain liturgical rubrics indicating the start and end of lections. The Old Testament lections were normally gathered together in the volume called the Prophetologion (see Chapter 3). The evidence of Laur. 5.38 suggests that this Octateuch was made for public recitation in a church. The large, clear script of Laur. 5.38, more easily legible than the script of the contemporary Vat. gr. 747 (clear but small), would facilitate such use. It is, therefore, reasonable that the illustrated Octateuch catena manuscripts were indeed made for private study by Constantinopolitan aristocrats, like Isaak Komnenos. How such patrons might have used the books, and in particular their images, are difficult questions that cannot be pursued here.

The *Letter of Aristeas* is a characteristic preface of Octateuch catena manuscripts (with and without miniatures), so the model for Isaak Komnenos's paraphrase was either the text in the book that was being made for him or the text in that book's model. As it happens, only one of the four other closely related

23   Anderson, "Seraglio Octateuch."
24   Lowden, *Octateuchs*, 32–33.
25   H. Belting and G. Cavallo, *Die Bibel des Niketas* (Wiesbaden, 1979); J. Lowden, "An Alternative Interpretation of the Manuscripts of Niketas," *Byz* 53 (1983): 559–74; J. Lowden, *Illuminated Prophet Books* (University Park, PA, 1988), 14–22; for a more recent study, see *In the Beginning* (n. 6 above), no. 69, pp. 234–35, 305–6.
26   A. Cutler, *The Aristocratic Psalters in Byzantium* (Paris, 1984), 63–71, 115–19. For the textual connection see G. Dorival, *Les chaînes exégétiques grecques sur les Psaumes: Contribution à l'étude d'une forme littéraire*, 4 vols. (Leuven, 1986–95), 1:246–48 and 4:418.

Octateuchs now contains the *Letter of Aristeas* (Vat. gr. 747), but this is doubtless because the other three (Smyrna A.1, Vat. gr. 746, and Vatopedi 602) lack their prefatory gatherings. We can be confident, therefore, that Isaak's model for the Topkapı Octateuch was another illustrated Octateuch. It might even have been the near-contemporary Smyrna manuscript. If so, the Kokkinobaphos Master could have provided a crucial link, because he worked on the Smyrna Octateuch as well as on Topkapı. But since the Smyrna manuscript has been destroyed, and can be studied only via the surviving photographs of its miniatures,[27] it is impossible to undertake the really detailed comparison with Topkapı that would be necessary to prove the point. Instead, we can turn to a different pair of illustrated Octateuchs to trace precisely how one such book (Vatopedi 602) was copied from another (Vat. gr. 746).

The direct dependence of the thirteenth-century Vatopedi 602 on the twelfth-century Vat. gr. 746 is revealed through a detailed comparison of their texts. The contents of a missing leaf in Vat. gr. 746 are also missing in Vatopedi (the scribe left blank pages, perhaps hoping to be able to supply the lacuna at some later date).[28] Less conspicuous, but incontrovertible, evidence is how a jumbled text in Vatopedi was produced by copying the misordered leaves of a quire in Vat. gr. 746 (which were subsequently rebound in the correct sequence).[29] We do not know for whom Vatopedi was made (perhaps a Palaiologos?—see above). Nor do we know why Vat. gr. 746 in particular was taken as a model, for unlike the Smyrna and Topkapı manuscripts—which share an artist—Vat. gr. 746 was well over a century old when copied in Vatopedi. But if we cannot say why Vat. gr. 746 was copied, we can certainly say how it was copied.

A most remarkable feature of Vatopedi 602 is how much the copying scribes and artist improved on the somewhat hasty workmanship that characterizes their model (compare Figs. 2 and 3).[30] This suggests that Vatopedi's scribe and artist were working slowly, providing the costly care that had probably been explicitly stipulated by the commission. The patron, for whom questions of artistic style seem to have been a serious concern, must have specified "I want a book like this, but better." The Palaiologan artist also for the most part suppressed characteristics of his own late thirteenth-century style (the architectural background in Fig. 3 is an exception). The widespread ability among book producers of the Palaiologan era, such as we see exercised in Vatopedi 602, to imitate

---

27 D.-C. Hesseling, *Miniatures de l'octateuque grec de Smyrne* (Leiden, 1909).
28 Lowden, *Octateuchs*, 38–39, figs. 21–24.
29 Ibid., 39–41, figs. 25–27.
30 Ibid., 45–53.

FIGURE 2 (top) Rome, Biblioteca Apostolica Vaticana, MS Vat. gr. 746, folio 457r, Joshua and Caleb (photo: Conway Library, Courtauld Institute of Art)

FIGURE 3 (bottom) Mount Athos, Monastery of Vatopedi, MS 602, folio 374r, Joshua and Caleb (photo: author)

Byzantine work of, say, the late tenth or eleventh century, probably reflects a quite widespread demand among the commissioning public.[31] Additionally, it is notable that the artist of Vatopedi 602 was working in a style that predated the style of his model by a century or more: he was not simply reproducing the style of Vat. gr. 746. This is intriguing. Was the Palaiologan artist adopting an archaizing style thoughtlessly? Or was he deliberately imitating work of circa 1000 because a manuscript of that era was known to have played some crucial role in the history of Octateuch illustration? Such questions are worth asking even if they cannot currently be answered.

The production of a new illustrated Octateuch catena manuscript in the Palaiologan era needed some specific motive. Earlier manuscripts—containing the same texts and to a large extent the same images—seem still to have been in circulation. But presumably they could not supply the demand. The eleventh-century Vat. gr. 747, for example, was still in use in the Palaiologan era, and its images, which had suffered severe losses due to flaking of the paint surface, were systematically overpainted in the 1320s to 1340s.[32] Given what must have been the condition of that book circa 1300 it can be readily understood that a patron might have wished for a less damaged copy. The Smyrna Octateuch had a new frontispiece added in the early Palaiologan period, so it too was still in use, but it seems to have been in the Peloponnese,[33] and hence not available to a patron in Constantinople. Vat. gr. 746, as we have seen, was put to use as a model for Vatopedi 602. In fact, of the five surviving fully illustrated Octateuchs only Topkapı has no evidence of Palaiologan use. Taken together the evidence suggests that the Vatopedi manuscript must have been intended to supply its patron with something that Vat. gr. 746 could not, something that detailed comparison of the two might be hoped to bring to light.

Miniature-by-miniature comparison of Vatopedi 602 with Vat. gr. 746 shows that the Palaiologan craftsman noted what must have appeared to him as oversights in his model, which he corrected. For example, he also added details to clarify the meaning of images. And in one case he introduced an image of the

---

31 The starting point is H. Buchthal and H. Belting, *Patronage in Thirteenth-Century Constantinople: An Atelier of Late Byzantine Book Illumination and Calligraphy*, DOS 16 (Washington, DC, 1978). See also R. S. Nelson and J. Lowden, "The Palaeologina Group: Additional Manuscripts and New Questions," *DOP* 45 (1991): 59–68; J. Lowden, "Manuscript Illumination in Byzantium, 1261–1557," in *Byzantium: Faith and Power (1261–1557)*, ed. H. C. Evans (New York, 2004), 259–69.
32 I. Hutter, "Paläologische Übermalungen im Oktateuch Vaticanus graecus 747," *JÖB* 21 (1972): 139–48.
33 Further references in Weitzmann and Bernabò, *Byzantine Octateuchs*, 15.

Fall of Jericho, which he derived from a different source, namely, the tenth-century Joshua Roll (BAV, Vat. palat. gr. 431). Unfortunately we do not know if this was because the Joshua Roll was in the possession of the patron of Vatopedi 602, or because the Palaiologan artist knew it by some other means. The most remarkable failing in Vat. gr. 746 involved the artist(s) misplacing ninety consecutive miniatures in Genesis, but as we lack the first volume of Vatopedi we do not know how the Palaiologan copyists coped with this problem.[34]

The single most conspicuous difference between Vat. gr. 746 and Vatopedi 602 is their size. Vat. gr. 746 is huge, now comprising 508 leaves, trimmed to about 39.5 × 31 cm (and rebound in two parts). The dimensions of Vatopedi 602, now about 34 × 24 cm, are little more than half that, but it is twice as long. Originally the Vatopedi Octateuch would have occupied about 950 folios (1900 pages) in two volumes, but only the second volume has survived (now 469 folios).

Despite the change in format, the miniatures in Vatopedi are for the most part very close in size to those in Vat. gr. 746, or even a little bigger. As a result they occupy a much larger portion of the page than do those in Vat. gr. 746, and the visual result is strikingly different.[35] It is conceivable that the decision to use smaller sheets of parchment for Vatopedi 602 was made for aesthetic reasons (that is, that the change to a smaller format was the patron's key demand, and hence might explain why Vatopedi was commissioned). But it is more likely, I think, that the decision to make a smaller format, two-volume Octateuch was forced on the Palaiologan patron and craftsmen by a shortage of parchment of large format. In contrast we can note that a comparably large format to that used in Vat. gr. 746 was also employed for Vat. gr. 747, Smyrna, and Topkapı, confirming that the absolute dimensions of a page in all these illustrated Octateuchs were considered important, and any change in them would occur through necessity.

As for Isaak Komnenos and the Topkapı Octateuch, it was not only Isaak's paraphrase that was left unfinished with spaces for images that were never executed. For some reason, the small team of artists who were involved left significant parts of the rest of the book unfinished.[36] Clearly, work was not proceeding through this book in a straightforward manner. Even within the unfinished quires it is evident that work did not progress—as might reasonably

---

34 Lowden, *Octateuchs*, 47–48; 50 (with figs. 51–52); 50–52 (with figs. 58–59); 71–72.
35 Ibid., figs. 4–5.
36 Moving by quires, folios 3–6 have (unfilled) spaces; fols. 7–9 have spaces; fols. 10–17 have spaces and one finished miniature; fols. 71–78 have spaces and unfinished miniatures; fols. 79–86 have spaces; fols. 111–18 have spaces; fols. 119–26 have some unframed miniatures. The miniatures in the other early quires were completed.

be expected—from the opening page, nor was it organized by the bifolium—two straightforward models for the production process. Jeffrey Anderson has suggested that in the quire composed of folios 71–79 the artist may have begun work on folio 74r because it corresponded to the start of a quire in his model.[37] Since the equivalent leaf in Vat. gr. 747 (folio 37r) begins a quire, a similar arrangement is indeed conceivable for the model of Topkapı gr. 8 (see further below). In contrast to what is observed in the early quires, however, the work of the Kokkinobaphos Master was much more consistent and methodical: he began his contribution at the start of a quire on folio 127, and ended at the end of a quire on folio 499, completing all the miniatures. Thereafter all fifty-one spaces for miniatures in the remaining folios 500–569 were left blank.

As a result of these unfinished images, we can be confident about the working processes of both artists and scribes in an illustrated Octateuch. Scribes worked first. They must have been instructed, as we have seen, as to what model or models to copy. In particular, they had to decide whether to make a page-for-page copy of their principal model, or to alter the layout drastically (as was done in Vatopedi 602). The reasons for working page for page were inherent in the complex layout of these illustrated catena manuscripts. Every page had a different layout, resulting from the need to accommodate varying amounts of biblical text, the relevant marginal catena, and images of differing size and shape. Laborious as it might seem to work a page at a time, it had the great advantage that it was not necessary to recalculate all the variables. Smyrna, so far as can be judged from the photographic record, generally resembled Vat. gr. 747 page for page and quire for quire. Since Smyrna was not a copy of Vat. gr. 747 (the evidence for this judgment is set out below), it follows that both were reproducing with great care the layout of a common model. Topkapı and Vat. gr. 746, however, both abandoned this layout. Since they both also employed a much larger script for the Septuagint text and catena, both were approximately twice as long as Smyrna and Vat. gr. 747. Topkapı, in particular, is much easier to read than Vat. gr. 747 (or presumably Smyrna), and it should not be ruled out—even if it seems banal—that greater legibility was among Isaak's motives in commissioning his book and specifying larger script. Whereas most Byzantine manuscripts did not reproduce, facsimile-like, the layout of their model, some catena manuscripts, with or without illumination, did follow their models page for page as we have observed in Vat. gr. 747 and Smyrna. Among illustrated Septuagint manuscripts, for example, the mid-tenth-century catena on the Prophet Books, Vat. Chisi. R. VIII.54, was copied

37 "Seraglio Octateuch" (n. 19 above), 101.

page for page in the early Palaiologan Vat. gr. 1153–54.[38] The late tenth-century Copenhagen, Royal Library, cod. GKS 6 was reproduced with facsimilizing attention to detail in the unillustrated Vienna, Österreichische Nationalbibliothek, cod. theol. gr. 11.[39] In general it can be said that the production of a biblical manuscript with marginal catena put far greater demands on Byzantine scribes than did books with incorporated catena (in which the biblical and commentary texts were organized as successive excerpts in a continuous sequence), or "normal" books, with no catena at all.

An essential part of the scribes' activities in the Octateuchs was to leave spaces for the miniatures, corresponding to what was found in their model. Although this was a routine scribal activity, it was considerably more complex in the Octateuchs than it was in most illuminated manuscripts. In every Octateuch the miniatures in any one manuscript vary greatly in size and shape, and in their location on the page.[40] But if we then look at the comparable images from different manuscripts, they generally display similar dimensions and shapes (Figs. 4–7).[41] The copying scribes must therefore have measured the miniatures in their model to reproduce spaces of appropriate size and shape in the manuscript they were making. Furthermore, it can be seen from adjustments they made, either stretching out or compressing their script near a miniature, that the precise point in the text at which the miniature was to be inserted was important. In Vat. gr. 747 (the evidence from the photographic record of Smyrna is too scant to permit more than an occasional comparison) it is clear that the location of miniatures was often, but by no means always, associated with the beginning of chapters (κεφάλαια), and the content of images might be suggested by the nearby chapter titles, at least in those cases when the images were not located as near as possible to the biblical text they depicted. This is closely comparable to what is found in the illuminated manuscript of 1–2 Samuel and 1–2 Kings, Vat. gr. 333, in which the *kephalaia* figured in the selection and location of miniatures.[42] It may be significant that Vat. gr. 333 is approximately contemporary to Vat. gr. 747.

When two or more Byzantine scribes collaborated on an illustrated Octateuch, they might leave valuable evidence of the arrangement of the text in their

---

38   Lowden, *Prophet Books* (n. 25 above), 41–45.
39   Belting and Cavallo, *Bibel des Niketas*; J. Lowden, "Alternative Interpretation" (both n. 25 above). For an edition of part of the text see *Catena Havniensis in Ecclesiasten*, ed. A. Labate (Brepols, 1992).
40   E.g., Lowden, *Octateuchs*, figs. 9, 14, 36, 74, 83, 87, 89.
41   Ibid., 36 and figs. 16–20.
42   In general on the manuscript see J. Lassus, *L'illustration byzantine du Livre des Rois* (Paris, 1973).

FIGURE 4 (top)　Rome, Biblioteca Apostolica Vaticana, MS Vat. gr. 747, folio 192r, Moses Expounds the Law to the Israelites (photo: Conway Library, Courtauld Institute of Art)

FIGURE 5 (bottom)　Formerly Smyrna [Izmir], Greek Evangelical School, MS A.1, folio 196r, Moses Expounds the Law to the Israelites (after Hesseling, *L'Octateuque de Smyrne*)

FIGURE 6   Istanbul, Topkapı Sarayı, MS gr. 8, folio 415r, Moses Expounds the Law to the Israelites (photo: author)

FIGURE 7 Rome, Biblioteca Apostolica Vaticana, MS Vat. gr. 746, folio 394r, Moses Expounds the Law to the Israelites (photo: Conway Library, Courtauld Institute of Art)

model. For example, the two scribes of Vatopedi arranged their collaboration around the quire divisions of their model, Vat. gr. 746. Scribe B of Vatopedi copied the content of precisely four quires of Vat. gr. 746.[43] Vat. gr. 746, on the other hand, was the work of three scribes. Scribe A adjusted the layout of his work to allow scribe B to begin at the start of a new quire, and scribe B did the same for scribe C. When we compare Vat. gr. 747 we discover that the text copied by Vat. gr. 746's scribe B corresponds exactly with the text in ten quires of Vat. gr. 747.[44] In one instance it is even possible to confirm that the Smyrna Octateuch also ended a quire at the identical point in the text as Vat. gr. 747 and Vat. gr. 746.[45] Since Vat. gr. 746 was not a copy of Vat. gr. 747 (evidence is set out below), the

43 Lowden, *Octateuchs*, 40–42, figs. 28–31.
44 Ibid., 42–43, figs. 32–35.
45 Ibid., 56–65, figs. 34–36.

correspondences must reveal the pagination and layout of the common model of Vat. gr. 747 and Smyrna. Surprisingly, the various copyists, especially in Vat. gr. 746, made little effort to harmonize their scripts. Such variety must have been acceptable to the patron. But it has to be said that a book that appears to be entirely by a single hand (e.g., Vat. gr. 747) may in fact be the product of several scribes, working to harmonize their contributions.

The use of the quire divisions of the model by the copying scribes to coordinate their activities and ensure that no text was omitted or duplicated would seem a rational process. As there was no pagination or foliation in these books, it would have been time-consuming to identify a specific passage of the text with certainty, especially given the formulaic and repetitive nature of much of the Septuagint. But not enough work has been done on Byzantine manuscripts to establish whether copying scribes often used the quire divisions of their model in this way or not. Clearly in a text such as the Four Gospels, the mainstay of Byzantine book production, each Gospel generally began a new quire. Thus although each Gospel could be the work of a different scribe, the resulting book would not reveal evidence about the quire division(s) of its model(s).

The artist or artists of an illustrated Octateuch received from the scribe(s) a pile of quires with spaces of varying sizes and shapes to be filled with images, and an exemplar to copy (unless the book they were working on had no exemplar). It is not surprising, therefore, that the comparable images in the five Octateuchs (excluding Laur. 5.38) resemble one another for the most part very closely. For example (Figs. 4–7), at Deuteronomy 12:12 is an image of an enthroned Moses expounding the law to a crowd of Israelite men. The image in the different versions is virtually identical in height (80–83 mm), but notably less wide in Vat. gr. 747 (73 mm as against the 94 mm of Vat. gr. 746). There is, however, a conspicuous unused blank space at the right side of the image in Vat. gr. 747, into which the artist could have expanded to make the miniature broader. Iconographically, the versions are virtually identical, apart from the presence of a dodecasyllabic title in Smyrna, Vat. gr. 746, and Vatopedi.

Overall, this pattern of scrupulous copying is different from the situation found in most illuminated Byzantine manuscripts, in which facsimile-like reproduction of a model was very much the exception. Of special significance, therefore, are those cases in which the Octateuchs differ among themselves over their choice of images or iconography. We need to ask on a case-by-case basis why such differences occurred, and what they might have meant for the books' users and makers. We have mentioned that the artist of Vatopedi added an image based on the Joshua Roll, making the Palaiologan manuscript different from any earlier Octateuch. But for the most part the differences between the Octateuchs bind together the three Komnenian manuscripts (Smyrna, Topkapı, and Vat. gr. 746), and distinguish them from Vat. gr. 747. For example, the scribes of the four manuscripts each left a space of similar size and shape in the Septuagint text beneath Exodus 1:17 (Vatopedi, it will be recalled, lacks Genesis and Exodus).[46] In Vat. gr. 747 we find the rare image of Pharaoh issuing his decree to midwives that sons born to Israelite women are to be killed (narrated in Exodus 1:15ff.). All three twelfth-century Octateuchs, however, substitute for this image a representation of the Birth of Moses (Exodus 2:2). Although also a highly unusual scene, it is based on a commonplace Byzantine iconographic formula, as employed elsewhere, for example, for the birth of John the Baptist or the birth of the Theotokos. The *kephalaion* that begins at Exodus 2:1, and its title (Περὶ τῆς γεννήσεως Μωϋσέως), presumably prompted the choice of this image.

A second example of what may be termed an alternative miniature can be cited here. Below Exodus 28:5 four Octateuchs (this part lacking in Vatopedi) have an image consisting of four small square panels in a row.[47] In Vat. gr. 747 each of the squares contains an element of the complex priestly garments of Aaron, as mentioned briefly nearby in Exodus 28:4 (and described in more detail later). But in all three twelfth-century Octateuchs the four squares are painted as four of the curtains of the tabernacle, described long before at Exodus 26:1–6. The curtains are composed of simple checkerboard squares and are inappropriate to the context in Exodus 28.

The likeliest explanation for these alternative miniatures is that the Komnenian artists (of Smyrna or another similar manuscript) occasionally found a miniature in the model hard to decipher. Rather than leaving the space for the image blank in the manuscript they were making, they substituted what seemed to them an adequate alternative. Looking at the flaked images of Vat. gr. 747, even those restored in the fourteenth century, we can see how miniatures could become difficult to read.

Were we to judge solely on the evidence of "alternative miniatures" (as defined above) it would appear safe to conclude that Vat. gr. 747 better represented the miniature cycle of the lost common model, and that the three Komnenian

---

46 Lowden, *Octateuchs*, 61, figs. 79–82; Weitzmann and Bernabò, *Byzantine Octateuchs*, 144–45, nos. 595–98.
47 Lowden, *Octateuchs*, 61, figs. 83–84; Weitzmann and Bernabò, *Byzantine Octateuchs*, 178–79, figs. 770–73. Two curtains already appeared in the image at Ex 25:36–37, flanking the menorah, in the 12th-century Octateuchs, but were omitted in Vat. gr. 747: see representations in Weitzmann and Bernabò, *Byzantine Octateuchs*, nos. 758–761b.

manuscripts represented a revised version. This explanation holds, though, for only a small minority of scenes. Elsewhere, for the most part, the images in Vat. gr. 747, in comparison with the other Octateuchs, can be seen to be simplified and sometimes truncated versions of the same scene. The simplification is partly a matter of technique. Beginning at the start of a quire on folio 37, the artist of Vat. gr. 747 abandoned the full palette of opaque pigments, and instead merely sketched the images, leaving the blank parchment as a highlight (the change is not obvious in black and white reproductions).[48] Presumably this was to hasten the production process. In addition, occasionally where the heavily incised and complex ruling pattern used by the scribe cut across the space left for an image, the artist narrowed the image in order to avoid some of the vertical rulings.[49] (These deep furrows caused the pigment to pool.) The resulting blank spaces alongside images look disturbing. And when the truncated image is compared with the version in the other Octateuchs it can be seen that the artist of Vat. gr. 747 simplified or compressed the iconography to fit the narrower space.[50] In general, therefore, the evidence that Vat. gr. 747 was copied from the lost common model at a time when it was more legible than in the Komnenian era has to be weighed against the evidence that the artist of Vat. gr. 747 simplified and sometimes truncated what he copied, making his version on such occasions less accurate; this is a complex and delicate analysis that must be undertaken without prejudice for each miniature. It is relatively easy to observe similarity or difference between the various Octateuchs, but much more difficult to interpret their significance.

An intriguing example of a small but significant difference among the illustrated Octateuchs is the representation of the serpent that tempts Eve in the garden of Eden as a non-biblical camel-like quadruped (an image that has been much discussed).[51] When we look in the Octateuchs, we find that the camel-like serpent is not present in the eleventh-century manuscripts (Vat. gr. 747 and Laur. 5.38 [Fig. 8]), but appears in the three closely related manuscripts of the second quarter of the twelfth century (Vat. gr. 746, the Smyrna Octateuch, and the Topkapı Octateuch [Fig. 9]). In 1982, Fernanda De' Maffei pointed out that in the Chronicle of Zonaras, a Constantinopolitan work contemporary with the Komnenian Octateuchs, the serpent is described as having feet, following a

48 Lowden, *Octateuchs*, 13–14.
49 Ibid., figs. 6, 9.
50 Ibid., 76–77.
51 See bibliography in Weitzmann and Bernabò, *Byzantine Octateuchs*, 33–34.

passage that goes back to Josephus's *Antiquities*.⁵² In the twelfth-century chronicle of Kedrenos, on the other hand, the serpent is explicitly said not to have had feet. The evidence appears unambiguous. The Komnenian Octateuchs seem to have changed the upright serpent, supported on its tail (as clearly seen in Laur. 5.38), into the quadruped serpent, presumably because this was a matter of debate in Constantinople at the time of their production. This is a matter to which we shall return.

Descendents of the lost common model for the Octateuchs permit us to envisage this manuscript with a surprising level of detail. From Vat. gr. 747, and to a lesser extent Smyrna (and the other Octateuchs), we know the model was a catena manuscript with certain prefaces and epilogues and a specific form of biblical (and catena) text. The Octateuch element of the model comprised 278 folios, measured about 40 × 30 cm, and was accompanied by 374 miniatures. It was page for page and quire for quire the same as Vat. gr. 747 and (for most of the cycle, it would seem) Smyrna. For the sake of discussion, we can allow the possibility that the lost common model was also the first example of this particular type of illustrated book. How then was it created?

It was not a "perfect" manuscript. It had mistakes. For example, two of the miniatures in Exodus are very similar in all the Octateuchs.⁵³ In the first miniature (Vat. gr. 747, folio 88r), Pharaoh pursues the Israelites (upper register) and the Israelites approach the sea (lower register). These events are narrated at Exodus 14:6–8, but the miniature is located in the Octateuchs at Exodus 13:15ff. In the second miniature the Israelites carry the bones of Joseph (Exodus 13:19), but the miniature is located in the Octateuchs at Exodus 14:11 (Vat. gr. 747, folio 88v). Clearly what has happened here is that the images have been entered in reverse order. The reversal must have taken place in the common model. And it must have happened at an early stage in the planning and production of that manuscript, for the two miniatures have different dimensions and proportions, appropriate to their different content (as transmitted by the Octateuchs), so it was not merely the artist of the common model who reversed the position of the images. The scribe must have made the mistake while leaving spaces for the miniatures as he worked on the lost common model.

52 F. De' Maffei, "Eva e il serpente, ovverossia la problematica della derivazione, o non, delle miniature vetero-testamentarie cristiane da presunti prototipi ebraici," *RSBN*, n.s., 17-19 (1980–82): 13–35.
53 Lowden, *Octateuchs*, 81, figs. 112–15; Weitzmann and Bernabò, *Byzantine Octateuchs*, nos. 700–703, 696a–99b *(sic)*.

FIGURE 8   Florence, Biblioteca Medicea-Laurenziana, MS plut. 5.38, folio 6r, Genesis scenes (photo: Florence, Biblioteca Medicea-Laurenziana)

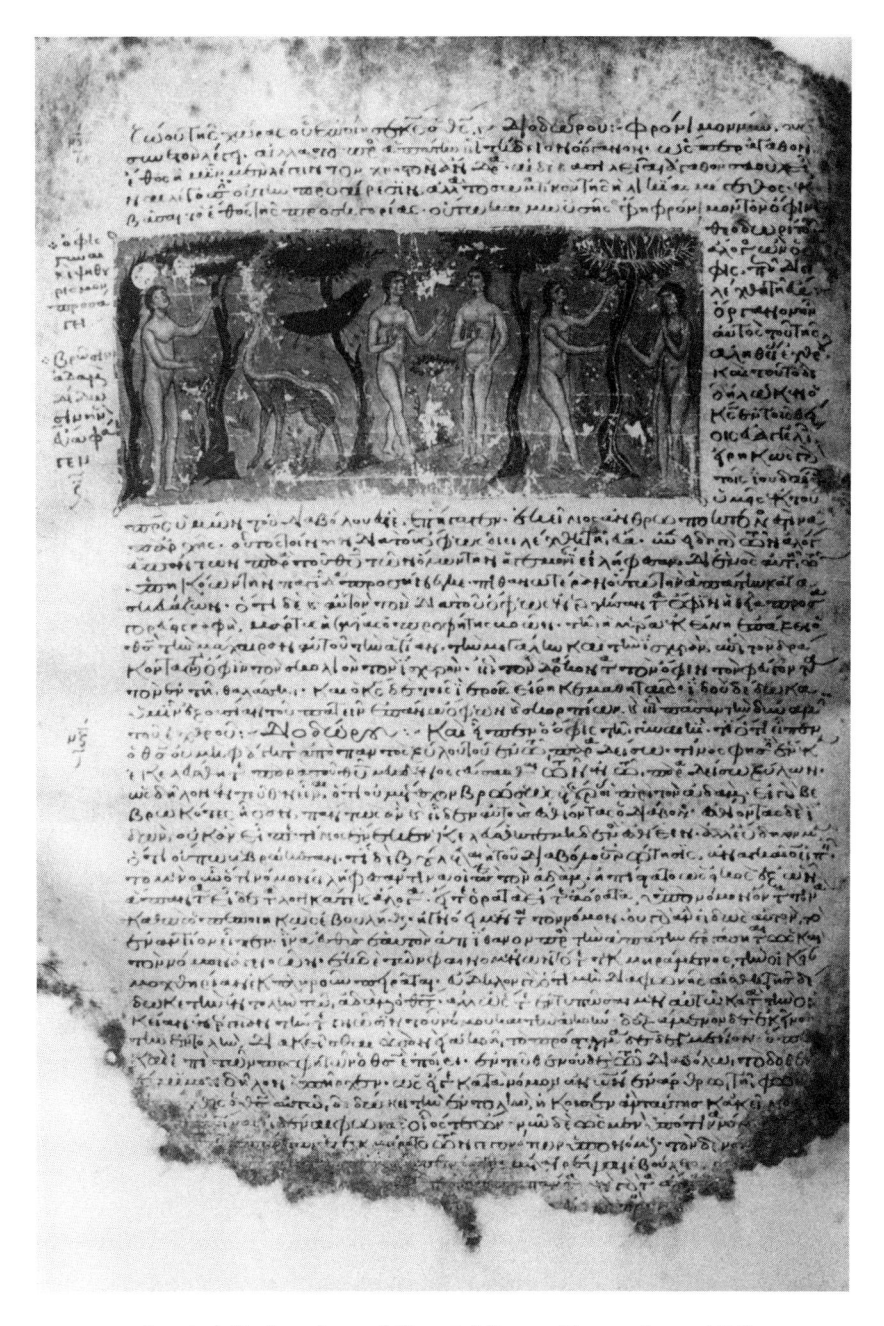

FIGURE 9 Istanbul, Topkapı Sarayı, MS gr. 8, folio 43v, Temptation and Fall, quadruped serpent (photo: author)

When it came to supplying the images in the common model, some were composed ad hoc from familiar formulas. For example, the model for the various "death of so-and-so" miniatures was generic and was provided entirely by the artist's training within the Byzantine iconographic tradition.[54] Often the artist provided more detail than the biblical text specified, placing the body in, for example, a shroud, and having it laid within a marble sarcophagus.

Next, some images were prompted by or based on a closely literal reading of the text. For example, the miniature of the dramatic account of the earth swallowing alive the men of Kore (and Dathan and Abiram), their houses, tents, and cattle (Numbers 16:30–33) includes precisely the details mentioned in the text, carefully distinguishing, for example, tent from house.[55] Such a composition was based on individual formulas familiar in a Byzantine context (gestures of grief, representations of buildings, animals, etc.). These were the individual blocks out of which the image was assembled. The end result of a miniature so put together, however, was not generic (like the "death of so-and-so" images), but specific to only one text.

Third, some images, while specific to the text, were included doubtless because they were already well known from their occurrence in a variety of "non-Octateuch" contexts. In this category would be the miniatures of the Crossing of the Red Sea, for example, or the Sacrifice of Isaak. These were images that would have been fully familiar to both the producers and the consumers of Byzantine art without recourse to an Octateuch. The well-known group of Moses and the Israelites from the Crossing of the Red Sea could then itself be repeated (as a formula) with minor adjustments for adjacent images in the Octateuchs' Exodus account.[56]

The fourth category, and the most intriguing, includes unusual images (not iconographic commonplaces) for which we nonetheless find a close parallel outside the family of the Octateuchs. These can be subdivided further into those for which the Septuagint text appears to form the underlying source, and those for which some other textual source must be postulated. The classic case of a

---

54   Noah, Sarah, Abraham, Rachel, Isaak, Jacob, Miriam, Aaron, Eleazar, Gideon, Jephthah, Samson; see Weitzmann and Bernabò, *Byzantine Octateuchs*, index under "burials. images of." The visual formula for "death of X" is also repeated in Vat. gr. 333: Lassus, *Livre des Rois* (n. 42 above), figs. 61, 65, 98, 99, 100, 102.

55   Lowden, *Octateuchs*, 62–64, figs. 34–39; Weitzmann and Bernabò, *Byzantine Octateuchs*, nos. 931–35.

56   See Weitzmann and Bernabò, *Byzantine Octateuchs*, nos. 692–95, 700–703, 704–7, 712–15.

Septuagint-based relative to the Octateuchs is provided by the Joshua rotulus. The most debated non-Septuagint source is provided by the illuminated manuscripts of the so-called *Christian Topography* of (so-called) Kosmas Indikopleustes. Whereas the first three categories outlined above, by their generalized nature, can hardly reveal anything specific about the date at which the common model was produced, the very specific nature of the connections in the fourth category promises insights into matters of chronology (but alas these connections prove not to be decisive).

The Joshua Roll was not merely the source (as we mentioned above) of a single image added to the cycle in Vatopedi, it was copied *in extenso* by the artist of the common model of the Octateuchs.[57] The Roll now consists of fifteen sheets of parchment, originally glued together to form a horizontal scroll, 30–31.5 cm high and 1064 cm long. The pictorial frieze is accompanied in the lower part by a series of biblical excerpts paraphrased from the Septuagint (unfortunately these are too short to provide decisive evidence as to the text type that was used, but it has some variants from the Vat. gr. 747/Vat. gr. 746 catena-group text). That the texts are interrupted at both the start and finish of the roll proves that at least one additional sheet is lost from each end. Blank spaces were left in the text on the Roll's sheets V, IX, X (Fig. 10), XI, and XIII. These gaps correspond to missing words or phrases, and most reflect closely the length of the missing passages. There are also some odd, unclear details in the picture frieze, for example, in the piles of bodies in the foreground of the battle scenes on sheet X (Fig. 10), or the missing implement (rope or spear) in the hands of the hangman on sheet IX. The obvious deduction from these gaps in the text and unclear or missing elements in the frieze is that the Joshua Roll must be a very careful copy of an earlier roll, a roll that in places was difficult to read or decipher. I have suggested that the surviving roll was made probably in an antiquarian enthusiasm to copy and record ancient artefacts and that its lost model was pre-Iconoclast, perhaps a sixth- or seventh-century roll, a conclusion

---

57   On the Joshua Roll, see in general K. Weitzmann, *The Joshua Roll: A Work of the Macedonian Renaissance* (Princeton, 1948); O. Mazal, *Josua-Rolle: Vollständige Faksimile-Ausgabe im Originalformat des Codex Vaticanus Palatinus Graecus 431 der Biblioteca Apostolica Vaticana* (Graz, 1984); Lowden, *Octateuchs*, 105–19; Weitzmann and Bernabò, *Byzantine Octateuchs*, 311–12, nos. 1147–1287b; H. Evans and W. Wixom, eds., *The Glory of Byzantium* (New York, 1997), cat. 162; most recently O. Kresten, "Biblisches Geschehen und byzantinische Kunst: Der Josua-Rotulus der Bibliotheca Apostolica Vaticana (Cod. Vat. Palat. gr. 431) und die illuminierten byzantinischen Oktateuche," Vortrag am 4. Februar 2002 in der Bayerischen Akademie der Wissenschaften, www.badw.de/aktuell/reden_vortraege/Reden_Texte/kresten/ (accessed 13 May 2009).

further developed by Otto Kresten in several recent publications.[58] Kresten has also proposed to identify the principal script of the roll with the hand of the Constantinopolitan scribe Basileios *kalligraphos*, and has in consequence dated the roll to ca. 955–75.[59]

If one assumes that the surviving roll was made as a facsimile of another Joshua roll, it is conceivable that either of these rolls could have served as a model for the Octateuchs. Consequently, the use of the Joshua Roll (or its model) cannot date the making of the lost common model of the Octateuchs, except possibly to a period in or after the sixth century. However, the production of a series of ivories, based closely on the Roll, enables the question of sources and their use to be approached in a different way.

The Joshua ivories consist of three short panels from a rosette casket, now in The Metropolitan Museum, New York, and one long panel, in the Victoria and Albert (V&A) Museum, London. These are astonishingly similar to the respective scenes on the Joshua Roll. The V&A ivory (7.5 × 27 cm) is assembled from three parts and shows, by comparison with the roll, the first appearance of the men of Gibeon before Joshua (from the join of sheets XII–XIII of the roll), and two messengers before Joshua (from the right end of sheet XIII).[60] Note, these scenes are not adjacent in the roll. The three Metropolitan panels (each about 6 cm tall) comprise Joshua's defeat of the men of Hai (Fig. 11; the lower half of a double register composition on sheet X of the roll); the king of Hai: before Joshua, and hanged (the left part of sheet XI; these two adjacent in the roll); and the men of Gibeon before Joshua, as in the V&A panel (from sheets XII–XIII of the roll).[61] All three Metropolitan panels have carved inscriptions. Most notably, the inscription on the panel showing Joshua's defeat of the men of Hai repeats the wording of the first part of the caption-like text in the Joshua Roll, including the two lacunae where the scribe of the roll could not decipher the text of his model (compare Figs. 10 and 11).

The ivories, whose manufacture would appear to be approximately contemporary with that of the (surviving) roll, that is, the third quarter of the tenth

---

58 Listed in Kresten, "Biblisches Geschehen."
59 Ibid.
60 A. Goldschmidt and K. Weitzmann, *Die byzantinischen Elfenbeinskulpturen des X.–XIII. Jahrhundert* (Berlin, 1930), 1:23–24, and pl. I. 4. But note that the evidence of the Joshua ivories was overlooked in Weitzmann and Bernabò, *Byzantine Octateuchs*.
61 Evans and Wixom, *Glory of Byzantium*, nos. 152 A–C. Goldschmidt and Weitzmann, *Elfenbeinskulpturen*, 1:23, and pl. I. 1–3.

century, were probably based directly and independently on the roll (rather than on its model). Comparison of the two ivory versions of the men of Gibeon before Joshua reveals a number of details in which the V&A ivory is more like the roll (the treatment of Joshua's seat and the first Gibeonite's tunic, for example). Yet the texts of the Metropolitan Museum ivory, with gaps, show that in this aspect it is a closer copy of the roll than the V&A panel. The ivories confirm that the Joshua Roll was known to a range of craftsmen in Constantinople in the tenth and perhaps eleventh centuries.

The continuous picture frieze of the Joshua Roll had to be adapted in various ways to provide the framed images in the lost common model of the Octateuchs. For example, across the join of sheets I–II is a long composition accompanied by a lengthy excerpt from Joshua 3:5–6—"And Joshua said to the people, 'Purify yourselves for tomorrow, for tomorrow among you the Lord will do wonders.' And Joshua said to the priests, 'Take up the ark of the covenant of the Lord, and go before the people.' And the priests took up the ark of the covenant of the Lord and went in front of the people" (NETS translation, modified). The image in the roll shows exactly this (Fig. 12): Joshua leading the Israelites, preceded by the priests carrying the ark. But when the scene came to be adapted for the common model of the Octateuchs, it was far too large and so had to be divided into two images. The resulting first image (Joshua leading the Israelites) was located in the Octateuchs, as in the roll, at Joshua 3:6 (Figs. 13–14). The resulting second image, the priests carrying the ark, was located on the next page in the Octateuchs at Joshua 3:15–16 (Figs. 15–16). The adjacent text reads: "And when the priests that bore the ark of the covenant of the Lord entered upon Jordan and the feet of the priests that bore the ark of the covenant of the Lord were dipped in part of the water of Jordan . . . then the waters that came down from above stopped. . . ." A comparison of the second scene in the Octateuchs with the right half of the composition in the roll shows that the lost common model of the Octateuchs must have added the water beneath the priests' feet and, at the right, the piled up Jordan. This was an intelligent and economical use of the model provided by the Joshua Roll, which adapted its images where necessary to their new function in a codex.

A second example of how the artist of the lost common model of the Octateuchs worked is provided by comparison with manuscripts of the *Christian Topography* of Kosmas Indikopleustes, a strange amalgam of geography, astronomy, theology, and biblical exegesis. The most striking Kosmas-related images appear in the Octateuchs as a series illustrating the provisions for the tabernacle

FIGURE 10 Rome, Biblioteca Apostolica Vaticana, MS Vat. palat. gr. 431, Joshua Roll, sheet X, lacunae in text (photo: Rome, Biblioteca Apostolica Vaticana)

and its equipment as recorded in Exodus 25–29.[62] In discussing and describing the tabernacle, Kosmas paraphrased the biblical account, so the relationship of his wording to the Septuagint can be complex and needs to be defined for each image. We can take a single test case in which the textual evidence is, fortunately, unambiguous.

62 D. Mouriki-Charalambous, "The Octateuch Miniatures of the Byzantine Manuscripts of Cosmas Indicopleustes" (PhD diss., Princeton University, 1970); L. Brubaker, "The Tabernacle Miniatures of the Byzantine Octateuchs," *Actes du XVe Congrès international des études byzantines*, vol. 2, *Art et archéologie: communications* (Athens, 1981), 73–92; Lowden, *Octateuchs*, 86–91; Weitzmann and Bernabò, *Byzantine Octateuchs* (with earlier bibliog.), nos. 750–85 (both n. 1 above). A cartographic world view at Gen 1:24 has also been linked to Kosmas (C. Hahn, "The Creation of the Cosmos: Genesis Illustration in the Octateuchs," *CahArch* 28 [1979]: 29–40; Weitzmann and Bernabò, *Byzantine Octateuchs*, 22–23).

FIGURE 11 New York, The Metropolitan Museum of Art, 17.190.135, Joshua ivory, lacunae in inscription (photo: New York, The Metropolitan Museum of Art)

135

FIGURE 12 (above and facing page) Rome, Biblioteca Apostolica Vaticana, MS Vat. Palat. gr. 431, Joshua Roll, sheets I–II, Priests take up the ark and go before the people (Joshua 3:5–6) (photo: Rome, Biblioteca Apostolica Vaticana)

Below Exodus 25:20 the Octateuchs have an image that is very similar to a miniature in the Kosmas manuscripts.[63] It represents the ark as a rectangular box with double doors, topped by the semicircle (half cylinder) of the mercy seat, flanked above by two cherubim and to either side by a standing priest, an old

---

63 Lowden, *Octateuchs*, figs. 120–22; Weitzmann and Bernabò, *Byzantine Octateuchs*, nos. 750–53 and fig. 35.

136   JOHN LOWDEN

man to the left, a younger to the right. The caption in Smyrna and Vat. gr. 746 identifies "the mercy seat, the cherubim, and the priests." The presence of the two priests is entirely inexplicable by recourse to the Septuagint text (or its catena), and the semicircular top to the ark is puzzling since this is not how the ark is described in the Bible. The text and illustrations of Kosmas, however, readily explain both anomalies. In *Christian Topography* 5.37, the priests are identified as Zacharias and Abia, and they are discussed at some length.[64] The ark is

---

64   W. Wolska-Conus, *Cosmas Indicopleustès, Topographie Chrétienne*, SC 141, 159, 197 (Paris, 1968–73), 2:65–69 (5.36–37); see also the long note to 5.37 on 2:66–67.

FIGURE 13 Rome, Biblioteca Apostolica Vaticana, MS Vat. gr. 747, folio 218r, Joshua leads the Israelites (photo: Conway Library, Courtauld Institute of Art)

FIGURE 14 Rome, Biblioteca Apostolica Vaticana, MS Vat. gr. 746, folio 442v, Joshua leads the Israelites (photo: Conway Library, Courtauld Institute of Art)

round-topped because (according to Kosmas's argument) it resembles the shape of the universe.[65] The visual parallels between the Kosmas and Octateuch miniatures are extremely close.

A comparison of the Octateuch versions with the Kosmas miniatures in the ninth-century Vat. gr. 699 and the eleventh-century Sinai gr. 1186 and Laur. 9.28 discloses that in this image (and other Kosmas-related images) the twelfth-century Octateuchs generally resemble the Kosmas manuscripts more closely than does Vat. gr. 747, and among the Kosmas manuscripts they are closer to Vat. gr. 699. A much-studied example that bears out this pattern of relationships is an elevated view of the tabernacle, enclosing the ark, table, and candlestick.[66]

65   Ibid., 2:64–66, note to 5.36.
66   Mouriki-Charalambous, "Octateuch Miniatures," 118–26; Brubaker, "Tabernacle," 76–80; Lowden, *Octateuchs*, 88–89, figs. 123–25; Weitzmann and Bernabò, *Byzantine Octateuchs*, nos. 762–65.

FIGURE 15 Rome, Biblioteca Apostolica Vaticana, MS Vat. gr. 747, folio 218v, Priests with ark reach the Jordan (photo: Conway Library, Courtauld Institute of Art)

FIGURE 16 Rome, Biblioteca Apostolica Vaticana, MS Vat. gr. 746, folio 443r, Priests with ark reach the Jordan (photo: Conway Library, Courtauld Institute of Art)

The common model of the Octateuchs must have derived images such as the ark flanked by priests from a Kosmas manuscript. Kosmas's text was even referred to by Photios in the ninth century as a *Commentary on the Octateuch*.[67] It was perhaps known to those involved in making the lost common model of the Octateuchs because one of them had recently worked on the production of such a book—the production of Laur. 9.28 and Sinai gr. 1186 suggests a particular demand for Kosmas in the eleventh century. But because Kosmas included illustrations as an integral part of his argument, the use of a Kosmas manuscript as a source for the common model of the Octateuchs is conceivable at any date after the completion of the *Christian Topography*, say from ca. 550 onward, right up to the period of the production of Vat. gr. 747.

A different kind of possible source for the lost model of the Octateuchs is more speculative. Was the Genesis cycle of the Octateuch's model based on a lost Genesis manuscript? The evidence for this is tenuous, but not to be ignored.

67 Photios, *Bibliothèque* (n. 1 above), 1:21, ἑρμηνεία εἰς τὴν Ὀκτάτευχον.

In part it is a matter of style. The Genesis images, with their fully-painted impressionistic backgrounds—most conspicuous in Vat. gr. 747—look quite different from the images in most of the rest of the Octateuch cycle. But they are not so different from the backgrounds of some of the Vienna Genesis images discussed further below. The iconographic program of Genesis in the Octateuchs is rich but without close parallel. The subject merits further investigation.[68]

Thus far it has been possible to trace the history of the illustrated Octateuch manuscripts with confidence. We have proceeded from the known toward the unknown, but of all the material discussed only the possible use of a lost Genesis manuscript is purely speculative. Kurt Weitzmann, however, believed it was possible to go much further, as he sought to demonstrate in numerous publications over his long scholarly career. Indeed it would hardly be an exaggeration to say that the topic of Octateuch illustration still owes much of its perceived importance to his treatment of it.[69]

By a series of linked hypotheses regarding surviving manuscripts, Weitzmann attempted to trace the origins of Old Testament illustration. These he located in the pre-Christian world of hellenized Jews, roughly speaking on a geographical arc between Alexandria and Antioch. Much of his work is pure speculation, but important aspects are derived from study of the Byzantine evidence, and it is therefore important for the present discussion to establish whether his treatment of the Byzantine manuscripts was well founded or not. We begin this analysis by briefly reconsidering three of the test cases treated above.

Weitzmann's view of the Joshua Roll and its relation to the Octateuchs was entirely different from the one proposed here. He denied that the Joshua Roll had a model in rotulus form, despite the blank spaces indicating copying problems in text and images. He completely ignored the text of the Roll as an indication of what its picture frieze represented, and instead supplied an interpretation of the images based on the Octateuchs. He proposed that the scenes in the Roll were derived in the tenth century from a lost Octateuch manuscript. And ignoring the evidence for a lost common model for the Octateuchs, he argued that Vat. gr. 747 was alone in having been copied from a "pre-Joshua Roll Octateuch." None of this corresponds to the evidence. The manner in which he ignored the witness of the text of the Roll, in particular, is surprising in a scholar whose method owed so much to philology and textual criticism.[70]

68   Mentioned in passing in Lowden, *Octateuchs*, 94.
69   Summed up, with further references in Weitzmann and Bernabò, *Byzantine Octateuchs*.
70   As set forth in K. Weitzmann, *Illustrations in Roll and Codex* (Princeton, 1947, rev. ed. 1970).

Weitzmann proposed a possible relationship between the Octateuchs and the Kosmas manuscripts much like the relationship between the Octateuchs and the Joshua Roll. Where Kosmas included Octateuch-related images, these were copied, he asserted, from an Octateuch manuscript. Vat. gr. 747, he said, was the most accurate copy of this hypothetical pre-Kosmas Octateuch (or possibly Pentateuch). Since Kosmas was writing in the mid-sixth century, the pre-Kosmas Octateuch had to be of an earlier date. But as with the Joshua Roll, this proposal failed to take adequately into account the textual evidence. The priests Zacharias and Abia, for example, must have found their way into an Octateuch from a Kosmas manuscript (not vice versa), and as they are present in all the Octateuchs, including Vat. gr. 747, they were certainly present in the lost common model of the Octateuchs (whatever its date).

The third test case is the representation of the camel-like serpent. Although the serpent is not so represented in Vat. gr. 747 (the miniature is flaked and hard to decipher), Weitzmann proposed that this representation was first incorporated into a lost illustrated Octateuch at an early date, having been derived from (an illustrated copy of) the *Pirke* of Rabbi Eliezer (a collection of aphorisms of the ninth or tenth century), or rather from the much earlier sources on which the *Pirke* drew.[71] Bernabò, with his greater knowledge of rabbinic and pseudepigraphic material, cited as a source for the non-biblical quadruped the (Hebrew) Genesis Rabbah, of circa 400, and for other extrabiblical elements a text close to the Syriac *Cave of Treasures* (of the sixth century), or rather the latter's midrashic sources.[72] The improbability of these hypotheses should be mentioned. No early illustrated examples of such texts have been found. Nor is it likely that Christian artists and patrons would have been familiar with such hypothetical manuscripts. The extrabiblical detail of the camel-like serpent in the twelfth-century Octateuchs is more plausibly explained by the twelfth-century chronicle evidence discussed above.

Why, it must be asked, did Weitzmann overlook crucial evidence for the Octateuch manuscripts in building his hypotheses? He defined the purpose of his study as "to find the iconographically purest version of the archetype."[73] This search inevitably led him into the first Christian centuries, for he argued

---

71 K. Weitzmann, "The Illustration of the Septuagint," reprinted in his *Studies in Classical and Byzantine Manuscript Illumination*, ed. H. L. Kessler (Chicago, 1971), 48 (originally published as "Die Illustration der Septuaginta," *Münchner Jahrbuch der bildenden Kunst*, 3–4 [1952–53]: 74 n. 59).
72 Weitzmann and Bernabò, *Byzantine Octateuchs*, 33–34, 317–18.
73 *Roll and Codex*, 183.

that biblical imagery was devised in the early period and that later (Byzantine or medieval) images or cycles were merely excerpts from lost early models. In his own words: "Biblical picture cycles of astounding wealth form the point of departure, and these, in turn, were excerpted and shortened during the Middle Ages."[74] The fifth- or sixth-century Cotton Genesis manuscript, with some 360 images in Genesis alone, was a crucial witness to this theory, and even it was said to have been based on still earlier, lost models.[75]

A further essential foundation to his analyses was his simplistic proposal that narrative images were invented to illustrate books (or scrolls), and then copied, often piecemeal, for use in other contexts. In his own words again: "Book illustration was the storehouse of iconography. Artists in all fields consulted and copied illustrated manuscripts … it is scarcely an exaggeration to assert that, in the last analysis, each 'narrative' cycle may be traced to an illustrated book."[76] The partial copying of the Cotton Genesis in the thirteenth-century mosaics of San Marco at Venice provided an example.[77] But surprisingly he did not cite the evidence of the Joshua ivories and their dependence on the Joshua Roll.

Taken together, these theories enabled Weitzmann to argue that any biblical image, whatever its context or medium, demonstrated the existence of an illuminated manuscript as source, and even a single such image pointed to the existence of a profuse cycle. From this it followed that an image from the Octateuch (or Pentateuch) in the synagogue at Dura in the mid-third century, for example, demonstrated (to him) the existence of a profusely illustrated Octateuch (or Pentateuch) manuscript in a Jewish context in the pre-Constantinian era. This was a very long way, in all senses, from the lost common model of the Octateuchs, the earliest form in which we can be truly confident that the Octateuch cycle, as known from surviving manuscripts, was in existence.

Weitzmann's arguments are as irrefutable as they are unprovable. The question remains, however, whether they are useful and plausible. To test this we can take a single example, much cited by Weitzmann. In the late 1930s, a relief

---

74 "Septuagint," 96–120.
75 K. Weitzmann and H. Kessler, *The Cotton Genesis: British Library Codex Cotton Otho B.VI* (Princeton, 1986), 42–43.
76 "Septuagint," 49. See also p. 48: "When analyzing a monumental picture cycle of narrative character … in most cases one is dealing with an epitome of an extensive miniature cycle. This holds true … also for the countless other forms of art which depend iconographically on miniature cycles."
77 K. Weitzmann, "The Genesis Mosaics of San Marco and the Cotton Genesis Miniatures," in Otto Demus, *The Mosaics of San Marco* (Chicago, 1984), 2:105–42, 253–57.

sculpture was discovered in excavations of the fifth- and sixth-century martyrion at Seleucia Pieria, near Antioch (the sculpture is now at Princeton).[78] The scene was identified by Weitzmann as Joseph in prison with Pharaoh's butler and baker (Fig. 17). This image has a visual parallel in the sixth-century Vienna Genesis (Fig. 18), but Weitzmann observed what he considered a closer parallel in the eleventh- and twelfth-century Octateuchs (Fig. 19). He emphasized, for example, "the cellar-like construction of the prison in each case."[79] Setting aside the evidence of the Vienna Genesis, he then concluded that the entire Octateuch cycle must have been in existence and available for consultation by the sculptor in Antioch in the sixth century.

On looking again at the comparison, however, it would seem that it is the Vienna Genesis and the Octateuchs that exemplify the closer parallel. In them, observe how Joseph is seated centrally between the two prisoners, the butler to the left lifting his arms in entreaty. The Antioch relief, on the other hand, shows four rather than three figures inside the prison. Any analysis must take account of these differences alongside the similarities. And when we note that the best evidence from Antioch is for the presence of one image among approximately 374 (accepting momentarily the validity of the comparison for the sake of argument), the weight that should be given to the 373 Octateuch images *not* found at Antioch seems to me overwhelming. A theory that is based on very limited similarity but that ignores widespread difference is hardly convincing. We can surely learn more about art in sixth-century Antioch from the sixth-century material (sculpture and Vienna Genesis in this case) than from middle Byzantine Octateuchs.

Weitzmann's theorizing about Octateuch illustration is so wide ranging as to appear nearly all-inclusive. Of special interest, then, is a composition on the so-called Adam and Eve ivory and bone caskets (Fig. 20),[80] which seems to stand outside his paradigms. Most of the scenes decorating these caskets can be readily paralleled in one or more of the many works having iconography of the Creation and Fall. But one scene, found in five examples, is otherwise unparalleled.

---

78   K. Weitzmann, "The Iconography of the Reliefs from the Martyrion," in *Antioch-on-the-Orontes*, vol. 3, *The Excavations 1937–1939*, ed. R. Stillwell (Princeton, 1941), 138–39 and pl. 20.
79   "Septuagint," 54.
80   Goldschmidt and Weitzmann, *Elfenbeinskulpturen* (n. 60 above), nos. 67e (Cleveland Museum of Art), 68d (St. Petersburg, Ermitage), 69e (Darmstadt, Landesmuseum), 76–77 (Milan, Museo delle arti decorative, Castello Sforzesco), 93 (New York, Metropolitan Museum); and discussion on pp. 48–49, 51, 54–55. These ivories were not discussed in Weitzmann and Bernabò, *Byzantine Octateuchs*.

FIGURE 17 Princeton, University Art Museum, c515-S630, stone sculpture from Antioch, Joseph in prison (photo: Princeton University Art Museum)

It shows Eve operating a pair of large bellows at a forge while Adam works as a smith, hammering a piece of metal that he holds in a pair of stout tongs. Because it is undoubtedly part of a narrative, but no trace of a written source for it has thus far come to light, it does not fit a Weitzmann paradigm. This exception has been largely overlooked, and not just by Weitzmann.[81] I suggest that we should consider the image to be part of a *visual* narrative, and a valuable witness to Byzantine representations of craftsmanship in the tenth century. Note how naturalistic are the bellows and tools. Observe how Eve has her head covered and her hair braided, her tunic belted, and kneels on the ground in a characteristic fashion. With or without a textual source, the scene of Adam and Eve at the forge merits further study.

Weitzmann's discussion of Octateuch illustration spread outward from the somewhat limited—but still vast—field of the illustrated Byzantine Octateuch manuscripts. To apply one of his own analogies from a different context, the pattern he perceived was like the ever-expanding ripples from a stone cast into a pond.[82] Chronologically and geographically, and in medium and context,

---

81 A notable exception is the article by H. Maguire, "Magic and Money in the Early Middle Ages," *Speculum* 72 (1997): 1037–54.

82 K. Weitzmann, "The Study of Byzantine Book Illumination, Past, Present, and Future," in K. Weitzmann et al., *The Place of Book Illumination in Byzantine Art* (Princeton, 1975), 1–60 at pp. 9ff.

FIGURE 18 Vienna, Österreichische Nationalbibliothek, cod. Theol. Gr. 31, f. 17 (pict. 33), Vienna Genesis, Joseph in prison (photo: Vienna, Bildarchiv ÖNB)

FIGURE 19   Istanbul, Topkapı Sarayı, MS gr. 8, folio 128r, Joseph in prison
(photo: author)

FIGURE 20 New York, The Metropolitan Museum of Art, 17.190.139, Adam and Eve at the forge (photo: New York, The Metropolitan Museum of Art)

Weitzmann widened analysis to include images that had some narrative basis in the Octateuch throughout Western art, from the beginnings of biblical illustration to the Renaissance. Yet the true situation of the Byzantine Octateuchs, as far as we can understand it today, was very different from how Weitzmann portrayed it. Octateuch illustration was not a Europe-wide, millennium-long phenomenon. There are no comparable illustrated Octateuch manuscripts in the Latin West (see below), or indeed in any other linguistic context. Had profusely illustrated Octateuchs been produced already in late antiquity, say in the sixth century, we might reasonably expect to find some trace of them at a later date (setting aside the circular argument of basing such a theory on the eleventh-century and later manuscripts). Rather, though, than "migrating" from an original source in some single archetypal Octateuch manuscript into other contexts, the iconographic riches of the Octateuchs resulted from a middle-Byzantine–era gathering of ideas and images from numerous earlier contexts, and a combining of these earlier elements with contemporary visual formulas. Yet if the Octateuchs are not important in the way that Weitzmann claimed,[83] it certainly does

---

83 Every scholar would wish to agree with at least one of Weitzmann's hypotheses: "The study of the Octateuchs will permit the establishment of general principles with regard to the process

not follow that they are unimportant. On the contrary, they are among the most ambitious achievements of Byzantine illumination.

In twentieth-century art-historical writing, the Byzantine Octateuchs were on occasion treated as though they had much in common with another family of even more profusely illustrated biblical manuscripts: the Bibles moralisées.[84] Both types of book were regarded, perhaps inevitably, primarily as invaluable repositories of iconographic exempla, but this meant that individual images were analyzed out of context, as visual comparanda, or sometimes as sources of possible "influence."[85] Comparison of the Octateuchs and Bibles moralisées can still be useful in my view, nonetheless, but this is because of the remarkable extent of their *dis*similarities. The resulting contrast is a useful reminder of some of the many differences between Byzantine and medieval Western phenomena. And in particular, comparison helps to draw attention to the limits of the Byzantine evidence and the silence of the Byzantine sources on many topics.

The first four surviving Bibles moralisées were all made in Paris circa 1220–35 (compare the three Komnenian Octateuchs made circa 1125–1155).[86] Whereas the Octateuchs contain the full biblical text, the Bibles moralisées contain only short biblical excerpts, and these are often paraphrases rather than quotations; in some cases they are in the vernacular. The linguistic situation in middle and late Byzantium was entirely different from that in medieval France.

The Octateuchs contain a very extensive marginal commentary, which does not appear to have influenced the content of any of the images. By contrast, the Bibles moralisées have only short passages of commentary (in the form of moralizations) but these are given status equal to that of the biblical passages, and both are accompanied by images. In other words, fully half the visual as well

---

of copying miniatures." See "The Octateuch of the Seraglio and the History of its Picture Recension," *Actes du Xe Congrès d'études byzantines* (Istanbul, 1957), 183.

84   For example, J. Zalten, *Creatio Mundi* (Stuttgart, 1979), 79–80. H. Minkowski, *Vermutungen über den Turm zu Babel* (Freren, 1991), 122–23, figs. 5, 11; 141, figs. 82–83. More recently, see M.-D. Gauthier-Walter, *L'histoire de Joseph* (Bern, 2003), 70–73, 322–27.

85   There is a possibility of direct contact: early in the Palaiologan period a frontispiece image of the Creator was added to the Smyrna Octateuch, an image seemingly derived from a Bible moralisée resembling Vienna, ÖNB cod. 1179. Lowden, *Octateuchs*, 18–20, figs. 12–13. On the problematic notion of "influence," see J. Lowden and A. Bovey, *Under the Influence* (Turnhout, 2008).

86   For what follows, see first J. Lowden, *The Making of the Bibles moralisées*, 2 vols. (University Park, PA, 2000).

textual content of the Bibles moralisées is based on the commentary. Whereas the catena in the illustrated Octateuchs was a scholarly text, the moralizations in the Bibles moralisées rarely show exegetical sophistication.

The Bibles moralisées were books for royalty, as the Octateuchs may also have been, but, unlike the Octateuchs, they made this fact clear by using images as a type of visual colophon. The Queen of France, Blanche of Castile, rather than a male (e.g., Isaak Komnenos), seems to have played a crucial role in commissioning the four early Bibles moralisées. Notably, the makers of the books were represented in the colophon images as equal in stature to the royal patrons (Louis VIII, Blanche of Castile, Louis IX), a prominence hard to parallel in any Byzantine context.

Especially in such basic matters as the transcription of the text and the provision of images, later Octateuchs were generally very close to their predecessors. The situation with the Bibles moralisées was totally different: each new manuscript was an attempt to surpass its predecessor(s), textually and visually, in a conspicuous manner. Not until the late thirteenth century do we find the first Bible moralisée that is indubitably a close copy of a specific model, and this manuscript was made (or later functioned) as a workshop model, not as a luxury book. However, both the Bibles moralisées and the Octateuchs, with the exception of Vatopedi 602, did reproduce the notably large dimensions of their relatives.

Whereas in the Octateuchs the layout of every page was different, in the Bibles moralisées, with the exception of frontispiece and colophon, the layout of every page was identical.

The Bibles moralisées were picture books, in which the act of consumption by the royal viewer was probably mediated through the explanatory comments of a favored household cleric. The Octateuchs were probably studied in private. Even the motive for including images in them is uncertain: doubtless the miniatures were more than simply a visual reward to the reader, but further understanding of this crucial topic requires further study.

In the Bibles moralisées the images played a vital role. Indeed, in the earliest such book the texts often read like explanatory captions of the images. In addition, the images were executed before the texts were inserted. In the Octateuchs the images were inserted after the text, and they are in all senses secondary. Whereas at least one of the Octateuchs was left with its miniature cycle unfinished (Topkapı), all four of the early Bibles moralisées were completed.

Where a mistake occurred in the text/image relationship in the Octateuchs, if it was noticed the image was erased (Vatopedi 602). But in a comparable situation in the Bibles moralisées, the images were retained and the text was erased.[87] Where a mistake in an image in a Bible moralisée was observed, it might be noted in the margin, with instructions to the artist as to how it was to be corrected.[88] In the Octateuchs no such notes can be found, nor have they been found in any other Byzantine manuscript.

The production of the first illustrated Octateuch manuscript (now lost) and—to a lesser but still significant degree—the production of subsequent exemplars (to judge by what survives) is evidence that the Octateuch had an unusual role to play in Byzantium. How and why should the volume containing the first eight books of the Old Testament have achieved this status, so different from its position in the medieval West? The starting point for finding answers to this basic but previously unasked question needs to be the Byzantine world in the tenth to thirteenth centuries.

Courtauld Institute of Art, University of London

87 Lowden, *Bibles moralisées*, 1:122–23.
88 Ibid., 1:158–65.

SIX

Old Testament "History" and the Byzantine Chronicle

ELIZABETH JEFFREYS

As the other chapters in this volume indicate, the Old Testament performed many roles and functions in the Byzantine world. In this, Byzantium is no different from any of the other groups that claim a special interest in the collection of texts that make up the Old Testament, be they Christian, Jewish, or Muslim. The purpose of this chapter is to explore the use made of the Old Testament by the Byzantine chronicle, a long-standing type of text that related a Christianized world history from creation to the time of each example's composition or compilation; these texts took over much Old Testament material in a form of historical appropriation. The relationship of Byzantine chronicles to their sources, often complex, in the case of the Old Testament, is certainly not direct, nor confined to a small range of dimensions. Because our sources themselves are often fragmentary or confused, and have survived haphazardly, research into the process of appropriation is difficult; there is usually no way to ascertain whether each played a primary or a secondary role in the appropriation. It seems most helpful

---

This paper is substantially as delivered at the Symposium and as such makes its arguments in a broad-brush manner that still reflects the original oral presentation. At a very late stage in its preparation, the author became aware of an excellent discussion by Mary Whitby on the biblical past as presented in Malalas's chronicle and the *Chronicon Paschale*; her work covers some of the points dealt with here but has a wider conclusion and focuses more on the later chronicle: M. Whitby, "The Biblical Past in John Malalas and the Paschal Chronicle," in *From Rome to Constantinople: Studies in Honour of Averil Cameron*, ed. H. Amirav and R. B. ter Haar Romeny (Leuven, 2007), 279–301. Other useful recent studies are K. Berthelot, "La chronique de Malalas et les traditions juives," in J. Beaucamp et al., eds., *Recherches sur la chronique de Jean Malalas I* (Paris, 2004), 37–52 and J. Beaucamp, "Le passé biblique et l'histoire juive: La version de Jean Malalas," in *Recherches sur la chronique de Jean Malalas II*, ed. S. Agusta-Boularot et al. (Paris, 2006), 19–34.

to work through the evidence systematically, providing bibliographical help at each stage for those whose interest might be aroused. Two brief biblical stories and their reflection in the chronicles are employed as concrete illustrations.

For Byzantium, the Old Testament is represented by what is referred to today as the Septuagint. The scholarly world has long been aware that this collection of Greek translations from the Hebrew of the Jewish Bible was made at various times and in various places, despite legendary ascription to intervention in the second century BCE by Ptolemy II Philadelphos, who supposedly ordered a translation of the Pentateuch to be made for the Jewish inhabitants of Alexandria.[1] However, neither Jews nor early Christians recognized a stable canon of scriptural books. It took time for the early Church to develop such a canon, for the New as well as for the Old Testament, as is revealed by the variations in the lists recorded from the third and fourth centuries (ascribed to, for example, Melito of Sardis, Origen, Athanasios, Cyril of Jerusalem, Epiphanios of Salamis, or Gregory of Nazianzos), or the contents of fourth- and fifth-century biblical manuscripts (such as the Codex Alexandrinus, the Codex Sinaiticus, or the Codex Vaticanus).[2] Quite apart from the issues of texts classified as pseudepigrapha and apocrypha, to this day the Roman Catholic, Protestant, and Orthodox Churches accord different status to a number of books within the Old Testament canon, most notably Judith and the several books of Maccabees.[3]

The Byzantine Christian tradition had many reasons for giving attention to the Old Testament. The primary, of course, was theological. The books that make up the Old Testament are interpreted as the gradual revelation of God's purpose for mankind, and as a statement of the Old Covenant that was

---

1 As recounted in the well-known *Letter of Aristeas*, produced at an unascertainable date between the second century BCE and the first CE, arguably as a piece of propaganda to glorify the Jewish people and Jewish law; see, for example, A. C. Sundberg, "The Septuagint: The Bible of Hellenistic Judaism," in *The Canon Debate*, ed. L. M. McDonald and J. A. Samson (Peabody, MA, 2002), 68–91. See also the discussion and bibliography above in Chapter 5, p. 111.

2 Melito of Sardis: in Eusebios, *Hist. eccl.* 4.26.14; Origen: in Eusebios, *Hist. eccl.* 6.25.1; Athanasios of Alexandria, *Ep. fest.* 39.4; Cyril of Jerusalem: *Catech.* 4.35; Epiphanius of Salamis: *Haer.* 1.1.8 and *Mens.* 4 and 23; Gregory of Nazianzos, *Iambi ad Seleucum* 2.51–88. For the contents of the fourth- and fifth-century uncial codices, see the tabulation in McDonald and Samson, *Canon Debate*, 588–89. This "instability" in the canon of accepted texts reflects a similar instability in Jewish practice, to which Josephus, *Contra Ap.* 1.38–42, is but one witness.

3 Of the copious literature on this topic, for useful recent surveys with good bibliographies see L. M. McDonald, *The Formation of the Christian Biblical Canon*, rev. ed. (Peabody, MA, 1995) and N. Fernández Marcos, trans. W. G. E. Watson, *The Septuagint in Context* (Leiden, 2000). On critical editions of the Septuagint see above, Chapter 3, pp. 60–61.

made repeatedly: to Noah (never again would mankind be subject to universal destruction: Gen. 9:11), to Abraham (that he would be the progenitor of God's chosen people: Gen. 15:18, 17:7), to Jacob (that God would watch over his people: Gen. 28:15), to Moses (the vehicle of God's commandments and wise leader of the chosen people: Exod. 19:5, 24:8). This Old Covenant, made with God's chosen people alone, had been superseded by the New Covenant, founded upon Christ's incarnation and redemptive acts, a covenant that was made with all peoples.[4] Thus the Old Testament with all its component parts is to be viewed as the precursor of the New Testament. Figures and episodes from the Old Testament prophesy, foreshadow, and validate figures and events from the New.[5] This process is an integral part of the Christian mindset and can be observed from very early on in the Christian tradition. Indeed it is present in the Gospels: the fulfillment of prophecies, for example, is conspicuous in Matthew (for example, Matt. 1:22–23, 2:5–6, 17–18) and underpins the Epistle to the Hebrews.[6] Typological referencing occurs throughout the Byzantine period and the Byzantine world. It is used both verbally and visually. It is responsible for much elaboration and allusiveness in hymnography and homilies as well as for the choice of motifs in church decoration; for instance, images of Abraham entertaining the three angels (Gen. 18:1–18) or being welcomed by Melchisedek (Gen. 14:18–20) are displayed in and around apses and sanctuaries because they can be read as Eucharistic prefigurations.[7]

But the Old Testament also has a role as "history" in a rather less theological sense. It narrates events involving the Jewish peoples, starting with their origins in remote myth and legend—at the dawn of time and the creation of mankind—and gradually becoming more historical. That is, from today's perspective, the kingdoms, especially that of Judah, can be observed meshing with other independently attested events in Near Eastern history involving the rulers of Babylon, Assyria, and Persia; these include historical figures such as Tiglath-Pileser

---

[4] The concept of the Covenant is based on many texts; Jeremiah 31:31–34 is the key Old Testament passage while such references are also frequent in the New Testament, as in Luke 22:20, 1 Corinthians 11:25, 2 Corinthians 3:6, and Hebrews 8:8, 9:15.

[5] This is a condensed and clumsy formulation of a complex topic; see, e.g., H. de Lubac, *Medieval Exegesis*, trans. M. Sebanc (Edinburgh, 1998), 1:225–67: "The Two Testaments."

[6] Hebrews possibly owes something to Philo's allegorizing treatment of Jewish Scriptures, which is most notable in his *Legum allegoriae*, and which is a form of typology; see H. W. Attridge, *The Epistle to the Hebrews* (Philadelphia, 1989), 28–29.

[7] Most notably at San Vitale in Ravenna. For a discussion of the symbolic importance of such decoration, see S. Gerstel, *Beholding the Sacred Mysteries: Programs of the Byzantine Sanctuary* (Seattle, 1999).

III (745–727 BCE), as well as Nebuchadnezzar, Cyrus, and Darius.[8] Nevertheless running through the narrative is the thread of an argument explicating the divine purpose for God's Chosen People, a parallel to, and justification for, the typological foreshadowings taken up in Christian usages. This narrative thread is set out in an evolving set of books (eventually categorized as Law, Prophets, and Writings) which, despite the weight of claimed Mosaic authority and the hovering hand of God, were clearly composed over several centuries and in many environments by writers with a range of agendas.[9] The strain of prophetic history finally slips into the unequivocally secular with the Books of Maccabees; Josephus (37–100 CE) in books twelve and thirteen of his *Jewish Antiquities* paraphrases much of 1 Maccabees as straight historical narrative.

Not to be overlooked are the many various apocryphal and pseudepigraphical texts, alluded to earlier, whose role in Byzantium's religious and literary culture deserves fuller exploration. Although these terms are often used interchangeably, a practical distinction limits "apocrypha" (literally, "hidden things") to those non-canonical books, such as Tobit or Ecclesiasticus (also known as Sirach), included in, for example, the King James Version of the Bible but regarded as non-canonical by the Protestant churches,[10] while the term "pseudepigrapha" (literally, "false writings," "falsely ascribed writings") is applied to "parabiblical" texts, such as *Joseph and Aseneth*, which are not used liturgically in any church.[11] The pseudepigraphical book (generally so-called) that most affected the Byzantine chronographic tradition is the *Book of Jubilees* or *Little Genesis*, written perhaps around 150 BCE; it is largely lost in Greek, though it survives fully in Ethiopic, and many Hebrew fragments were found among the Qumran scrolls.[12] This is a purposeful reworking of the account of the patriarchs in

---

8 For the type of interlocking evidence that emerges from the archaeology of the Middle East, see, e.g., H. Tadmor, *The Inscriptions of Tiglath-Pileser III, King of Assyria* (Jerusalem, 1994). The analysis of the archaeological evidence is a vast and well-charted field, which is well reported in serious commentaries such as the Anchor Bible (1964–); see also A. Mazar and E. Stern, *Archaeology of the Land of the Bible*, 2 vols. (New York, 1990, 2001).
9 For an appreciation of the main issues, see the works cited in notes 1 and 3 above.
10 The term "apocrypha" was first applied by Jerome to the works found in the Septuagint but not in the Hebrew version of the Old Testament. The status of the books classed as apocryphal varies between the Churches. Orthodox Bibles use the term "anaginoskomena" ("read," "permitted to be read"). See above, Chapter 3, p. 73.
11 Again, the situation is complex, and, for example, the *Book of Jubilees* is part of the Bible in the Ethiopian Church.
12 For the full Ethiopic text, with English translation and discussion of the textual transmission, see J. C. VanderKam, *The Book of Jubilees*, 2 vols., CSCO, Ser. Aethiop. 87–88 (Leuven,

Genesis and the beginning of Exodus, onto which has been layered a chronology of days, weeks, months, and years in cycles of seven, which culminate in the Jubilee after every forty-ninth year, and the Great Jubilee in the fiftieth Jubilee period.[13] Another relevant pseudepigraphon is the *Book of Iannes and Iambres*, likewise from the late second century BCE, from Egypt; substantial papyrus fragments have now been identified and, relatively recently, published.[14] *Iannes and Iambres* deals quite elaborately with the activities of two magicians, a tale whose resonances arguably reach as far as the fanciful career of Simon Magus (who clashed with St. Peter during the reign of Nero), and even further into the European literary tradition, to the Faust legend.[15]

Thus, in broad terms, the Old Testament had an ambiguous role as both a factual and, as it were, a transcendent text in the Jewish environment, which provided the initial incentive for these books' construction, and also in the later Christian and Byzantine one.

The Christian World Chronicle

This ambiguity—the blurring of secular history and sacred history—is apparent in many aspects of the Christianized environment of Byzantium. It is especially apparent in the Christian world chronicle, a series of texts that have been frequently categorized as quintessentially Byzantine. Here the Old Testament narratives, but more particularly the genealogies, provided the spine for calculations

---

1989). R. H. Charles, ed., *The Apocrypha and Pseudepigrapha of the Old Testament* (London, 1913) remains a useful resource; see also J. H. Charlesworth, *The Old Testament Pseudepigrapha*, 2 vols. (London, 1983–85).

13 Leviticus 25 decrees that in a Jubilee year Israelite slaves are to be freed and alienated land is to be restored to its Israelite owner; in the Great Jubilee period the entire Israelite people were released from bondage in Egypt and entered their land that had been taken by Canaan (J. C. VanderKam, *The Book of Jubilees* [Sheffield, 2001], 96). This combination of chronological symbolism and precision would have appealed to Byzantine chronographers such as Synkellos, who seems to have known *Jubilees* in a version interpolated into Josephus's *Jewish Antiquities* (W. Adler and P. Tuffin, *The Chronography of George Synkellos* [Oxford, 2002], liii). *Jubilees* also informed the ninth-century (?) *Palaia*; though few independent manuscripts of the *Palaia* survive in Greek (there is a widely circulating Slavic translation), this emerges in late medieval vernacular Greek texts such as the *Kosmogenesis* of Georgios Choumnos (ed. G. A. Megas [Athens, 1975]).
14 A. Pietersma, *The Apocryphon of Jannes and Jambres the Magicians* (Leiden, 1994).
15 Ibid., 24–36, 67–70; Iannes and Iambres appear in the *Palaia* (A. Vassiliev, ed., *Anecdota graeco-byzantina pars prior* [Moscow, 1893], 188–292, at 231). Apart from his appearance in Acts 8:9–24, Simon Magus is prominent in the apocryphal Acts of Peter, which lie behind the clash between Simon and the Apostle Peter in Malalas's chronicle (10.32–33 [190–92]).

of the lapse of years since creation, or from Adam, thus providing what became the basic Byzantine dating structure, also known as annus mundi, onto which were added notices of events not derived from the biblical narratives; the anno Domini dating system, from the year of Christ's birth, invented unobtrusively in the sixth century, was never widely used in the East.[16]

The story of the development of the Byzantine world chronicle has been told more than once. Gelzer's exhaustive study of 1885 is still in most respects the unchallenged statement of the fundamental chronological structures, though recent studies have placed Gelzer's conclusions in a framework that is more helpful to today's readers.[17] Key stages in the world chronicle's development are the chronicle of Sextus Julius Africanus (fl. ca. 220 CE), of which only fragments remain, but whose calculations were regularly referred to; the work of Eusebios, most notably his chronicle (ca. 280 CE), although most of its tables are lost in Greek and must be reconstructed from Jerome's amplified Latin translation of ca. 380 and the much later Armenian translation. The sequence then continues—there are major world chronicles, or texts that can reasonably be put under that heading, from virtually every century throughout the Byzantine period: Malalas (ca. 530–65), the *Chronicon Paschale* (ca. 640), George Synkellos (d. ca., 810) and his continuator Theophanes the Confessor (d. ca. 817), George the Monk (ca. 850), the wide-ranging chronicle that goes under the name pseudo-Symeon (most of which is still unpublished; late 10th century), the slightly mysterious Kedrenos (late 11th century), the verbally elegant Manasses (ca. 1144), Zonaras (mid-12th century), and the chronicle attributed to Skoutariotes (mid-13th century);[18] this list passes over those texts that have survived in part only,

---

16 V. Grumel, *La Chronologie* (Paris, 1958), 224; see also "Chronology," in *OHBS*: it should be remembered that competing calculations for the annum mundi coexisted for much of the Byzantine period.

17 H. Gelzer, *Sextus Julius Africanus und die byzantinische Chronographie*, 2 vols. (Leipzig, 1885); recent work includes A. A. Mosshammer, *The Chronicle of Eusebius and Greek Chronographic Tradition* (Lewisburg, 1979); W. Adler, *Time Immemorial: Archaic History and Its Sources in Christian Chronography from Julius Africanus to George Syncellus* (Washington, DC, 1989); B. Croke, "The Origins of the Christian World Chronicle," in *History and Historians in Late Antiquity*, ed. B. Croke and A. Emmett (Sydney, 1983), 116–31; A. Karpozilos, Βυζαντινοί Ιστορικοί και Χρονογράφοι (Athens, 1997–2002). There is useful material in G. Marasco, ed., *Greek and Roman Historiography in Late Antiquity, Fourth to Sixth Century, A.D.* (Leiden, 2003) and D. Rohrbacher, *The Historians of Late Antiquity* (London, 2002).

18 Discussions of these texts and lists of editions to 1977 can be found in H. Hunger, *Die hochsprachliche profane Literatur der Byzantiner* (Munich, 1978), 1:243–504; for more recent editions and (English) translations, see *OHBS*, "Historiography."

like the late sixth- or early seventh-century John of Antioch,[19] or those whose existence, like that of the *Epitome* of Traianos (early 8th century), must be surmised from their ghostly presence in later writers.[20] There are other writers for whom we have only names and just enough of a hint at the contents of their work to give license for speculation about what they might have written; prime examples are Eustathios of Epiphaneia (early sixth century), much respected by Evagrios later in the century,[21] and Hesychios Illoustrios (mid-sixth century), though perhaps his chronological fragments never formed a complete text.[22]

What these chronicles have in common is the system instigated by Africanus—the meshing together of ruler lists from the Hellenic and Roman chronographic traditions with a chronology derived from the Old Testament genealogical lists; in this way a time scheme was formed that took mankind's history back to creation.[23] Much material, containing elements both of dating systems and of narrative, was taken over by one author from another, at times with debate and correction (Synkellos was especially prone to chide his predecessors),[24] more usually without acknowledgment (as seems to have been the case with John of Antioch, and is most conspicuously true of Malalas).[25] To

---

19 The problems over the date and content of the history associated with the name John of Antioch are set out in two recent editions: U. Roberto, *Ioannis Antiocheni: Fragmenta ex Historia chronica* (Berlin, 2005), and S. Mariev, *Ioannis Antiocheni Fragmenta quae supersunt omnia* (Berlin, 2008); see also P. Sotiroudis, *Untersuchungen zum Geschichtswerk der Johannes von Antiocheia* (Thessalonike, 1989). W. Treadgold has recently attempted to solve the Gordian knot of the relationship between Malalas and John of Antioch by attributing their overlapping material to use of a common source, Eustathios of Epiphaneia, in the process labeling Malalas a fraudulent plagiarist (*The Early Byzantine Historians* [Basingstoke, 2007], 311–29, and in more detail, "The Byzantine World Histories of John Malalas and Eustathius of Epiphaneia," *The International History Review* 29 [2007]: 709–44); the case is, however, overstated—see, for example, the review by Darius Brodka, in Clio-online, 20 August 2007, http://hsozkult.geschichte.hu-berlin.de/rezensionen/2007-3-130.pdf (accessed 4 December 2007).
20 On Traianos, see Hunger, *Literatur*, 1:337, and C. Mango and R. Scott, *The Chronicle of Theophanes Confessor* (Oxford, 1997), lxxxviii–xc.
21 E.g., Evagrios, *Eccl. hist.* 3.27–30, with a comment on his elegant style; cf. P. Allen, *Evagrius Scholasticus, the Church Historian* (Leuven, 1981), 120–21, 138–40, 238–40.
22 See Photios, *Biblioteca*, cod. 69 and T. Preger, ed., *Scriptores Originum Constantinopolitarum* (Leipzig, 1901), 1:1–18.
23 This is laid out in detail in the first part of Gelzer, *Sextus Julius Africanus* (n. 17 above).
24 E.g., he reproaches Eusebios for faulty chronological reasoning (*Ecloga* 197.18–198.9, ed. Mosshammer) and for combining Eusebios, Africanus, and Panodoros (*Ecloga* 391.1–397.10, ed. Mosshammer); Synkellos names many of his sources: Adler and Tuffin, *Chronography of Synkellos* (n. 13 above), lx–lxix.
25 The relationship of Malalas's text to that of the sources named and apparently quoted has caused much debate: most cannot have been consulted directly. For a survey see E. Jeffreys,

call this plagiarism is anachronistic: it is part of a mindset that is different from that of today.

However, we should be aware that the reworking or re-edition of a world chronicle in each generation, to speak in general terms, does not imply that each new version was a simple extension of the earlier. Arguably each writer who put together a world chronicle had an agenda, visible in programmatic statements and in small changes to a predecessor's work. There was the universal purpose, common to all, to show the temporal working out of man's salvation and the divine plan, but there were also individual agendas. Africanus was concerned to demonstrate that Christ's birth took place in the year 5500.[26] Eusebios was concerned more straightforwardly with the management of time sequences, to show that Christ's lifetime could be fixed in secular time within the chronologies of the Roman Empire and to demonstrate the relationship between biblical and Greco-Roman antiquity.[27] Malalas argued that the sixth millennium had come and gone.[28] The anonymous author of the *Chronicon Paschale* was preoccupied with constructing tables for the date of Easter,[29] George the Monk, by the wish to write an ideologically acceptable account of world history in the post-Iconoclast world;[30] George Synkellos's careful calculations are designed to show that every major event of Christ's life was paralleled by events in the week of creation.[31] Thereafter the need to be compendious seems to have overcome particular agendas—the tenth-century pseudo-Symeon is a good example of encyclopaedism.[32] Perhaps John of Antioch is an early case of the wish to be all

---

"Malalas' Sources," in *Studies in John Malalas*, ed. E. Jeffreys, B. Croke, and R. Scott (Melbourne, 1990), 167–216; for a polemical judgment, see Treadgold, "Byzantine World Histories." In late-antique historical writing it is more common not to identify a source than to name it. In Malalas's case, of course, the problem is compounded by detectable distortions

26   As quoted in Synkellos's *Ecloga* 395.19–20 (ed. Mosshammer); cf. Gelzer, *Sextus Julius Africanus*, 1:47.

27   Mosshammer, *Chronicle of Eusebius*, 31–37. See also R. W. Burgess, *Studies in Eusebian and Post-Eusebian Chronography* (Stuttgart, 1999), 67–74.

28   *Chronographia* 10.2 and 18.8 (ed. Thurn); see the discussion in E. Jeffreys, "Chronological Structures in the Chronicle," in *Studies in Malalas*, at 119–20. Malalas was not alone in his millennial preoccupations, which were shared by, amongst others, the patriarch Severus of Antioch (P. Beatrice, *Anonymi Monophysitae Theosophia* [Leiden, 2001], xlviii), though Malalas's particular version does not seem to have been widespread.

29   *Chronicon Paschale* 3–31 (ed. Dindorf); cf. J. Beaucamp and others, "Temps et Histoire I: Le prologue de la Chronique Paschale," *TM* 7 (1979): 229–301; M. Whitby, "Biblical Past" (unnum. n. above), 293.

30   *Chronicon* 2.16–5.3 (ed. de Boor and Wirth).

31   *Ecloga* 1.15–28, 388.22–390.31 (at A.M. 5533) (ed. Mosshammer).

32   A. Markopoulos, *Η χρονογραφία του Ψευδο-Συμεών και οι πηγές της* (Ioannina, 1978) remains the most helpful study of the broad range of this text.

inclusive, for the filleted remains that survive of his chronicle suggest that his discourse was that of a full narrative history.[33]

Malalas and the Old Testament

The impetus for this chapter comes from the chronicle of Malalas, from two passages that perhaps typify how the Old Testament is used in the Byzantine Christian world chronicle. Malalas's text is an appropriate subject if only because—despite all its textual problems—it is the earliest extant world chronicle to be transmitted virtually complete.[34] The first passage concerns the naming of the two magicians who oppose Moses at Pharaoh's court (Malalas, *Chronographia* 3.13) and is based on Exodus 7–15. The second recounts the Assyrian Sennacherib's foiled attack on Jerusalem in the fourteenth year of the reign of King Hezekiah of Judah (5.40–42),[35] which is narrated through an extensive and almost verbatim quotation from Isaiah 36:22–37:21, which also appears in 2 Kings (4 Kingdoms LXX) 18:37–19:20, 32–37.

To put these passages in context, it is first necessary to outline what Malalas might be said to have taken from the Old Testament, however historical or otherwise it might seem:[36] the Old Testament, or rather Moses, is indeed acknowledged in Malalas's preface as one of the authorities he consulted, though the closeness of the consultation is—as noted already—debatable. There are many overt references: in 1.2 [5.34] Moses' account is cited with reference to Enoch being "taken up" (as in Gen. 6:2, 4), and then (1.3 [5.49–50]) in connection with the "stubborn giants" (cf. Gen. 6:3); in 2.10 [25.22] (cf. Gen. 10:25) Moses is cited on the patriarch Phalek appearing at the midpoint of time, which is picked up later in 10.2 [173.21].[37] In 3.14 [47.6], referring to Exodus 14, the Israelites walked

---

33 Although the old debate on the distinction between chronicle and history still surfaces occasionally, the issue today has become that of literary interpretation, and any distinctions imposed by genre have been elided; see, e.g., the papers included in P. Odorico, A. Agapitos, and M. Hinterberger, eds., *L'Écriture de la mémoire: la littérarité de l'historiographie* (Paris, 2006).

34 Though in a battered state: the text in the main manuscript (Oxford, Barocc. 182) is abbreviated and has to be supplemented by later excerpts and translations; see *Studies in Malalas* (n. 25 above), 245–312.

35 All references to Malalas's *Chronographia* are taken from Thurn's edition, with book and paragraph number followed by page and line number in square brackets. All translations are from E. Jeffreys, M. Jeffreys, and R. Scott, *The Chronicle of Malalas: A Translation* (Melbourne, 1986).

36 See also Beaucamp, "Passé biblique," and Whitby "Biblical Past" (both unnum. n. above).

37 Note that Malalas, unlike his ultimate source, Sextus Julius Africanus (Africanus F16c [30.7 ed. Wallraff], from Synkellos), for whom the date of Phalek's death was significant, does not specify whether this refers to his birth or death.

through the "sea's waves—the Red Sea—as if on dry land." In these cases, Malalas's allusions can be located in the Old Testament. However, in 4.7 [53.32–33] a verse text ascribed to Orpheus is quoted to the effect that "men were moulded from earth by God and took a rational soul from him," and Moses cited as corroboration; Genesis 1 is somewhere in the background to this statement but the connection is not verbally close. Elsewhere Moses is regularly described as a "very wise chronographer" or "very wise" (as are all those cited by Malalas as sources). Moses is also associated with other non-scriptural texts, which will be discussed later.

Other Old Testament material is referred to vaguely by Malalas as the "Hebrew Scriptures," in phrases such as ἐν ταῖς Ἑβραϊκαῖς γραφαῖς: there is a certain overlap with the references to Moses. Thus the references in his preface to authorities and in 1.2 to Enoch link the Hebrew Scriptures with Moses' name, though this is not the case later in 1.4 [6.79] in a reference to the Flood, where there is a general recollection of the wording of Genesis, nor in 3.8 [43.74] on Joseph, where again there is a hazy rephrasing based this time on Exodus. In 3.13 [45.67] occurs the first of the passages to be examined in greater detail below, derived from Exodus and dealing with Moses, Pharaoh, and the release of the Jews. In 4.12 [58.65] Sampson's mystic knowledge and miracle working have an undefined backing in Hebrew Scripture—mystic knowledge being a recurring theme in Malalas.[38] In 6.14 [124.13] Judith's entanglement with Holofernes has added support from an attestation to Eirenaios (probably Irenaeus of Lyons, ca. 200 CE) but the Old Testament book of Judith underlies this section.

Elsewhere allusions to ἐν ταῖς θείαις γραφαῖς (in the sacred Scriptures) refer to the New Testament, a distinction being made between Jewish and Christian traditions. Thus sacred Scriptures in 10.2 [174.42] support Malalas's millennial date for Christ's incarnation and crucifixion, the slaughter of the innocents (10.4 [175.77]), John the Baptist's strictures on Herod's marriage (10.11 [179.90–91]), and the opening of graves at Christ's crucifixion (10.14 [182.70]).

All these references allude to material in the chronicle that is loosely linked to the relevant Old Testament passages. Far more clearly derived from the Old Testament narratives are the dates that form the backbone of Malalas's text,

---

38   See E. Jeffreys, "Malalas' World View," in *Studies in Malalas*, 55–66, at 63; eadem, "Literary Genre and Religious Apathy? The Presence or Absence of Theology and Religious Thought in Late Antique Secular Writing," in *Religious Diversity in Late Antiquity*, ed. D. Gwynn and S. Bangert (= *Late Antique Archaeology* 5.1; Leiden, forthcoming); and also A.-M. Bernardi, "Les *mystikoi* dans la chronique de Jean Malalas," in *Recherches sur la chronique de Jean Malalas I*, ed. J. Beaucamp (Paris, 2004), 53–64.

which give a chronological framework of years from Adam, though with cumulative totals that are not consistent with the biblical ones.[39] Thus we find:

> From Adam till the angels desire women (in the year 2122;
>   *Chronographia* 1.2 [5.36–37] = Genesis 6:4),[40]
> From Adam to Noah's Flood (2522; 1.4 [6.79–80] = Gen. 6:13–7:10),
> From Adam to the Tower of Babel (2922; 1.5 [8.19–20] = Gen. 11:1–9),
> From Adam to Phalek (3000; 2.10 [25.23] = Gen. 10:25),
> From Adam to Abraham (3445; 3.3 [42.29–30] cf. Gen. 17),
> From Adam to the birth of Moses (4036; 3.10 [44.86–87] cf. Exod. 2),
> From Adam to the death of Moses and Aaron (4156; 3.10 [44.89–90]
>   cf. Deut. 34),
> From Adam to David (4755; 5.39 [112.14] cf. 1 Kings 2:11),
> From Adam to Solomon (4795; 5.39 [112.21] cf. 1 Kings 6–7 and 1 Kings 11:42),
> From Adam to Hezekiah (5266; 5.39 [112.28] cf. 2 Kings 18:2),
> From Adam to Manasses (5321; 5.43 [116.34] = 2 Kings 21:1),
> From Adam to Eliakim and Joachim (5365; 5.43 [116.42] = 2 Kings 21:19).

Although there are several intervening staging points for the construction of these calculations, those listed here provide the chronicle's main structure.[41] There is much room for speculation on the significance of these dates and on the sources that Malalas used to calculate these figures; worth noting is that many of the concepts embedded in the narrative passages reflecting Genesis have close parallels in the *Book of Jubilees*.[42] However, to comment in detail here would be to enter an ultimately unproductive antiquarian maze: its windings have been explored thoroughly elsewhere, initially by Gelzer and more recently by William Adler.[43] After the reference to Eliakim and Joachim, Malalas ceases to use Old

---

39   Unlike the *Chronicon Paschale*, which builds on the figures in Genesis for the ages and generations of the patriarchs (Gelzer, *Sextus Julius Africanus* [n. 17 above], 1:142–44).
40   In this list the Old Testament passages confirm the event, but not the dating; for a discussion on Malalas's often idiosyncratic from-Adam datings see Gelzer, *Sextus Julius Africanus*, 2:129–41.
41   For a fuller listing and discussion, see Jeffreys, "Chronological Structures" (n. 28 above).
42   E. Jeffreys, "The Chronicle of John Malalas, Book 1: A Commentary," in *The Sixth Century: End or Beginning?* ed. P. Allen and E. Jeffreys (Brisbane, 1996), 52–74.
43   On these dates, see Gelzer, *Sextus Julius Africanus*, 2:133–35; for a discussion that develops Gelzer's materials, see Adler, *Time Immemorial* (n. 17 above), and Adler and Tuffin, *Chronography* (n. 13 above), especially xxxv–xlviii. The *Synopsis scripturae sacrae*, a summary of events in the Old and New Testaments attributed to Athanasios of Alexandria (PG 28:254–437) and also to John Chrysostom (*CPG* 4559; PG 56:313–86), which was used by later Byzantine historians, seems not to have been known to Malalas.

Testament staging points and switches to "Hellenic" ones. Thus, the next from Adam date occurs in 6.17 [125.45]; it is insolubly corrupted and its reference point is not clear (it may allude to a narrative about Picus Zeus in book 1 or simply refer to Philip of Macedon from the beginning of the previous paragraph). There follow two staging points involving Alexander (8.2 [147.33–34], 8.4 [195.69–70]). Thereafter there is a reference back to Phalek in the discussion of the incarnation and crucifixion date (10.2 [172.12–20]). The final from Adam dates come under Zeno and Justinian (15.16 [318.35] and 18.8 [357.66–67]) and have to do with Malalas's millennial agenda.

But if Malalas is making this material the main framework for his chronicle he is also, like his predecessors, combining it with material from the secular chronographic tradition—as demonstrated with the numerous fragmented ruler lists and the narratives dealing with legendary or mythological characters from the Hellenic literary traditions who appear at intervals in the first books of the chronicle. One might look for synchronisms. Indeed, one of the points at issue for Africanus and Eusebios, which ultimately derived from the Hellenized Jewish intellectual circles that produced the Septuagint, was the relative dating of the Greek and Jewish intellectual traditions: which had temporal priority? What was the temporal relationship between Plato and Moses?[44] Malalas, however, gives very few explicit synchronisms of any sort. Ruler lists of city-states, which in the chronographical tables of Kastor of Rhodes (first century BCE), for example, or in Eusebios's chronicle were regularly correlated, are located only vaguely by Malalas, whose disjointed lists represent the last stage in a paraphrasing process.[45] Thus a sequence of references to the Argive kings appears in 2.6 [21.10] (cf. 4.1 [48.3–11]) after the completion of the tower of Babel in the year 2922 (1.5 [8.19–20]), while Moses is by implication synchronized with Inachos of Argos, seemingly around 4156 from Adam (3.10 [44. 87–90] but cf. 4.2 [48.18–20]).[46] This imprecision contrasts with, for example, Africanus's explicit synchronization of Moses and Inachos in 3652 from Adam (or Synkellos's date of 3662).[47]

---

44   Cf. Eusebios, *Praep. ev.* 10.2; Josephus, *Contra Ap.* 1.4–8.
45   More complete versions of the ruler lists that lie behind those of Malalas appear in the chronicle that forms part of the *Excerpta barbari* (C. Frick, *Chronica minora* [Leipzig, 1893], 184–371 and Beatrice, *Theosophia* [n. 28 above], 74–134; cf. F. Jacoby, "Excerpta Barbari," *PW* 6.2 [1909]: 1566–76).
46   For a discussion of Malalas's ruler lists and their synchronizations, parallels and sources, see Jeffreys, "Chronological Structures," 124–38.
47   Gelzer, *Sextus Julius Africanus*, 1:143; Synkellos, *Ecloga* 145.5 (ed. Mosshammer). The linking of Moses and Inachos was in fact a common Christian synchronism; cf. Eusebios, *Praep. ev.* 10.9–10.

Mythological personages are euhemerized, that is, treated as historical beings, and are also given an implied chronology: Persephone, for example, is located in the same period (3.12 [44.98–45.19]).

Interesting not so much as a synchronism but as an indication of the key role of the Old Testament narrative is the role given to the sons of Noah: by the logic of postdiluvian history, because of the universal destruction wreaked by the Flood, all subsequent individuals and peoples must be descended from Noah through one of his sons. This thought is pursued only intermittently in Malalas's text (and will not be pursued here) but, for example, in 1.8 [9.47–10.65] Kronos and his son Picus Zeus, who are slotted in after the building of the tower of Babel 2922 years from Adam, are stated to be of the tribe of Shem.[48]

Malalas's Text

One perennial, and fundamental, question about Malalas's chronicle concerns the state of the text and the extent to which it can be taken as accurately representing what Malalas wrote. Thurn's 2000 edition, which uses all the many extant witnesses, though at times in a questionable manner,[49] reproduces reasonably well a literary artifact that was in something like this state in the latter years of the sixth century. Another question is, how credible is Malalas's chronicle, whether as history or as a statement of the beliefs of his day? It certainly contains a farrago of nonsenses, and when it can be tested against predecessors, the distortions are many and obvious. So, for example, in ruler lists from other ancient authorities, such as Kastor of Rhodes, fragmentary or reconstructed, the names and numbers are far more coherent than those in Malalas's text.[50]

Although it continues to be a tenable position to argue that one guiding authorial hand formed the text of Malalas as it survives in the extant witnesses, it is nevertheless valid to question how much in the chronicle is due to Malalas himself, and how much to his immediate predecessors and sources named or otherwise.[51] The issue of Malalas's sources has not ceased to be vexed. For present

---

48 For an intensive analysis of the Picus Zeus material in Malalas, see now B. Garstad, "The Excerpta Latina Barbari and the 'Picus-Zeus Narrative,'" *Jahrbuch für internationale Germanistik* 34 (2002): 259–313.

49 Most conspicuously in the "reverse translation" of the Slavic witnesses and the inconsistent italicizing of inserted passages.

50 As was set out by Gelzer, *Sextus Julius Africanus*, passim.

51 The argument of E. Jeffreys' now rather elderly article, "The Attitudes of Byzantine Chroniclers towards Ancient History," *Byzantion* 49 (1979): 199–238, that a distinct authorial personality can be seen in the idiosyncratic selection of material in Malalas's chronicle, underlies the

purposes, it simply needs to be pointed out that in several places in the early books of his chronicle, use is demonstrably being made of an early sixth-century text that recent work suggests combined ruler lists and chronicle narrative with pagan oracles foretelling Christ and the Trinity: studies by Pier Beatrice (2001) convincingly link what is known as the *Excerpta barbari* (a chronicle of sorts) with what is known as the *Tübingen Theosophy* (a set of pagan oracles, foretelling the coming of Christ).[52] Both chronicle and oracles have complex transmission histories that obscure their original state. Beatrice suggests that the chronicle and oracles originally formed a *Theosophia* arguably composed in 502/3 CE. The question still remains, however, of how many veils of authorities there are between this demonstrable source and the text of Malalas that now exists on Thurn's printed page: suspected intermediaries include Timotheos, otherwise unknown but acknowledged by Malalas,[53] and Eustathios of Epiphaneia, known but not extant, whom Malalas acknowledges.[54]

Malalas and Pharaoh's Magoi

The passages mentioned at the beginning of this chapter exemplify two uses to which Old Testament material is put in Malalas's chronicle. In 3.13–14 we have the account of how Moses persuaded Pharaoh to "let his people go." The Old Testament basis for Malalas's drastically curtailed narrative is Exodus 1:6–14 and 7:28–15:21. The most obvious omissions are the details of the ten plagues (Exodus 8–11), concealed by the reference to the "sevenfold wrath" (3.13 [46.43]; probably influenced by the *Book of Jubilees*, which calculates in sevens), the institution of the Passover (Exodus 12), and Moses' song of triumph at the crossing of the Red Sea (Exodus 15). What has been retained are the most basic elements of the Exodus story: the oppression of the Jews by the Egyptians, the clash between Moses and Pharaoh, as represented by the magi (Exodus 7:8–25), Pharaoh's obduracy and its weakening through the demonstrations of the power of the God of Israel, the departure of the Jews, their crossing of the sea and the drowning of Pharaoh.

---

contributions by B. Croke ("Malalas, the Man and His Work") and R. Scott ("Malalas and His Contemporaries") in *Studies in Malalas* (n. 25 above), 1–26 and 67–86 respectively.

52 Beatrice, *Theosophia* (as in note 28); see also the comments in *Studies in Malalas*, passim, especially 195, which are based on Erbse's now superseded edition.

53 There are two figures named Timotheos amongst Malalas's sources, one of them associated with millennial arguments, the other seemingly a contemporary oral informant; see *Studies in Malalas*, 194–96.

54 Eustathios cited by Malalas at 16.10 (326.44–45).

Of note are several elements of nonbiblical origin. There is a synchronism at the beginning of the passage (3.13 [45.20–21]): Moses is synchronized with Erechtheus, ruler of the Assyrians. Erechtheus is not present in any list of Assyrian rulers surviving in the Greek chronographic tradition, although—as indicated above—Malalas does seem to have been working with something like the lists in the *Excerpta barbari*, which ultimately go back to Kastor. The pharaoh is named as Petissonius; this is not a name of any known pharaoh; the meaning of his epithet κωμωδός is puzzling (the "Pharaoh who was mocked" found in the 1986 English translation was a counsel of despair). The statement (3.13 [45.23–25]) on the increasing number of Jews in Egypt summarizes the biblical narrative (cf. Exodus 1:7–8), as indeed does that on the brick-making oppression of the burgeoning Jewish population (3.13 [45.29–34]; cf. Exodus 1:11–13). Iothor (Jethro) is indeed one of the names given for Moses' father-in-law in Exodus (3.13 [45.26]; Exodus 3:1), but it looks a little odd that he is called the "chief priest of the Hellenes." And this sits somewhat oddly with the statement that "Moses had been educated in all the wisdom of Egypt" (3.13 [45.28]).

The clue to what is going on has been given already in the reference to Pharaoh's *magoi* (3.123 [45.22]). *Magoi* and their activities are something of a leitmotif in Malalas, appearing not only at Christ's nativity (10.4 [174–75]), where today they have come to be expected as part of the traditional narrative (Matt. 2:1–12), but as wonderworkers, usually Persian priests,[55] while Simon Magus has a prominent role in book 10 (10.32–35 [190.9–193.8]). The *magoi* in this passage in book 3 are named Iannes and Iambres—they are not named in Exodus—and with them the reader is taken into the world of apocryphal Jewish literature. The narrative here is recognizably derived from the *Book of Iannes and Iambres*, a text that bobbed below the surface of literary perception but to which allusions floated up in the magical papyri, in Pliny (*Natural History* 30.2.11), in Apuleius (*Apologia* 90), and most notably in 2 Timothy 3:8, where the author (traditionally St. Paul) knows Iannes and Iambres to be Moses' opponents. Reasonably substantial papyrus fragments have now been identified, sufficient to permit the structure of the *Book of Iannes and Iambres* to be established, more or less. It is a tale of two brothers, their magical contests, the slaying of the one by the other and how he is brought back to life. However, the wide dissemination of the story

---

55 E.g., 2.12 [28.11]; 6.3 [118.26]; 18.30 [371.13]; 18.69 [393.3]; for Malalas the role of *magoi* seems to be not dissimilar to that of the wonder-working *mystikoi* whose identity ranges from Picus Zeus through Augustus to the *comes* Maurianos, who foretold the accession of Zeno (cf. Bernardi, "Les *mystikoi*," as in note 38 above).

has produced many variants that do not easily fit into a coherent whole.⁵⁶ The elements that have been taken over in the version found in Malalas's text include the transformation of rods into serpents and the victory of Moses' rod (a variant on Exodus) and the transformation of the bloody river (again a variant on the Exodus narrative). However, the situation is somewhat circular: Malalas's narrative is as much evidence for the contents of the *Book of Iannes and Iambres* as a witness to his indebtedness to it.⁵⁷ The presence of the names provides the key. Nonetheless, despite the divergence from the Exodus narrative, Malalas's chronicle unequivocally attributes the episode to "the Hebrew Scriptures" (ταῖς Ἑβραϊκαῖς γραφαῖς; 3.13 [46.67]).

What then of the oracle in Memphis (3.13 [46.70]), consulted by Pharaoh in bafflement after the defeat of his *magoi*? This prophetic foreshadowing of Christian Trinitarian theology ("father son of himself thrice-blessed") is attested independently from Malalas's text, appearing in the remains of the *Theosophy* (and is part of the nexus of material derived from the *Excerpta barbari–Theosophy* combination).⁵⁸ But the prophecy does not seem ever to have been part of the *Book of Iannes and Iambres*, despite that text's apparently loose structure. The two texts had different purposes: *Iannes and Iambres* was a narrative of conflict and resolution arguably with resonances from its time of composition, while the *Theosophy* was a propaganda or missionary document for use in, probably, Monophysite circles, to combat intellectual paganism.⁵⁹ One might venture to suggest that the combination of these two elements, from *Iannes and Iambres* and from the *Theosophy*, is attributable to Malalas himself, or at least to his immediately proximate source, if Malalas is to be given no credit for independence. The combination would have been constructed between ca. 503 (the most likely date for the composition of the *Theosophy*) and ca. 530, when the first edition of Malalas's chronicle was completed.⁶⁰

From this passage, what can we conclude about the role of the Old Testament in this chronicle? Clearly, the Old Testament narrative was of prime importance, for it provides the assumed chronological underpinning and the narrative around which variants are woven. But it is also clear that alternative interpretations were willingly entertained. There are para-theological elements (for want

---

56 Pietersma, *Jannes and Jambres* (n. 14 above), 48–72.
57 Ibid., 30.
58 Beatrice, *Theosophia*, 24 (1.50).
59 Ibid., xxxiv–xxxv.
60 Ibid., xli–xlv. On the evidence for dates of the editions of Malalas's chronicle, see Croke, "Malalas, the Man and His Work," in *Studies in Malalas*, 17–25.

of a better term), products of semirational attempts to interpret the unfathomable. This combination is the product of the mindset that led Malalas's contemporary Kosmas Indikopleustes to model the world on Moses' Tabernacle in his *Christian Topography;* less dramatically, in later centuries the combination led to the *Erotapokriseis* of Anastasios of Sinai (late 7th century),[61] and to the *Amphilochia* of Photios (mid-9th century).[62] But Malalas was not alone among Byzantine chronographers in turning to apocryphal texts: some three centuries later Synkellos referred often to the *Book of Jubilees*, and indeed he is a source for much of what can be attributed to *Jubilees* in Greek, though it must be admitted that *Jubilees*' precise calculations are rather different from the curious episodes of the *Book of Iannes and Iambres*.[63]

But what use did writers in the chronicle tradition make of Moses' clash with these *magoi*? Only a few of the later excerptors of Malalas took this episode over in its entirety—John of Nikiu, pseudo-Symeon, followed, as so often, by Kedrenos, and the Slavonic translation—that is, those excerptors who went in for uncritical scissors and pasting.[64] But the names of Iannes and Iambres have a recurring typological presence, one that is valid despite the blurred authenticity of their origin. In their opposition to Moses they became emblematic of an evil opposition to the forces of good. Most strikingly, the typology was later used in depicting the Iconoclast patriarch John Grammatikos, whose learning lent itself particularly well to charges of lekanomancy (dish divination) and so forth made by fervent Iconophiles such as George the Monk, for whom this John, or Ioannes, is the "new Iannes and Iambres." The similar insistence in Theophanes Continuatus that Ioannes the patriarch is to be called Iannes "because of his impiety" also picks up on this resonance.[65] Of course this cannot be attributed solely to the effect of Malalas's narrative: the reference in 2 Timothy, reinforced by Pauline commentators such as Theodoret, John Chrysostom, and Eusebios, would have kept the typology alive.

---

61 J. Haldon, "The Works of Anastasius of Sinai: A Key Source for the History of the Seventh-Century East Mediterranean Society and Belief," in *The Byzantine and Early Islamic Near East*, vol. 1, *Problems in the Literary Source Material*, ed. Av. Cameron and L. Conrad (Princeton, 1992), 107–48.
62 A. Louth, "Photius as a Theologian," in *Byzantine Style, Religion and Civilisation: In Honour of Sir Steven Runciman*, ed. E. Jeffreys (Cambridge, 2006), 206–23.
63 Not all chroniclers, however, were so accepting. Glykas, for one, in the mid-twelfth century was sceptical of the value of *Jubilees*, known to him as *Lepte Genesis*: e.g., *Annales* (ed. Bekker), 392.18–393.1, cf. 198.2, 206.8.
64 As mentioned above, Iannes and Iambres also appear in the ninth-century *Palaia*.
65 George the Monk, *Chronicon*, 778.13 (ed. de Boor and Wirth); Theophanes Continuatus, *De Theophilo* 26, *De Michaele* 6 (121.6, 154.12; ed. Bekker).

Malalas and Sennacherib

The second passage to be considered takes a different approach to the Old Testament. Book 5 of Malalas's chronicle, having opened with a synchronism between Priam, ruler of Ilion, and David, the son of Jesse who had been appointed king of the Jewish people (*sic*; rather than Israel: 4.20 [66.51]), deals at length with the Trojan War, in a narrative that is not without problems.[66] There follows a brief series of dates from Adam (5.39 [112.11–29]), referring to David, Solomon, and Hezekiah. Then (5.40–42 [113.30–116.33]) there appears, located in the fourteenth year of the reign of Hezekiah, a virtually verbatim quotation from the Old Testament books of Isaiah and 2 Kings,[67] recounting Sennacherib's attempted siege of Jerusalem, the speeches of his envoy Rabshakeh, or perhaps *the* Rabshakeh—a title, "cup-bearer," rather than a proper name—Rabshakeh's attempts to induce treachery, and the miraculous rescue of the city when the angel of the Lord slew the Assyrians by night. This is a striking event, dated quite reliably to 701 BCE, recorded in Assyrian inscriptions with a triumphalist outcome and by Herodotus (2.141), who gives to mice the credit for the unexpected victory, these having nibbled the aggressors' bow-strings.[68] It passed into the imaginations of a certain generation of English-speaking schoolchildren via Byron's poem: *The Assyrian came down like the wolf on the fold, And his cohorts were gleaming in purple and gold*. This episode is rich in interpretative possibilities for historical theology—but that is not our concern here. The questions to ask are, how does this episode fit in with Malalas's patterns of thought, and why is it quoted at such length.

Malalas's quotations, like his sources, are notoriously problematic. Unlike many Byzantine authors—of any period—he names a great many authorities as his sources, but—and this is the problem—many of these names seem pure invention and, when a correlation can be established between a source and the quoted information, which is not often, there are usually huge discrepancies. In other places, his use of a particular source can be clearly demonstrated—the

---

66 Malalas avoids the Homeric version and claims to be using the eyewitness diaries of Dictys of Crete that had been recast by the otherwise unattested Sisyphos of Kos: see Jeffreys, "Malalas' Sources" (n. 25 above), 176–77, 192–93.

67 Isaiah 36.1–37.21; 2 Kings (4 Kingdoms LXX) 18.13–20.37. It might be hoped that this passage, coming from a secular context, would provide interesting insights into the nature of the recension available to Malalas; a collation with the Göttingen edition of Isaiah (ed. Ziegler) indicates unexciting affinities with the late third-century (?) Lucianic recension.

68 On the archaeology see Mazar and Stern, *Archaeology* (n. 8 above), 1:417–35 (discussing the fortifications at Jerusalem attributable to defense works against Sennacherib) and 2:4–10.

Excerpta barbari referred to earlier is a case in point—but there is no acknowledgment. Only a few texts are quoted very precisely, such as the passages attributed to Orpheus that have been edited as Orphic fragments and which in the examples found in Malalas are derived from the *Theosophy* in another rather circular situation.[69] Some passages suggest a close knowledge of the cited source, such as the lines from Euripides' *Iphigeneia in Tauris* (5.32–34 [104.56–107.24]), which are precise and are of some relevance for the textual history of that tragedy; the longer extracts, also in book 5, purporting to be from the diaries by Dictys of Crete and Sisyphos of Kos of eyewitness experiences in the Trojan War are far less straightforward, since the transmission history of Dictys is complex. Nevertheless it is possible to suggest reasons why these quotations should be given with precision: the Orphic material chimes in with the para-theological streak already noted, the lines from *Iphigeneia in Tauris* deal with Antiochene antiquities (a preoccupation of Malalas), and the Dictys material is para-Homeric, Homer being a central figure in Byzantine literary culture. All these being so, why should a long passage from Isaiah/Kings be quoted without paraphrase?[70]

There are two reasons: typology and topicality. Sennacherib and the Assyrians could be read typologically as Persians; the besieged and threatened inhabitants of Jerusalem could be read as the Byzantines, or more precisely the inhabitants of Malalas's native Antioch. The passage was topical since, although Anastasios's Persian War came to an end with a truce in 506, tensions rumbled on even if actual warfare did not break out again until 528.[71] The latter was a fateful year for Malalas's chronicle—the year of a great earthquake and the year into whose record was inserted a major chronographical and millennial calculation (18.8 [357.64–358.95]).[72] In 529, on the evidence of Malalas, a Persian raiding force, led by Persia's Arab ally Al-Mundhir, made inroads into First Syria "as far as Antioch"; in 531 Christian captives in Persian hands petitioned in Antioch for their ransoms.[73] The Persian incursions persisted, culminating in the sack of

---

69 O. Kern, *Orphicorum Fragmenta* (Berlin, 1922), nos. 62, 65, 233, and 299.
70 This passage is also presented without attribution. It was not taken up by any of the later chronicles: the parallels found in the *Chronicon Paschale* are due to that text's systematic working through the Old Testament; e.g., *Chronicon Paschale*, 215 (ed. Dindorf) on Sennacherib.
71 F. Haarer, *Anastasius I: Politics and Empire in the Late Roman World* (Cambridge, 2006), 47–65; G. Greatrex, *Rome and Persia at War, 502–532* (Leeds, 1998), 114–18, 151–65.
72 The importance for Malalas of these natural disasters is brought out in Thurn's edition, where reverse translation from the Slavic text has brought "fall [i.e., earthquake] of Antioch" into the titles of books 17 and 18.
73 Al-Mundhir's raids in 529: Malalas, 18.32 (372.30–31); the petitions of 531: Malalas, 18.59 [386.38–397.74].

540 reported so graphically by Prokopios and so laconically by Malalas.[74] It is an attractive thought that the miraculous prevention of the disaster that seemed to await Hezekiah should be read as an apotropaic aspiration by an Antiochene whilst the threatening hordes collected, especially when this thought is combined with recognition of Malalas's habitual anachronisms, which can lead him to present biblical as well as mythological material in phrases drawn from contemporary concerns.[75] That this passage in book 5 was ignored by all later excerptors suggests that its implications were particular to the moment of composition and the meaning soon lost. Similarly, Malalas's millennial arguments, expressed in passages in books 10 and 18, which were idiosyncratic and apparently topical, were also ignored by virtually every subsequent excerptor.

Conclusion

The Old Testament provided the fundamental chronological underpinning for the Byzantine worldview. Further, typology was important in the reception of Old Testament material into the Byzantine world chronicle, as this chapter has tried to suggest with two cases selected from the chronicle of Malalas. But this is typology in an extended form; it moves beyond the linking of the Old and the New Covenants, from the use of Abraham's feast as a type of the Eucharist. It assumes that the Old Testament is linked not only with Christianity in general but with Byzantium in particular. Why should the Byzantines make this assumption? The first answer is that this embracing of the old and the new is entirely natural for Christians of any sort. At some point though, Byzantine rhetoric, both theological and political, developed the view that the Byzantines in particular were the New Israel, the new Chosen People, God's New Elect.[76] By the twelfth century this cliché was used as regularly as the cliché that Byzantium—Constantinople—was the New Rome: in court rhetoric the two

---

74 Prokopios, *Wars* 2.5–9, cf. *Buildings* 2.10; Malalas, 18.87 [405.65–66]. See also G. Downey, *A History of Antioch in Syria from Seleucus to the Arab Conquest* (Princeton, 1961), 533–46.
75 Emphasized by Whitby, "Biblical Past" (unnum. n. above), 287–88, commenting on Malalas's non-biblical details on Abraham's father (3.1 [41.3–10]); cf. *Studies in Malalas*, 64. That Malalas presented the mythological past in terms of sixth-century realities has been acknowledged; see R. Scott, "Malalas' View of the Classical Past," in *Reading the Past in Late Antiquity*, ed. G. W. Clarke (Canberra, 1990). Whitby has also suggested that the siege of Jerusalem may have been included as a counterpart to the immediately preceding, lengthy, account of the siege of Troy ("Biblical Past," 288).
76 This is, of course, a restriction of the New Testament and patristic claim that the Church is the Chosen People, and limits the concept to those within Byzantine political boundaries.

are combined with results that can be bizarre.[77] It is not easy to trace the moment at which this equation became explicit, and in secondary literature on this subject airy statements are frequent but hard references few. Dagron takes the Avar and Persian problems in the early seventh century during the reign of Heraklios as a key moment in the development of the concept of the "chosen people," who are both protected and chastized, adducing the homilies of Theodore Synkellos.[78] But explicit statements before the twelfth century remain sparse: Constantine VII (d. 959) called the army "the New Chosen People," Mavropous (d. ca. 1080) referred to the Byzantine people as the "New Israel."[79] The best discussions remain those of Otto Treitinger in 1938 and Paul Alexander in 1962.[80] Both emphasize the importance of the symbols of empire, the *pignora imperii*, which were held in Constantinople: the staff of Moses, the throne of Solomon, and the Constantinian Cross, which "related the emperors to their Israelite prototypes and their Byzantine predecessors."[81] Both argue that the empire's Christianization inevitably led to Old Testament typology, with emperors compared to Moses, Elijah, David, and so forth, or even, playing with the ambivalent nature of the emperor as priest-king, a ruler of the order of Melchisedek. The early seventh century and the reign of Heraklios provide, once again, one of the key moments in this development, as witnessed by the imagery of the David plates—this time with reference to Heraklios's deeds in the Persian wars.[82] However, this typology is applied to the emperor rather than to the people as a whole. A stage is missing.

[77] The poet known as Manganeios Prodromos, whose work is not yet fully edited, offers some resounding examples; see, for example, the discussion in E. Jeffreys and M. Jeffreys, "The 'Wild Beast from the West': Immediate Literary Reactions in Byzantium to the Second Crusade," in *The Crusades from the Perspective of Byzantium and the Muslim World*, ed. A. Laiou and R. Mottahedeh (Washington, DC, 2001), 101–16.
[78] Theodore Synkellos, *Analecta Avarica*, ed. L. Sternbach (Cracow, 1900), 297–334; G. Dagron, "L'Église et la chrétienté byzantines entre les invasions et l'iconoclasme (VIIe–début VIIIe siècle)," in *Évêques, moines et empereurs (610–1054)*, ed. G. Dagron, P. Riché and A. Vauchez, Histoire du Christianisme des origines à nos jours 4 (Paris, 1993), 9–91, at 20; cf. H. Ahrweiler, *L'Idéologie politique de l'empire byzantin* (Paris, 1975), 110.
[79] H. Ahrweiler, "Un discours inédit de Constantine VII Porphyrogénète," *TM* 2 (1967): 393–404; Mavropous: P. Lagarde, *Ioannis Euchaitensis quae in cod. vat. gr. 676 supersunt*, Acad. hist.-philosoph. Classe Göttingen 28.1 (1881), at 140.
[80] O. Treitinger, *Die oströmische Kaiser- und Reichsidee nach ihrer Gestaltung im höfischen Zeremoniell* (Jena, 1938); P. Alexander, "The Strength of Empire as Seen through Byzantine Eyes," *Speculum* 37 (1962): 339–57.
[81] Alexander, "Strength of Empire," 343.
[82] "The Cyprus plates would seem to be the product of an historical moment when the concept of Old Testament kingship and the reality of contemporary governance found uncanny concordance": S. H. Wander, "The Cyprus Plates and the 'Chronicle' of Fredgar," *DOP* 29 (1975): 346.

There are perhaps a few hints in Malalas's choice of phraseology throughout the chronicle that show how this gap is bridged and how the concept was developing in the course of the sixth century, indications of the formation of the idea that all the inhabitants of Byzantium—the empire of East Rome—were indeed the Chosen People, that is, the New Israel. Malalas refers to the many natural disasters, especially earthquakes, that afflicted the Byzantine world, and not only the Antiochenes, as θεομηνία, "the wrath of God"; on several occasions this is also expressed as God's φιλανθρωπία, "benevolence," perhaps to be interpreted as "benevolent chastisement." A possible interpretation is that these disasters are a demonstration of God's especial concern. For how else could he nurture his Chosen People if he did not benevolently chastize them for their errors? It was for Malalas's readers to make the identification.

University of Oxford

SEVEN

Old Testament Models for Emperors in Early Byzantium

CLAUDIA RAPP

During the Great Persecution under Diocletian and Galerius, a group of five Christians from Egypt was subjected to gruesome tortures. When the judge asked them to identify themselves, they refused to relate their given names, which had idolatrous associations. Instead, they called themselves Elijah, Jeremiah, Isaiah, Samuel, or Daniel, and indicated Jerusalem as their place of residence. Eusebios of Caesarea describes this event in his *Martyrs of Palestine* as part of the great project of proving that the Old Testament foreshadows the New Testament and that God's past history with his people, the Old Israel and the New, continues in the present until it finds its fulfillment at the end of days.[1] One expression of this idea of teleological continuity in the history of God's people is the association of individuals, whether living or dead, with figures from the Old Testament.

The most prominent individual in Byzantine society to invite such association was the emperor, because of his role as general, lawgiver, model of conduct, and leader of a Christian people.[2] Employing various kinds of writing and pursuing differing agendas, different authors chose to set emperors in relation to Old

---

1 Eusebios of Caesarea, *De mart. Pal.* 11. 8, ed. E. Schwartz and T. Mommsen, rev. F. Winkelmann (Eusebios, *Werke*) (Berlin, 1999), 2.936, lines 13–937, line 5.
2 Bishops, holy men, and saints are also frequently compared to Old Testament models, especially in hagiographical literature. See C. Rapp, "Comparison, Paradigm and the Case of Moses in Panegyric and Hagiography," in *The Propaganda of Power: The Role of Panegyric in Late Antiquity*, ed. Mary Whitby (Leiden, 1998), 277–98. A rare instance of a high administrative office being placed in relation to biblical precedent is found in Cassiodorus, *Variae* 6.3.1, ed. T. Mommsen, MGH, Auct. Ant. 2 (Berlin, 1898), 176, lines 1–4, trans. S. Barnish (Liverpool, 1992), 94–96, where the model for the Praetorian Prefecture is said to be Joseph at the court of Pharaoh.

Testament figures. Moses and David served as positive models of leadership or meekness, while Pharaoh and Ahab were invoked as negative examples of tyrannical and cruel rulers. Eusebios set the trend for the development of Byzantine imperial ideology. He claimed that Constantine had received special favors from God and stood in a privileged relationship to him. Accordingly, scholarship has tended to focus on the emperor's relation to Christ, his *mimesis theou*, and the connection between monotheism and monarchy within a Christian historico-political mindset.³ It is within this context that Old Testament models for emperors also find mention in scholarly writing.⁴ As Gilbert Dagron remarks: "No new event was wholly true nor any new emperor wholly authentic until they had been recognized and labeled by reference to an Old Testament model. In Byzantium, the Old Testament had a constitutional value; it had the same normative role in the political sphere as the New Testament in the moral sphere."⁵

This chapter seeks to scrutinize the use of Old Testament models in authors of the fourth to the seventh century, though occasionally drawing on supplementary evidence from later centuries. During this period Christianity, recently strengthened by imperial recognition and support, was seeking to find its voice and establish its presence within the existing framework of ancient culture. Christian authors, many of whom were bishops and well educated, experienced the new reality of engaging with an emperor who shared their religion. They were faced with the need to develop new expressions in their representation of imperial rule. Two sets of interlocking questions guide this study: the first is the degree to which the position of the author vis-à-vis Christianity determines the frequency of his use of Old Testament models. Crucial in this context is not only an author's allegiance to Christianity, but also the literary genre in which he was writing. Bishops who made a direct address to the emperor on behalf of the new religion were the first to invoke connections to Old Testament models on a large scale. Historians and panegyrists, by contrast, were much slower to do so, because they were following classical models in expression and style. The second issue to be explored is the quality of the relationship between emperor and Old

---

3   See the interesting comparative overview by A. Al-Azmeh, "Monotheistic Kingship," in *Monotheistic Kingship and Its Medieval Variants*, ed. A. Al-Azmeh and J. M. Bak (Budapest, 2004), 9–29, esp. 14–23.
4   F. Dvornik, *Early Christian and Byzantine Political Philosophy: Origins and Background*, 2 vols. (Washington, DC, 1966), 2:645. A useful study for the Latin authors of the late fourth to mid-seventh century is M. Reydellet, "La Bible miroir des princes du VIe au VIIe siècle," in *Le monde antique et la Bible*, ed. J. Fontaine and C. Pietri (Paris, 1985), 2:431–53.
5   *Emperor and Priest*, trans. J. Birrell (Cambridge, 2003; first published in French as *Empereur et prêtre: Étude sur le "césaropapisme" byzantin* [Paris, 1996]), 50.

Testament model that these texts establish. How is the emperor set in relation to his model? In a positive or negative way? Does he engage in conscious imitation? Does he follow a historical model of the past, or does he bring a typological figure to its full realization in the present?

Two main modes of establishing a relationship to Old Testament models can be identified, the Roman mode of the *exemplum* and the Christian mode of typology. In Roman political thought and Latin historiography, the dominant vehicle to express ideas of imitation was the *exemplum*. The ancient *exemplum* (Greek: ὑπόδειγμα or παράδειγμα) in word and deed is defined by rhetorical theorists, beginning with Aristotle and continuing through the author of the *Rhetorica ad Herennium* (first century BCE) and Quintilian (first century CE). It is a rhetorical device that may also serve a moral purpose. It always refers to a deed or saying of a person from a nostalgically glorified past, and it provides an illustration for or serves as a point of comparison with the present. In addition to simply describing or illustrating a person's deeds or character, the *exemplum* can also have a moral function, when an author registers approval for the successful imitation of a great model or expresses the desire that the model may be followed in the immediate future. *Exempla* were essential to Roman education and a staple of Latin historiography.[6] Following the *exempla maiorum* and becoming in turn an *exemplum* for future generations were the highest goals of the Roman statesman. As Thomas Wiedemann observes: "When Roman writers deploy the theme that the history they are writing is useful, what is meant is not that it provides a framework for understanding human nature or the possible ways in which communities can be controlled politically, but that they are providing a storehouse of further *exempla* to assist decision-making," so that "historical material is seen as a series of *exempla*."[7] This is the significance of Augustus's proud statement in the *Res gestae divi Augusti*: "By new laws passed on my proposal I brought back into use many exemplary practices of our ancestors [*exempla maiorum*] which were disappearing in our time, and in many ways I myself transmitted exemplary practices [*exempla*] to posterity for their imitation."[8]

---

6 For the application of *exempla* from history or legend in late antique literature, see L. Cracco Ruggini, "La funzione simbolica di eroi, re e imperatori nella cultura greca e romana del Tardoantico," in *Politica retorica e simbolismo del primato: Roma e Costantinopoli (secoli IV–VII); Atti del convegno internazionale (Catania, 4–7 ottobre 2001)*, ed. F. Elia (Catania, 2002), 355–83.
7 "Reflections of Roman Political Thought in Latin Historical Writing," in *The Cambridge History of Greek and Roman Political Thought*, ed. C. Rowe, M. Schofield et al. (Cambridge, 2000), 517–31, esp. 512f., 522.
8 *Res gestae divi Augusti* 8, ed. J. Gagé (Paris, 1977), 86: "Legibus nouis me auctore latis multa exempla maiorum exolescentia iam ex nostro saeculo reduxi et ipse multarum rerum exempla

Accordingly, the highest praise was to align a person with the great models of the past. Themistius, the prominent pagan orator of the late fourth century, followed the practice when, in his speech on the fifth anniversary of the accession of Valens in 369, he remarked that the immortality based on fame and a good reputation "continually renews the reign of Augustus, keeps Trajan from growing old, and revives Marcus Aurelius each day; among whom I would like our king to be numbered."[9] In late antiquity, Christian authors began to adapt this trope to their own purposes and selected their *exempla* from the Old or the New Testament, or from the stories of the holy men and women.[10] Thus Sozomen explains why he included monastic founding figures in his *Church History*: "I would wish to leave behind me such a record of their manner of life that others, led by their example, might attain to a blessed and happy end."[11] The emperors of the foundational period of Byzantine history—Constantine, Theodosius I, and Justinian—were regarded as prominent historical *exempla* in subsequent centuries.[12] At the birth of the son of the emperor Maurice and his wife Constantina in 583, for instance, the Blues and the Greens entered into a shouting match about the name of the future emperor, the former advocating Justinian, because of the length of his reign, and the latter Theodosius, because of his orthodoxy.[13] By definition, then, *exempla* are located in the historical past and

---

imitanda posteris tradidi." Trans. P. A. Brunt and J. M. Moore, *Res gestae divi Augusti: The Achievements of the Divine Augustus* (Oxford, 1967), 23.

9   Themistius, *Oration* 8.173, ed. G. Downey (Leipzig, 1964), 173, lines 14–19; trans. D. Moncour in P. Heather and J. Matthews, *The Goths in the Fourth Century* (Liverpool, 1991), 30. On the use of *exempla* from ancient history in early Byzantine writing about emperors, see M. Whitby, "Images for Emperors in Late Antiquity: A Search for New Constantines," in *New Constantines: The Rhythm of Imperial Renewal in Byzantium, 4th–13th Centuries*, ed. P. Magdalino (Aldershot, 1994), 83–93, esp. 84–86.

10 An excellent recent study is E. Goldfarb, "Transformation through Imitation: Biblical Figures as Moral Exempla in the Post-Classical World" (PhD diss., UCLA, 2005). Late-antique authors presaged the importance of *exempla* in later medieval literature, when it served a pedagogical purpose as a teaching tool, or indeed as an "instrument of conversion." See C. Bremond and J. LeGoff, *L'"Exemplum,"* Typologie des sources du moyen âge occidental 40 (Turnhout, 1982), 48–50. For the application of *exempla* among Christian authors of late antiquity, see also R. Cantel and R. Ricard, "Exemplum," *DSp* 4:1885–1902. For the use by Latin Christian authors of Old Testament figures as *exempla* for fourth-century emperors, see F. Heim, "Les figures du prince idéal au IVe siècle: du type au modèle," in *Figures de l'Ancien Testament chez les Pères*, Cahiers de Biblia Patristica (Strasbourg, 1989), 2:277–301.

11 1.1.19, ed. J. Bidez and G. C. Hansen (Berlin, 1960), 10, lines 12–16; trans. E. Walford, *The Ecclesiastical History of Sozomen* (London, 1855), 12.

12 J. F. Haldon, "Constantine or Justinian? Crisis and Identity in Imperial Propaganda in the Seventh Century," in Magdalino, *New Constantines*, 95–107.

13 P. Maas, "Metrische Akklamationen der Byzantiner," *BZ* 21 (1912): 28–51, 29, n. 1. The episode is mentioned in a *scholion*, written in a tenth-century hand, accompanying Theophylaktos

are re-enacted through imitation in the present. *Exemplum* depends on the active effort of the imitator and looks backward in time.

Typology, the second imitative mode under consideration here, is a specifically Christian hermeneutical strategy that connects the present with the biblical past of the Old Testament. Etymologically, "typos" derives from τύπτω = "to strike a blow," hence it literally means an "impression," as for example on a coin, and thus an "image" that reproduces and reflects the "archetype."[14] The first author to apply the notion of *typos* to the interpretation of Scripture was Philo of Alexandria (but in a very specific sense, influenced by Platonism); some of the New Testament epistles show the influence of his thought. Thus 1 Peter 3:21 explains that baptism is the *antitypos* (that which receives the imprint) to the *typos* of Noah's Ark; at Romans 5:14 Paul calls Adam "a type of the one who was to come" (τύπος τοῦ μέλλοντος), in the sense that both Adam and Christ's humanity were created by God without sin and Adam was the foreshadowing of Christ. Thus, typology provides the essential link of complete and continuous unity between the Old and the New Testament. Old Testament events and people are the prefiguration of the work that God would bring to completion with the New Covenant in Christ.

It is in its relation to historical time that *typos* radically differs from *exemplum*. In the words of Jean Daniélou: "There is no question of nostalgia for some remote ideal, as in the case of the Greek descriptions of a Golden Age. The past is only recalled as a foundation for future hope.... The essence of typology... is to show how past events are a figure of events to come."[15] In the thinking of Byzantine theologians, the extension of Old Testament time reached only partial fulfillment with the coming of Christ into the world, and it continues on

---

Simokattes, in cod. Vat. gr. 977, f. 184v, as well as in a fourteenth- or fifteenth-century manuscript of Prokopios's *Wars*.

14 For a useful lexical study of *typos*, see K. J. Woollcombe, "The Biblical Origins and Patristic Development of Typology," in G. W. H. Lampe and K. J. Woollcombe, *Essays on Typology*, Studies in Biblical Theology 22 (London, 1957), 60–65. The most detailed treatment is by J. Daniélou, *From Shadows to Reality: Studies in the Biblical Typology of the Fathers*, trans. W. Hibberd (London, 1960; first published in French *Sacramentum Futuri: Études sur les origines de la typologie biblique* [Paris, 1950]). On Old Testament *typoi* in the ascetic project of Athanasios of Alexandria, see D. Brakke, *Athanasius and Asceticism* (Baltimore–London, 1995), 165–70. For a general overview of typology, with relevance to early Christian art, see S. Schrenk, "Typologie: Biblische Typologie; Frühchristliche Literatur," *Lexikon des Mittelalters* 8:1183. For the continued relevance of typology (Latin: *figura*) in medieval and Renaissance thought, see E. Auerbach, "Figura," *Archivum Romanicum* 22 (1938): 436–89. On typology as an interpretive strategy of patristic authors, see J.-N. Guinot, "La typologie comme technique herméneutique," in *Figures de l'Ancien Testament* (n. 10 above), 2:1–34.

15 *From Shadows*, 12.

into the present until the Second Coming and the end of the world. *Typoi* are thus, in a sense, the figures of Old Testament history who cast their long shadows into the historical time of the here and now, where they are fully realized. As the image of a coin being struck suggests, they give new shape to those who receive their imprint.

Early Byzantine authors made frequent application of these two imitative modes, invoking Old Testament figures in a kind of hermeneutical shorthand that instantaneously conveyed an entire story along with its moral and thus provided an ethical lesson and elicited an emotional response.

Let us now examine the way in which early Byzantine authors invoked Old Testament models of emperors, whether as *exempla* or as *typoi*. This is to a large degree determined by the literary genre they are employing and the agenda they might be pursuing. There are three literary contexts in which emperors were set in relation to figures of the Old Testament. First, Old Testament models were employed by authors of historical narratives, where they served a descriptive function, as a kind of iconic sign-posting. Two rhetorical strategies were available to authors for this purpose: *exemplum* and *comparatio*. Proceeding in linear fashion, *exemplum* was used to demonstrate that the emperor was a worthy imitator of earlier models and the pinnacle of a long line of eminent predecessors. The word *exemplum* thus has a dual meaning, either the historical figure as a point of reference in the past, or the method of direct comparison with such a figure. *Comparatio* (Greek: σύγκρισις) resembles a zig-zag movement, making detailed comparisons between the emperor and earlier models, culminating in the conclusion that he surpassed them all.[16]

Direct addresses to the emperor provided the second context for the invocation of Old Testament figures. These addresses to the emperor, whether declarative or descriptive, could be positive or negative in tone, and they always harbored a further agenda: to exhort the emperor to imitation of Old Testament models, or to castigate him for the failure to do so. They could be pronounced on public occasions—at the delivery of panegyrics or the performance of acclamations—or they could be written down for reading in a more confined

---

16 H. Lausberg, *Handbook of Literary Rhetoric*, ed. D. E. Orton and R. D. Anderson, trans. M. T. Bliss, A. Jansen, and D. E. Orton (Leiden, 1998; first published in German, *Handbuch der literarischen Rhetorik* [Ismaning bei München, 1960]), 191–92 and 196–200. On *synkrisis* in rhetorical theory and its application in Greco-Roman literature, see F. Focke, "Synkrisis," *Hermes* 58 (1923): 327–68.

setting.[17] In both these contexts, the historical and the paraenetic, it is an identifiable author or speaker who suggests the association between emperor and Old Testament figure.

Exemplum and *typos* were applied by historians, chroniclers, and encomiasts. Writing in their own voice, they used these devices to describe and pass judgment on the emperor's qualities. There is a third, more oblique way in which historians sometimes set an emperor in relation to Old Testament models. In these instances, authors did not make explicit statements, but rather crafted their descriptions in such a way as to hint that an emperor's conduct was evocative of an Old Testament figure. According to the church historians Sozomen and Theodoret, Theodosius I modeled David when he abased himself before Ambrose to atone for the massacre at Thessalonike, while reciting David's penitential Psalm 99 (98): 25: "My soul cleaveth unto the dust: quicken thou me according to thy word."[18] That same Psalm 99 (98): 137 was also on the lips of the emperor Phokas shortly before his execution: "Righteous art thou, O Lord, and upright are thy judgments."[19] It is ironic that Phokas's dying words proclaimed his own association with David in front of Heraklios, who successfully usurped the throne and who would invoke Davidic associations for himself and his family on an unprecedented scale. The new emperor called one of his sons David, and was himself dubbed a "new David" by Theodore Synkellos already in 627, not long before the glorious conclusion of Heraklios's grand campaign against the Sasanians, which was celebrated by the creation of a set of silver plates narrating the story of David, including his fight with Goliath.[20] These reports of imitative conduct of emperors are, however, scarce. While they underscore the extent of the pervasiveness of Old Testament models, in that emperors themselves shaped their behavior according to this mold—at least according to the reports of their

---

17   On paraenetic writing addressed to rulers in general, see P. Hadot, "Fürstenspiegel," *RAC* 8:555–632.

18   Sozomen, *Church History* 7.25.1–7, ed. Bidez and Hansen, 338, line 24–340, line 4; Theodoret, *Church History* 5.18.19, ed. L. Parmentier, rev. G. C. Hansen (Berlin, 1998), 312, line 13–16. See also H. Leppin, *Von Constantin dem Grossen zu Theodosius II: Das christliche Kaisertum bei den Kirchenhistorikern Socrates, Sozomenus und Theodoret*, Hypomnemata 110 (Göttingen, 1996), 114–20. The David-like repentance of Theodosius, at least according to *Vita Ambrosii* by Paulinus, was integrated into the Byzantine liturgical cycle by the tenth century, and some version of this was known to Constantine VII. See Dagron, *Emperor and Priest* (n. 5 above), 105–6, and 120.

19   Theophylaktos Simokattes, *Historiae* 8.11.3, ed. C. de Boor, rev. P. Wirth (Leipzig, 1972), 305, lines 6–8. cf. Dagron, *Emperor and Priest*, 150.

20   M. Mundell Mango, "Imperial Art in the Seventh Century," in Magdalino, *New Constantines* (n. 9 above), 109–38, esp. 122–27.

historians or observers—they do not shed much light on the literary strategies of Byzantine authors regarding the imitative process, which is the focus of the present study, and thus shall be left aside.

The use of Old Testament models for emperors begins, like so much of Christian Greek writing, with Constantine and Eusebios. The reign of Constantine, the first Roman emperor to grant legitimacy to Christianity and to extend his personal patronage to the Church and her representatives, rings in a period of experimentation in all areas of politics and cultural expression. This includes imperial ideology and literature, and in both of these Eusebios of Caesarea established new trends. Of particular relevance are his *Church History*, the first of its kind, circulated in several editions and finally published in 325, and his *Life of Constantine*, written shortly after 337. Eusebios, like many authors after him, infused the pagan tradition of rhetoric with Christian theology and exegesis.[21] Take, for example, the *Life of Constantine*, a hybrid of history, biography, and panegyric. In this work, Eusebios invokes historical *exempla* (King Cyrus of Persia, Alexander the Great) alongside Old Testament figures, especially Moses. As Moses escaped from Pharaoh's court, Constantine fled from the court of Diocletian, and just as Moses had led the Israelites across the Red Sea, Constantine was leading the new and true Israel, that is, the Christians, into a new realm of religious freedom. A focal point is the Battle of the Milvian Bridge, where Constantine's adversary Maxentius drowned miserably in the Tiber, as had Pharaoh in the waters of the Red Sea. These are just the most obvious instances in a narrative that is constructed to depict the progression of the life of Constantine as parallel to the life of Moses. One might even say that Moses serves as a *typos* for Constantine.[22] After Eusebios's narrative, "Pharaoh" became the shorthand for any enemy of the faith, a negative model to be applied to any persecutor of Christians or any political adversary of the reigning emperor.[23] By the seventh century,

---

21 On this theme in general, see Av. Cameron, *Christianity and the Rhetoric of Empire: The Development of Christian Discourse* (Berkeley, 1991).
22 R. Farina, *L'impero e l'imperatore cristiano in Eusebio di Cesarea: La prima teologia politica del Cristianesimo* (Zurich, 1966), 189–90; A. Wilson, "Biographical Models: The Constantinian Period and Beyond," in *Constantine: History, Historiography and Legend*, ed. S. N. C. Lieu and D. Montserrat (London–New York, 1998), 107–35, esp. 113 and n. 39, and 116–21; M. Hollerich, "The Comparison of Moses and Constantine in Eusebios of Caesarea's Life of Constantine," in *StP* 19 (Leuven, 1989): 80–85; idem, "Religion and Politics in the Writings of Eusebius: Reassessing the First 'Court Theologian,'" *Church History* 59 (1990): 309–25; C. Rapp, "Imperial Ideology in the Making: Eusebius of Caesarea on Constantine as 'Bishop,'" *JTS*, n.s., 49 (1998): 685–95; Eusebios, *Life of Constantine*, ed. and trans. Av. Cameron and S. G. Hall (Oxford, 1999), 35–39.
23 B. Isele, "Moses oder Pharao? Die ersten christlichen Kaiser und das Argument der Bibel," in *Die Bibel als politisches Argument: Voraussetzungen und Folgen biblizistischer Herrschaftslegitimation*

Heraklios's enemy, the Persian King Chosroes, was identified by George of Pisidia as "new Pharaoh," which made Heraklios not only into a new Moses but also, indirectly, into a new Constantine.

By contrast, in his *Church History*, completed more than a decade earlier, Eusebios only once used an Old Testament model for an emperor, on the occasion of Constantine's victory over Maxentius at the Milvian Bridge.[24] Maxentius's death in the Tiber reminds the author of the drowning of Pharaoh in the Red Sea at the time of Moses. This association is first underlined with a quotation from Exodus 15:4–5, and then reinforced by the suggestion that the soldiers of Constantine replicated the actions of the Israelites who followed Moses: "So that suitably, if not in words, at least in deeds, like the followers of the great servant Moses, those who had won the victory by the help of God might in some sort hymn the very same words which were uttered against the wicked tyrant of old."[25] Constantine's victory is, in Eusebios's view, nothing less than a reenactment of Moses' triumph: "These things, and such as are akin and similar to them, Constantine by his very deeds sang to God the Ruler of all and Author of the victory."[26]

Eusebios's uneven application of the Moses imagery for Constantine, which dominates his *Life of Constantine* but is barely present in his *Church History*, suggests that Old Testament models were favored in only certain genres of writing and not in others. Historians, even Church historians, were surprisingly reluctant to evoke such associations. The fifth-century continuators of Eusebios's *Church History*, though taking their inspiration from Eusebios and putting forward a specifically Christian ideal of rulership, were equally restrained in their application of Old Testament models to emperors.[27] Socrates, who composed his *Church History* in Constantinople in ca. 439, did invoke Old Testament models for both Constantine and Theodosius II, during whose reign he was writing. He seems to establish this relation both typologically and historically. Constantine's

---

in der Vormoderne, ed. A. Pecar and K. Trampedach, Historische Zeitschrift, Beihefte, n.F. 43 (Munich, 2007), 103–18.

24   I have considered only Books 8 to 10, which cover the period from Diocletian to Constantine. Eusebios's speech on the dedication of the church at Tyre (*Church History* 10.4.2–72) is mentioned below.

25   Eusebios, *Church History* 9.9.8; E. Schwartz and T. Mommsen, *Die Kirchengeschichte*, rev. F. Winkelmann, GCS 6 (Berlin, 1999), 2.2:830, lines 13–16; K. Lake, trans., *The Ecclesiastical History* (Cambridge, MA, 1926–38), 2:363. Cf. *Church History* 9.9.5, ed. Schwartz, 828, lines 23–24; trans. Lake, 361.

26   Eusebios, *Church History* 9.9.9, ed. Schwartz, 830, lines 21–23; trans. Lake, 363.

27   G. F. Chesnut, *The First Christian Histories* (Paris, 1977), 223–49; Leppin, *Von Constantin* (n. 18 above), 195–97.

preparation for his war against Persia is said to include the creation of "a tabernacle of fine and varied linen made in the model of a church (ἐκκλησίας τύπον), just like (ὡς) Moses had made in the desert."[28] Socrates' manner of comparison here suggests direct imitation. Likewise, when Socrates compared Theodosius II's actions in times of war to those of Moses or David, he did so very much in historical mode. "And if ever war occurred, he took refuge in God in the manner of David (κατὰ τὸν Δαυίδ)."[29] Theodosius II's victory against the usurper John is given additional luster with the invocation of Moses' generalship (ἐπὶ Μωυσέως) in the crossing of the Red Sea, even though it was not Theodosius himself who led his troops, but his generals.[30] Later in the text, Socrates suggests that what was said about Moses as the model of meekness may now be said about Theodosius II, who surpassed all the clergy in this virtue.[31] Here, the application of the rhetorical device of *comparatio* between the emperor and the clergy indicates that Socrates saw the emperor as the worthy imitator of the example of Moses.

Socrates' contemporary Sozomen also wrote his *Church History* in Constantinople, but slightly later, during the last decade of the reign of Theodosius II. He invoked imperial Old Testament models only once, in his dedicatory preface to Theodosius II, which is really a panegyric *en miniature*. To illustrate the emperor's love of learning, Sozomen mentioned prior examples from classical antiquity (such as the appreciation of Homer shown by the Cretans), and then finally invoked Solomon as a comparison: "You know the nature of stones and the power of roots and the forces of remedies no less than the wisest Solomon, son of David. Rather, you even surpass him in virtues."[32] With this *comparatio* to an Old Testment example, Sozomen skilfully brings to a grand conclusion a sequence of *exempla* that includes Solomon.

Theodoret wrote his *Church History* in Cyrrhus, where he was bishop, sometime between 429 and his death ca. 466. He mentioned the Old Testament only twice, both times negatively, to castigate non-Christian and heretical emperors by juxtaposing them to Pharaoh, who failed to heed the message of the ten plagues: when the emperor Julian continued in his plans to rebuild the temple in Jerusalem, despite terrifying signs and miracles, he is said to have hardened his

---

28   Socrates, *Church History* 1.18.12, ed. G. C. Hansen (Berlin, 1995), 59, lines 19–60, line 2. Unless otherwise noted, translations are mine.
29   Socrates, *Church History* 7.22.19, ed. Hansen, 370, lines 18–20. See also Leppin, *Von Constantin dem Grossen zu Theodosius II*, 137–38.
30   Socrates, *Church History* 7.22.21, ed. Hansen, 370, lines 25–27.
31   Socrates, *Church History* 7.42.2, ed. Hansen, 390, lines 24–391, line 1.
32   Sozomen, *Church History* Prologue 10, ed. Bidez and Hansen, 3, lines 7–10. See also Leppin, *Von Constantin*, 138.

heart "similar to Pharaoh (τῷ δὲ Φαραὼ παραπλησίως)."[33] And when the emperors Valens and Valentinian persisted in their support of Arianism, although they should have followed the advice of the holy man Aphraat and should have been warned by the untimely death of a bath attendant, they are said to have hardened their hearts against him "in the manner of Pharaoh (κατὰ τὸν Φαραώ)."[34] Theodoret's choice of expressions merely alludes to the historical precedent of the Bible to castigate the unpopular measures of certain emperors, but refrains from completely equating imitator and model. The anonymous *Church History*, formerly attributed to Gelasius of Cyzicus, which was composed around 480 largely on the basis of prior authors, is entirely devoid of any associations between emperors and the Old Testament; so also is the *Church History* of Evagrios Scholastikos, which covers events from 428 to 592.

On the whole, then, early Byzantine church historians, beginning with Eusebios, employed Old Testament comparisons for emperors only sparingly. In the few cases where an emperor is set in relation to an Old Testament figure, this is most commonly achieved by invoking the model as a historical *exemplum*. Only rarely is a typological relation established between the Old Testament prototype and its imperial counterpart.

In historical narratives that focus on the emperor and the empire, by contrast, Old Testament models are entirely absent.[35] Authors of historical accounts who adopt a classicizing style, such as Prokopios and Agathias in the sixth century, avoid any mention of biblical figures or allusions to Christianity in general, because such words and concepts would not have been known to their stylistic models from classical antiquity, especially Herodotus and Thucydides. Even Theophylaktos Simokattes, who wrote his *History* in the early seventh century from an unabashedly Christian viewpoint but with all the stylistic aspirations to *mimesis* of the ancients, does not include Old Testament references in his descriptions of emperors and their deeds.

The absence of Old Testament models for emperors in historical narratives is the result of the stylistic requirements of a genre that had deep roots in the

---

33 Theodoret, *Church History* 3.20.8, ed. Parmentier and Hansen, 200, line 6.
34 Theodoret, *Church History* 4.26.9, ed. Parmentier and Hansen, 266, lines 18–19.
35 The following depends on extensive searches for Old Testament names (David, Moses, Solomon, Melchisedek, Noah, Jonah, Pharaoh, Ahab, Jezebel) in the relevant authors in the Thesaurus Linguae Graecae online. These names are often mentioned when the authors discuss them in their own context in the history of Israel, when they refer to their actions either in the biblical past or as having a model character in later periods, or when they quote or refer to something the biblical figures have said. Since such mentions have no bearing on the present question, they have not been charted here.

classical tradition. This would lead one to expect a larger number of such references in a new kind of historical writing that gained popularity in late antiquity, the Christian world chronicle. After all, chroniclers employ a Christian frame of reference, beginning their coverage at a date that is significant for Christian history—whether the creation of the world or the reign of Diocletian—and focusing on the Christians, preceded by the Israelites, as the people who "make history." But such associations are very rare. In this instance, it is not the literary tradition but the narrative format of year-by-year recording that does not allow for elaborations in the authorial voice. Eusebios's *Chronicle*, as it survives in Jerome's Latin translation, contains only telegraph-style information, with no opportunity for rhetorical flourishes such as Old Testament comparisons. Even the sixth-century chronicler John Malalas is very restrained in his application of Old Testament models, despite his broad application of the Old Testament elsewhere (see above, Chapter 6). He uses this literary device only once, when he reports a pun that does not throw an entirely positive light on the modesty of the empress Eudokia. According to Malalas, when the empress rebuilt the wall of Jerusalem on her journey to the Holy Land, she exclaimed with pride: "It was of me that the prophet David spoke when he said, 'In thy good pleasure (εὐδοκία), O Lord, the walls of Jerusalem shall be built (cf. Psalm 51 [50]:18).'"[36] This dearth of Old Testament models left room for elaboration by later imitators. Malalas was extensively used by John of Nikiu in his *Chronicle*, which was originally composed in Greek in the late seventh century, but now survives only in an Ethiopian translation of an earlier Arabic version. Where Malalas has: "When the Samaritans learnt of the emperor's anger against them, they rebelled and crowned a bandit chief, a Samaritan named Julian,"[37] John of Nikiu elaborates: "And he [Julian the Samaritan] seduced many of his people by his lying statement when he declared: 'God hath sent me to re-establish the Samaritan kingdom'; just as (Je)roboam the son of Nebat who, reigning after the wise Solomon the son of David, seduced the people of Israel and made them serve idols."[38] Here we see at work a chronicler whose embellishment of his source includes the introduction of a negative model from the Old Testament. Finally, the *Chronicon*

---

36 John Malalas, *Chronographia* 14.8, ed. J. Thurn (Berlin–New York, 2000), 278, lines 37–39 (Dindorf, 357–58), trans. E. Jeffreys, M. Jeffreys, and R. Scott, *The Chronicle of John Malalas: A Translation* (Melbourne, 1986), 195.
37 John Malalas, *Chronographia* 18.35, ed. Thurn, 373, lines 50–52 (Dindorf, 445–46), trans. Jeffreys, 260.
38 John of Nikiu 93.5, trans. R. H. Charles, *The Chronicle of John Bishop of Nikiu* (London–Oxford, 1916), 147.

Paschale, a product of the reign of Heraklios, is strikingly devoid of any reference to Old Testament figures in conjunction with ruling emperors.

As the example of John of Nikiu's use of Malalas shows, there can be some variation in the application of Old Testament models even between chroniclers of roughly the same period. The same holds true for the chroniclers of the late eighth and early ninth centuries. Whereas Theophanes in his *Chronographia*, composed ca. 813, frequently compared emperors to Old Testament figures, such allusions are entirely absent in Theophanes' main source, the *Chronicle* of George the Synkellos. They are also lacking in the late eighth-century *Breviarium* by the Patriarch Nikephoros, which is closely related to Theophanes' text. The *Breviarium* is told as a consecutive narrative, which should have allowed the author greater leeway for rhetorical flourishes than the annalistic style employed by Theophanes.

The latter's use of Old Testament figures occurs mainly as criticism of heretical and iconoclast emperors.[39] King Ahab serves as a comparison for Valens's rage against the monk Isaac, who had challenged him because of his pro-Arian policy[40] and for the iconoclast persecutions unleashed by Constantine V.[41] The emperor Nikephoros is even called a "new Ahab" for his unwise campaign against the Bulgarians, which cost him his life,[42] and he is reported to have prided himself on possessing the harshness of Pharaoh when confronted with a request to relax his taxation policy.[43] In some instances, Theophanes reiterated imperial connections to Old Testament models that he found in his sources. He picked up on the imagery established by Eusebios when he compared Maxentius's drowning in the Tiber to the death of Pharaoh,[44] and for his equation of Constantine and David (in his description of the emperor's escape from a plot on his life by Galerius and Maximian), he depended on Alexander the Monk.[45]

On a rather modest scale and with largely polemical intent, Theophanes employed Old Testament models to demonstrate the historical continuity

---

39 See also F. H. Tinnefeld, *Elemente der Kaiserkritik in der byzantinischen Historiographie von Prokop bis Niketas Choniates* (Munich, 1971).

40 Theophanes, *Chronographia*, AM 5870, ed. C. de Boor, vol. 1 (Leipzig, 1883; repr. Hildesheim, 1963), 65, line 14.

41 Theophanes, AM 6258, ed. de Boor, 439, line 16.

42 Theophanes, AM 6303, ed. de Boor, 489, line 23. Cf. 490, line 13.

43 Theophanes, AM 6303, ed. de Boor, 489, lines 32–490, line 1. Cf. the self-identification with Jonah of the Patriarch Germanos as he resisted Leo's condemnation of icons: Theophanes, AM 6221, de Boor, 409, line 7.

44 Theophanes, AM 5802, ed. de Boor, 14, line 10.

45 Theophanes, AM 5793, ed. de Boor, 9, line 26, with commentary by C. Mango and R. Scott, *The Chronicle of Theophanes* (Oxford, 1997), 14, n. 8.

between Old Testament history and his own day. Pointing to Ahab and Pharaoh as paradigmatic "bad rulers," he implicitly criticized unpopular emperors and at the same time reassured his like-minded, iconophile audience that they were siding with the true Israel and would also be granted deliverance. The connection of Old Testament models with criticism and praise will concern us again soon.

Theophanes was the only chronicler to use the Old Testament models. Since the chroniclers' primary task was to report, rather than to depict or analyze events, there was little opportunity for them to establish connections between emperors and Old Testament models. Their simple and accessible style did not lend itself to literary flourishes such as comparisons or exclamations, which encompass an element of interpretation, unless—as in the case of Theophanes—they wished to express strong negative sentiments, for which Old Testament comparisons may become a vehicle.

Old Testament models are most prevalent in direct addresses to the emperor, which were regular features at ceremonial occasions. Whether the emperor was present or not, he would be praised in acclamations in various contexts and locations: at the horse races in the hippodrome, during ceremonies in the palace involving the Blues and Greens, at meetings of the senate for the approval of laws,[46] or in assemblies of bishops at church councils. These expressions of the collective will of the people are accessible to us only if historians reported the relevant event, archivists maintained a record of the protocol for specific ceremonies (as in the *Book of Ceremonies*), or the redactors of the *acta* of church councils preserved them. For our period of interest at least, references to Old Testament figures in acclamations to the emperor seem to be uttered predominantly by groups of bishops in the context of church councils. Their earliest occurrences are from the middle of the fifth century, at roughly the same time when the Church assumed a larger role in confirming imperial power through the participation and prayers of the clergy in the accession ceremonies.[47] Their appearance may thus signal a new chapter in the relation between emperor and bishops, when the latter assumed a more assertive position in defining the parameters of Christian rulership.

The great watershed in the invocation of Old Testament models for the emperor seems to have been the time of the Council of Chalcedon (451), when bishops found different ways to insinuate such associations for the emperor. They

---

46 J. Harries, *Law and Empire in Late Antiquity* (Cambridge, 1999), 65–69.
47 A. E. R. Boak, "Imperial Coronation Ceremonies in the Fourth and Fifth Centuries," *Harvard Studies in Classical Philology* 30 (1919): 37–47.

did so not just collectively in acclamations at the council itself but also in letters of advocacy for a particular cause sent by groups of bishops. Like all rhetoric of praise, these expressions establish a gold standard of conduct and character for the emperor, sometimes with the subtle implication that it may yet await fulfillment. Prior to the Council of Chalcedon, Bishop Sabinian addressed an urgent letter to the emperors Valentinian and Marcian, requesting an investigation into the circumstances of his forcible ordination to the episcopate. He begins his missive by praising the emperors for their piety and just rulership, which is why God might also address them: "I added help to one who was powerful; I exalted one chosen from my people. I found David my slave; with my holy oil I anointed him (Ps 89:19–20 [88:20–21] NETS modified)."[48] In this purposeful flattery, the bishop assumes the voice of the psalmist who pronounces God's words to suggest that the emperor may be (or ought to be) re-enacting David's piety.

The sessions of the Council of Chalcedon are rife with Old Testament evocations in praise of emperors. The sixth session, on 25 October 451, concluded the doctrinal discussions with the approval of the definition of faith, ratified by the bishops and endorsed through lengthy acclamations. In this context, the models of the Old and New Testament are invoked on the same plane as those of Christian imperial history: "To Marcian, the new Constantine, the new Paul, the new David! The years of David to the emperor!"[49] These pronouncements are ostensibly a statement of fact ("Marcian has proved himself to be like Constantine, Paul, David"), yet also exhort the emperor to imitate their example ("We hope, Marcian, that you will act like these predecessors"). They are also a prayer to God to grant that this may come to pass, which is especially obvious in the wish for the longevity of David. These acclamations indicate that a Christian interpretation of imperial rulership that was universalist not only in its geographical but also in its historical claims was beginning to take a firm hold in Byzantine society. Not only did the extent of imperial rule encompass the Christian *oikoumene*, but its *raison d'être* reached back beyond Roman times all the way to the Israelites.

The trend established by the bishops at Chalcedon for addressing the emperor within a biblical context continued under Marcian's successor, Leo I (457–474). Early in his reign, Leo removed the non-Chalcedonian Timothy Aelurus from the patriarchal throne in Alexandria—a measure for which many Eastern

---

48 Mansi 7:316D.
49 Mansi 7:169C. *ACO* 2.1.2:155, lines 12–13. Trans. R. Price and M. Gaddis, *The Acts of the Council of Chalcedon* (Liverpool, 2005), 2:240.

bishops expressed their approval in letters to the emperor. The letter of the bishops of Isauria to Leo offers a masterly combination of Old Testament typology with historical *exemplum*. It begins by equating the purity of the emperor's sacrifice with that of Abel. Then a second point of comparison is introduced, this time with a historical figure. Leo is said to be a zealous imitator of Constantine, who himself is considered "a living image of Abel" in eternity, who stands before God "like David as a king and a prophet," and who shines forth along with Peter and Paul, as a near likeness of them.[50] Leo's imitation of Abel is thus refractured to make him an imitator of Constantine, and—through him—of the biblical king and the Christian apostles. The bishops of the province of Lycia who assembled at a synod in Myra praised the emperor for extending his wise judgment "like the most great Moses."[51] Likewise the bishops of Europe wrote to Leo I proclaiming that he would be known as the "imitator of David the most mild,"[52] while the bishops of Armenia Prima sent a letter in which they asserted that God had appointed him to the throne "like a new David."[53] In these passages, Old Testament models were evoked variously as historical precedent worthy of imitation or as typological prefigurations of the present reign. What the Church historians of the 430s and 440s—following the ideas floated by Eusebios a century earlier—had very tentatively put into circulation, the bishops of the 450s trumpeted with great fanfare: imperial rule was rooted as much in the Roman tradition as in Judeo-Christian history.

This is roughly the same period when the involvement of the patriarch of Constantinople in the imperial succession seems to have become common.[54] The oldest known text of the imperial coronation ritual begins with a prayer by the patriarch reminding God that, through Saul, he selected David and anointed him king of Israel; it then asks God to do the same at the present moment.[55] The

---

50   This, like the following two letters, is accessible only in a Latin version, in Mansi 7:559C–D: "Abel sacrificiorum puritate fecistis: in quo enim aequale est sacrificium cum veritate fidei et amicitia pacis. Zelatus es actibus tuis, tranquilissime imperator, Constantinum illum memoriae immortalem, maximum, pium, amatorem Christi, et indubitanter apud omnes beatum, qui Abelis vivens imaginem in animabus hominum possidit in aeternum: qui cum David quidem sicut rex et propheta stat apud Deum, cum Petro autem et Paulo et tonitrui [?] filiis quasi similis eis, in praedicationibus veritatis effulget."

51   Ibid., 7:576D–577A: "sicut Moyses maximus."

52   Ibid., 7:539A: "mansuetissimi David imitator."

53   Ibid., 7:587C: "quodam secundo David."

54   For a detailed discussion of imperial accessions and the ceremonies that were created or adapted for these occasions, see Dagron, *Emperor and Priest* (n. 5 above), 54–69.

55   Bibliotheca Vaticana, Barberini gr. 336, fols. 176v–177r, ed. S. Parenti and E. Velkovska, *L'Euchologio Barberini gr. 336 (ff. 1–263)* (Rome, 1995), 194–95. The same text, from ms. Grottaferrata

invoking of God's prior interventions is meant to solicit analogous divine actions in the present, a typological reference to past events in the hope of future fulfillment, in a kind of anamnestic prayer. The ritual is preserved in the oldest Byzantine liturgical manuscript, the Barberini Euchologion, which dates from the mid-eighth century, but the coronation prayers themselves may well predate the manuscript. Equally hard to date with any accuracy are two objects associated with the Old Testament that played an important part in imperial ritual: Solomon's Throne, located in the central apse of the Magnaura, a reception hall in immediate proximity of the great palace in Constantinople, and the Rod of Moses, which the emperor Constantine was believed to have brought to the capital.[56]

In the mid-fifth century bishops first championed the use of Old Testament models in acclamations to praise and exhort the emperor. Already a century earlier, they had adopted these models in a negative sense, for the chastisement of emperors in invectives and letters. For instance, Athanasios of Alexandria's descriptions of Constantius II show how the choice of biblical models depended on political context and literary genre. Athanasios, as a strong adherent of Nicene Christology, found himself at odds with the emperor's pro-Arian policies. He used positive models to coax the emperor into imitation, negative models to illustrate the intensity of his censure of the emperor.[57] In his *Apology to the Emperor Constantius*, written in 356–57, Athanasios pleads with the emperor to give a fair hearing to his case, reminding him, in two separate places, that he ought to follow the example of David, who refused to give heed to false accusations, and mentioning that Solomon had the good sense to avoid unnecessary and untrue rumors.[58] Slightly later, in 358, when Athanasios wrote his *History of*

G.b.I ("Bessarion"), fols. 122–23, in J. Goar, *Euchologion sive Rituale graecorum* (Venice, 1730; repr. Graz, 1960), 726. Cf. M. Arranz, "Couronnement royal et autres promotions de cour: Les sacrements de l'institution de l'ancien euchologe constantinopolitain," *OCP* 56 (1990): 83–133, at 85 and 93.

56 For imperial associations with Solomon, see Constantine Porphyrogenitus, *Three Treatises on Imperial Military Expeditions*, ed. and trans. J. Haldon (Vienna, 1990), 178–79. For detailed documentation of both objects, see O. Treitinger, *Die oströmische Kaiser- und Reichsidee nach ihrer Gestaltung im höfischen Zeremoniell*, 2nd ed. (Darmstadt, 1956), 134–35.

57 For historical context, see L. W. Barnard, "Athanase, Constantin et Constance," in *Politique et théologie chez Athanase d'Alexandrie*, Actes du Colloque de Chantilly, 23–25 septembre 1973, ed. C. Kannengiesser (Paris, 1974), 127–43; Dvornik, *Political Philosophy* (n. 4 above), 2:731–42; Isele, "Moses oder Pharao?" (n. 23 above), 110–14. See also R. Flower, "Polemic and Episcopal Authority in Fourth-Century Christianity" (PhD diss., Cambridge, 2007).

58 Athanasios, *Apologia ad Constantium imp.* 5 and 20, ed. J.-M. Szymusiak, *Apologie à l'empereur Constance*, SC 56 (Paris, 1958).

the Arians, his characterization of Constantius II shows his displeasure with the emperor's support for the Arian position. In this work he compares the emperor three times to Pharaoh, and also to Ahab, Belshazzar, and the cruelty of Saul.[59]

Similarly scathing criticism is leveled by Gregory of Nazianzus against Julian the Apostate. In one of his homilies against Julian, Gregory establishes a laundry list of Old Testament representatives of specific vices whom Julian is said to imitate: Ieroboam (apostasy), Ahab (bloodthirstiness), Pharaoh (harshness), Nebuchadnezzar (sacrilege); and the combined impiety of all.[60] The rhetorical trope he applies is that of *comparatio*: the enumeration of individual virtues or vices in their Old Testament impersonations, which culminates in the statement that Julian does not merely embody one or another of these, but surpasses their combined total.

Thus, bishops of the late fourth century who found themselves in conflict with the emperor combined an optimistic expression regarding the possibility of a change of heart in the emperor with dire condemnations, should he fail to do so. We see here a feature of *exemplum* and *typos* as imitative modes: in the context of praise, *exemplum* and *typos* may both be used, while invective employs only the *typos*. The *exemplum* assumes the possibility of agency and indeed encourages the effort to conform to an ancient model. *Typos*, by contrast, asserts that someone extends an established pattern to the present. Since negative models are held up, not for imitation, but only for condemnation, they are always invoked in the mode of the *typos* that shapes its imprint, not the *exemplum* that invites imitation.

Texts on the nature of rulership, including Mirrors of Princes, might be expected to yield rich material for the interpretation of the emperor's role in a biblical mold. But in the early Byzantine works that theorize about imperial rule and attempt to draw an idealized picture of the emperor, Old Testament models are conspicuously absent, perhaps as a consequence of the authors' classicizing tendencies to shun any overt reference to Christian writing—a pattern that has already been noted for historical narratives. Old Testament figures appear neither in Agapetos's *Capitula admonitoria*, nor in the anonymous dialogue *On*

---

59 Athanasios, *Historia Arianorum* 45.24, ed. H.-G. Opitz, *Athanasius Werke* (Berlin, 1940), 2.1:209, line 29: "a new Ahab and second Belshazzar in our time." Further comparison with Ahab: *Hist. Ar.* 53.3, ed. Opitz, 213, line 33; the emperor is worse than Ahab: *Hist. Ar.* 68.1, ed. Opitz, 220, line 18–19. Comparison with Pharaoh: *Hist. Ar.* 30.4, ed. Opitz, 199, lines 18–19; and 34.3, ed. Opitz, 202, lines 12–13. A second Pharaoh: *Hist. Ar.* 68.1, ed. Opitz, 220, line 21. He strives to imitate the model of Saul: *Hist. Ar.* 67.3–4, ed. Opitz, 220, lines 6–11.
60 Gregory of Nazianzus, *Oratio 5 Contra Iulianum* 2.3, PG 35:668A.

Political Science.⁶¹ Neither are they featured in a further work of the sixth century, John the Lydian's *On Magistracies*.

Panegyrics are a different matter. Eusebios, as has been noted, is the master of allusions to Old Testament models in his praise for Constantine. However, his application of these references is as uneven in his speeches of panegyrical nature as in his narratives of historical character, discussed above. While they do not appear in his celebration of three decades of Constantine's rule in the *De laudibus Constantini*, they are quite predominant in his speech on the occasion of the inauguration of the newly built church in Tyre, which may with some justification be classified as a panegyric. Eusebios begins this speech, which he later included in his *Church History*, by addressing the emperor, who was present in the audience: "One should call thee a new Bezalel the architect of a divine tabernacle, or Solomon the king of a new and far goodlier Jerusalem, or even a new Zerubbabel who bestowed upon the temple of God that glory which greatly exceeded the former."⁶² The theme of Constantine as a temple builder is resumed again later, when he is called "our most peaceful Solomon."⁶³ Eusebios also praises Constantine for the priestly role he received from God, as a "new Aaron or Melchizedek."⁶⁴ This is one of the very few instances where Melchisedek, king and priest, is invoked by an early Byzantine author in conjunction with an emperor. Eusebios here does not merely use expressions of parallel and comparison, but consciously employs the language of complete, typological equation. Constantine's participation in the divine *logos*, a recurrent theme in Eusebios, extends to his typological participation in everything that these Old Testament models represent. But Eusebios, who was a bishop as well as a historian, biographer, and panegyrist, was an exception: in general, authors of Mirrors of Princes and panegyrists prior to the seventh century were extremely reluctant to take up Old Testament models for emperors. This may not only be rooted in their indebtedness to classical models for their genre but also stem from their intellectual outlook and formation as authors who do not represent the Church.

After Eusebios, it was a long time before the authors who wrote panegyrics accepted Old Testament figures as a point of reference. Such mentions

---

61 Agapetos Diakonos, *Der Fürstenspiegel für Kaiser Iustinianos*, ed. R. Riedinger (Athens, 1995). *Menae Patricii cum Thoma referendario De scientia politica dialogus*, ed. C. M. Mazzucchi (Milan, 1982).
62 Eusebios, *Church History* 10.4.3, ed. Schwartz, 862, line 24–864, line 2, trans. Lake, 399.
63 Eusebios, *Church History* 10.4.45, ed. Schwartz, 876, line 6–7, trans. Lake, 427.
64 Eusebios, *Church History* 10.4.23, ed. Schwartz, 869, line 28, trans. Lake, 413.

are certainly absent in Themistius, the pagan orator at the Christian court of Constantinople from 355 to ca. 384, during the reigns of Constantius II, Jovian, Valens, and Theodosius I. Corippus's Latin verse panegyric on the emperor Justin II, for all its references to Christianity and the Mother of God, does not mention Old Testament models, but instead reports the acclamations of the senators at the inauguration of Justin as consul in 566 that invoke historical precedent: "You have renewed the ancient age of Augustus Caesar; but yours is more famed and greater."[65] Likewise, Prokopios of Gaza, in his panegyric on the emperor Anastasios I, avoids references to biblical models. Instead, he highlights the emperor's character as a *nomos empsychos* who provides an example to his subjects; Prokopios then gives a detailed *comparatio* with great men of ancient history, Cyrus of Persia, Agesilaos of Sparta, and Alexander the Great, culminating in the affirmation that Anastasios surpasses them all in his combination of virtues.[66]

It was only during the reign of Heraklios that Old Testament models became an important component of panegyric. More than any emperor before him, Heraklios's imperial rule was associated with the model of David.[67] Biblical imagery abounds in the homily delivered by Theodore Synkellos after the dual siege of Constantinople by Persians and Avars in 626 had been thwarted by the miraculous intervention of the Mother of God. The author very explicitly employs the language of biblical typology, explaining that what Isaiah had announced (προδιαγράψας) "by shadow and type" (ἐν σκιᾷ καὶ τύπῳ) about the Jerusalem of old had now come to pass under "the David who is emperor in our times" (τοῦ Δαυὶδ τοῦ καθ' ἡμᾶς βασιλεύοντος).[68] This expression is significant. More than just a "new David," Heraklios *is* the *same* David who had lived in biblical times, now transposed to the present. The David theme is resumed at the end of the homily, when the author explains that Heraklios *is* David because of his piety toward God and gentleness (πραότης) toward his subjects, but also because of

---

65 Corippus, *In laudem Iustini minoris* 4.135, ed. and trans. Av. Cameron (London, 1976), 77, trans. 113.
66 Prokopios of Gaza, *In imperatorem Anastasium panegyricus* 23, ed. K. Kempen (Bonn, 1918), 14, lines 22–25; and chapter 24, 15, lines 13–15.
67 See above, note 20.
68 Theodore Synkellos 38, Greek text ed. L. Sternbach, "Analecta Avarica," repr. with French trans. by B. Tátray and comm. by F. Makk, *Traduction et commentaire de l'homélie écrite probablement par Théodore le Syncelle sur le siège de Constantinople en 626*, Acta Universitatis de Attila József Nominatae, Acta Antiqua et Archaeologica 18, Opuscula Byzantina vol. 3 (Szeged, 1975), 313, lines 35–314, line 1.

his victoriousness and because of the wisdom and peaceful disposition of his son, qualities that resemble those of Solomon.[69]

The last great panegyrist before the lull in literary—or, more precisely: non-theological—production during the so-called Dark Centuries was George of Pisidia. He composed several verse panegyrics on the emperor Heraklios, praising his victorious exploits against the Avars and the Persians. Favoring the complete equation of imitator with archetype, he called Heraklios a "new Moses," an "imitator of Elijah of old," and "the Noah of the new *oikoumene*."[70] The guiding principle of George of Pisidia's praise of Heraklios, however, was the comparison with David, as Claudia Ludwig has meticulously demonstrated.[71] The parallels are many: the unexpected accession to the throne (Heraklios's coup d'état of 610), the fight against a formidable enemy (the Persians), and the return of a sacred object to Jerusalem (the Holy Cross).

George of Pisidia carefully chose the verbs to indicate the imitative relationship between the emperor and his Old Testament models.[72] *Mimeisthai*, "to imitate," is the usual word, and it is frequently employed. But he also used the rarer verb *eikonizein*, "to model, to signify," on three occasions. For example in *De expeditione Persica*, line 135: "Immediately after the celebration of Easter, you led the troops against the second Pharaoh, in the image of Moses (εἰκονίζων Μωσέα), if it were not a mistake to call 'second' (Pharaoh) him who in reality was the first with regard to his sin."[73] A cursory check in the Thesaurus Linguae Graecae reveals that the verb *eikonizein* was little used in the pre-Christian centuries but enjoyed great currency among Christian authors in Byzantium. George of Pisidia employed it to indicate an essential connection between the imitator and his archetype. The identification he suggested is qualitatively different from the historicizing mode of the *exemplum* and the biblicizing mode of the *typos*. Heraklios participates in the essence of his Old Testament predecessors and models them for his subjects in a communicative process that reaches

---

69 Theodore Synkellos, ch. 52, ed. Sternbach in Makk, 320, lines 20–24.
70 *De expeditione Persica* 3.415, ed. A. Pertusi, *Poemi* (Ettal, 1959), 184; *Bellum Avaricum* 496, ed. A. Pertusi, 198. *Heraclias* 2.133, ed. Pertusi, 257. *Heraclias* 1.84, ed. Pertusi, 244.
71 "Kaiser Herakleios, Georgios Pisides und die Perserkriege," *Poikila Byzantina* 2, Varia 3 (Bonn, 1991), 73–128.
72 Cf. A. Pertusi, *Il pensiero politico bizantino*, ed. A. Carile (Bologna, 1990), 66–68; Mary Whitby, "A New Image for a New Age: George of Pisidia on the Emperor Heraclius," in *The Roman and Byzantine Army in the East: Proceedings of a Conference held at the Jagiellonian University, Kraków in September 1992*, ed. E. Dabrowa (Cracow, 1994), 197–225, esp. 201, 208.
73 *De expeditione Persica* 1.135, ed. Pertusi, 90.

up toward the divine realm and mediates it to humanity in the same way that an icon does.

In contrast to their earlier counterparts, panegyrists at the time of Heraklios had fully embraced the Old Testament as a frame of reference. The late sixth and early seventh century represented a conceptual watershed when, as Averil Cameron noted, "the division of literary genres into 'classical' and 'ecclesiastical' [that was] still observed, though sometimes indeed with effort and difficulty, under Justinian, now broke down, as the 'Roman' side of imperial ideology fell away."[74] The popularity of Old Testament figures, often in conjunction with models from ancient history or mythology, would continue among later authors. In this case at least, practice seems to have preceded theory: it took until the tenth century for the Byzantine rhetorical treatises that dispensed schoolbook advice on the crafting of speeches to recommend setting the emperor in relation to Old Testament figures.[75] Thus the anonymous treatise *On the Eight Parts of Rhetorical Speech* suggests that in panegyrics, the suitable models with which to compare the emperor are David, Moses, and Joshua the son of Nun.[76] Indeed, in the sixteen imperial panegyrics composed between 1204 and 1330 analyzed by Dimiter Angelov, David is the most popular model of kingship, closely followed by Alexander the Great.[77] The imperial chancery made a different choice. The collection of twenty *prooimia* of legal documents issued by the emperor that is preserved in the early fourteenth-century cod. Palat. Gr. 356 invokes only Moses as Old Testament precedent.[78] Clearly, the selection of models was determined by the context of their use. The panegyrists' emphasis on divinely appointed rulership proved by military might invited comparisons with David, while the emperor's legal documents evoked his relation to Moses the lawgiver.

---

74 "Images of Authority: Elites and Icons in Late Sixth-Century Byzantium," *Past & Present* 84 (1979): 3–35, esp. 23–24, reprinted in her *Continuity and Change in Sixth-Century Byzantium* (London, 1981).

75 G. L. Kustas, *Studies in Byzantine Rhetoric*, Analekta Blatadon 17 (Thessalonike, 1973), 25 n. 1. An example of the addition of scriptural references to a classical rhetorical treatise is the twelfth-century adaptation of Hermogenes in the *Rhetorica Marciana*, preserved in the fourteenth-century cod. Marc. gr. 44, fols. 25–91, partially edited by V. de Falco, "Trattato retorico bizantino (Rhetorica Marciana)," *Atti della Società Linguistica di Scienze e Lettere di Genova*, vol. 9, fasc. 2 (Pavia, 1930).

76 Περὶ τῶν ὀκτὼ μερῶν τοῦ ῥητορικοῦ λόγου, ed. C. Walz, *Rhetores Graeci* (Stuttgart–Tübingen, 1834), 3:599, lines 23–25.

77 D. Angelov, *Imperial Ideology and Political Thought in Byzantium, 1204–1330* (Cambridge, 2007), 85–91; on the importance of the Davidic model from the ninth century onward, see esp. 127–31.

78 H. Hunger, *Prooimion: Elemente der byzantinischen Kaiseridee in den Arengen der Urkunden*, WByzSt 1 (Vienna, 1964), 222, 228, 230; cf. 200–203.

What became commonplace in the late Byzantine period had very tentative and uneven roots in the formative phase of the fourth to seventh century that has been considered here. The lasting trend in the application of biblical models of rulership was pioneered in the mid-fifth century, and it came not from the orbit of the imperial court and its panegyrists or from theoreticians of rulership, but from bishops. A century after Constantine's patronage of Christianity propelled it to new prominence in culture and politics, the bishops were successful in asserting their ability to offer a new framework for the articulation of imperial power. Whether the representation of the emperor in relation to Old Testament figures was in effect the elevation of a mortal earthly ruler to the timeless realm of historical continuum and typological identity, or whether it demoted a divinely appointed monarch who had originally claimed to be Christ-like or at least equal to the apostles to the lesser status of an Old Testament leader, would bear further investigation.[79]

This very cursory overview of the first three and a half centuries of the Byzantine Empire has also, I hope, helped to sharpen our tools for recognizing two modes of connection to Old Testament models used by Byzantine authors: *exemplum* and *typos*. The selection of mode depended upon the outlook and training of the author and on the literary genre in which he wrote. Historians favored the *exemplum*, while theologians preferred the *typos*, but both groups shared an appreciation of the Old Testament as the root, baseline, and standard against which their present had to be measured.

University of California, Los Angeles

---

79 The latter approach is advocated, in general terms, by F. Kolb, *Herrscherideologie in der Spätantike* (Berlin, 2001), 125–38. For the tension between the two approaches, see M. Meier, "Göttlicher Kaiser und christlicher Herrscher?" *Das Altertum* 48, no. 2 (2003): 129–60.

EIGHT

The Old Testament and Monasticism

Derek Krueger

Christian monasticism claimed an Old Testament heritage from its very beginnings. Already in the fourth century, Athanasios of Alexandria described how Antony the Great gained knowledge of his own life from "the career of the great Elijah, as from a mirror."[1] Jerome, who had practiced monasticism in Syria and observed it in Palestine, reported that some regarded the prophet Elijah to have been the first monk.[2] A monk's retreat from society, the restriction of diet, and the renunciation of family reprised the lives of Old Testament prophets. In monastic conversation and literature from the fourth century on, biblical figures represented qualities that monastics might invoke in the cultivation of Christian ascetic virtues. Monastic theologians allegorized Old Testament stories for insights into the Christian's movement toward God and salvation. Monastic liturgies revoiced Old Testament texts from the Psalms and the canticles in worship, while other biblical verses provided words to say in times of trouble. The Old Testament thus shaped the monastic imagination, monastic identities, and the rhythms of devotion.

In all these processes, Byzantine monasticism also reshaped the Bible. Christian monastics systematically and consistently read biblical narratives through the lens of their own rigorous practice.[3] The Old Testament was refigured,

---

1 *Vie d'Antoine*, ed. G. J. M. Bartelink (Paris, 1994), 154 (chap. 7; and see 155 n. 2); trans. R. C. Gregg, in *The Life of Antony and the Letter to Marcellinus* (New York, 1980), 37.
2 *Life of Paul* 1, see also 13. Edition: W. Oldfather et al., *Studies in the Text Traditions of St. Jerome's Vitae Patrum* (Urbana, 1943), 36–42. In later centuries, the prophet's ascent to heaven prompted the dedication of numerous monastic foundations to Elijah throughout the Byzantine Empire. R. Janin, *Les églises et les monastères des grands centres byzantins* (Paris, 1975), 143–46.
3 See E. A. Clark, *Reading Renunciation: Asceticism and Scripture in Early Christianity* (Princeton, 1999).

however improbably it might seem to modern readers, as an ascetic text, licensing and endorsing the renunciation of sexuality in particular. The Old Testament was used selectively, creating a canon within the canon. In addition to the Psalms, which monks chanted during the devotional offices throughout the day, monks regularly heard only those stories and prophecies of ancient Israel that were included in the lectionary, the cycle of liturgical readings. Despite Epiphanios of Cyprus's teaching that "reading the Scriptures is a great safeguard against sin," and that "ignorance of the Scriptures is a precipice and a deep abyss,"[4] only the more learned monks engaged in scriptural study of complete biblical books. Compilations of excerpts deemed useful to cenobitic life, called florilegia, appeared from the eighth century onward; they drew most heavily from the wisdom books: the Psalms, Proverbs, and Ecclesiasticus (Sirach).[5] Monastic literature frequently extolled Old Testament heroes for their virtues without reference to the stories in which these virtues were practiced. Monks participated in a culture of biblical reference that used the Old Testament as it was useful to the practice of monasticism.

This chapter considers the place of the Old Testament in Byzantine monastic culture in the early and middle periods—that is, from the fourth through the seventh century and from the eighth through the twelfth century—primarily among men, charting how monks employed the Old Testament as a tool for understanding and participating in the monastic life. The foundational writings of early Byzantine monasticism, some of which would take on a canonical status of their own, established the patterns for the deployment of Old Testament characters, stories, and texts. The *Apophthegmata patrum*, the *Longer Rules* of Basil of Caesarea, and the Macarian homilies, for example, contain references to the Old Testament that would typify Byzantine monastic discourse for centuries to come. In monastic foundation documents, in hagiography, and in the writings of major monastic theologians, various patterns of biblical reference employed in these early and classic texts continued in use through later antiquity and the middle Byzantine period.

---

4   *Apophthegmata patrum* (hereafter *AP*) Epiphanius 9 and 10 (PG 65:165); trans. B. Ward, *The Wisdom of the Desert Fathers: The Alphabetic Collection* (Oxford, 1975), 58. For an introduction to the *AP*, see W. Harmless, *Desert Christians: An Introduction to the Literature of Early Monasticism* (Oxford, 2004), 167–273.
5   M. Richard, *Opera minora* (Leuven, 1976), vol. 1, parts 1–5.

The Sayings of the Fathers and the Illustration of Virtues

The heroes of the Old Testament provided Byzantine monks with models that they might strive to emulate. Biblical figures such as Abraham, Moses, David, and Daniel embodied the practices and modes of being that monasticism valued. A passage from the late fifth-century anthology of sayings of earlier desert fathers demonstrates how Old Testament worthies could serve to indicate key virtues.

> A brother questioned an old man saying, "What good work should I do so that I may live?" The old man said, "God knows what is good. I have heard it said that one of the Fathers asked Abba Nisteros the Great, the friend of Abba Anthony, and said to him, 'What good work is there that I could do?' Abba Nisteros answered, 'Are not all [good] deeds equal? Scripture says that Abraham was hospitable and God was with him. Elijah loved interior peace [ἡσυχία] and God was with him. David was humble, and God was with him. So, do whatever you see your soul desires according to God and guard your heart.'"[6]

As this passage from the alphabetical series of the *Apophthegmata patrum* illustrates, biblical heroes played important roles in shaping early Byzantine monastic moral teaching.[7] A patriarch, a prophet, and a king exemplify fundamental monastic virtues: hospitality, quietude, and humility. Abraham and perhaps especially David might seem odd exemplars for a form of life requiring the renunciation of the world and a commitment to celibacy, and Elijah's period of solitary withdrawal might not seem an obvious model for men living stably in

---

6   *AP* Nisteros 2 (PG 65:305–6; trans. Ward, 154, modified). The saying appears also as *AP, Systematic Collection* 1.18. Edition: J.-C. Guy, *Les Apophtegmes des Pères: Collection systématique*, 3 vols., SC 387, 474, 498 (Paris, 1993–2005). The literary compilation of the *Apophthegmata* likely occurred in the final decades of the fifth century, possibly in Palestine. The alphabetic collection appears to have been assembled first, after which a subsequent redactor collected many of the same and other sayings into the systematic collection, arranged topically by key virtues. Pelagius (later Pope Pelagius I) began a Latin translation of the systematic collection in the 530s; a Syriac translation dates from 534. See Guy, *Apophtegmes*, 1:23–35, 79–84; L. Regnault, "Les Apophtegmes des pères en Palestine aux Ve–VIe siècles," *Irénikon* 54 (1981): 320–30; C. Faraggiana di Sarzana, "*Apophthegmata Patrum*: Some Crucial Points of their Textual Transmission and the Problem of a Critical Edition," *StP* 29 (1997): 455–67.

7   On the role of the Bible in the *Apophthegmata*, see D. Burton-Christie, *The Word in the Desert: Scripture and the Quest for Holiness in Early Christian Monasticism* (New York, 1993); for a brief discussion of this text, see p. 168.

community with each other and thus having a different set of expectations and realities. For the purpose of moral instruction, however, these biblical figures have been reduced to the virtues they exhibited at individual moments in their story: Abraham is brought forward for his hospitality to the three divine visitors in Genesis 18; Elijah for the inner peacefulness exhibited in his stints alone in the wilderness at the brook called Cherith and at Mount Horeb in 1 Kings 17 and 19 when "the Lord came to him"; and David for the humility of his self-abasement after the murder of Uriah the Hittite in 2 Samuel 12.

Perhaps the saying attributed to Nisteros assumes an audience familiar with the entirety of each biblical story, but the text requires familiarity only with those incidents in which the men of the Old Testament exhibit their key virtue. Or perhaps it requires no such familiarity at all. In Abba Nisteros's saying, each biblical hero stands free of his narrative to embody a single virtue. In an anthology devoted to teaching monastic virtues, the heroes of the Old Testament point neither to themselves nor to their narratives but to a way of Christian life.

As Nisteros's invocation of biblical exemplars suggests, the holy men of the Old Testament provided early Byzantine monks a lens through which they might understand themselves and their ascetic goals. Even in the absence of significant direct quotation of Old Testament verses, the *Apophthegmata* reveal an extensive culture of biblical reference, in which the monks read themselves and their monastic forebears in the image of biblical heroes. At the same time, the monks reread the biblical narratives as a repository of monastic ideals. In fact, the saying attributed to Nisteros establishes not one but two parallel strands of tradition. The first invokes biblical exemplars: Abraham, Elijah, and David; the second traces a chain of monastic transmission, backward from the late fifth-century written compilation, to a story about a brother questioning an older monk, and then through an oral tradition ("I have heard it said") to Nisteros, a friend of Antony, himself remembered as the founder of monasticism.[8] To illustrate godly virtues the text both reveals and entwines these two sorts of authority: the wisdom of the desert fathers and the examples of the biblical heroes. Within the anthology, biblical heroes and monastic heroes stand side by side, inhabiting and exhibiting the same virtues. Indeed, in a book on the role of Scripture in the desert tradition, Douglas Burton-Christie has argued, "because the words of the leaders were valued so highly in the desert, there was no clear

---

8 On the significance of the chains of transmission in a great number of the *Apophthegmata*, see ibid., 78–79.

distinction between the words which came from the sacred texts and the words which came from the holy exemplars."⁹

The intertwining of the biblical and the monastic within the *Apophthegmata* is even more clearly observable in a saying about Abba John the Persian.

> Someone said to Abba John the Persian, "We have borne great afflictions for the sake of the kingdom of heaven. Shall we inherit it?" The old man said, "As for me, I trust [πιστεύω] I shall obtain the inheritance of Jerusalem on high, which is written [ἀπογεγραμμένην] in the heavens.... Why should I not trust? I have been hospitable like Abraham, meek like Moses, holy like Aaron, patient like Job, humble like David, a hermit like John, filled with compunction like Jeremiah, a master [διδάσκαλος] like Paul, full of faith like Peter, wise like Solomon. Like the thief, I trust that he who of his natural goodness has given me all that, will also grant me the kingdom."¹⁰

John catalogues a long list of biblical figures and their virtues. Once again Abraham is remembered for his hospitality, and David for humility. This highly reductive technique distills each personage to a single and differentiable virtue. John's list of biblical worthies includes figures from both the Old Testament and the New, and not in canonical or chronological order. John the Baptist appears between David and Jeremiah, and Solomon follows both Paul and Peter. Thus while Old Testament figures may tend to predominate in the monastic invocation of biblical exemplars, they do so as part of a larger biblical repository of moral instruction. In the absence of narrative context and order, the biblical exemplars inhabit a nearly timeless realm, a gallery of ancient holy men who stand iconically for cardinal elements of Christian moral life.

In contrast to the biblical figures invoked in his speech, John the Persian himself, however, practices not one but all their virtues. He represents the entire canon of biblical morality in a single person. The text does not seem concerned that John the Persian's statement might be boastful, manifesting the vices of pride or vainglory. Instead it represents the frank confidence of a self-reflective monk who with God's help has taken instruction from the biblical narrative to learn how to live in accord with God's command. The text is just as interested to present John the Persian as an exemplar as it is to promote any of the biblical

9   Ibid., 108.
10 *AP* John the Persian 4; trans. Ward 108, modified.

figures. The saying asserts that the proper practice of monasticism re-enacts and re-presents all the modes of biblically sanctioned behavior.

David's moral complexity became particularly useful for monastic spiritual development. Rather than ignoring David's lack of chastity, monastic teachers cited David's penance after unchastity as a potent model for the disciplining of the monastic self. Another saying in the *Apophthegmata* demonstrates how David's example might be profitable: "A brother asked Abba Poemen, 'What shall I do, for fornication and anger war against me?' The old man said, 'In this connection David said, "I pierced the lion and I slew the bear" [cf. 1 Sam. 17:35–36]; that is to say: I cut off anger and I crushed fornication with hard labor.'"[11] This persistent interest in David's penance and humility in the face of inner turmoil also appears in the seventh century in Maximos the Confessor's *Chapters on Love*: "Humility and distress free man from every sin, the former by cutting out the passions of the soul, the latter those of the body. The blessed David shows that he did this in one of his prayers to God, 'Look upon my humility and my trouble and forgive all my sins [Ps. 24:18].'" Here David's psalm provides in a verse a model for penitence that the monk could—and did—regularly repeat.[12]

The *Apophthegmata* and their invocation of Old Testament worthies as exemplars of key virtues had a very long afterlife in Christian monasticism. The Latin translation carried out in the 530s by Pelagius and John of the systematic sayings collection soon influenced Western monasticism. In Byzantium, the complexity of the manuscript tradition of both the alphabetical–anonymous collection and the systematic collection attests the copying, reading, reuse, redaction, and rearrangement of these materials in monasteries throughout the empire. There was no one version of the text, but rather multiple dossiers of the sayings of the fathers.[13] In the eleventh century, Paul Evergetinos (died 1054) included a significant portion of these sayings in a massive new anthology of earlier Christian ascetic literature for the Monastery of the Theotokos Evergetis outside the walls of Constantinople. This compilation, known as the *Synagoge* or *Evergetinon*, tremendously influenced subsequent Byzantine monasticism and survives

---

11 *AP* Poemen 115; trans. Ward, 184, modified. For a parallel, see *AP Systematic Collection* 5.11 (ed. Guy).
12 *Chapters on Love* 1.76. Edition: Maximos the Confessor, *Capitoli sulla carità*, ed. A. Cerasa-Gastaldo (Rome, 1963); trans. G. C. Berthold, in Maximos Confessor, *Selected Writings* (New York, 1985), 43.
13 On the manuscripts leading to the editio princeps, see J.-C. Guy, *Recherches sur la tradition grecque des* Apophthegmata Patrum (Brussels, 1962). See also J. Wortley, "The Genre and Sources of the *Synagoge*," in *The Theotokos Evergetis and Eleventh-Century Monasticism*, ed. M. Mullett and A. Kirby (Belfast, 1994), 321.

in more than eighty copies.¹⁴ Paul transmits from the *Apophthegmata* many sayings that invoke Old Testament exemplars, thus ensuring the persistent impact of the *Apophthegmata*'s pattern of citing Old Testament figures for their individual virtues.¹⁵

Invocations of Old Testament precedents, although they persisted in the literature we have just considered, are not common in the monastic foundation documents known as *typika*, which lay out the rules and character of individual monastic communities. When such references do occur, they suggest familiarity with the patterns and style of the *Apophthegmata* or other literature of the patristic period. In some cases they restate the commonplace that Elijah and John the Baptist were the founders of monasticism. For example, Isaac Komnenos's twelfth-century typikon for the Kosmosoteira monastery—citing an oration of Gregory of Nazianzos—envisions the monastic ideal as "Elijah's Carmel and John's [the Baptist's] desert."¹⁶ In a similar vein, the thirteenth-century typikon of the Monastery of St. Neophytos on Cyprus includes a prayer to be recited for a new leader, or "recluse," calling on Christ, "who strengthened and shed thy grace on Elijah of Tishbe in the old days and more recently upon John thy Forerunner and Baptist so that they led the solitary and eremitic life and achieved the angelic life on earth (emulating their life and following on their footsteps were Antony, Euthymios, Onouphrios and their companions)."¹⁷ This same typikon, where it requires a full, regular reading of the monastery's rule and canons, cites Moses's practice of regular oral recitation of the Law (Deut. 31:11) and mentions how Josiah rent his clothes after hearing the law and realizing that his peo-

---

14 Paul Evergetinos, Συναγωγὴ τῶν θεοφθόγγων ῥημάτων καὶ διδασκαλιῶν τῶν θεοφόρων καὶ ἁγίων πατέρων, ed. V. Matthaiou, 4 vols. (Athens, 1957–66). An English translation is in press: *The Evergetinos: A Complete Text*, trans. Chrysostomos et al. (Etna, CA, 1988–). A second English translation is in progress at Queen's University, Belfast as part of the British Academy Evergetis Project. See R. Jordan in *BMFD*, 2:454–55; J. Richard, "Florilèges spirituels grecs," *DSp* 5 (1964): 502–3. See Wortley, "Genre and Sources," 306–24; B. Crostini, "Towards a Study of the Scriptorium of the Monastery of the Theotokos Evergetis: Preliminary Remarks," in *The Theotokos Evergetis*, ed. M. Mullett and A. Kirby, 177–78. For a number of studies of the source material for the *Synagoge*, see *Work and Worship at the Theotokos Evergetis 1050–1200*, ed. M. Mullett and A. Kirby (Belfast, 1997).
15 For the use of Old Testament examples in sayings culled from the tradition of the *AP*, see for example *Synagoge* 1.40.33 (cf. *AP Systematic Collection*, ed. Guy 7.46); 1.45.18 (cf. *AP* John the Dwarf 20); 1.45.38 (cf. *AP* Poemen 71); 2.15.10 (cf. *AP* Poemen 178); 2.22.16 (cf. *AP* Sisoes 23). A full study of the use and effect of the Bible in the *Synagoge* would further illuminate the place of Old Testament exemplars in middle Byzantine monastic literature.
16 Kosmosoteira 29; *BMFD*, 2:801; see Gregory of Nazianzos, *Oration* 14.4 (PG 35:861).
17 Neophytos 14; *BMFD*, 4:1356.

ple had gone astray (2 Kings 22:12).[18] The typikon thus functions like the Torah (Νόμος) and in a peculiar way comes to substitute for it.

The commonplace of Abraham's hospitality continued to serve as a model, although the variety of uses to which the typika put him suggests no single way to interpret his philanthropy. In one case, the biblical patriarch offers a type for the monk who might also "receive God in his soul";[19] in another, he provides an example for how the hospice host might maintain his fasting and abstinence while showing "appropriate hospitality ... do[ing] as Abraham, the archetype of hosts," who did not eat with his guests.[20]

The evidence of the apophthegmatic literature and the infrequent references to Old Testament figures in the typika affirm that one of the primary ways monks encountered the Old Testament was through stock invocation of biblical figures as exemplars of monastic virtue. One result was that monasticism acquired an enduring biblical veneer, such that the practice of asceticism and the cultivation of virtue engaged in a reprise of biblical narrative: the monk formed himself in the image of biblical heroes. A second result was the reflexive reconception of the Bible as a monastic text: monks found the Old Testament relevant to the extent that it contributed to the monastic way of life.

Old Testament Models in Monastic Hagiography

The tendency to see monasticism as a reenactment of biblical modes of life features prominently in early Byzantine hagiography, where the citation of biblical precedents serves as an apologia for the veneration of Christian saints.[21] In his *Religious History*, written in the 440s, Theodoret of Cyrrhus associates the Christian holy men and women of northern Syria with a wide variety of biblical heroes. He compares the hermit turned bishop James of Nisibis with six Old Testament figures, including Moses, Elijah, and Elisha, as well as with the apostles, especially Peter, and with Christ himself.[22] His treatment of Symeon the Stylite compares the saint's origins as a shepherd to Jacob, Joseph, Moses, David, and Micah; he compares his fasting to the fasting of Moses and Elijah. Theodoret

18   Neophytos 11; *BMFD*, 4:1354.
19   Eleousa (eleventh century) 15; *BMFD*, 1:185.
20   Roidion (twelfth century) [B]8; *BMFD*, 1:433.
21   See for example D. Krueger, "Typological Figuration in Theodoret of Cyrrhus's *Religious History* and the Art of Postbiblical Narrative," *JEChrSt* 5 (1997): 393–419, reprinted in *Writing and Holiness: The Practice of Authorship in the Early Christian East* (Philadelphia, 2004), 15–32.
22   *Religious History* 1. Edition: *Histoire des moines de Syrie*, ed. P. Canivet and A. Leroy-Molinghen, 2 vols., SC 234, 257 (Paris, 1977–79).

explains Symeon's innovative practice of standing on a pillar by asserting its continuity with the peculiar asceticisms of the biblical prophets Isaiah, Jeremiah, Hosea, and Ezekiel.[23] The *Syriac Life of Symeon the Stylite* associates Symeon's fasting with Moses, Elijah, and Daniel, and implicitly connects his ascending the pillar with Moses on Sinai and Elijah in the chariot.[24] Drawing correspondences between events in the biblical narrative and in the lives of the saints, hagiography reread monasticism through the lens of the Bible.

Occasionally authors of monastic hagiography would shape an entire hagiographical narrative on the account of a biblical hero, as in the case of John Rufus's late fifth- or early sixth-century *Life of Peter the Iberian*. Throughout the work, John stresses how Peter's deeds reenact events in the life of Moses. The allusions go beyond the standard invocations of Moses' asceticism to include his journey toward the Holy Land and his visit to Mount Nebo. Peter's life becomes a recapitulation of Moses's. At a key point in the narrative, Peter visits Moses's tomb.[25] Such efforts result in an integration of the biblical narrative and the monastic saint's *Life*. This level of intertextual correspondence stresses the biblical character of monastic heroes and thus governs and shapes perceptions of monasticism for hagiography's audiences, both monastic and lay. In a mirroring way, the Old Testament came to be regarded as a hagiographical text, that is, as a text that told of the holy men of old.[26]

The Old Testament books of histories and the prophets were not the only parts of Scripture recapitulated in monastic literature. Ascetic wisdom might also reprise or extend biblical books of wisdom. The early fifth-century *Life of Synkletike* presents that ascetic mother's teaching as biblical in character. She humbly instructs the community of women that she leads to regard Scripture as sufficient nourishment in a life of rigorous fasting. "We draw spiritual water from the same source; we suck milk from the same breasts—the Old and the New Testaments."[27] Meanwhile the author of her biography presents the saint's own teaching as an expansion of biblical wisdom literature, especially Proverbs.

---

23 Ibid. 26.
24 *Syriac Life of Symeon the Stylite* 108 (trans. in R. Doran, *The Lives of Simeon Stylites* [Kalamazoo, 1992], 176–77); and *Syriac Life of Symeon the Stylite* 41–42 (trans. Doran, 125–26).
25 John Rufus, *Petrus der Iberer: Ein Charakterbild zur Kirchen- und Sittengeschichte des fünften Jahrhunderts* (Leipzig, 1895). For an excellent discussion of Mosaic themes in the text, see B. Bitton-Ashkelony and A. Kofsky, *The Monastic School of Gaza* (Leiden, 2006), 62–81.
26 See Krueger, *Writing and Holiness*, 30–31.
27 *Life of Synkletike* 21 (PG 28:1500); trans. in E. B. Bongie, *The Life and Regimen of the Blessed and Holy Teacher Syncletica* (Toronto, 1996), 19. For a discussion of this aspect of the text, see Krueger, *Writing and Holiness*, 144–46.

While other authors presented the saints as latter-day prophets and miracle workers, this anonymous male author invoked the model of the Old Testament sage to portray his monastic heroine. The *Life of Synkletike* proved popular in subsequent centuries, and Paul Evergetinos excerpted a significant percentage of the text in his *Synagoge*, thus ensuring that monastic teachers could be seen in the model of biblical wise men.

The connection to biblical figures could also function more statically, abstracted from biblical action and teaching. Hagiographers trained their audiences to see the Bible in monks' faces.[28] The anonymous late fourth-century author of the *History of the Monks of Egypt* relates that the hermit John of Diolkos "looked like Abraham and had a beard like Aaron's."[29] One finds such comparisons in the *Apophthegmata Patrum* as well, where Abba Arsenios's appearance is "angelic, like that of Jacob," and Abba Pambo "was like Moses, who received the image of the glory of Adam when his face shone."[30] The fragmentary Coptic *Life of Makarios of Alexandria* (24) remembers that the saint was "gentle like Moses [Num. 12:3]."[31] Engaging in what Georgia Frank has called "biblical realism," hagiography asserted that the world of the Bible continued to live on in the world of Christian ascetics.[32]

After the seventh century, sustained reference to Old Testament figures in Byzantine hagiography became less common; however, incidents in monastic saints' lives continued to provide opportunities for comparison with Old Testament figures. Thus, the eighth-century *Life of David of Thessalonike* compares him to Elijah and contrasts the empress Theodora's treatment of David with Jezebel's persecution of the prophet.[33] In the eleventh-century *Life of Symeon the New Theologian*, when the young mystic surpasses his elders in asceticism and

---

28 G. Frank, *The Memory of the Eyes: Pilgrims to Living Saints in Christian Late Antiquity* (Berkeley, 2000), 134–70. For Old Testament overtones in Christian monasticism in the Egyptian desert, see C. Rapp, "Desert, City, and Countryside in the Early Christian Imagination," in *The Encroaching Desert: Egyptian Hagiography and the Medieval West*, ed. J. H. F. Dijkstra and M. van Dijk (Leiden, 2006), 93–112.

29 *History of the Monks of Egypt* 26. Edition: *Historia monachorum in Aegypto*, ed. A.-J. Festugière, SubsHag 53 (Brussels, 1971).

30 *AP* Arsenios 42; trans. Ward, 97 (parallel in the *Systematic Collection* 15.11). *AP* Pambo 12; trans. Ward, 197. Frank, *Memory of the Eyes*, 160.

31 T. Vivian, trans., *Four Desert Fathers: Pambo, Evagrius, Macarius of Egypt, and Macarius of Alexandria: Coptic Texts Relating to the* Lausiac History *of Palladius* (Crestwood, NY, 2004), 162.

32 See Frank, *Memory of the Eyes*, 29–33.

33 *Leben des Heiligen David von Thessalonike*, ed. V. Rose (Berlin, 1887), 16.31. David lived in the fifth century. See A. Vasiliev, "The Life of David of Thessalonica," *Traditio* 4 (1946): 123.

becomes their leader, Niketas Stethatos compares Symeon's precociousness with that of the "great prophet Daniel."[34] The travails of Daniel and the three Israelite boys continued to fascinate. Their song (Dan. 3:35–65 LXX) had been chanted at morning prayers since the fourth century and in conjunction with their feast day on December 17th from the middle Byzantine period. In the ninth century the Italo-Greek saint Elias the Younger headed toward Persia to see the place where they had contended (ἀγωνιστήριον).[35]

Old Testament typology continued to be a useful tool for denying charges of innovation and asserting the legitimacy of monastic leaders. Both vitae of Athanasios of Athos, who died around 1001, compare the founder of the Great Lavra to biblical precursors to assert that Athanasios did not "destroy the ancient rule and customs" of earlier Athonite monastic patterns.[36] *Vita A*, which Dirk Krausmüller dates before 1025, stresses that when Michael Maleinos died, his spirit came to rest "twofold" on the young Athanasios, just as Elijah's transferred to Elisha and Moses's to Joshua.[37] Indeed, Athanasios had taken Michael's cowl when he left Mount Kyminas, continued to wear it for protection, and finally was buried with it.[38] Narratively, the cowl functions like the mantle of a prophet. In praising Athanasios's "virtue and wisdom," the early twelfth-century *Vita B* states that "he possessed the moderation [σωφροσύνη] of Joseph and the sincerity [ἄπλαστον] of Jacob and the hospitality of Abraham. He was a leader of people like the great Moses and his successor Joshua."[39] Moving on from Old Testament exemplars to a series of earlier Christian monastic leaders, the passage

---

34 *Vie de Syméon le Nouveau Théologien*, ed. I. Hausherr, *OCA* 12 (1928): 30 (chap. 20).

35 *Vita di Sant'Elia il Giovane*, ed. G. Rossi Taibbi (Palermo, 1962), 32 (chap. 22). On the place of the Benedicite in the monastic office, see R. Taft, *The Liturgy of the Hours in East and West: The Origins of the Divine Office and Its Meaning for Today*, 2nd ed. (Collegeville, 1993), 88–89. See the readings for Vespers and Orthros on December 16 and 17 in *The Synaxarion of the Monastery of the Theotokos Evergetis: September–February*, ed. and trans. R. H. Jordan, BBTT 6.5 (Belfast, 2000), 280–81, 287–91.

36 Both *Lives* appear in J. Noret, *Vitae duae antiquae sancti Athanasii Athonitae*, CCSG 9 (Turnhout, 1982). Quotation at *Life of Athanasios A* chap. 114. On Athanasios and Athonite monasticism, see K. Ware, "St Athanasios the Athonite: Traditionalist or Innovator," in *Mount Athos and Byzantine Monasticism*, ed. A. Bryer and M. Cunningham (Belfast, 1996), 3–16.

37 *Life of Athanasios of Athos A* chap. 72. For the dates of the lives, see D. Krausmüller, "The Lost First *Life of Athanasios the Athonite* and Its Author Anthony, Abbot of the Constantinopolitan Monastery of *Ta Panagiou*," in *Founders and Refounders of Byzantine Monasteries*, ed. M. Mullett, BBTT 6.3 (Belfast, 2007), 63–86.

38 *Life of Athanasios A* chap. 240; *Life of Athanasios B* chaps. 12 and 65. See R. Morris, *Monks and Laymen in Byzantium, 843–1118* (Cambridge, 1995), 102.

39 *Life of Athanasios B* chap. 64. *Life of Athanasios A* chaps. 219–21, which invokes Abraham, Jacob, and Joseph in similar terms, is clearly related.

invokes the Egyptian desert-father Arsenios, Sabas the founder of the Great Lavra in the Judean Desert, Pachomios, and Antony. In the following section, the author suggests continuity between Athanasios's monastic program and that of Theodore Stoudites.[40] Thus the *Vita B* uses the Old Testament figures as the foundation of a lineage for Orthodox monasticism, a lineage that culminates—or at least passes through—the great Athonite reformer. At the same time, listing both biblical and monastic leaders reifies an essentially monastic reading of the patriarchs and prophets as protomonks, perhaps even as proto-abbots.

In general, hagiography about monastic figures worked to form an onlooker's understanding of an ascetic hero, providing a view of a glorious other, encouraging reverence and veneration.[41] Hagiographers prompted their audiences, whether lay or monastic (or both), to understand the monasticism of others as a continuation of biblical patterns for self-discipline and miracle working; hagiography tended to do so by situating the reader or listener as an onlooker, framing the gaze from the outside. The role of biblical typology in the enterprise was to apply one set of precedents to establish and enhance another. Allusion to biblical precursors was thus a persistent feature of the hagiographical genre. Hagiographers employed key figures and stories from the Old Testament in the literary construction of monasticism.

Old Testament Models for Monastic Discipline

In contrast to hagiography, which trained the eye on the saint, other monastic literature trained the eye on the self. It was in such a reflexive and normative mode that Basil of Caesarea used Old Testament figures in his *Longer Rules*. Written and then revised by Basil shortly before his death in 379, the *Rules* underwent additional redaction in the sixth century and became one of the great foundational texts of the Byzantine monastic tradition.[42] Basil arranged this *Asketikon* in the form of questions and answers, reflecting conversations between the

---

40 *Life of Athanasios B* chap. 65.
41 On this aspect of hagiography, see P. Brown, "The Saint as Exemplar in Late Antiquity," in *Saints and Virtues*, ed. J. S. Hawley (Berkeley, 1987), 3–14; P. C. Miller, "Strategies of Representation in Collective Biography: Constructing the Subject as Holy," in *Greek Biography and Panegyric in Late Antiquity*, ed. T. Hägg and P. Rousseau (Berkeley, 2000), 209–54; S. A. Harvey, "The Sense of a Stylite: Perspectives on Symeon the Elder," *VChr* 42 (1988): 376–94.
42 Basil, *Longer Rules*, PG 31:901–1305; trans. M. M. Wagner, *Saint Basil: Ascetical Works* (Washington, DC, 1962), 223–337. J. Gribomont, *Histoire du texte des Ascétiques de S. Basile* (Louvain, 1953). J. Quasten, *Patrology* (Westminster, MD, 1950), 3:212–14.

ascetic leader and his monks.⁴³ In his preface, Basil frames the monastic life as a fulfillment of divine commandments, implicitly tying his *Rules* to the commandments of Scripture. This same Scripture offers examples of men who kept God's laws, particularly for maintaining a proper interior disposition. Basil asks, "How shall I be worthy of the company of Job—I who do not accept even an ordinary mishap with thanksgiving? How shall I who am lacking in magnanimity toward my enemy stand in the presence of David? Or of Daniel, if I do not seek for God in continual constancy and earnest supplication?"

For Basil, these Old Testament worthies stand within a broader communion of holy people: Basil also asks how he might stand in the presence of "any of the saints, if I have not walked in their footsteps."⁴⁴ Thus the canon of the Old Testament does not set a limit to the rolls of the holy, rather it sets the standard. Basil himself, of course, engages in a "speech-in-character [προσωποποιΐα]," a common rhetorical technique through which he models an appropriate interior dialogue for the Christian ascetic, a series of self-accusations that underscore the gap between the self and the biblical and saintly exemplars.⁴⁵ The figures of the Old Testament begin a long and continuing series of holy personages that Basil can invoke to mark his own failures and to set goals for his monks.

Old Testament figures appear again in Basil's discussion of self-control in food consumption. Basil warns his monks against ἀκρασία, here meaning "gluttony," and encourages them to practice ἐγκράτεια, in this context "abstemious eating."⁴⁶ He teaches that a monk should chastize his body and bring it under submission, to practice "that abstinence from pleasures which aims at thwarting the will of the flesh for the purpose of attaining the goal of piety."⁴⁷ In addition to the words of Paul, he cites Old Testament fasters:

> Moses, through long perseverance in fasting and prayer [Deut. 9:9], received the law and heard the words of God, 'as a man is wont to speak to a friend' [Ex. 33:11], says the Scripture. Elijah was deemed worthy of the vision of God

---

43 For an extensive discussion of the text, see P. Rousseau, *Basil of Caesarea* (Berkeley, 1994), 190–232, 354–60.
44 Basil, *Longer Rules*, preface; trans. Wagner, 229.
45 For a similar modeling of self-accusation for lay Christians, see D. Krueger, "Romanos the Melodist and the Christian Self in Early Byzantium," in *Proceedings of the 21st International Congress of Byzantine Studies, London, 2006*, vol. 1, *Plenary Papers*, ed. E. Jeffreys (Aldershot, 2006), 247–66.
46 For Christian teaching on fasting in late antiquity, see T. Shaw, *The Burden of the Flesh: Fasting and Sexuality in Early Christianity* (Minneapolis, 1998).
47 *Longer Rules* Q16; trans. Wagner, 270.

when he also had practiced abstinence [ἐγκράτεια] in like degree [1 Kgs. 19:8]. And what of Daniel? How did he attain to the contemplation of marvels? Was it not after a twenty-day fast [Dan. 10:3]? And how did the three children overcome the power of the fire? Was it not through abstinence [Dan. 1:8–16]?

Basil reinterprets Daniel's and his companions' refusal to eat foods prohibited to Jews as ascetic dietary practice. The association of these biblical figures with fasting endured in Byzantium. Indeed, the twelfth-century typikon of the Monastery of St. John the Forerunner of Phoberos requires fasting in the period after Pentecost: "For both Moses [Ex. 34:28] and Elijah fasted for forty days and for three weeks Daniel 'ate no pleasant bread, and no flesh or wine entered into my mouth [Dan. 10:2–3].'"[48] Note, however, that Basil's catalogue of biblical examples slips effortlessly from one testament to the other, suggesting that in his search for precursors to the monastic life, Basil saw a continuity of biblical forms of life. "As for John [the Baptist]," he continues, "his whole plan of life was based on the practice of continency [ἐγκράτεια] [Matt. 3:4]." And to top it all off, Basil reminds his audience, "Even the Lord Himself inaugurated His public manifestation with the practice of this virtue."[49] The ascetic virtues practiced in the New Testament replicated those already exhibited in the Old.

Basil's search for Old Testament models extends to costume as well. Considering the ζώνη, the belt or cincture tied about the waist that was part of the monastic garb, Basil argues, "The saints long before us have demonstrated the necessity of the ζώνη. John bound his loins with a leather girdle [ζώνη], as did Elijah before him." Indeed, 2 Kings (1:8) describes Elijah as "a hairy man with a girdle of leather about his loins." Basil's list of exemplars oscillates between Old Testament and New Testament figures, from John the Baptist to Elijah, to Peter, Paul, and Job, ending with the apostles themselves, whose use of girdles is proved "by the fact that they were forbidden to carry money in their girdles [see Matt. 10:9]."[50] In virtues, dress, and diet, Basil presents monasticism as a biblical form of life.[51]

---

48   Phoberos 28; trans. R. Jordan in *BMFD*, 3:917.
49   *Longer Rules*, Q16; trans. Wagner, 269–70 modified. On Jesus' asceticism in patristic literature, see D. B. Martin, *Sex and the Single Savior: Gender and Sexuality in Biblical Interpretation* (Louisville, 2006), 91–102.
50   *Longer Rules* Q23; trans. Wagner, 284–85.
51   For an assessment of Basil's impact on subsequent monasticism, see *BMFD*, 1:21–32.

Old Testament Allegory and Spiritual Progress

The appeal to Old Testament figures as positive models for monastic comportment in moral and practical discourse contrasts with the use of Old Testament narratives in spiritual exegesis. In the latter, distinctions between the Old Testament and the New come to the fore, such that the narratives of ancient Israel represent fleshly prefigurations of heavenly and immaterial realities. Already in the third century, Origen of Alexandria had distinguished two modes of Christian biblical exegesis beyond the literal sense of the text. The first was moral, whereby most Christians derived basic edification and moral instruction. The other was spiritual, and involved searching after the higher (or deeper) and allegorical meanings embedded in the text. Significantly, Basil of Caesarea and Gregory of Nazianzos included the relevant sections of Origen's treatise *On First Principles* (namely, book 4, chapters 1–3) in the *Philokalia*, their anthology of works beneficial to the monastic life. Even after the condemnation of parts of Origen's theology in the sixth century, these chapters of Origen continued to be read by Byzantine monastics and to inform monastic exegesis.[52]

Monastic spiritual interpretation of Scripture stressed the fulfillment of Old Testament prophecy in the person of Jesus Christ and the supersession of Christianity over the religion of Israel. While the *Apophthegmata*'s and Basil's invocations of biblical figures to illustrate monastic virtues and modes of life valorized the Old Testament holy men, this spiritual exegesis regarded Old Testament narratives as mere shadows of hidden truths. The fourth-century *Spiritual Homilies* attributed to Makarios the Egyptian, but likely composed in Syria, provide a good and popular example of this discourse.[53] A number of these homilies invoke the story of Moses at Sinai. Recalling Moses' ascent, forty-day fast, communion with God, and his descent from Mount Sinai with his face aglow, the homilist writes, "All this, which happened to him, was a figure of something else. For that glory now shines splendidly from within the hearts of Christians."[54] The glowing face of Moses on his descent from Sinai (Ex. 35:29–35) offers a prefiguration

---

52 Origen, *Traité des principes*, ed. H. Crouzel and M. Simonetti, vol. 3, SC 268 (Paris 1980) contains both the *Philokalia* text and Rufinus's Latin translation. English trans. K. Froehlich, *Biblical Interpretation in the Early Church* (Philadelphia, 1984), 48–78.
53 *Die 50 Geistlichen Homilien des Makarios*, ed. H. Dörries, E. Klostermann, and M. Kroeger (Berlin, 1964); trans. G. A. Maloney in pseudo-Makarios, *Fifty Spiritual Homilies and the Great Letter* (New York, 1992). For a summary of arguments on the provenance of these texts, see ibid., 6–7.
54 *Spiritual Homilies* 12.14; trans. Maloney, 102.

of the bodily resurrection to come and of the interior life of Christian holy men in the present.

> [B]lessed Moses provided us with a certain type through the glory of the Spirit which covered his countenance upon which no one could look with steadfast gaze. This type anticipates how in the resurrection of the just the bodies of the saints will be glorified with a glory which even now the souls of the saintly and faithful people are deemed worthy to possess within, in the indwelling of the inner man.[55]

To be sure, the Macarian homilies also recall Old Testament narratives to present examples of virtue: the ninth homily invokes episodes in the stories of Joseph, David, Moses, Abraham, and Noah to illustrate the virtue of perseverance in the endurance of difficulties.[56] But the homilist's general practice is to treat the Old Testament figures as a series of types for a superior and spiritualized monastic life. "The ancient law is a shadow of the New Covenant. The shadow manifests in advance the truth, but it does not possess a service of the Spirit. Moses, having been clothed in the flesh, was unable to enter into the heart and take away the sordid garments of darkness. . . . Circumcision, in the shadow of the Law, shows the coming of the true Circumcision of the heart. The baptism of the Law is a shadow of true things to come."[57] Allegorical readings of the Old Testament provided an instrument for Christian monastic theological exploration, and in the process offered ways of understanding monks' aspirations and expectations of salvation. Theological speculation grounded itself in Old Testament narrative even as it claimed to transcend it.

Following in the tradition of the Macarian homilies, Maximos the Confessor frequently allegorized familiar Old Testament episodes to illustrate the flight of the monk's mind from the realm of matter in the contemplation of the divine. Many of these allegories appear in works composed in complex prose, and their allusions to Scripture are often obscure, suggesting that they were inaccessible to uneducated monks. Nevertheless they typify the use of allegory in charting a path for monastic theology. The mantle that Elijah gave to Elisha, which he had

---

55 *Spiritual Homilies* 6.10; trans. Maloney, 74. On the glowing face of Moses see M. Plested, *The Macarian Legacy: The Place of Macarius-Symeon in the Eastern Christian Tradition* (Oxford, 2004), 34, 56.
56 *Spiritual Homilies* 9.2–6; trans. Maloney, 84–85. For a later instance of the use of Old Testament exempla to encourage the patient endurance of trials see Barsanouphios and John of Gaza, *Correspondence*, ed. L. Regnault and P. Lemerle (Solesmes, 1972), letter 31.
57 *Spiritual Homilies* 32.4; trans. Maloney, 194.

previously used to strike the Jordan and cross on dry land and which his disciple would use subsequently in the same way (2 Kings 2:6–14), "accomplished by way of a figure" the "mortification of the flesh in which the magnificence of the good moral order is firmly grounded." The mantle serves as an "ally of the spirit in the struggle against any enemy force and as a blow against the unstable and flowing nature figured by the Jordan so that the disciple be not held back from crossing over to the Holy Land by being swamped in the mud and slipperiness of the craving for matter."[58] In a similar vein, Moses's pitching the tent of meeting outside the Israelite camp, where "every one who sought the Lord would go" (Ex. 33:7), indicates that Moses began to adore God only after having "installed his free will and his understanding outside the visible." "Having entered the darkness, the formless and immaterial place of knowledge, he remains there to accomplish the most sacred rite. Darkness is a formless, immaterial, and incorporeal state which bears the exemplary knowledge of beings. The one who enters into this state as another Moses understands things invisible to his moral nature."[59] As these examples demonstrate, Maximos's allegories turn on small details in the biblical narratives.[60] Since Maximos neither quotes nor paraphrases the stories, they must have been familiar in their written form to his intended monastic audience, either because they were read regularly enough in short pericopes during the Divine Liturgy or, more likely, during Vespers, or read as devotional readings at other times. It is possible that these allegories developed from discussions in monastic Bible study.

Episodes in the Old Testament continued to offer points of departure for theological reflection in the middle Byzantine period, most notably for Symeon the New Theologian. In the first of his *Ethical Discourses* an extended reading of Genesis's account of creation and the fall of Adam frames a distinctly monastic account of salvation in Christ and the kingdom of heaven.[61] The second *Ethical Discourse* similarly allegorizes episodes from early human history

---

58 Maximos the Confessor, *Commentary on the Our Father*, lines 361–71; ed. P. van Deun, *Maximi confessoris opuscula exegetica duo*, CCSG 23 (Turnhout, 1991), 27–73; trans. Berthold, 108–9.
59 Maximos, *Chapters on Knowledge* (*Capita theologica et oecumenica*) 1.84–85 (ed. PG 90:1084–1173); trans. Berthold, 144. For additional allegories in the *Chapters on Knowledge* see 2.13–16 (Moses and Elijah); 2.26 (Abraham); 2.31 (Joshua); 2.50–53 (David, Saul, and Samuel); 2.74 (Elijah).
60 For an example of extensive Old Testament allegories in his more esoteric texts, see Maximos the Confessor, *Ambigua* 10; trans. A. Louth, in *Maximus the Confessor* (London, 1996), 94–154.
61 Symeon the New Theologian, *Ethical Discourses* 1.1–2. Edition: *Traités théologiques et éthiques*, ed. J. Darrouzès, SC 122 (Paris, 1966); trans. A. Golitzin in Symeon the New Theologian, *On the Mystical Life: The Ethical Discourses*, 3 vols. (Crestwood, NY, 1995–97), 1:21–31.

as prefigurations of Christ. Concerning God's taking Adam's rib, Symeon reasons, "Just as the portion was taken from the whole body of Adam and built up into a woman, so, in turn, the same portion set aside from the woman should be built up into a man and become the new Adam, our Lord Jesus Christ."[62] Noah's ark, carrying those to be saved from the flood, figures as "a type of the Theotokos and 'Noah' of Christ."[63] To some extent, Symeon deploys commonplace typological readings of biblical history, but always with an eye to monastic instruction. Symeon could use the same story in diverse ways. For example, he was fond of the translation to heaven of Enoch (Gen. 5:24) and Elijah (2 Kings 2:11), and invoked them in tandem variously to reproach his monks for their unworthiness,[64] to illustrate how these events were mere types of salvation,[65] to stress "that our minds are completely dependent on someone to lift them up to heaven,"[66] and to show that even after the Fall, God honored those who pleased him.[67] This flexibility attests not only the range of theological interpretations that Old Testament narratives afforded to monks but also the degree to which Scripture had been assimilated into the monastic imaginary.

Hearing and Speaking Old Testament Texts

Quite apart from the invocation of exemplars and the exegesis of Scripture, some texts of the Old Testament themselves resounded in the monastic life. Monks with access to complete books of the Bible might read them aloud for themselves and others, but much more prevalent was the ritual reading of scriptural passages in the course of worship. In this context, the Bible was less a library of ancient books and more a source of liturgical lections employed to shape the rhythms of the liturgical year. Indeed, to a large extent the Bible was a liturgical text in Byzantium. Since the primary tendency of emerging lectionaries was to follow the narrative of the Gospels, the lectionary usually fragmented the Old Testament

---

62 Symeon the New Theologian, *Ethical Discourses* 2.2; trans. Golitzin, 1:91.
63 Symeon the New Theologian, *Ethical Discourses* 2.4; trans. Golitzin, 1:99. That is, the Theotokos is the "Noah" of Christ, bearing him to safety.
64 Symeon the New Theologian, *Catecheses* 5.449–53. Edition: *Catéchèses*, ed. B. Krivochéine, SC 96 (Paris, 1963); trans. C. J. de Catanzaro in Symeon the New Theologian, *The Discourses* (New York, 1980), 102.
65 Symeon the New Theologian, *Hymns* 51.66, 104. Edition: *Hymnes*, ed. J. Koder, SC 156, 174, 196 (Paris, 1969–73).
66 Symeon the New Theologian, *Theological Discourses* 1.408–15 (ed. J. Darrouzès); trans. P. McGuckin in Symeon the New Theologian, *The Practical and Theological Chapters and the Three Theological Discourses* (Kalamazoo, 1982), 121.
67 Symeon the New Theologian, *Ethical Discourses* 1.2.106; trans. Golitzin, 1:30.

narratives to offer correspondence and counterpoint to the story of the life of Christ. Thus, not only did the Bible give shape to the liturgical calendar, but the liturgy and the liturgical calendar reshaped the meanings of the biblical texts.

Until the seventh century, selections from the Old Testament were read during the first portion of the synaxis or Divine Liturgy. After the seventh century, Old Testament lections were appointed only for the Vespers service, the Mass of the Presanctified Gifts during Lent, and vigils of major feasts. The service book known as the *Prophetologion* contained these readings as well as other texts proper to each day.[68] On the one hand, this meant that after the seventh century, Byzantine monks who observed the monastic hours heard much more of the Old Testament than lay Christians attending only the Divine Liturgy and the occasional vigil. On the other hand, monks ordinarily heard only those passages that were in the lectionary and in a context where they were keyed to New Testament passages, and where for the most part their selection had been determined by the sequence of the Gospel narratives.[69]

One book of the Old Testament was recited regularly and—usually in the course of a week—in its entirety. The Psalter served as the soundtrack of Byzantine monasticism from its very origins. Monks chanted the psalms at seven appointed times of the day. As a saying attributed in the *Apophthegmata patrum* to Epiphanios of Cyprus illustrates, David featured not only as the author of the Psalms but as an example of how to pray them. "David the prophet prayed late at night; waking in the middle of the night he made entreaties before dawn; at the dawn he stood [before the Lord]; at the morning hour [πρωΐας] he interceded; in the evening and at midday he made supplication; and this is why he said, "Seven times a day have I praised you [Ps. 118:164 (LXX 119)]."[70] The Psalter stood at the center of monastic prayer life.

According to Athanasios of Alexandria in his *Letter to Marcellinus*, the Psalter holds the very heart of Scripture, containing in one book a précis of sacred

---

68   J. Mateos, *La célébration de la parole dans la liturgie Byzantine* (Rome, 1971), 131–33. The eleventh-century typikon of the Monastery of the Black Mountain seeks to prevent readings from the Prophetologion outside of Vespers: Black Mountain 92; *BMFD*, 1:416. For more developed discussion of the Prophetologion see James Miller's contribution here, Chapter 3.
69   *Prophetologium*, ed. C. Høeg, G. Zuntz, and G. Engberg, 2 vols. (Copenhagen, 1970–81).
70   *AP* Epiphanios 7; my translation. On the Egyptian monastic office in the fourth century, see Taft, *Liturgy of the Hours* (n. 35 above), 57–73. And see also *AP* Epiphanios 3 and its parallel in the *Systematic Collection*, ed. Guy 12.6. For a broader overview see R. Taft, "Christian Liturgical Psalmody: Origins, Development, Decomposition, Collapse," in *Psalms in Community: Jewish and Christian Textual, Liturgical, and Artistic Tradtions*, ed. H. W. Attridge and M. E. Fassler (Atlanta, 2003), 7–32.

history and divine instruction. "[The Book of Psalms] chants those things in modulated voice that have been said in the other books in the form of detailed narrative.... It also legislates.... It narrates at times about the journeying of Israel, and prophesies concerning the Savior."[71] Revoicing the words of David, the Psalms teach one how to pray. Athanasios explains that in chanting the Psalms one recognizes the words as his own, and the one who hears the psalms "is deeply moved, as though he himself were speaking." Although Marcellinus, the ostensive recipient of the letter, was most likely a layman, the letter reflects Athanasios's familiarity with desert asceticism. Indeed the letter was subsequently popular among monastics for explaining what was happening in the performance of psalmody.[72] In chanting the Psalms, a monk conforms his voice and his thoughts to the patterns of the Bible. When one sets aside the exclusively prophetic content, "he who recites the Psalms is uttering the rest as his own words, and sings them as if they were written concerning him."[73] Since all the monks were reciting the same Psalms (eventually in the same order and at the same times of the day), the result was not individuality, where each monk might come to think of himself as different, but rather identity: the monk identified himself with and as the speaker of the Psalms. In the monastic office, the monks assumed biblical identities through liturgical performance. The monk became Scripture's mouthpiece, and the Psalms scripted the monk's interior self-reflection and outward self-presentation.

Athanasios also recommended psalms for recitation in specific situations, such as when one wished to express praise, offer thanksgiving, arouse shame, or confess sins.[74] This practice of reciting psalms especially in times of distress endured throughout Byzantine monasticism, as evidenced by a number of tenth- to thirteenth-century psalters that include supplementary texts recommending

---

71 Athanasios, *Letter to Marcellinus* 9 (text: PG 27:12–45); trans. Gregg (n. 1 above), 107.
72 A complete study of the reception of the *Letter to Marcellinus* in Byzantine monasticism would be useful. The earliest copy appears in the fifth-century Bible manuscript *Codex Alexandrinus*, where it serves as an introduction to the Book of Psalms. The text, or parts of it, preface a number of psalters of monastic provenance; excerpts from the *Letter* appear in monastic catenae (anthologies of patristic commentary) of Psalms from the sixth century on (the earliest being a Syriac translation). For some of the manuscripts and codicology, see M. J. Rondeau, "L'Épître à Marcellinus sur les Psaumes," *VChr* 22 (1968): 176–80.
73 Athanasios, *Letter to Marcellinus* 11; trans. Gregg, 109–10. See also P. R. Kolbet, "Athanasius, the Psalms, and the Reformation of the Self," *HTR* 99 (2006): 85–101; J. Ernest, *The Bible in Athanasius of Alexandria* (Leiden, 2004), 332–36; D. Brakke, *Athanasius and the Politics of Asceticism* (Oxford, 1995), 194–96.
74 For example, Athanasios, *Letter to Marcellinus* 14, 21.

psalms to recite when attacked by thoughts of despondency or lust, when remembering injuries done to one, or when held captive by an evil thought, and so forth.[75] A teaching related by John Moschos in *The Spiritual Meadow*, written early in the seventh century, encapsulates the power of the psalms both to attract and to ward off demons.

> [T]here is nothing which troubles, incites, irritates, wounds, destroys, distresses and excites the demons and the supremely evil Satan himself against us, as the constant study of the Psalms. The entire holy Scripture is beneficial to us and not a little offensive to the demons, but none of it distresses them more than the psalter.... For when we meditate on the psalms, on the one hand, we are praying on our own account, while, on the other hand, we are bringing down curses on the demons."[76]

For this reason, monks also recited the psalms while performing manual labor. Moschos relates a cautionary tale about a monk who failed to pay attention to the proper texts of the psalms he recited while plaiting baskets; while his mind wandered, a demon entered his cell in the form of a dancing Saracen boy.[77] Basil of Caesarea encouraged prayer and psalmody during work, a recommendation repeated in the eleventh-century typikon of Gregory Pakourianos for the Monastery of the Mother of God Petritzonitissa at Bačkovo, which states that while monks "work with their hands they should offer up psalms with their mouth."[78]

The use of biblical verses to combat demons offers another, more peculiar example of the efficacy of Scripture in formative spiritual practice. In his *Antirrheticus*, or *Talking Back*, Evagrios Pontikos (died 399) anthologized biblical sentences for a monk to use to answer the demonic thoughts that attacked him: gluttony, lust, greed, sadness, anger, boredom, vainglory, and pride.[79] For the

---

75 For the text and the manuscripts that contain it, see G. Parpulov, "Toward a History of Byzantine Psalters" (PhD diss., University of Chicago, 2004), 268–69, and his chapter in this volume.
76 John Moschos, *The Spritual Meadow* 152 (PG 87:3018–20); trans. J. Wortley, in John Moschus, *The Spiritual Meadow* (Kalamazoo, 1992), 125–26.
77 John Moschos, *The Spiritual Meadow* 160 (PG 87:3028).
78 Basil, *Longer Rules* 37; Pakourianos, 14; trans. R. Jordan, *BMFD*, 2:538.
79 The critical edition of the Syriac version of the text appears in W. Frankenberg, *Evagrios Ponticus*, AbhGött, Philol.-hist.Kl., Neue Folge 13.2 (Berlin, 1912), 472–544. For a partial translation see M. O'Laughlin, "Evagrius Ponticus: *Antirrheticus* (Selections)," in *Ascetic Behavior in Greco-Roman Antiquity: A Sourcebook*, ed. V. L. Wimbush (Minneapolis, 1990), 243–62. See D. Brakke, "Making Public the Monastic Life: Reading the Self in Evagrius Ponticus' *Talking Back*," in *Religion and the Self in Antiquity*, ed. D. Brakke, M. L. Satlow, and S. Weitzman (Bloomington, 2005),

struggle against each of these vices, Evagrios assembled a list of verses, "words required to confute the enemies."[80] Evagrios explains that these words "cannot be found quickly enough in the hour of conflict, because they are scattered through the Scriptures.... Therefore I [Evagrios] have carefully chosen [certain] words from the holy Scriptures, so that equipped with them, we can drive the Philistines out forcefully as we stand to the battle."[81] (We note the use of typology here in the monks' reenactment of David's battle against the Philistines.) For each of the eight evil thoughts Evagrios prescribes different verses, usually in their canonical order in the two testaments of the Bible, and keyed to particular situations. In the section on anger, Evagrios writes: "For the anger that rises up against a brother and makes one's mind unsettled at the time of prayer—'Every sincere soul is blessed, but the passionate soul is ugly.'"[82] The quotation is Proverbs 11:25 (LXX), although, like all Evagrios's selected verses, it is given without citation or context. In the section on greed, in the instance where the demons counsel the monk to get one of his "relatives or some rich person to send money," Evagrios suggests a verse from Genesis: "I stretch out my hand to the most high God, who made heaven and earth, that I will not take anything from all that is yours (Gen. 14:22–23)."[83] Removing the verse far from its narrative context, Evagrios makes no reference to its place in the story of Abraham's visit to the king of Sodom. Fragmented into useful bits, the Old Testament provided part of the arsenal for spiritual warfare. And although Evagrios's text ceased to be copied among Greek monks after the sixth century, he does provide early witness to a style of monastic rhetoric in which a monk's speech was heavily seasoned with biblical tags and quotations.

For Byzantine monks, the Old Testament was familiar in the deepest sense: on monks' tongues and in the air. Byzantine monasticism sang, taught, interpreted, embodied, and reenacted Scripture. Monastic teachers employed Old Testament heroes in moral instruction; hagiographers structured monastic biographies along the lines of Old Testament narratives; monastic theologians allegorized

---

222–33; D. Brakke, *Demons and the Making of the Monk: Spiritual Combat in Early Christianity* (Cambridge, MA, 2006), 48–77; M. O'Laughlin, "The Bible, the Demons, and the Desert: Evaluating the *Antirrheticus* of Evagrius Ponticus," *Studia Monastica* 34 (1992): 201–15; G. Bunge, "Evagrios Pontikos: Der Prolog des *Antirrhetikos*," *Studia Monastica* 29 (1997): 77–105.
80 Evagrios Pontikos, *Antirrhetikos*, prologue; trans. O'Laughlin, 246.
81 Evagrios Pontikos, *Antirrhetikos*, prologue; trans. O'Laughlin, 246–47.
82 Evagrios Pontikos, *Antirrhetikos*, Anger 17; trans. O'Laughlin, 258.
83 Evagrios Pontikos, *Antirrhetikos*, Greed 1; trans. O'Laughlin, 248.

Old Testament texts in spiritual exegesis; and key Old Testament readings were regularly repeated in monastic worship and prayer. Indeed, the monastic Bible consisted not so much in a canon of texts as in a canon of gestures toward those texts. All these uses converged to infuse monasticism with a biblical character, a form of life always in dialogue with Scripture, even as it reformed this Scripture in its own image.

University of North Carolina at Greensboro

NINE

New Temples and New Solomons
The Rhetoric of Byzantine Architecture

ROBERT OUSTERHOUT

For Rick Layton, in gratitude

At the Orlando, Florida theme park "The Holy Land Experience," the Temple of the Great King stands out as the dominant attraction.[1] A grandiose building, its design is based on the Temple of Jerusalem. Nearby, the divine presence, the *shekinah*, is recreated nightly with smoke and lights. The Tomb of Christ, represented by General Gordon's Garden Tomb, simply pales by comparison.[2] The striking contrast between the two monuments may be exaggerated for one simple reason: the Tomb still exists (and thus verisimilitude is in order), while the Temple does not. The official website differentiates them for us, explaining that the Tomb is an "exact replica," whereas the Temple is "a breathtaking representation."[3] The brainchild of Reverend Marvin Rosenthal, a Baptist pastor who had converted from Judaism, the Holy Land Experience has been criticized by local Jewish groups who claim its real purpose is to convert Jews to Christianity. To be sure, although Old Testament sites and monuments are represented in the theme park, they are given a New Testament spin.

This holds true for the Byzantine period as well. Although the Jewish Temple of Jerusalem had disappeared long before the Byzantine period, the idea of the Temple loomed large then as it does now. As at the Holy Land Experience,

---

1   A. Wharton, *Selling Jerusalem: Relics, Replicas, Theme Parks* (Chicago, 2006), 189–232.
2   Perhaps in response to Protestant criticism of the "shabby theatre" at the Church of the Holy Sepulchre, in 1886 General Charles Gordon popularized an alternative site for Christ's Resurrection, the so-called "Garden Tomb," near the Damascus Gate, which subsequently became the focus of Protestant devotion. Although its authenticity has been consistently discounted by historians, it "conforms to the expectations of simple piety"; see J. Murphy-O'Connor, OP, *The Holy Land* (Oxford, 1980), 146–48.
3   See http://www.theholylandexperience.com (accessed 22 February 2008).

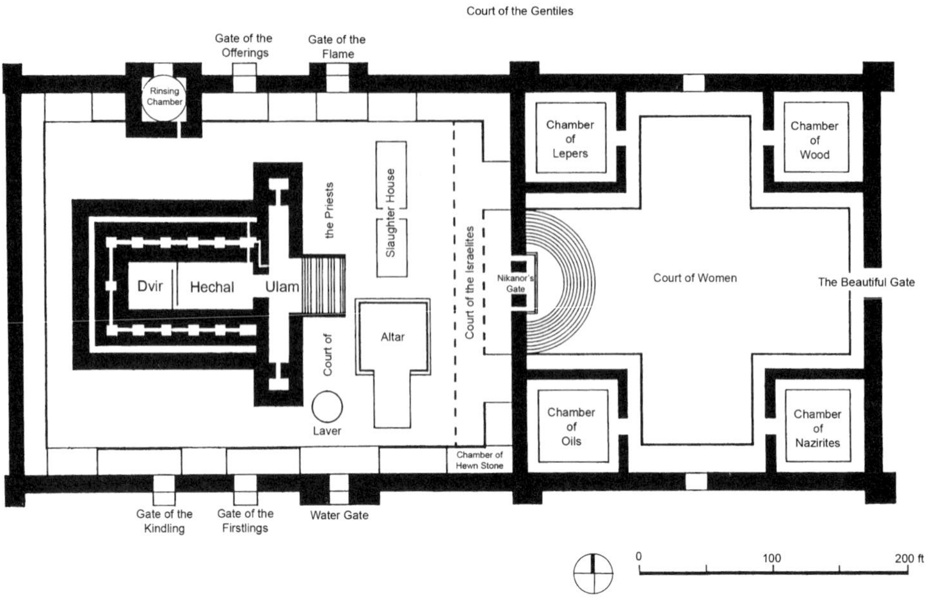

FIGURE 1 Jerusalem, Herod's Temple, hypothetical reconstruction (after J. Comay, *The Temple of Jerusalem* [New York, 1975], 166)

however, in Byzantine times the Temple was invariably viewed through the lens of Christianity. Just as the Old Testament was never interpreted as a Jewish book but instead read in relationship to the New Testament, the idea of the Temple of Solomon was also Christianized. For the Byzantines, it offered a potent if problematic architectural image—or rather images. The Tabernacle, Solomon's Temple, Zerubbabel's Temple, Herod's Temple, and the visionary temple of Ezekiel all had distinct identities that may have come to the fore in particular contexts, but in the polyvalent allegorical language of the Byzantines they were often conflated.[4] Nevertheless, the basic features, proportions, and dimensions were known from a variety of sources; from these the Temple could have been replicated (Figs. 1–2).[5] Indeed, with the possible exception of Noah's Ark, the Temple is the sole architectural exemplar presented in the Old Testament. All the same,

---

4 The literature on the Temple is voluminous; for a convenient summary with extensive bibliography, see B. Narkiss, "Temple," *Encyclopaedia Judaica* (Israel, 1971), 15:942–88; for a popular survey, J. Comay, *The Temple of Jerusalem* (New York, 1975); and more recently, M. Goldhill, *The Temple of Jerusalem* (Cambridge, MA, 2004).

5 For the descriptions, see 1 Kings 6; 7:13–51; 2 Chronicles 3–4; Ezekiel 40–48; Ezra 1–6; Josephus, *Jewish Wars* 5, among others.

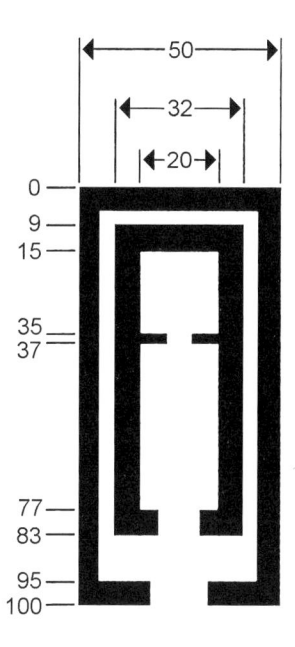

FIGURE 2 Ezekiel's Temple, hypothetical reconstruction, with measurements in cubits (after J. Wilkinson, *From Synagogue to Church: The Traditional Design* [London, 2002])

there were scriptural objections to its reconstruction: Christ had prophesied the destruction of the Temple, and according to Christian thought it should remain in ruins until the end of time. Thus, the challenge for the Byzantine builder would have been how to represent symbolically the sanctity, the divine presence of the Temple, without falling into theological error or, in the worst-case scenario, bringing about the Apocalypse.

In this chapter, I attempt to come to grips with the metaphorical language of Byzantine architecture, in which the Temple figures prominently as a powerful, potent, and multivalent image. As an architectural historian, however, I am interested not so much in the nuances of the text as in how its language might assist us in interpreting architectural forms. The distinctions noted in the Holy Land Experience may be important for the Byzantine architectural context as well. There is a difference between a "replica," based on a physical model, and a "representation," based on a textual description. Similarly, in Byzantine architecture, it is important to distinguish between the language of words and the language of forms. Byzantine rhetoricians often used metaphor to equate a Byzantine church with the Temple in ways that are both allegorical and anagogical, even when there was very little if any physical similarity between buildings. Indeed, *any* Byzantine church could become an "image" of the Temple through the appropriation of its terminology: the worship space is called a *naos*, and its sanctuary *to hagion ton hagion*. The application of Temple terminology to the church building seems to begin with Eusebios, appearing for the first time in his dedicatory speech at the cathedral of Tyre, delivered in ca. 315–17, but the terms were to become common in Byzantine usage.[6] In the so-named "Panegyric on the Building of the Churches, Addressed to Paulinus, Bishop of Tyre," Eusebios explores the spiritual meaning of the Temple as he develops a complex, three-fold parallelism: the church built by Paulinus is the image of the worldwide Church, founded by Christ, which the Jerusalem Temple prefigured.[7] The new Christian Church was to be understood in continuity with the Temple, which it replaced. The speech was included in book 10 of Eusebios's *Church History*, and he no doubt intended it to be widely circulated, to be read and followed. Indeed, it may have set the standard for Temple symbolism in the Byzantine church.

In his description of the church at Tyre, Eusebios clearly follows the familiar descriptions of the Temple, part by part, detail by detail, to symbolic ends, as John Wilkinson has analyzed.[8] Moreover, at the outset, Eusebios addresses the patron, Bishop Paulinus, wondering, "whether one indeed should wish to call you a new Beseleel, the builder of a divine tabernacle, or a Solomon, king of a new and far better Jerusalem, or even a new Zorobabel, who bestowed far greater glory than the former on the temple of God."[9]

This may be the first instance of what would become a topos in Byzantine panegyric, although Eusebios here significantly pins the metaphor on a bishop and not an emperor. He later states, "And these, also, our most peace-loving Solomon (ὁ εἰρηνικώτατος ἡμῶν Σολομών), wrought... so that the above-mentioned prophecy is no longer a word but a fact, for the last glory of this house has become and now truly is greater than the former."[10]

Johannes Koder, Gilbert Dagron, and others have assumed that ὁ εἰρηνικώτατος ἡμῶν Σολομών refers to Constantine.[11] However, because the speech was written before Constantine parted ways with Licinius, I suspect Eusebios—at least initially—is more likely referring again to the founder Paulinus. This conclusion

---

6 J. Wilkinson, "Paulinus' Temple at Tyre," *JÖB* 32, no. 4 [= Akten II/4, XVI. Internationaler Byzantinistenkongress] (1982): 553–61.
7 T. Barnes, *Constantine and Eusebius* (Cambridge, MA, 1981), 162–63.
8 "Paulinus' Temple."
9 Eusebios, *Church History* 10.4.2–72; trans. R. Defferari, FOTC 29 (New York, 1955), 2:244.
10 Ibid.; trans. 2:259.
11 G. Dagron, *Constantinople imaginaire: Études sur le recueil des "Patria"* (Paris, 1984), 293–309; J. Koder, "Justinians Sieg über Salomon," Θυμίαμα στη μνήμη της Λασκαρίνας Μπούρα (Athens, 1994), 135–42, esp. 136.

is reinforced by the organization of the *Church History*, for the following chapter begins with the Edict of Milan, which is credited to both Constantine and Licinius.

With well-constructed metaphors, Eusebios laid out for succeeding generations the meaning of the church building with respect to the Temple. But how much did the descriptions of the Temple influence *actual* church planning? John Wilkinson has proposed that the proportional systems underlying the design of many early Christian basilicas referred directly to those of the Temple.[12] He notes a variety of examples in which the elongated nave seems to repeat the 1:3 proportional system of the Temple, with a square bema (sanctuary) that would correspond to the Holy of Holies. The interpretation of the proportional system depends on the points from which the measurements were taken. Moreover, the proportions of the Temple are so simple and so common that it may be impossible to determine if and when their employment was intended symbolically.

Although the basilica at Tyre does not survive, we can be certain it looked nothing like the Temple. To begin with, as Richard Krautheimer has taught us, a basilica is not a temple.[13] A basilica is simply a large hall designed for large crowds of worshippers to gather inside. In contrast, the interior of a temple (and most certainly of *the* Temple) was off-limits to most worshippers, and most ceremonies took place outside the temple, where the altar was located. Although symbolic associations with the Temple may have been introduced into early churches, the typologies of the buildings remained inherently different. Krautheimer sees the formal distinctions as meaningful—there could be no visual confusion between a temple and a basilica; the latter, rising prominently on the skyline of a late Roman city, would advertise the presence of the new religion as if a billboard—a subject nicely developed recently by Dale Kinney.[14] Krautheimer made this distinction concerning the development of a new architecture in Rome. The temples to which he referred were pagan and not Jewish, but I believe his basic point holds.

Meaning is a different matter. Does the application of an allegorical language to architecture automatically signal the replication of meaningful forms? Symbols and metaphors are elusive and difficult to pin down—both in texts

---

12 *From Synagogue to Church: The Traditional Design; Its Beginning, Its Definition, Its End* (London, 2002).
13 "The Constantinian Basilica," *DOP* 21 (1967): 115–50.
14 "The Church Basilica," *Acta ad Archaeologiam et Artium Historiam Pertinentia* 15 (2001): 115–35.

and in buildings. By contrast, although a building may be the passive receptor of applied meanings, its architectural form is fixed and concrete. And although symbols and metaphors may be hard to isolate, their very elusiveness may also be the basis of their power. By definition and etymology, a metaphor transposes or transports its subject. A symbol, on the other hand, represents or associates a subject with something else, something that exists beyond it in time and space. In this respect, architectural form is passive; symbol and metaphor become its active manipulators.[15] As an architectural historian confronting the rhetorical symbolic language of architecture, it may be important to distinguish between word-driven meanings (which usually fall into the category of metaphors) and image-driven meanings (which usually fall into the category of symbols). The former would be applied from the outside, usually in the form of a text that tells us how to interpret a building or its parts; the latter is embedded or encoded within the architectural forms of the building itself. There may be significant overlap between the two systems, and in many instances the architectural symbolism will exist within a larger program of applied meaning.

In his famous study of the iconography of medieval architecture, Krautheimer concentrated on the latter system—the replication of forms—to situate the study of medieval architecture within the mainstream of contemporary art historical discourse, drawing upon Panofsky's studies of iconography and iconology.[16] Krautheimer's basic proposition was that meaning is transferred in architecture through the repetition of significant, identifiable forms. While concentrating on medieval architectural "copies," he emphasized the importance of texts or inscriptions for verification of the architectural relationship.[17] Krautheimer's overemphasis on form as the carrier of meaning has unnecessarily complicated subsequent discussions of architectural symbolism, by suggesting that meaning is inherent in architectural form, that form is the primary conveyor of meaning, but this need not be the case. As a rhetorical trope, a metaphor may be

---

15 See the study by R. Webb, "The Aesthetics of Sacred Space: Narrative, Metaphor, and Motion in 'Ekphraseis,'" *DOP* 53 (1999): 59–74.
16 R. Krautheimer, "Introduction to an 'Iconography of Medieval Architecture,'" *JWarb* 5 (1942): 1–33; reprinted in idem, *Studies in Early Christian, Medieval, and Renaissance Art* (New York, 1969), 115–50, following E. Panofsky, *Studies in Iconology* (New York, 1939). For a more recent assessment, see P. Crossley, "Medieval Architecture and Meaning: The Limits of Iconography," *The Burlington Magazine* 130 (1988): 116–21; note also N. Goodman, "How Buildings Mean," *Critical Inquiry* 11 (1985): 642–53, who offers a somewhat anachronistic system of interpretation.
17 This was something Krautheimer failed to do in the second part of his study, as I have discussed elsewhere: see R. Ousterhout, "The Temple, the Sepulchre, and the *Martyrion* of the Savior," *Gesta* 39, no. 1 (1990): 44–53.

only loosely related to a specific architectural form, or not related at all, but following Krautheimer, we expect a connection.

For example, the sanctuary of a Byzantine church was regularly viewed in association with the Temple, in reliance on a long textual tradition, again beginning with Eusebios at Tyre. He writes, following Old Testament models, "Lastly, in the center, [Paulinus] placed the most holy altar (τὸ τῶν ἁγίων ἅγιον θυσιαστήριον), fencing it round . . . with wooden chancels to make it inaccessible to the general public." A similar barrier in the atrium prevented "unhallowed and uncleaned feet" from treading on the "holy places within."[18] Marking zones of sacrality and hierarchy, the barriers echo those of the Temple, and the association helps to legitimize the sacred space of the church by conjuring its predecessor, as Joan Branham has discussed.[19] For the Byzantine sanctuary, the Temple symbolism continued: Paul the Silentiary refers to the sanctuary of Hagia Sophia as "set aside for the bloodless sacrifice."[20] Prokopios calls the sanctuary "the part of the church which is especially inviolable and accessible only to the priests."[21] The patriarch Germanos I, writing in the eighth century, explains the meaning of the chancel as follows: "The cancelli (*kangella*) denote the place of prayer, and signify that the space outside them may be entered by the people, while inside is the holy of holies which is accessible only to the priests."[22]

These and other writers judiciously borrow the language of the Temple to enhance their descriptions. The parts and furnishings of the church thereby become "hooks" on which the writers hang their meanings. All the same, they do not force a one-to-one relationship, nor do they tell us that the plan of the sanctuary and the details of the cancelli are modeled on the Temple and its parts. The borrowed language never says the church *is* the Temple, rather it suggests that meanings associated with the Temple may enlighten our understanding of the church as sacred space. We might also view this relationship in terms of medieval memory theory: informed by the text, the features of the sanctuary

---

18 Wilkinson, "Paulinus' Temple" (n. 6 above), 556.
19 "Sacred Space in Ancient Jewish and Early Medieval Architecture" (PhD diss., Emory University, 1993): 63–70; eadem, "Sacred Space under Erasure in Ancient Synagogues and Early Churches," *AB* 74 (1992): 375–94, esp. 380–82; eadem, "Penetrating the Sacred: Breaches and Barriers in the Jerusalem Temple," in *Thresholds of the Sacred*, ed. S. Gerstel (Washington, DC, 2006), 7–24.
20 M. L. Fobelli, *Un tempio per Giustiniano: Santa Sofia di Costantinopoli e la* Descrizione *di Paolo Silenziario* (Rome, 2005), 76–77, lines 682–84.
21 Prokopios, *Buildings*, trans. H. P. Dewing (Cambridge, MA, 1971), 1.1.64–65.
22 *Historia mystagogica* 7; see C. Mango, *The Art of the Byzantine Empire 312–1453: Sources and Documents* (Toronto, 1986), 143.

FIGURE 3 Mt. Nebo, chapel of the Theotokos, detail of the sanctuary mosaic floor depicting the Temple (from S. Saller, *The Memorial of Moses on Mount Nebo* [Jerusalem, 1941])

recall—that is, they call to our memory and act as loci of contemplation for—the meaning of the Temple.[23]

A few unusual examples move from the loosely applied textual metaphor to the more specifically identified architectural symbol. The sixth-century Chapel of the Theotokos on Mt. Nebo offers a unique example in which the association with the Temple is visually manifest. Between the chancel barrier and the altar, a schematic representation of the Temple appears in the floor mosaic (Fig. 3). A fire burns before the Temple, and the building is flanked by two bulls, whose presence is explained by the inscription, from Psalm 51 (50): "They shall lay calves upon thy altar." Here the phrase identifies the bulls as sacrificial, and, as Sylvester Saller noted, the verse was repeated in the early Jerusalem liturgy when the offerings were placed upon the altar.[24] In the Mt. Nebo inscription, the Temple is invoked in a fairly specific way, but its parts have been conflated: the altar of sacrifice and the Holy of Holies merge, for in Christian terms the Eucharist represents both the sacrifice and the divine presence. In the end, the

23 See M. Carruthers, *The Craft of Thought: Meditation, Rhetoric, and the Making of Images, 400–1200* (Cambridge, 1998), esp. 7–21.
24 *The Memorial of Moses on Mount Nebo* (Jerusalem, 1941), 235–37; see also Branham, "Sacred Space under Erasure," 381–82 and figs. 11–12.

relationship of the Byzantine sanctuary to the Temple is more metaphorical than mimetic; beyond the presence of a barrier and an altar, there seems to have been no attempt to replicate the Temple's forms.

The association of the bema with the Temple became a commonplace in Byzantine art and architecture.[25] In Christian Egypt, for example, it seems to have been standard to associate the sanctuary screen with the veil of the Temple or the tabernacle, at least after the thirteenth century, as Elizabeth Bolman has discussed recently.[26] There is tantalizing earlier evidence, however, such as a seventh-century graffito from Kellia depicting what is apparently a church sanctuary, which is inscribed as "the tabernacle of testimony."[27]

In Byzantine art, the setting for the Presentation of the Virgin in the Temple is the sanctuary of a Byzantine church, as we see in narthex mosaics of the Chora, now the Kariye Camii, Istanbul (Fig. 4).[28] The hymns associated with the feast of the Presentation of the Virgin emphasize the theme of Mary as the true temple, prefiguring the Nativity.[29] The Chora image is set in the inner narthex on axis above the entrance to the naos, so that anyone entering the church would see the image of the Temple in relationship to the bema—perhaps connecting the manna fed to the Virgin with the Eucharist offered at the bema.[30] The mosaic with its Temple imagery is thus situated within the larger thematic program of the Chora, building upon the common theme. A similar thematic connection, joining art and architectural elements, is found in a recently published painted templon (chancel barrier) from Cappadocia.[31] At the thirteenth-century (?) Ağaçlı Kilise in Güzelöz, the templon was formed by a solid, painted wall. Now dismantled, in the reconstruction proposed by Rainer Warland, the

---

25 See for example I. Shalina, "The Entrance to the Holy of Holies and the Byzantine Sanctuary Barrier," in *The Iconostasis: Origins—Evolution—Symbolism*, ed. A. Lidov (Moscow, 2000), 52–71 (in Russian, with English summary, 719–20).
26 E. Bolman, "Veiling Sanctuary in Christian Egypt: Visual and Spatial Solutions," in Gerstel, *Thresholds*, 70–104.
27 Ibid., 88, n. 81, and fig. 23.
28 P. Underwood, *The Kariye Djami* (New York, 1966), 1:72–73; R. Ousterhout, "The Virgin of the Chora," in *The Sacred Image East and West*, ed. R. Ousterhout and L. Brubaker (Urbana, 1995), 91–109, esp. 99–100.
29 R. Taft and A. Weyl Carr, "Presentation of the Virgin," *ODB* 3:1715; I. E. Anastasios, "Eisodia tes Theotokou," *Threskeutike kai Ethike Enkyklopaideia* (Athens, 1962–68), 5:451–54; J. Lafontaine-Dosogne, *Iconographie de l'enfance de la Vierge dans l'empire byzantin et en occident*, 2 vols. (Brussels, 1964), 1:136–67.
30 Ousterhout, "Virgin of the Chora," 99–100.
31 R. Warland, "Das Bildertemplon von Güzelöz und das Bildprogram der Karanlık Kilise/Kappadokien," in *Architektur und Liturgie*, ed. M. A. Altripp and C. Nauerth (Wiesbaden, 2006), 211–21 and pls. 32–34.

FIGURE 4 Istanbul, Kariye Camii, inner narthex. Mosaic of the Presentation of the Virgin in the Temple (courtesy of Dumbarton Oaks Visual Resources)

outer surface is decorated with the scene of the Presentation of the Virgin in the Temple, organized so that the central arched opening is surmounted by the painted columns and arches that represent the Temple.[32] Here it appears as if the Virgin is introduced into the bema itself.

In fact, references to the Temple appear frequently in the metaphorical language of early Christianity, in a variety of contexts and often without reference to specific architectural forms. Ambrose, for example, introduced it into his explanation of the baptismal rite. He calls the baptistery the *sancta sanctorum* and refers to the officiants as levites.[33] "The Holy of Holies was unbarred to you," he writes, contrasting the accessibility of the baptistery to the lack of access at the Temple. Here he must be developing a theme that appears in the Epistle to the Hebrews: that in the New Covenant, Christ is both high priest and sacrifice, bringing the benefits of the Temple to his followers with the promise of a

32 Ibid., pl. 34, fig. 1.
33 *De mysteriis* 2.5–7.

heavenly sanctuary (Hebrews 9:11–14). Indeed, this conflation may lie behind the Temple symbolism of the altar noted above. The idea that the Temple lived on in the Christian community and their ceremonies is a theme developed as early as the writings of Ignatios of Antioch and it became widespread in the early centuries of Christianity.[34]

In short, the Temple provided a common metaphor for a variety of architectural forms, and to a variety of ends. At its simplest, an association with the Temple could offer a convenient shorthand for sacred space. On a theological level, it could emphasize the relationship of the Old and the New Covenants—that a Christian church or specifically the sanctuary of the church represents the New Covenant. Viewed more broadly, by situating the Temple symbolism amid the congregation, it could even signal that the Christians are the new chosen people.

In what follows, I examine a few well-known examples of Byzantine architecture in which the Temple figured prominently as metaphor or symbol, to question what the association with the Temple signified in each specific context, and if and how it was expressed in architectural terms. In the first part, I look at the Church of the Holy Sepulchre, for which the description by Eusebios parallels contemporaneous exegetical writings—that is, the Temple was invoked to theological ends to provide a special identity to Constantine's church. For the second part, I turn to the thorny issue of the interpretation of Justinian's Hagia Sophia and related buildings. Here I believe the theological message, so powerful at the time of Constantine, is overshadowed by a political message, that the Temple was invoked as an expression of an imperial ideology grounded in Old Testament kingship.

In his description of Constantine's building program at the Church of the Holy Sepulchre in Jerusalem, Eusebios applies a vocabulary similar to what he had developed at Tyre:

> New Jerusalem was built at the very Testimony to the Savior, facing the famous Jerusalem of old, which after the bloody murder of the Lord had

---

34 See the fascinating essay by R. Young, "Martyrdom as Exaltation," in *Late Ancient Christianity*, ed. V. Burris, A People's History of Christianity 2 (Minneapolis, 2005), 70–92, who relates the concept of Christian martyrdom to Temple sacrifice; note also R. McKelvey, *The New Temple: The Church in the New Testament* (Oxford, 1969); W. Schoedel, *Ignatius of Antioch: A Commentary on the Letters of Ignatius of Antioch*, ed. H. Koester (Philadelphia, 1985).

been overthrown in utter devastation, and paid the penalty of its wicked inhabitants. Opposite this then the Emperor erected the victory of the Savior over death with rich and abundant munificence, this being perhaps that fresh new Jerusalem proclaimed in prophetic oracles, about which long speeches recite innumerable praises as they utter words of divine inspiration.[35]

In addition to referring to the new church complex as the new Jerusalem, Eusebios calls the Tomb of Christ the "holy of holies." He thus invites us to contrast Constantine's new church complex to the ruins of the Temple. As Jonathan Z. Smith comments, "We should accept the invitation."[36] In the fourth century, the two buildings stood in visual opposition, facing each other across the Tyropoeon Valley. An imposing new work of architecture could testify to the success of the New Covenant, just as the empty and abandoned remains of the Temple opposite it could represent the failure of the Old Covenant. Although it is easy in retrospect to jump to the conclusion that the Holy Sepulchre became the New Temple, Eusebios's rhetorical strategy is a bit more subtle, for he is simultaneously comparing and contrasting the two buildings.[37] While the two buildings had almost no formal similarities, they shared a few common features (Figs. 1, 5).[38] Both had their entrances facing the rising sun, and according to the late fourth-century pilgrim Egeria, the dedications were related, as she explains:

---

35   Eusebios, *V. Const.* 3.33.1–2, trans. Av. Cameron and S. G. Hall, *Life of Constantine* (Oxford: Oxford University Press, 1999), 135, with extensive commentary, 273–91: "It is worthy of note that it is the building itself which is described as the 'new Jerusalem' and identified with that spoken of by the prophets ('perhaps that fresh new Jerusalem proclaimed in prophetic oracles'; cf. Rev. 3:12, 21. 2)," (p. 284).
36   J. Z. Smith, *To Take Place: Toward Theory in Ritual* (Chicago, 1987), 83.
37   As I have discussed elsewhere: R. Ousterhout, "Temple" (n. 17 above), from which much of the following discussion derives.
38   The standard monograph remains H. Vincent and F.-M. Abel, *Jérusalem nouvelle* (Paris, 1914), vol. 2. The history of the building is summarized in R. Ousterhout, "Rebuilding the Temple: Constantine Monomachus and the Holy Sepulchre," *JSAH* 48 (1989): 66–78; and idem, "Architecture as Relic and the Construction of Sanctity: The Stones of the Holy Sepulchre," *JSAH* 62 (2003): 4–23. V. C. Corbo, *Il Santo Sepolcro di Gerusalemme*, 3 vols. (Jerusalem, 1981), is indispensable and has superseded all previous publications on the subject, but without providing a full analysis of its architectural remains. A less satisfactory account, with imaginative reconstruction drawings, is provided by C. Coüasnon, *The Church of the Holy Sepulchre in Jerusalem* (London, 1974). See the more recent J. Taylor and S. Gibson, *Beneath the Church of the Holy Sepulchre* (London, 1994), for important observations on the site of the Constantinian building, although their attempts at reconstruction are less useful. M. Biddle, *The Tomb of Christ* (Stroud, 1999), offers important observations on the building's history while focusing on the present condition of the tomb.

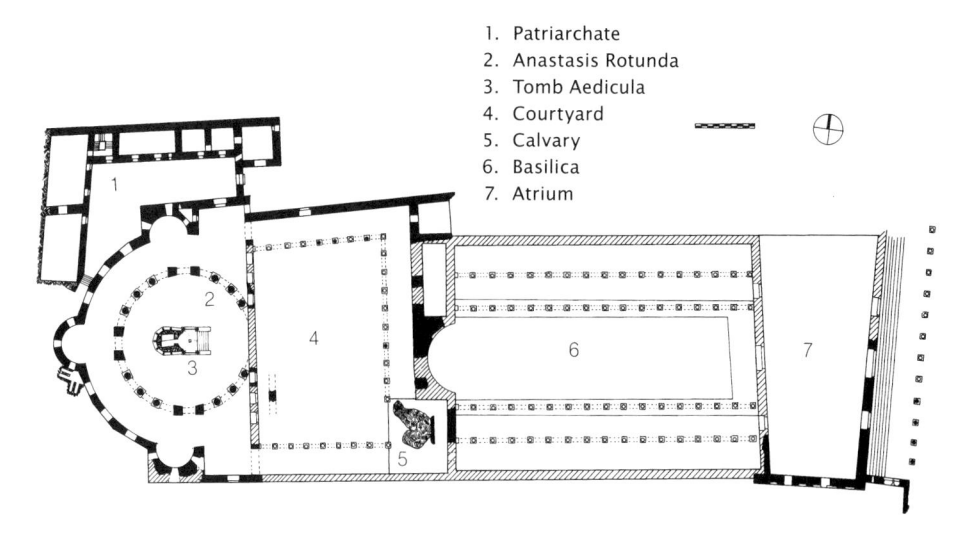

1. Patriarchate
2. Anastasis Rotunda
3. Tomb Aedicula
4. Courtyard
5. Calvary
6. Basilica
7. Atrium

FIGURE 5 Jerusalem, Holy Sepulchre, plan as of mid-fourth century (author with A. Papalexandrou, after V. Corbo, *Il Santo Sepolcro di Gerusalemme* [Jerusalem, 1981], pl. 3)

The date when the church on Golgotha (called Martyrium) was consecrated to God is called Encaenia, and on the same day, the holy church of the Anastasis was also consecrated, the place where the Lord rose again after his passion. The Encaenia of these holy churches is a feast of special magnificence, since it is on the day when the cross of the Lord was discovered.... You will find in the Bible that the day of Encaenia was when the House of God was consecrated, and Solomon stood in prayer before God's altar, as we read in the book of Chronicles.[39]

An association seems to have been formed on the basis of function; the timing and organization of the individual celebrations, as well as the ordering of the liturgical calendar, reflect Jewish worship. John Wilkinson has suggested that parts of the early liturgical celebration at the Holy Sepulchre were structured following the model of the ceremonies at the Temple.[40] The synagogue service may have provided a liturgical intermediary, but many elements of the liturgy seem to relate directly to the Temple. For example, the timing of the morning whole-offering at the Temple is paralleled in the weekday morning hymns at the

---

39   Egeria 48.1; J. Wilkinson, *Egeria's Travels to the Holy Land* (Warminster, 1981), 146.
40   "Jewish Influences on the Early Christian Rite of Jerusalem," *Le Muséon* 92 (1979): 349–59; idem, *Egeria's Travels*, 298–310. Note also M. Barker, *The Great High Priest: The Temple Roots of Christian Liturgy* (London, 2003).

Holy Sepulchre. Both began at cockcrow with the opening of the doors; morning prayers or hymns began at daylight. Subsequently in the Temple service, the high priest and the other priests entered the Temple and prostrated themselves. At the Holy Sepulchre, the bishop and the clergy entered the tomb aedicula for prayers and blessings. Then, in both ceremonies, the officiants emerged to bless the people.[41]

In other site-specific ceremonies described by Egeria, a parallelism seems to be developed: the Tomb of Christ takes the place of the Temple, or perhaps more specifically the holy of holies. The ever-burning lamp in the tomb might be likened to the menorah in the Temple, and the rock of Calvary may have assumed the role of the altar of sacrifice on Mount Moriah. In addition, the stone of the angel in front of the Tomb of Christ—the rolling stone from the original rock-cut tomb—is described not as round but as a "cube," which would liken it to the altar of incense at the Temple.[42]

A liturgical reflection of the Temple would accord with the exegetical emphasis of fourth-century Christian apologists; that is, it mirrors the desire of writers like Eusebios to ground the recently accepted faith on the signs and prophecy of the Old Testament. In fact, the symbolic association of the Temple and the Holy Sepulchre may have been initiated by Eusebios himself. As at Tyre, his purpose in describing Constantine's new church in Jerusalem was to demonstrate the continuity from Temple to Church, and to show the fulfillment of Haggai's prophecy that "the last splendor of this house shall be great beyond the first" (Hag. 2:9, NETS).[43] Moreover, the language used by Eusebios to describe the discovery of the site of the Tomb of Christ and the subsequent Constantinian building project at the Holy Sepulchre follows the same pattern. From the beginning, he refers to the site as the *martyrion* of the Savior's resurrection.[44] By the end of the fourth century—and in modern scholarship—the term *martyrion* is used in a somewhat different sense. But Eusebios must have intended it in the same way Cyril of Jerusalem explains a few decades later, namely, in reference to the prophecy of Zephaniah: "Wherefore expect me, says the Lord, in the day of my resurrection at the *martyrion*" [Διατοῦτο ὑπόμεινόν

---

41 Wilkinson, "Jewish Influences," 354.
42 Ibid., 357.
43 Trans. A. Pietersma, *New English Translation of the Septuagint* (Oxford, 2000); Wilkinson, "Paulinus' Temple" (n. 6 above) 557; Eusebios, *V. Const.* 4.45.
44 *V. Const.* 3.28; trans. Wilkinson, *Egeria's Travels*, 165.

με, λέγει Κύριος, εἰς ἡμέραν ἀναστάσεώς μου εἰς μαρτύριον].⁴⁵ The Tabernacle is called the σκηνὴ τοῦ μαρτυρίου in the Septuagint; the "place of witness" in an Old Testament sense would imply a witness to divine presence.⁴⁶ This verse could be translated in a variety of ways; the New English Translation of the Septuagint renders it, "Therefore wait for me, says the Lord, for the day of my arising as a witness." I suspect Cyril has subtly altered its meaning to suit his own ends, as both Anastasis and Martyrion were toponyms at the Holy Sepulchre. He explains in the next paragraph: "Now for what reason is this place of Golgotha and of the Resurrection called, not a church . . . but a martyry [μαρτύριον]? It was perhaps because of the prophet who said, 'in the day of my resurrection at the martyry.'"

Eusebios also preached at the dedication of the basilica at the Holy Sepulchre in 336. The sermon has not survived, although he notes in the *Life of Constantine* that he "endeavored to gather from the prophetic visions apt illustrations of the symbols it displayed."⁴⁷ In consideration of this and his references elsewhere, Wilkinson concludes that Eusebios interpreted the *"martyrion* of the Savior" as the new Temple of Jerusalem in the dedicatory sermon.⁴⁸

The connection of the Holy Sepulchre with the Temple, then, seems to have existed from the inception of the church. While seen most clearly in the shaping of the liturgy and in the language of Eusebios, the relationship does not appear to have had a clear architectural manifestation—that is, it was expressed in metaphors but not in symbols. The only possible exception to the latter is the articulation of the tomb aedicula, which looks suspiciously similar to the early representations of the Temple. For example, the image of the Temple above the scroll niche in the synagogue of Dura Europos and similar images on the coinage of Bar Kochba may be compared with the images of the Holy Sepulchre on late sixth-century pilgrims' ampullae.⁴⁹ But verisimilitude was not critical here;

---

45 Zeph. 3:8; Wilkinson, "Jewish Influences," 352; idem, *Egeria's Travels*, 324, n. to p. 165; Cyril of Jerusalem, *Cat.* 14.6, PG 33.832, trans. L. McCauley and A. Stephenson, FOTC 64 (Washington, DC, 1970), 35–36.
46 Young, "Martyrdom" (n. 34 above) esp. 71, makes an important association of the early Christian and contemporaneous Judaic concept of martyrdom (*martyria*) with the Temple sacrifice.
47 *V. Const.* 4.45; trans. Wilkinson, *Egeria's Travels*, 302.
48 Wilkinson, "Jewish Influences," 351–52.
49 Ousterhout, "Temple" (n. 17 above) 48 and figs. 4–6.

as the exegetical strategy contrasted the two sites, the Holy Sepulchre might be better understood as replacing, rather than replicating, the Temple.

The association of the two sites developed in the folklore of the early Christian period with a blatant literalism. To be more readily understood, the elusive literary metaphor of Eusebios needed to be made physical and concrete. Thus, "holy sites" and relics previously associated with the Temple migrated to the Holy Sepulchre complex. For example, in the fourth century the Pilgrim of Bordeaux saw on the Temple Mount "an altar which has on it the blood of Zacharias—you would think it had only been shed today—as well as the footprints of the soldiers who killed him."[50] In the sixth century, the author of the *Breviarius* saw the "altar where holy Zacharias was killed, and his blood dried there," in front of the Tomb of Christ.[51] Sometime before the seventh century, the *omphalos* or navel of the world was also relocated inside the Church of the Holy Sepulchre.[52]

Events from the life of Christ associated with the Temple were transferred as well. For example, pilgrims in the sixth century were told that the inner courtyard of the Holy Sepulchre was the Temple court "where Jesus found them that sold the doves and cast them out."[53] In addition, Christian pilgrims saw an evocative collection of Old Testament relics: the horn used for the anointing of the Jewish kings, the ring of Solomon, and the altar of Abraham. Unmentioned in the Jewish sources, the horn of the anointing is first noted by Egeria in the late fourth century; she says that it was venerated along with the wood of the Cross and the ring of Solomon on Good Friday.[54] The ring of Solomon was apparently a seal-ring, decorated with a pentagram. A Jewish legend, well known in the early Christian centuries, claimed that King Solomon had employed it to seal the demons and thereby gain power over them. While under his control, the power of the demons was channeled to aid in the construction of the first Temple.[55] Elsewhere in the Basilica of Constantine, pilgrims saw the vessels in which Solomon had sealed the demons.[56]

The altar of Abraham marked the site where he had offered his son Isaac as a sacrifice on Mount Moriah, and this was identified commonly with the altar of

---

50 Pilgrim of Bordeaux, *Travels*, 591; trans. J. Wilkinson, *Egeria's Travels*, 157.
51 *Breviarus*, 3; trans. Wilkinson, *Jerusalem Pilgrims before the Crusades* (Warminster, 1977), 60.
52 Adomnan, *De locis sanctis*, 1.11.4; Bernard the Monk, *A Journey to the Holy Places and Babylon*, 12; trans. Wilkinson, *Jerusalem Pilgrims*, 99, 144.
53 *Breviarus*, 3; trans. Wilkinson, *Jerusalem Pilgrims*, 60.
54 Egeria, 37.3; trans. Wilkinson, *Egeria's Travels*, 137.
55 G. Vikan, *Byzantine Pilgrimage Art* (Washington, DC, 1982), 35 and fig. 27; C. C. McCown, *The Testament of Solomon* (Leipzig, 1927), 10.
56 *Breviarius*, 2; trans. Wilkinson, *Jerusalem Pilgrims*, 59.

the Temple. The event figured prominently in Christian thought, juxtaposing Abraham's sacrifice of Isaac with the sacrifice of Christ. According to the *Breviarius* (ca. 500), the sacrifice of Isaac occurred "in the very place where the Lord was crucified."[57] Golgotha thus became Mount Moriah and also was regarded as the place where Adam was created and where he was buried. The altar is also mentioned by the Piacenza Pilgrim and by Alculf as recorded by Adomnan (ca. 679–88), and it is represented in the Holy Sepulchre plans that accompany the texts of Arculf.[58]

The early situation at the Holy Sepulchre provides a fascinating combination of antithesis and assimilation. Eusebios clearly intends us from the beginning to *contrast* the two buildings—the glory of one is to stand in meaningful opposition to the ruin and abandonment of the other. At the same time, the repetition of such key terms as *anastasis, martyrion,* and *holy of holies,* the ordering of the service, and the orientation of the building encourage the reader to view the two sites in relationship to each other. Nevertheless, with the possible exception of some details of the tomb aedicula, there seems to have been no attempt to replicate the architectural forms of the Temple.

Let me now turn to Justinian's Hagia Sophia (Fig. 6). For a building of unrivaled architectural grandeur, it is a bit odd how we invariably turn to a text to explain it, to the *ekphraseis* of Prokopios or Paul the Silentiary or even the tales recorded in the *Diegesis peri tes Hagias Sophias,* when our own words fail us.[59] Justinian's Hagia Sophia may have been meant to evoke the Heavenly Jerusalem, or the Throne of God, or the Temple of Jerusalem, or quite possibly all three. Prokopios writes, echoing descriptions of the Temple: "Whenever anyone enters to pray, he understands at once that it is not by human power and skill, but by God's will that this work has been so finely finished. His mind is lifted up to God and floats on air, feeling that God cannot be far away, but must especially love to dwell in this place, which He has chosen."[60]

57   Wilkinson, *Jerusalem Pilgrims,* 60.
58   Piacenza Pilgrim, *Travels from Piacenza,* 19; Adomnan, *De locis sanctis,* 6.2; trans. Wilkinson, *Jerusalem Pilgrims,* 83, 89.
59   For the texts on Hagia Sophia see Mango, *Art of the Byzantine Empire* (n. 22 above), 72–102; for the architecture see, among others, R. Mainstone, *Hagia Sophia: Architecture, Structure and Liturgy of Justinian's Great Church* (New York, 1988); T. F. Mathews, *The Early Churches of Constantinople: Architecture and Liturgy* (University Park, PA, 1971), 105–80; C. Mango, *Hagia Sophia: A Vision for Empires* (Istanbul, 1997).
60   *Buildings* 1.1.61–62 (trans. Dewing).

FIGURE 6 Istanbul, Hagia Sophia, nave interior, view to east (courtesy of Dumbarton Oaks Visual Resources)

Prokopios emphasizes the quality of light in the building: "Indeed, one might say that its interior is not illuminated from without by the sun, but that the radiance comes into being within it, such an abundance of light bathes this shrine."[61] Set within the context of the general evocation of the Temple, this may refer to the appearance of the *shekinah*, or presence of God, in the Temple. Similar themes echo in the ninth- or tenth-century, semilegendary *Diegesis*, which recounts that the bricks of the building were stamped with the verse of Psalm 45, reading "God is in her midst, she shall not be moved"—a verse that may have been spoken at the dedication ceremony. Gilbert Dagron extends the metaphor to suggest that as Hagia Sophia increased in prestige, it came to be regarded as the new Temple of Solomon, thereby equating Constantinople with Jerusalem.[62]

Romanos the Melode also evokes the Temple in relation to Hagia Sophia in his *Hymn* 54, which tells of Justinian's rebuilding.

> If anyone looked to Jerusalem [21]
> and the magnificent temple
> That all-wise Solomon in a very prosperous time
> Raised up, adorned, and embellished with infinite wealth,
> He will see how it was given over to pride and destroyed.
> And still remains fallen; it was not restored.
> Then he may see the grace of this church
> which offers
> eternal life.
> The people of Israel were deprived of their Temple [22]
> but we instead of that,
> Now have the holy Anastasis and Sion
> Which Constantine and the faithful Helena
> gave to the world
> Two hundred and fifty years after the fall.
> But in our case, just one day after the disaster
> Work was begun on having the church restored.
> It was brilliantly decorated and brought to completion.[63]

---

61 Ibid., 1.1.29–30.
62 G. Dagron, *Constantinople imaginaire* (n. 11 above), 293–309.
63 Romanos the Melode, *Hymnes*, ed. J. Grosdidier de Matons (Paris, 1981), 5:470–99; E. Topping, "On Earthquakes and Fires: Romanos' Encomium to Justinian," *BZ* 71 (1978): 22–35; also M. Carpenter, trans., *Kontakia of Romanos, Byzantine Melodist*, vol. 2, *On Christian Life* (Columbia, MO, 1973), 237–48, esp. 246–47.

In the following strophe [23], he elaborates the metaphor, insisting that "the very structure of the church / was erected with such excellence / That it imitated Heaven, the divine throne."[64] Similar themes resonate in a sixth-century kontakion,[65] as well as in Corippus's *In laudem Iustini*, both of which contrast the two buildings; a direct comparison is avoided. "Let the description of Solomon's Temple now be stilled," concludes Corippus.[66]

Was the comparison of the two buildings ever more than simply a literary motif? Georg Scheja once suggested a physical similarity, noting the possible proportional relationships: at Hagia Sophia, the length, if one included the narthex (but not the exonarthex), would be approximately 300 ft., the width of the nave 100 ft., and the height of the first dome would have been, perhaps, 150 ft.[67] These measurements would repeat the Temple's proportions of 3:1:1.5. Scheja also wondered if the cherubim in the pendentives might be a reference to the vision of Ezekiel.[68] The proportions of the Temple are so simple, however, one can find them almost anywhere, depending on how one measures; also, the height of the first dome remains uncertain. To be sure, no one has ever successfully explained the proportional system of Hagia Sophia.[69] Whether cherubim or seraphim, the six-winged creatures in the eastern pendentives date from the late Byzantine period following the reconstruction of ca. 1355; those in the western pendentives had been almost completely destroyed and were repainted in the nineteenth and twenty-first centuries; it is unclear when they first appeared in this position and how they should be interpreted.[70]

To my mind, the best point of comparison between Hagia Sophia and the Temple lies in the fact that neither site had any particularly significant

---

64   Carpenter, 247; a reference to Rev. 4:2.
65   C. A. Trypanis, *Fourteen Early Byzantine Cantica*, WByzSt 5 (Vienna, 1968), 139–47; A. Palmer, "The Inauguration Hymn of Hagia Sophia in Edessa: A New Edition and Translation with Historical and Architectural Notes and a Comparison with a Contemporary Constantinopolitan Kontakion," *BMGS* 12 (1988): 137–49.
66   Flavius Cresconius Corippus, *In laudem Iustini Augusti minoris libri IV*, ed. Av. Cameron (London, 1976), 4.283.
67   G. Scheja, "Hagia Sophia und Templum Salomonis," *IM* 12 (1962): 44–58, esp. figs. 1–2.
68   Ibid., 55.
69   How the central nave space relates proportionally to the side aisles is problematic; note the "simple" explanation of B. Pantelić, "Applied Geometrical Planning and Proportions in the Church of Hagia Sophia in Istanbul," *IM* 49 (1999): 493–515.
70   A. M. Schneider, "Die Kuppelmosaiken der Hagia Sophia zu Konstantinopel," *Nachrichten der Akademie der Wissenschaften in Göttingen, I Philologisch-Historische Klasse* 13 (1949): 345–55, esp. 352–53; C. Mango, *Materials for the Study of the Mosaics of St. Sophia at Istanbul*, DOS 8 (Washington, DC, 1962), 85–86. Both cite Choniates and Sphrantzes, who refer to the dome as the "second firmament."

associations, religious or otherwise, prior to construction. Aside from an angelic pronouncement at the threshing floor, "there is nothing inherent in the location of the Temple in Jerusalem. Its location was simply where it happened to be built."[71] Hagia Sophia housed no significant relics when it was founded and commemorated no specific event.[72] But, like the Temple, sanctity came to inhabit the building by virtue of its architectural magnificence and the piety of its founder. Thus, Russian pilgrims would "visit" other churches, but they would "venerate" Hagia Sophia.[73] Robert of Clari noted that its columns—rather than the relics—had curative powers.[74] I would argue, following the ritual theory of Jonathan Z. Smith, that, as at the Temple, the construction of sanctity at Hagia Sophia was a political act.[75] It was also part of a historical process. Hagia Sophia's collection of relics developed only gradually and was not essential to its foundation. Among those displayed in the building were the Rod of Moses, the ark of the covenant, the tablets of the Law, Elijah's robe, the horn of the anointing of David, and Joshua's trumpets from Jericho.[76] All these objects were associated with or kept in the Temple and would have complemented the Old Testament associations the architecture may have been meant to evoke. At the same time, the Old Testament relics did not exist in isolation, for New Testament relics were also displayed at Hagia Sophia.

The excavation and study of the church of St. Polyeuktos, built immediately before Hagia Sophia by Justinian's political rival, Anicia Juliana, encourage an interpretation of Hagia Sophia based on Old Testament traditions.[77] As the excavator Martin Harrison has argued, St. Polyeuktos replicated the Temple of Solomon in its measurements, translated into Byzantine cubits: measuring 100 royal cubits in length, as was the Temple, and 100 in width, as was the Temple

71 J. Z. Smith, *To Take Place: Toward Theory in Ritual* (Chicago, 1987), 8.
72 See most recently J. Wortley, "Relics and the Great Church," *BZ* 99 (2006): 631–47, who suggests that the lack of corporeal relics at Hagia Sophia might reflect the building's association with the Temple.
73 G. Majeska, *Russian Travelers to Constantinople in the Fourteenth and Fifteenth Centuries*, DOS 10 (Washington, DC, 1984), 199.
74 Robert of Clari, *La conquête de Constantinople*, ed. A. Pauphilet, *Historiens et chroniqueurs du moyen âge* (Paris, 1952), 84.
75 Smith, *To Take Place*.
76 G. Majeska, "St. Sophia: The Relics," *DOP* 27 (1973): 71–87; Dagron, *Constantinople imaginaire* (n. 11 above), 301–3; Wortley, "Relics."
77 R. M. Harrison, *Excavations at the Saraçhane in Istanbul* (Princeton, 1986), vol. 1, esp. 410–11; idem, *A Temple for Byzantium* (Austin, 1989); idem, "The Church of St. Polyeuktos in Istanbul and the Temple of Solomon," *Okeanos: Essays Presented to Ihor Ševčenko on His Sixtieth Birthday by His Colleagues and Students*, ed. C. Mango, O. Pritsak, and U. Pasicznyk (Cambridge, MA, 1984): 276–79.

FIGURE 7 Istanbul, Archaeological Museum. Marble block from St. Polyeuktos, with a fragment of the nave inscription (author)

platform—following both the unit of measure and the measurements given in Ezekiel 42:2–3. Harrison estimates the sanctuary of the church to have been 20 royal cubits square internally, the exact measurement of the Holy of Holies, as given in Ezekiel 41:4. Similarly, the ostentatious decoration compares with that described in the Temple; if we let peacocks stand in for cherubim, as Harrison suggests, cherubim alternate with palm trees, bands of ornamental network, festoons of chainwork, pomegranates, network on the capitals, and capitals shaped like lilies (Fig. 7).[78]

A powerful noblewoman who could trace her lineage back to Constantine, Anicia Juliana was one of the last representatives of the Theodosian dynasty. When her son was passed over in the selection of emperor in favor of Justin I and subsequently Justinian, the construction of St. Polyeuktos became her statement of familial prestige. It was the largest and most lavish church in the capital at the time of its construction. The adulatory dedicatory inscription credits

78 Ibid.

Juliana with having "surpassed the wisdom of the celebrated Solomon, raising a temple to receive God."[79] In this context, Hagia Sophia could be seen as part of a larger, competitive discourse between political rivals. Justinian's famous, if legendary, exclamation at the dedication, *"Enikesa se Solomon!"* "Solomon, I have vanquished thee!" may have been directed more toward Juliana than toward Jerusalem.[80] In addition to the *double entendre*, there might also be a pun here: *Enikesa: Anikia*. Prokopios uses similar Temple-like language about Hagia Sophia, insisting that God "must especially love to dwell in this place which He has chosen."[81] The discourse was ultimately more about the construction of divinely sanctioned kingship than about sacred topography. Clearly, both Juliana and Justinian understood the symbolic value of architecture, with which they could make powerful political statements that could not be put into words.

Recent studies have offered a more nuanced history to the architectural discourse, suggesting that SS. Sergios and Bakchos appeared as an intermediary between St. Polyeuktos and St. Sophia, and suggesting revisions for the dates of the first two churches. Based on a reanalysis of the brickstamp evidence from St. Polyeuktos, Jonathan Bardill dates the bricks from the substructure to the period 508/9 to 511/12, and those of the superstructure to 517/18 to 521/22.[82] He suggests that the project was begun under Areobindos, that there was a five-year gap corresponding to a period of religious and political crisis, and that work resumed at the death of Anastasios. Although the proposed chronology would place the initial construction into a somewhat different context than the rivalry between Juliana and Justinian, Bardill insists that the construction of St. Polyeuktos "was doubtless intended to make a striking political and religious statement."[83] He suggests the church may have been begun as a prominent public reminder of the authority of the Theodosian dynasty. However, when Juliana's son Olybrios was passed over in the election of a new emperor, in favor of Justin, the change of

---

79 Harrison, *Excavations*, 5–7.
80 Ed. Preger, *Scriptores originum Constantinopolitanarum*, 2 vols. (Leipzig, 1901), 1:105; Dagron, *Constantinople imaginaire*, 303–9; Harrison, "Church of St. Polyeuktos," 276–79.
81 Prokopios, *Buildings*, 1.1.61–62.
82 J. Bardill, *Brickstamps of Constantinople*, 2 vols. (Oxford, 2004), 1:62–64 and 111–16; see also review by Robert Ousterhout in *BZ* 98 (2005): 575–77; and J.-P. Sodini, "Remarques sur les briques timbrées de Constantinople," *REB* 63 (2005): 225–32, esp. 226–28.
83 J. Bardill, "A New Temple for Byzantium: Anicia Juliana, King Solomon, and the Gilded Ceiling of the Church of St. Polyeuktos in Constantinople," in *Social and Political Life in Late Antiquity*, ed. W. Bowden, A. Gutteridge, and C. Machado (Leiden, 2006), 339–70, with a thorough bibliography; note esp. 339–40.

emperors nevertheless marked the restoration of pro-Chalcedonian orthodoxy, which Juliana had championed. Thus, in its final form, the church would have added the commemoration of the orthodox victory to its political message. Following the Solomonic overtones in the architecture, Bardill suggests that Juliana's church was intended to be "an earthly copy of a new and better Temple, foreseen in the scriptures, a Temple surpassing Solomon's because it was a pure Christian shrine 'to receive God,' who had departed long ago from the defiled Jewish Temple."[84]

Bardill also offers some important emendations to Harrison's reconstruction, insisting—correctly, in my view—that Juliana's church was covered by a wooden roof, rather than a dome.[85] There are also notable similarities in the descriptions of the gilded wooden ceilings of the Temple, of Constantine's basilica at the Holy Sepulchre, and of St. Polyeuktos that encourage a symbolic connection.[86] All the same, it is difficult to argue—as Bardill and Milner have done[87]—that the *specific* model for Juliana's church was Ezekiel's Temple, particularly since the dedicatory inscription refers to Solomon. Whereas the underlying symbolism derives from the Temple, most likely it was not a representation of one particular Temple, although Ezekiel's or Solomon's might have been called to the fore as the political or religious occasion prompted.

Brian Croke proposes that SS. Sergios and Bakchos was Justinian's immediate response to St. Polyeuktos.[88] Through a careful reconsideration of the historical circumstances, he dates the building to the mid-520s, when Justinian was resident at the Hormisdas Palace. This dating would place its construction immediately after the completion of St. Polyeuktos as redated by Bardill. Indeed, several scholars have proposed to view the two churches in relationship to each other.[89] Both were lavishly decorated, and in both, epigrams concern-

---

84 Ibid., 342.
85 Ibid., 345–60.
86 Ibid., 356–57.
87 Ibid., 342–45; C. Milner, "The Image of the Rightful Ruler: Anicia Juliana's Constantine Mosaic and the Church of Hagios Polyeuktos," in *New Constantines: The Rhythm of Imperial Renewal in Byzantium, 4th–13th Centuries*, ed. P. Magdalino (Aldershot, 1994), 73–81.
88 B. Croke, "Justinian, Theodora, and the Church of Saints Sergius and Bacchus," *DOP* 60 (2006): 25–63; I am grateful to A.-M. Talbot for bringing this to my attention and Brian Croke for permission to read it in advance of publication.
89 C. Connor, "The Epigram in the Church of Hagios Polyeuktos in Constantinople and Its Byzantine Response," *Byzantion* 69 (1999): 479–527, esp. 511–12; J. Bardill, "The Church of Sts. Sergius and Bacchus in Constantinople and the Monophysite Refugees," *DOP* 54 (2000): 1–11, esp 4; I. Shahîd, "The Church of Sts. Sergius and Bakchos at Constantinople: Some New

ing their founders encircled the nave. The piety expressed in the Sergios and Bakchos epigram stands in sharp contrast to the hubris that characterizes Juliana's inscription. The reference to "other sovereigns" in the Sergios and Bakchos epigram, to those "dead men whose labor was unprofitable," may be read as a not-so-subtle critique of Juliana, her vaunted ancestry, and her imperial pretensions.[90] In the experimental nature of its vaulting and in the subtle geometric complexities of its design, the church of SS. Sergios and Bakchos is conceptually far advanced beyond its rival, signaling the important innovations that characterize Justinianic architecture. On the other hand, no underlying symbolic message seems to have been manifest in its architectural forms—at least, none comparable to that of St. Polyeuktos. A symbolic response would have to wait until Justinian asserted his imperial authority—that is, until the construction of Hagia Sophia.

Did Justinian "vanquish" Solomon? It is recounted that Justinian had a statue of Solomon set up in the Basilica, overlooking Hagia Sophia, and that the figure appeared to clutch his cheek, "as one who had been outdone in the building of the New Jerusalem."[91] The reference sounds a bit suspicious, to say the least; Dagron suggests that this was originally a statue of Theodosios I, "rebaptisée avec humour."[92] And whether or not Justinian ever scampered up the ambo of Hagia Sophia and shouted the legendary utterance, the Solomonic theme was very much in the air by the early sixth century. Following Harrison, Irfan Shahîd has suggested similar symbolism in other Justinianic foundations, notably the Nea in Jerusalem.[93] Like the Temple, the Nea was raised on a high platform on a site with no previous religious associations and fronted by two majestic columns; indeed, the motivation behind the construction of a new church on virgin territory in a city where virtually every stone is imbued with symbolic significance

---

Perspectives," in *Byzantium State and Society: In Memory of Nikos Oikonomides* (Athens, 2003), 465–80, esp. 476–80.

90   Croke, "Justinian, Theodora."

91   Ed. I. Bekker, *Annales* (Bonn, 1836), 498; as noted by P. Magdalino, "Observations on the Nea Ekklesia of Basil I," *JÖB* 37 (1987): 58, n. 42; *Patria Konstantinoupoleos*, 2.40; ed. Preger, 171; discussed by Dagron, *Constantinople imaginaire* (n. 11 above), 138, 268. The statue was later transferred to the substructures of the Nea, discussed below.

92   Dagron, *Constantinople imaginaire*, 138.

93   R. M. Harrison, "From Jerusalem and Back Again: The Fate of the Treasures of Solomon," in *Churches Built in Ancient Times: Recent Studies in Early Christian Archaeology*, ed. K. Painter (London, 1994), 239–48; J. Taylor, "The Nea Church: Were the Temple Treasures Hidden Here?" *Biblical Archaeology Review* (Jan.–Feb. 2008), 50–60. I thank Prof. Shahîd for generously sharing his ideas with me.

is far from clear. One wonders if the return to Jerusalem of the Temple's relics, recovered from the Vandals in 532, might have inspired its construction, as both Harrison and Shahîd suggest.[94]

At the same time, Byzantine rulership was regularly cast in Old Testament terms, emphasizing the position of emperor as head of the chosen people. "In Byzantium, the Old Testament had a constitutional value," Gilbert Dagron writes; "it had the same normative role in the political sphere as the New Testament in the moral sphere."[95] The *Life of St. Sylvester*, popularly disseminated in the fifth and sixth centuries, set Christian kingship in relation to the Old Testament kings: according to it, the empress Helena is supposed to have written to her son Constantine advising him to "enter into possession of the *basileia* of David and the wisdom of Solomon," and to join them as a mouthpiece of God.[96] References to Davidic virtues abound in imperial panegyric; similarly, royal builders could be lauded as new Solomons; both became commonplaces in Byzantine times.[97] But when does the metaphorical use of the Temple for political ends actually begin? If, as I argue, Eusebios's Solomonic reference is to Paulinos and not to Constantine, then our first imperial Solomon or, as Shahîd calls him, "Better-Than-Solomon" may be in the Justinianic period.[98]

The underlying allusions to the Temple at Hagia Sophia, then, took many directions. As a new Temple rebuilt by Justinian at the heart of Constantinople, it transformed the city into a new Jerusalem, emphasizing its sacred character,

---

94 Ibid.; Prokopios, *History of the Wars*, trans. H. B. Dewing (Cambridge, MA, 1914), 4.9.5–9: "And among these were the treasures of the Jews, which Titus, the son of Vespasian, together with certain others, had brought to Rome after the capture of Jerusalem. And one of the Jews, seeing these things, approached one of those known to the emperor and said: 'These treasures I think it inexpedient to carry into the palace in Byzantium. Indeed, it is not possible for them to be elsewhere than in the place where Solomon, the king of the Jews, formerly placed them. For it is because of these that Gizeric captured the palace of the Romans, and that now the Roman army has captured that [of] the Vandals.' When this had been brought to the ears of the Emperor, he became afraid and quickly sent everything to the sanctuaries of the Christians in Jerusalem."
95 *Emperor and Priest: The Imperial Office in Byzantium*, trans. Jean Birrell (Cambridge, 2003), 50.
96 Ibid., 146–47.
97 Koder, "Justinians Sieg" (n. 11 above); F. Dvornik, *Early Christian and Byzantine Political Philosophy*, 2 vols. (Washington, DC, 1966). For the expression of the theme in art, see H. Maguire, "Davidic Virtue: The Crown of Constantine Monomachos and Its Images," in *The Real and Ideal Jerusalem in Jewish, Christian and Islamic Art*, ed. B. Kuehnel (Jerusalem, 1998), 117–23 (published as the journal *Jewish Art* 23–24 [1997–98]); and S. Spain Alexander, "Heraclius, Byzantine Imperial Ideology, and the David Plates," *Speculum* 52 (1977): 217–37, among others.
98 I. Shahîd, "The Church of Hagios Polyeuktos in Constantinople: Some New Observations," *Greco-Arabica* 9–10 (2004): 354.

without necessarily replicating its forms.⁹⁹ It also bolstered Justinian's claims to imperial authority, grounding his rule in the divinely sanctioned kingship of the Old Testament. These themes—the religious and the political metaphors provided by the Old Testament, by Solomon and his Temple, expressed in architectural terms—overlap in the time of Justinian, and they merge again in later centuries. They are clearly in the air during the period of Basil I and Leo VI (ca. 867–912), as Shaun Tougher and others have discussed.¹⁰⁰ Basil had a statue of Solomon placed in the foundations of his famed church of the Nea Ekklesia in Constantinople; according to Leo the Grammarian, Basil had the statue, known as the "Victory" of Justinian, taken from the Basilica and renamed (or possibly recarved) after himself.¹⁰¹ Dagron views all of this as a pretentious parody; he suggests that Basil had the statue tossed into the foundations in a sort of imitation sacrifice for the dedication in 880.¹⁰² It seems more likely that the statue was displayed in a chapel in the substructures. In addition, Basil may have been responsible for the introduction into the Nea of the horn with which Samuel anointed David.¹⁰³ Even though they were not expressed in architectural terms, there were clearly Solomonic overtones in the Nea church that paralleled contemporary imperial panegyric. In the same period, other Solomonic relics were to be found in Hagia Sophia: the chalice of Solomon was attested in Hagia Sophia in the ninth century; a table of Solomon was noted there in the tenth.¹⁰⁴

Like Justinian, a great builder could be compared to Solomon. During the mid-eleventh century, in the mosaic image of the Anastasis at Nea Mone on Chios, Solomon is uniquely represented as bearded, having been given the features of the monastery's imperial patron, Constantine IX Monomachos (Fig. 8).¹⁰⁵ Constantine was renowned as a patron of architecture, and his

---

99 See my comments in R. Ousterhout, "Sacred Geographies and Holy Cities: Constantinople as Jerusalem," in *Hierotopy: The Creation of Sacred Space in Byzantium and Medieval Russia*, ed. A. Lidov (Moscow, 2006), 98–116.
100 S. Tougher, "The Wisdom of Leo VI," in *New Constantines: The Rhythm of Imperial Renewal in Byzantium, 4th–13th Centuries*, ed. P. Magdalino (Aldershot, 1994), 171–79.
101 Leo the Grammarian, ed. Bekker (n. 91 above), 257–58; Dagron, *Constantinople imaginaire* (n. 11 above), 269, 309.
102 Ibid., 269; but see Tougher, "Wisdom," 174–75.
103 As Magdalino, "Observations on the Nea" (n. 91 above), 58, suggests.
104 Discussed by Tougher, "Wisdom," 174; see I. Ševčenko, "The Greek Source of the Inscription on Solomon's Chalice in the *Vita Constantini*," in *To Honor Roman Jakobson: Essays on the Occasion of His Seventieth Birthday, 11 October 1966* (The Hague, 1967), 3:1806–17; A. A. Vasiliev, "Harun-Ibn-Yahya and His Description of Constantinople," *Seminarum Kondakovum* 5 (1932): 477–87.
105 D. Mouriki, *The Mosaics of Nea Moni on Chios*, 2 vols. (Athens, 1985), 1:137; R. Ousterhout, "Originality in Byzantine Architecture: The Case of Nea Moni," *JSAH* 51 (1992): 48–60, esp. 59.

FIGURE 8 Chios, Nea Mone, naos interior. Mosaic of the anastasis, detail showing David and Solomon (author)

support for construction projects extended from Constantinople westward to Monte Cassino and Rome, eastward to Euchaita, northward possibly to Kiev, and southward to Chios, Mt. Galesion, Myra, and Jerusalem.[106] The last is perhaps most significant, for Constantine had rebuilt (or at least completed the rebuilding of) the Church of the Holy Sepulchre, which had been destroyed earlier in the century.[107] If the Holy Sepulchre stood as the new Temple, then Constantine Monomachos could be justly lauded as the new Solomon—but curiously, in image alone, not in a surviving text.

The Byzantine reconstruction of the Holy Sepulchre seems to have had an impact on the liturgy of Constantinople. Recently Sysse Engberg brought to my attention the Byzantine enkainia ceremony, which she has examined as a part of her study of the Prophetologia.[108] The enkainia are the readings used in ceremonies for the dedication of a church. In 38 of the 66 manuscripts that include the enkainia, the text is that used at the feast for the dedication of the Holy Sepulchre, and is listed as such, with the date either 13 or 14 September, to correspond with the Feast of the Elevation of the Cross. Ten manuscripts have the Enkainia of the Great Church—that is, Hagia Sophia—and if a date is given,

106   C. Bouras, *Nea Moni on Chios: History and Architecture* (Athens, 1982), 23–24.
107   Ousterhout, "Rebuilding the Temple" (n. 38 above); Biddle, *Tomb of Christ* (n. 38 above), 77–81, has questioned the attribution of the Byzantine reconstruction to Constantine Monomachos, preferring his predecessor Michael IV (1034–41). The association with Constantine Monomachos was recorded after ca. 1165 by William of Tyre, based on local tradition, although the reconstruction may have been begun several decades earlier than the time of Monomachos.
108   S. Engberg, *Profetie-Anagnosmata-Prophetologion*, vol. 1, *The History of a Greek Liturgical Book* (forthcoming), chap. 7.7. I thank Dr. Engberg for sharing this chapter with me in advance of publication.

it is set at 23 December. The first manuscript to specify a particular church for the ceremony appears only in the tenth century and it is for the Enkainia of the Great Church, although Engberg assumes its common appearance before this time. The *idea* of the enkainia had been taken directly from the Jewish calendar, as Egeria's account testifies, although the surviving texts of the Byzantine ceremony are much later in date than Egeria's account.[109] The Enkainia of the Anastasis Church first appeared in the eleventh century, and by the fourteenth century it held a near-monopoly in the headings of manuscripts that reflect the liturgical practice of Constantinople. Engberg speculates that Byzantine imperial participation in the reconstruction of the Holy Sepulchre "would justify the creation in Hagia Sophia of a yearly feast for the Dedication of the Anastasis church," which was not mentioned in Constantinople prior to that time.[110]

The lections read in the ceremony have great resonance:

Solomon stood before the altar of the Lord
    (1 Kings [3 Kingdoms LXX] 8:22–23a, 27bc, 28–30)
The Lord by wisdom founded the earth (Prov. 3:19–34)
Wisdom built herself a house (Prov. 9:1–11)

These lections could refer with equal appropriateness to the Temple of Solomon, the Church of the Holy Sepulchre, or Hagia Sophia. What is perhaps more important is that the same verses could have been used in the dedication of *any* Byzantine church. That is, although the allusions to the Temple have a powerful resonance at Hagia Sophia and the Holy Sepulchre, the association was neither exclusive nor all-encompassing.

The preceding analysis raises a difficult question for the architectural historian: What does this chapter have to do with architecture? For if a building is to be a bearer of meaning, what is a building's formal language and how does it communicate? That is, can we—and *should* we—understand the relationships I have just discussed as part of an "iconography" of Byzantine architecture? Are any of these buildings "copies" of the Temple in the Krautheimerian sense?[111] In the final analysis, neither the Holy Sepulchre nor Hagia Sophia looked anything

109 Egeria 48–49; trans. Wilkinson, *Egeria's Travels*, 146–47.
110 Engberg, *History*.
111 Krautheimer, "Introduction" (n. 16 above); it is important to recognize that Krautheimer wrote his essay *as an introduction* and not as the last word on the subject.

like the Temple, no matter how much we want them to and depite rhetoricians of the time standing by to tell us they did. In this respect, St. Polyeuktos, with its replication of measurements and imagery, stands as an audacious anomaly, never to be repeated, and one that does not figure prominently in the later history of Constantinople—nor in the later history of Byzantine architecture.

Byzantine architecture was capable of subtlety and nuance—more often than we are willing to credit. The above discussion should encourage us to develop new strategies for the interpretation of built forms, for meanings may be attached to architecture in more than one way. Moreover, as Krautheimer recognized, multiple meanings could be ever-present to "vibrate" together in the same building.[112] I would argue that the churches of the Holy Sepulchre and Hagia Sophia succeed as works of architecture precisely because their symbolism is multivalent. By contrast, the symbolic potential of St. Polyeuktos, as a "copy," seems much more restricted. Both the Holy Sepulchre and Hagia Sophia created an identity for their city, standing as powerful images; both celebrate the triumph of Christianity, both are imbued with tangible evidence of imperial patronage, both testify to the order and harmony of the Christian cosmos. Although they could be compared and contrasted with the Temple in all of its manifestations—as they no doubt were intended to be—this was never an exclusive meaning; moreover, they needed to function for the daily liturgy and to respond to its ceremonies.

With rare exception, the connection with the Temple is made by words, ceremonies, and relics, but not by specific architectural forms, or by visual imagery. Even in an image like the Chora narthex mosaic, we "see" a bema; we need the inscription to tell us it is the Temple. Understanding the liturgical service and the textual tradition may aid in the interpretation of Byzantine architecture, but words and images, ceremonies and settings, communicate in different ways. This fact should not diminish the potential impact of the associations with the Temple, which remained powerful, if multivalent, as a symbol and as a metaphor in Byzantine architecture, just as it did in the other arts. It is often said that Byzantine writers and artists preferred complex metaphors to simple allegories—that is, to hold in dynamic tension several levels of meaning simultaneously—and we should expect no less of the architecture.[113] In this respect, a Byzantine church could act as a sort of resonating vessel, responding to and interacting with

---

112   Ibid., 122, following Johannes Scotus Eriugena, *Versus Ianinis Scotti ad Karolum Regem*, *MGH Poetae* 3, v. 45, on the symbolism of the number eight.
113   A point emphasized throughout the important study by L. Brubaker, *Vision and Meaning in Ninth-Century Byzantium: Image as Exegesis in the Homilies of Gregory of Nazianzus* (Cambridge, 1999).

the ceremonies it housed, with different meanings coming to the fore as usage required. Finally, buildings, even great monuments, do not exist in isolation; nor should they be interpreted out of their historical or social context. Byzantium's "monuments of unageing intellect" were products of a literate, visually oriented culture, in which words and images mattered greatly, and we should attempt to understand its architecture as being as resonant and as meaning-full as its art and literature.[114]

University of Pennsylvania

---

114 W. B. Yeats's poem "Sailing to Byzantium" (1926) is quoted in full and discussed by R. Nelson in *Hagia Sophia 1850–1950: Holy Wisdom Modern Monument* (Chicago, 2004), 129–54.

TEN

Old Testament Models and the State in Early Medieval Bulgaria

Ivan Biliarsky

The state of the Bulgars was one of the most important in central and southeastern Europe in the early medieval epoch. It had spread its power throughout the greater part of the Balkan Peninsula to the north of the Haemus Mountains and fiercely attacked Thrace and Macedonia. Bulgaria at this time had acquired some traits typical of a barbarian state, because the bellicose tribe of the Bulgars had imported the Turkic traditions of the great steppes into the Balkans.[1] The creation of the identity of the state and power of early medieval Bulgaria on this periphery of Eastern Christendom is the focus of this study, which is based on research into the texts forming its political ideological complex during the period of the transition from a pagan barbarian state to a Christian imperial one, dating to the reign of Tsar Symeon (893–927). The epoch of his rule is extremely important for the creation of the foundations of the medieval Bulgarian identity, culture, and state ideology.[2] It is essential for our study too

---

1   I. Bozhilov, "El nacimiento de la Bulgaria medieval: Problemos metodológicos, termológicos y typológicos," *Revista de la Universidad Compultense* (1988): 41ff.; idem, "Razhdaneto na srednovekovna Bŭlgariia: Nova interpretatsiia," *Istoricheski pregled*, nos. 1–2 (1992): 3–34.
2   The era of Tsar Symeon has been the object of much research. Here we refer to only a few publications: I. Bozhilov, *Tsar Simeon Veliki (893–927): Zlatnijat vek na Srednovekovna Bŭlgarija* (Sofia, 1983); idem, "L'idéologie politique du tsar Syméon: Pax Symeonica," *Byzantinobulgarica* 8 (1986): 73–88; F. Thomson, "The Symeonic Florilegium—Problems of Its Origin, Content, Textology and Edition, Together with an English Translation of the Eulogy of Tzar Symeon," *Palaeobulgarica* 17 (1993): 1, 37–53; L. Simeonova, *Diplomacy of the Letter and the Cross: Photios, Bulgaria and the Papacy; 860s–880s*, Classical and Byzantine Monographs 41 (Amsterdam, 1998); J. Shepard, "Bulgaria: The Other Balkan 'Empire'," in *New Cambridge Medieval History* (Cambridge, 1999), 3:567–85; A. Nikolov, *Politicheska misŭl v rannosrednovekovna Bŭlgarija (sredata na IX—kraja na X vek)* (Sofia, 2006).

because of its transitional character. We focus mainly on two important texts of Palaeobulgarian literature: the *List of the Names of Bulgar Princes (Khans)* and the *Bulgarian Apocryphal Chronicle of the Eleventh Century*. Both monuments attest to the ambivalence of the transitory Bulgarian state, which created its new identity on the basis of models borrowed from the Old Testament tradition. The thesis of this study is that the dominant themes of these two texts were borrowed from the Bible, and they substituted for pagan beliefs and images of authority.

The Two Principal Texts

The *List of the Bulgar Princes (Khans)*[3] is a brief list of the names of rulers. It begins with the purely mythological Avitochol and his son Irnik, who were said to have lived and ruled three hundred years and one hundred fifty years, respectively.[4] They are followed by a list of more or less historical leaders of the Bulgar people. The structure of the text is quite simple: the name of the khan is followed by the number of the years he ruled or lived, the name of his clan, and the date of the beginning of his reign according to the Bulgar calendar. The *List* appears within the larger work known as the *Hellenic Chronicle*—an original composition originating in the south Slavic, probably Bulgarian, milieu.[5] A special study on this topic has been published elsewhere; here we shall mention only our conclusions.[6]

It is clear from an examination of the *Hellenic Chronicle* that the compiler followed the biblical narration of the establishment and the history of the kingdom of Israel: the text includes the acts of the prophet Samuel and a list of the Old Testament rulers, as well as the entire text of 2 Kings. The *List*, beginning with the mythical Avitochol, is located in the *Chronicle* after the tale of Nebuchadnezzar and the end of the kingdom of the People of Israel, making it appear that the kingdom of Israel ends with the beginning of the Bulgar rulers. In no way does the *List* appear to constitute a separate text in the *Hellenic Chronicle*—and so the reader is left with the impression that it is a part of the preceding

---

3   M. Moskov, *Imennik na bŭlgarskite khanove (Novo tŭlkuvane)* (Sofia, 1988) and the literature cited there; I. Biliarsky, "Ot mifa k istorii ili Ot stepi k Izrailju," *Zbornik radova Vizantološkog instituta* 42 (2005): 7–22.
4   Moskov, *Imennik*, 19–20.
5   A. Popov, *Obzor khronografov russkoĭ redaktsii* (Moscow, 1866), 2:19; Arkhimandrit Leonid, "Drevniaia rukopis," *Russkiĭ arkhiv*, no. 4 (April 1889): 3ff.; Biliarsky, "Ot mifa k istorii," 9.
6   Biliarsky, "Ot mifa k istorii."

biblical text. So, in the opinion of some authors,[7] the *List* is presented in the *Hellenic Chronicle* as a part of the preceding scriptural text and thus the names of the Bulgar rulers are merely a continuation of the list of the kings of Israel and Judah. In this way the whole conception of the state—the land and the people—appears as an image of the promised land and the chosen people.

This context expresses a certain approach to universal history and the Bulgars' place in it. One of the most important representations of the pagan Bulgarian state's ideology entered a Christian chronicle, a Christian synthesis of time and history.[8] The pagan mythological text became a part of the Christian sacred history, the history of salvation, because some authors perceived it as a continuation of the second book of Kings.[9] This proves significant since, as we mentioned earlier, the *List* was included in this context in Bulgaria during the reign of Tsar Symeon in the tenth century.[10] Thus, we see how the new Christian identity is created through identification with certain scriptural phenomena, the most important of which is surely that of the Chosen People of God.

There are also several Russian chronicles, mostly from Novgorod, that show heavy influence from Old Testament history. This interest in the Old Testament gave rise to a bitter controversy in the Russian church linked to the heresy of the so-called "Judaizers."[11] The phenomenon of chronicles centered on the Old Testament is usually classified as Russian and is quite atypical for Byzantine, Western, and even medieval Jewish historiography.[12] It is usually linked to the western Russian lands of the Grand Duchy of Lithuania, where there was a large Jewish population, and to Novgorod, which preserved the traditions of Kievan Rus'.[13] The use of the biblical chronicle as evidence of collaboration between

---

7 B. von Arnim, "Wer war Avitokhol? Zur Fürstenliste," *Sbornik v chest na prof. L. Miletich* (Sofia, 1933), 574–75; Moskov, *Imennik*, 18; Biliarsky, "Ot mifa k istorii," 19.
8 Popov, *Obzor khronografov russkoĭ redaktsii*, 58–66.
9 von Arnim, "Wer war Avitokhol?" 574; Moskov, *Imennik*, 18; Biliarsky, "Ot mifa k istorii," passim.
10 von Arnim, "Wer war Avitokhol?" 575; E. Pritsak, *Die bulgarische Fürstenliste und die Sprache der Protobulgaren* (Wiesbaden, 1955), 13–14.
11 About this, see C. G. De Michelis, *La Valdesia di Novgorod: "Giudaizzanti" e prima riforma (sec. XV)* (Turin, 1993); L. R. De Michelis, *Eresia e Riforma nel Cinquecento: La dissidenza religiosa in Russia* (Turin, 2000).
12 M. Pljukhanova, "Biblejskie khronografy," *Biblija v dukhovnoj zhizni i kul'ture Rossii i pravoslavnogo slavjanskogo mira: K 500–letiju Gennadievskoj Biblii* (Moscow, 2001), 83. Attention should also be drawn to the very interesting study of Moshe Taube, "The Fifteenth-Century Ruthenian Translations from Hebrew and the Heresy of the Judaizers: Is There a Connection?" in *Speculum Slaviae Orientalis: Muscovy, Ruthenia and Lithuania in the Late Middle Ages*, ed. V. V. Ivanov et al., UCLA Slavic Studies 4 (Moscow, 2005), 185–208.
13 Pljukhanova, "Biblejskie khronografy," 82.

Pontic Jews and the people of Rus' is quite problematic and cannot be confirmed by the chronicles alone, but it is linked to these territories, where the influence of hesychast literature (from the fourteenth century onward) was slight.[14] Maria Pljukhanova wrote that in the tradition preserved in Novgorod, the literature reflects the archaic forms and the heritage of the Bulgarian empires, thus confirming our argument relating the Old Testament theme to the tradition of the city of Preslav.[15] We find in the very creation of the chronography a link to the archaic traditions of the First Bulgarian Empire and so to the *List*.

The second text is the so-called *Bulgarian Apocryphal Chronicle of the Eleventh Century* or the *Tale of How the Prophet Isaiah Was Brought by an Angel to the Seventh Heaven* (hereafter *Apocryphal Chronicle*).[16] The manuscript containing this text disappeared and was lost to scholars for almost a century. It was only in the last decade of the twentieth century that the Russian scholar A. A. Turilov rediscovered it in Moscow.[17]

Usually the *Apocryphal Chronicle* is presented as a more-or-less original Bulgarian text, but understood as showing influence from other Old Testament apocryphal texts such as the *Vision of Isaiah*, the *Apocalypse of Daniel*, and so forth.[18] The connection to the Hebrew messianic and apocalyptic literature is obvious; some parts of the *Apocryphal Chronicle* are also related to the near eastern tradition, which indicates that it is probably a compilation.

The inclusion of certain historical events in the text of the chronicle makes it appear that the final version was prepared in the eleventh century, approximately a century and a half after the period that concerns us here. References in the text of the *Apocryphal Chronicle* to the Cometopouloi and especially to Peter Deljan (d. after 1041), the grandson of Tsar Samuel and son of Tsar Gabriel-Radomir, leave no doubt that the text as we have it dates from the middle of the eleventh century or even later. Nevertheless, in its composite character we detect traces of narrative typical of the transitional epoch between the pagan state and the Orthodox Empire (Orthodox Tsarstvo); this epoch we date to the last decades

---

14   Ibid., 81, 87.
15   Ibid., 87.
16   L. Stojanović, "Stari srpski hrisovulii akti, biografije, letopisi, tipici, pomenici, zapisi i dr.," *Spomenik* 3 (1890): 190–93; J. Ivanov, *Bogomilski knigii i legendi* (Sofia, 1927), 273–87. See the most recent publication of the text in V. Tapkova-Zaimova and A. Miltenova, *Istoriko-apokaliptichnata knizhnina vŭv Vizantija i v srednovekovna Bŭlgarija* (Sofia, 1996), 192–206.
17   A. A. Turilov, "Kichevskij sbornik 'Bolgarskoj apokrificheskoj letopisju,'" *Palaeobulgarica* 19, no. 4 (1995): 2–39.
18   Tapkova-Zaimova and Miltenova, *Istoriko-apokaliptichnata knizhnina*, 192–93; Ivanov, *Bogomilski knigi i legendi*, 273ff.

of the ninth and the beginning of the tenth century. The *Apocryphal Chronicle* includes many different parts that have been adopted from other literary works. Those of biblical origin cannot help us to date the text from which they derive. There are, however, some historically relevant citations that certainly refer to an epoch earlier than the eleventh century. To cite only one example: the Arab name of Aref/Arethas given to one of the rulers is suggestive of the cultural situation in the Balkans in the first half of the ninth century.[19] Of course, another argument confirming the use of earlier texts in the compilation of the *Apocryphal Chronicle* as we have it is provided by the traces of some pre-Christian beliefs in the narrative.

What was known in early medieval Bulgaria of the texts of the Old Testament? The Old Testament texts, which are the fundamental source of ideas relevant to our study, were transmitted primarily in three ways: complete books of the Old Testament; liturgical lectionaries (the so-called "*Prophetologion*" or "Books of *paroimiai*"); and a narrative text of the events in the Old Testament (the historiographical compendiums called the Historical Palaea or *Palaea chronographica*, and the Interpreted Palaea or *Palaea interpretata*).

There is no consensus among scholars regarding the date of the translation of the complete text of the Old Testament books into Slavonic. There are some textual references to the translation of the Bible by Saint Methodios during his mission in Greater Moravia. In chapter 25 of his extended *Vita* it is noted that "he translated for six (eight)[20] months all of the books of the Old Testament from Greek into Slavonic, except the Books of Maccabees, with the help of only two (three) 'tachygraph' priests"[21] In the introduction to his translation of John of Damascus's *De fide orthodoxa*, John the Exarch indicates that St. Methodios translated all sixty books of the Old Testament in Greater Moravia.[22] There is also a mention in the *Archival Chronicle (Chronograph)*—a fifteenth-century

---

19 I. Biliarsky, "One More Arab King in the Balkans?" Ἐκκ.Φάρ. 89 [n.s. 18] (2007): 42–48.
20 The discrepancy in the numbers results from the difference between the Glagolitic and Cyrillic systems of alphabetical numeration. We find the same problem in the number of the "'tachygraph' priests" who helped St. Methodios.
21 Kliment Okhridski, *Sŭbrani sŭchinenija*, vol. 3, *Prostranni zhitija na Kiril i Metodij*, ed. B. St. Angelov and Kh. Kodov (Sofia, 1973), 191. We also find this assertion concerning the translation of the sixty Old Testament books by St. Methodius in the Synaxarion of the *Vitae* of SS. Cyril and Methodius, which dates from the tenth century (P. Lavrov, *Matrialy po istorii vozniknovenija drevnejshej slavjanskoj pis'menosti* [Leningrad, 1930], 100–101.) Unless otherwise indicated, all translations are my own.
22 L. Sadnik, ed., *Des hl. Johannes von Damascus* Ἔκθεσις ἀκριβὴς τῆς Ὀρθοδόξου πίστεως *in der Übersetzung des Exarchen Johannes*, Monumenta linguae slavicae dialectis veteris 5 (Wiesbaden, 1967), 2–6, 212–13.

Russian text with vestiges of its tenth-century Bulgarian prototype—of a translation of the Holy Scriptures from Greek into Slavonic by Gregory the Presbyter during the time of Tsar Symeon, son of Boris.[23] We shall not deal here with data concerning later translations or redactions of the Old Testament such as the fourteenth-century translation of St. Euthymios the Patriarch, and the like.

There is also no consensus on the meaning of the reference in the *Life of St. Methodios* to the translation of the entire corpus of the Old Testament and subsequent work on it in the capital city of Preslav in eastern Bulgaria.[24] The textual data appear to contradict the *Life*'s assertion. Obviously, it is doubtful that such an enormous task could be accomplished in six or eight months. Questions remain as to the number and format of the Old Testament books included in this translation, as well as the means by which the codices were able to reach Bulgaria after the collapse of the Moravian mission. In light of this discussion, the work of Gregory the Presbyter is viewed as either a new translation of the biblical text or a redaction of the earlier translation.[25] These issues, however, are clearly outside the scope of our brief presentation on the knowledge of Old Testament texts in early medieval Bulgaria. It is clear that the new society of tenth-century Bulgaria was familiar with some parts of this biblical corpus from which it obtained its ideas and stories about the history of the chosen people.

While the text of the Greek Bible developed from the complete books of the Bible to the miscellany of liturgical lections, the Slavonic Bible formed in the opposite manner.[26] The first Slavonic translations of the Old Testament, that is, the Psalter and the Prophetologion, are linked to the liturgical use of the Holy Scriptures.[27] The mission of the brothers SS. Cyril and Methodios among the Slavs in central Europe was to introduce Christianity, using their vernacular in the divine service as an apostolic dialect. This is why the first translations they prepared were of the Gospels, the Acts and Epistles, and the Psalter.[28]

---

23   S. Nikolova, "Problemŭt za izdavaneto na nebogosluzhebnite bŭlgarski srednovekovni tekstove na Starija Zavet," in *Starobŭlgarskijat prevod na Starija Zavet*, vol. 1, *Kniga na dvanadesette prorotsi s tŭlkuvanija*, ed. R. Zlatanova (Sofia, 1998), 1:XIII.

24   See the most recent publications on this topic: A. A. Alekseev, *Tekstologija slavjanskoj Biblii* (St. Petersburg, 1999), 153–63ff.; F. J. Thomson, "The Slavonic Translation of the Old Testament," in *The Interpretation of the Bible: The International Symposium in Slovenia*, ed. J. Krašovec (Sheffield, 1998), 638ff.

25   Nikolova, "Problemŭt," XVII; Alekseev, *Tekstologija slavjanskoj Biblii*, 167–69.

26   Thomson, "Slavonic Translation," 719.

27   Alekseev, *Tekstologija slavjanskoj Biblii*, 23–25; Thomson, "Slavonic Translation," 719ff. For more on the Prophetologion, see the article by James Miller in this volume.

28   See *Vita Methodii* 15—Kliment Okhridski, *Sŭbrani sŭchinenija* (n. 21 above), 3:191; I. Karachorova, "Kŭm vŭprosa za Kirilo-Metodievija starobŭlgarski prevod na Psaltira,"

The liturgical lections from the Old Testament are found in the Prophetologion. This is a collection of *paroimiai*: readings designed to convey the theme of the service. The Slavonic text is very archaic, and most scholars believe that the Prophetologion was one of the books translated by SS. Cyril and Methodios in Greater Moravia.[29] One should note especially the thesis of M. A. Johnson about the consequences of the introduction of the Typikon of the Great Church for the destiny of the Slavic Prophetologion.[30]

The Old Testament texts are integrated into the divine liturgy directly as lections and indirectly as quotations.[31] Both uses familiarized Bulgarians with the Old Testament. More importantly, the Old Testament images were often used in the service as archetypes and models for events and persons of the New Testament, and thus the structure of the service itself directed neophytes to seek models of their own identity in the Old Testament.

The translation and compilation of both the *Historical Palaea* and the *Interpreted Palaea* are thought to have occurred in the tenth century, which is later than the two other types of Old Testament texts mentioned above. The earliest translations of the Palaea are preserved only in Russian copies, so it is questionable whether these texts were disseminated among the south Slavs. One point of view asserts that the translation or compilation was prepared in tenth-century Bulgaria, and the other affirms that it was created among the eastern Slavs.[32]

The *Historical Palaea* presents the events of the Old Testament from the creation up to the reign of King David the Prophet and includes some apocryphal commentary and supplementary material.[33] Therefore, this compilation largely

---

Kirilo-Metodievski studii 6 (1989): 130–245; A.-M. Totomanova, "Prevodi na Kiril i Metodij," and I. Karachorova, "Psaltir," both in *Starobŭlgarska literatura: Entsiklopedichen rechnik*, ed. D. Petkanova (Sofia, 1992), 361, 379–80 (with cited bibliography); A. Naumow, *Idea-Immagine-Testo: Studi sulla letteratura slavo-ecclesiastica* (Alessandria [Italy], 2004), 117ff.

29 A. Miltenova, "Parimijnik," in *Starobŭlgarska literatura*, 320.
30 "Observations on the Hymnography of Certain Medieval Slavic Parimejniks," *Srpski jezik* 2, nos. 1–2 (1997): 363–76.
31 Naumow, *Idea-Immagine-Testo*, 117.
32 Thomson, "Slavonic Translation," 870–73; T. Slavova, "Za protografa na Tŭlkovnata Paleja (vŭrkhu material ot palejnija Shestodnev)," *Palaeobulgarica* 15, no. 3 (1991): 57–69; idem, "Arkhivskijat khronograf i Tŭlkovnata Paleja," *Palaeobulgarica* 18, no. 4 (1994): 48–63; idem, *Tŭlkovnata Paleja v konteksta na starobŭlgarskata knizhnina* (Sofia, 2002). These articles present contrary points of view and give rich citations of the earlier literature.
33 A. N. Popov, "Kniga bytija nebesi i zemli (Paleja istoricheskaja) s prilozheniem sokrashchennoj Palei russkoj redakcii," *Chtenija otdela istorii i drevnostej rossijskikh* 1 (1881); M. N. Speranskij, "Jugoslavjanskie teksty 'Istoricheskoj Palei' i russkie ee teksty," in *Iz istorii russko-slavjanskikh svjazej*, ed. M. N. Speranskij (Moscow, 1960), 104–47; R. Stankov, "Istoricheskaja Paleja—pamjatnik drevnej bolgarskoj kul'tury," *Palaeobulgarica* 10, no. 4 (1986): 55–63.

coincides with the two texts on which our present study is focused. The apocryphal nature of these two texts and their close link to Old Testament history are very important, and we strongly believe that the *Historical Palaea* should be examined as one of the main sources of ideas of the *List* and the *Apocryphal Chronicle*. With this assertion we do not want to diminish the importance of the Interpreted Palaea[34]—as we strongly believe that this polemical text was also a possible source of knowledge of biblical history.

Thus, these three basic varieties of the Old Testament were available in tenth-century Bulgaria. Texts used liturgically were the most influential, since they brought the stories closer to the believers and created a link between the literary and oral traditions. In this way medieval Bulgarian society quite early achieved a fundamental awareness of Old Testament narrative.

The People and the Kingdom—the New Israel in the New Promised Land

The introduction of the *Apocryphal Chronicle* draws from the Old Testament prophetical tradition as borrowed from the "Vision of Isaiah": God sends Isaiah with a special mission to his people (Isaiah 6). Isaiah was the one who condemned the sins of the people of Israel (Isaiah 1:1–10) and predicted their punishment in exile, the subsequent creation of a renewed Israel, free of sins (Isaiah 5:13ff.), and the calling of many peoples to the faith of the "mountain of the Lord, to the house of the God of Jacob" (Isaiah 2:3). All this is linked to the prophecy of the Messiah (Isaiah 9:6) and makes the book of Isaiah of special interest for Christian interpretations and particularly relevant to the present study. The history, related later, is presented as the result of the special mission of the prophet Isaiah to disclose the destiny of the "last people" in the "last times."[35] So too the Bulgarian people are presented in the *Apocryphal Chronicle* as having such a special mission in world history. We would like to stress some points in the text that reveal to us noteworthy ideas of the medieval author.

In the *Apocryphal Chronicle* the Bulgarians adopt a vision of a new chosen people that has strong ethnic characteristics. The text develops certain elements of similarity between the Bulgarians and the children of Israel. God takes the prophet to the heavens to charge him with a special mission concerning "the third part of the Comans, called Bulgarians." Their history is especially emphasized: the prophet went to the Comans on the "left of Rome," separated a third

---

34   Slavova, *Tŭlkovnata Paleja*, 105ff., 109ff., 160ff., 275ff., 335–48.
35   Tapkova-Zaimova and Miltenova, *Istoriko-apokaliptichnata knizhnina* (n. 16 above), 195.

of them and conducted them to the "Land of Karvuna." He, the prophet of God, promoted a king for them and organized their kingdom as the prophet Samuel had organized Israel. From then on the entire history of the new people is closely linked to the history of humanity, which is the history of salvation: this new people were first to abandon pagan beliefs and from them came the first Christian empire in the person of St. Constantine. The finding of the Holy Cross and the foundation of Constantinople, called the "new Jerusalem" (events related to salvation), are linked to Constantine. Finally, the Bulgarian kingdom, established by the prophet Isaiah, is linked to the last days, revealed in a manner suggesting the Apocalypse with attacks of savage barbarian peoples.[36]

The land of this new chosen people in many ways replicates the Holy Land, geographically as well as historically and religiously. For the People of Israel, the Promised Land is an essential part of their covenant with God. A reference to it in the Palaeobulgarian texts indicates the state's attempt to form an individual identity based on an Old Testament model. Certain geographical characteristics unite the land presented in our sources with the biblical archetype, that is, features of the natural landscape of Canaan. Most especially, the *Apocryphal Chronicle* develops this particular similarity between the biblical promised land and the land of the Bulgars: the new Patria is a fertile territory located between two waters.

There are several references to rivers in the *List* and in the *Apocryphal Chronicle*. Although they differ somewhat, they share certain key elements. In the *List* the idea of the kingdom is not well developed in its geographical characteristics. The text is restricted mostly to the enumeration of the princes with the dates of their reigns. We do find, however, some references about the land in the passage "These five princes ruled for five hundred and fifteen years beyond the Danube with shaved heads. After them the prince Isperich came on this side of the river. And it is the same until now."[37] So, the former period is characterized by the Bulgars being settled beyond the great European river. We see, therefore, the passage of the people to the new land, presented as a crossing of the river of Danube. Their settlement in the New Patria is obviously a turning point in their history, which is how it is presented also in the *Apocryphal Chronicle*. The journey of the people is separated into two parts: before and after the conquest of the present lands. The arrival of the Bulgarians in their promised land is presented exactly according to the paradigm of the arrival of the people of Israel

36   Ibid., 196–98.
37   Moskov, *Imennik* (n. 3 above), 20.

in the promised land of Canaan. They crossed the river Jordan and entered the land. The very crossing of the river is especially stressed in the scriptural text. It happened miraculously with divine intervention when the Levites under God's inspired command of Joshua stopped in the river and the people passed through it (Joshua 3). Obviously, this incident is reminiscent of the text on crossing the Red Sea and marks a crucial moment in the history of the covenant of the chosen people with God.

With the mention of the river and also of the sea the Holy Land is presented as a median between the two. It is important to emphasize the geography of the land where the prophet led the Bulgar people: the *Apocryphal Chronicle* mentions it as the "Land of Karvuna" or the land between the Danube and the Black Sea, which was formerly inhabited by the Hellenes and the Romans.[38] This is modern-day Dobrudja, the territory on the right bank of the lower Danube that lies between the great European river and the Pontus. This terrain is similar to that of the Holy Land: a large strip of land between two bodies of water (the Jordan River and the sea), fertile and abundant.

The land of the Bulgarians is presented in our sources not only as a geographical but also as a religious replica of the Holy Land. It is the land appointed by God for them (as the promised land for the Hebrews): that is why he sends the prophet Isaiah of the *Apocryphal Chronicle* on his mission. It is the land of the "people of the last days," an expression giving an eschatological dimension.

The reference to the "Kingdom of Jerusalem" is linked to the activities of the emperor Constantine,[39] who is himself an image of the Holy Emperor Constantine the Great, but his connection—in the framework of the *Apocryphal Chronicle*—to the Bulgarian Kingdom, established by the Prophet Isaiah, is strongly emphasized: he is born in the Bulgarian land under Tsar Peter to a young, wise and righteous widow.[40] He created the city of Constantinople, also known as the "New Jerusalem," in a deserted territory situated again between two waters, two seas. All this is somehow linked to the discovery of the Holy Cross.[41]

---

38   Tapkova-Zaimova and Miltenova, *Istoriko-apokaliptichnata knizhnina*, 195.
39   Ibid., 197.
40   Ibid., 196.
41   Here is the text of the *Apocryphal Chronicle*, presenting the birth, life, and activities of the "tsar Constantine": "Then, during the reign of the holy tsar Peter, there was in the Bulgarian land a widow and she was young and wise and very righteous; her name was Helena. And she gave birth to Tsar Constantine, a holy and righteous man. He was son of Constantine the Green and mother Helena; that Constantine, called Porphyrogenitus, was the Roman emperor. . . . And an angel of God appeared to him and announced to him about the Holy Cross from the East. He gathered his warriors, took his mother, and went to the East by sea, to the place of Calvary. There was a

Thus the history of the Bulgarians is intermingled with that of the Romans, and the "Kingdom of Jerusalem" of the first Christian emperor is inhabited, according to the text, by Bulgarians. The Bulgarian and Roman lands are deliberately confused in the *Apocryphal Chronicle* and both together with "Jerusalem's land," since all three are described as "the dominion of the tsar Constantine."[42]

The King

In this conception of the state as the unity of the land, the people, and the king, it should be understood that the king should be seen not merely as the ruler but as a synthesis of the other two—the land and the people—and that he is their personified and incarnate representative. Now the king is not a typical figure among the leaders of Israel (1 Samuel 8). The act of creating a terrestrial kingdom of the chosen people was perceived in the beginning as a destruction of the power of God, who was considered the one and only king of Israel. The leaders of the Hebrews are therefore not just their kings, but also their prophets and judges, and so the paradigm for Christian rulers is not only the king of Israel or Judah but also the patriarch, the judge, and, most of all, the prophet.

Speaking about the conception of the kingdom as a replica of the Old Testament kingdoms of the chosen people is not so extraordinary, surprising, or original. We find it brilliantly expressed in Byzantium,[43] giving the archetype and main patterns of the medieval Bulgarian culture. We can say that this is the exact source of ideas for the creation of the Old Testament models in the state of the neophytes to the north of the Balkan Mountains. Even more, we find an excellent expression of these ideas in the *Vita Cyrilli* in the words of the very apostle of the Slavs and in a text undoubtedly known in Bulgaria.[44] Let us look at how the paradigm of Christian rulers as kings, patriarchs, and prophets is reflected in the *List* and the *Apocryphal Chronicle*.

---

little town called Byzantium. And when he arrived at this place and saw the deserted area from sea to sea, he thought: 'If I go to Calvary and find the Holy Cross, on Which Christ was crucified, and come back again to this deserted place, I shall build a city and I shall give it the name of New Jerusalem—habitation of the saints and adornment of the kings.'" Tapkova-Zaimova and Miltenova, *Istoriko-apokaliptichnata knizhnina*, 196–97.

42   This is in the paragraph explaining the "bad tsar" Symeon the Wise: "And he made perish the Bulgarian land, Jerusalem's and the Roman, the dominion of the tsar Constantine." Tapkova-Zaimova and Miltenova, *Istoriko-apokaliptichnata knizhnina*, 197.

43   See G. Dagron, *Emperor and Priest: The Imperial Office in Byzantium* (Cambridge, 2003), 48–50.

44   Kliment Okhridski, *Sŭbrani sŭchinenija* (n. 21 above), 3:99ff.

Not only are the names of the kings cited in the *Apocryphal Chronicle*—the brothers Moses, Aaron, and Samuel, born miraculously to a woman who was both widow and prophet[45]—the names of biblical prophets, but we find those same names in the political history of Bulgaria during the second half of the tenth and the beginning of the eleventh century.[46] The four Cometopouloi brothers, David, Moses, Aaron, and Samuel, lived in the western part of Bulgaria and restored the empire that had been occupied by the *Romaioi*. It is revealing that all four were given names of great Old Testament prophets, a practice highly atypical for the Bulgarian milieu.[47] Certainly the name of the ruler is an identity marker of ideological character; in this case, the identification of these four brothers with the leaders of the children of Israel is certain.

The next and probably the most interesting and controversial element of the *Apocryphal Chronicle* relates to the "apparition" of the Bulgar khan Asparuch (ca. 650–ca. 700), called Ispor in the *Apocryphal Chronicle*. One should stress here his miraculous appearance in the world. The chronicle states that he was "a child brought for a period of three years in a basket."[48] It is not explicitly written that the basket floated in a river, but all the later activities of Ispor occur in the context of the Danube. Thus Ispor's story strongly suggests the story of the prophet Moses and the myth about the "miraculously appearing child" who had a special destiny in history. The latter generated great interest in Bulgarian

---

45 The theme of the miraculously born child is of special importance to the chronicle. It is usually interpreted in Bulgarian historiography as a reminiscence of the pagan believers, but it has a strong scriptural basis as well. In Isaiah 8:3 we find mention of a virgin who conceived and bore a son. We return to this topic later.

46 Tapkova-Zaimova and Miltenova, *Istoriko-apokaliptichnata knizhnina*, 197. There are many studies on the history of Cometopouloi and here we shall cite only a few of them: G. Schlumberger, *L'épopée byzantine à la fin du dixième siecle*, 3 vols. (Paris, 1896–1905); V. N. Zlatarski, *Istorija na bŭlgarskata dŭrzhava prez srednite vekove* (Sofia, 1927), 1.2:633–790; N. Adontz, *Samuel l'Arménien, Roi des Bulgares*, Études Arméno-Byzantines (Lisbon, 1965), 347–407; W. Seibt, "Untersuchungen zur Vor- und Frühgeschichte der bulgarischen Kometopulen," *Handes Amsorya* 89 (1975): 65–98; S. Pirivatrić, *Samuilova drzhava: Obim i karakter* (Belgrade, 1997), subsequently translated into Bulgarian (Sofia, 2000); I. Bozhilov in *Istorija na srednovekovna Bŭlgarija VII–XIV vek*, vol. 1 of *Istorija na Bŭlgarija v tri toma* (Sofia, 1999), 308–38.

47 Here I shall not discuss the well-known thesis about the Armenian origin of the Cometopouloi. It is not relevant to this article and, moreover, it does not at all explain why they have names of the great Old Testament prophets.

48 Tapkova-Zaimova and Miltenova, *Istoriko-apokaliptichnata knizhnina*, 196. There is a problem with this text. Some scholars have taken this opportunity to develop a whole theory on the mythological basis of the story and to link it to pagan mythological patterns—T. Mollov, *Mit, epos, istorija* (Veliko Tŭrnovo, 1997), 34–35. We follow the majority position in reading the word as "basket," which is not only logical but also corresponds to the Old Testament text about the childhood of the prophet Moses. The mistake can be accounted a scribal error.

historical literature, as there is a general tendency to seek pagan roots in the country's Christian tradition. This is mainly the focus of folklore studies, where the citations of medieval texts are usually used only as an auxiliary support. Even the scriptural models are interpreted as borrowed from the Near Eastern pagan past, which is seen as a precursor of the Bible and a source of biblical topoi and ideas. We shall leave this type of interpretation aside in our study in order to try to identify the scriptural basis of the Bulgarian Christian tradition.

Thus, we arrive at the Moses paradigm for the king, the image of the ruler as the "new Moses," which was familiar in the Middle Ages. Much earlier, Eusebios of Caesarea, in the *Vita Constantini*, had used the pattern in his glorification of the emperor Constantine.[49] Constantine's life is presented as a replica of Moses' from cradle to grave: he is a servant of God and fulfills His will on the Earth. Eusebios provided a literary model in the European and Mediterranean east, and his work had a great influence on all the countries of the Byzantine commonwealth.[50] Recent research shows that this model existed in Bulgaria as well.[51]

The great prophet is the leader of the people of Israel, their liberator from the pharaoh's yoke, their guide to the promised land. Coming from the house of Levi and organizing the cult of the Hebrews, Moses figures not only as a priest but also as a legislator and secular ruler, the king. It is important to mention the "Rod of God," given to the prophet. This rod had special importance during imperial ceremonies in Byzantium, where it was brought by Constantine as one of the *pignora imperii*.[52]

The Mosaic paradigm for Bulgarian rulers is mentioned in a few places other than the *Apocryphal Chronicle*. R. Rashev emphasizes a phrase from a letter of Patriarch Nicholas Mystikos to Tsar Symeon in which the Bulgarian ruler is

---

49 M. Hollerich, "Religion and Politics in the Writings of Eusebius: Reassessing the First 'Court Theologian,'" *Church History* 59, no. 3 (Sept. 1990): 321–25; idem, "The Comparison of Moses and Constantine in Eusebius of Caesarea's *Life of Constantine*," *StP* 19 (1989): 80–95; A. Wilson, "Biographical Models: The Constantinian Period and Beyond," in *Constantine: History, Historiography and Legend*, ed. S. N. C. Lieu and D. Montserrat (New York, 1998), 107–35; Eusebios, *Life of Constantine*, trans. Av. Cameron and S. G. Hall (Oxford, 1999), 36ff.

50 The Moses paradigm is very popular in Byzantium, and not only for Constantine. See Dagron, *Emperor and Priest* (n. 43 above), 98, 109–10, 127ff., 253, 282ff., 276–81, 313–18.

51 R. Rashev, "Tsar Simeon: prorok Mojsej i bŭlgarskijat Zlaten vek," *1100 godini Veliki Preslav*, ed. T. Totev (Shumen, 1995), 1:66–69; idem, "Tsar Simeon—'nov Mojsej' ili 'nov David,'" *Preslavska knizhovna shkola* 7 (2004): 366–76; idem, *Tsar Simeon: Shtrihi kŭm lichnostta i deloto mu* (Sofia, 2007), 60–72.

52 A. Grabar, *L'empereur dans l'art byzantin* (Paris, 1936), 29; Dagron, *Emperor and Priest*, 98, 143ff., 231; Rashev, "Tsar Simeon—'nov Mojsej' ili 'nov David,'" 372ff.; Rashev, *Tsar Simeon: Shtrihi*, 67–68.

compared to the image of the great prophet.[53] We view this as a continuation not only of the general trend to perceive the king as the new Moses, which was borrowed from Byzantium, but also of the native tradition presented in the *Apocryphal Chronicle*, which was based directly on the Old Testament narrative.

The first two rulers in the *List* are purely mythological, despite their identification by certain scholars as Attila, the leader of the Huns, and his son Ernac.[54] The text, though, is purely mythological and presents the pagan "religious" conceptions of power in the Bulgar state and society.[55] The rulers of the Bulgarian state appear in it not only as leaders of their people but as descendants of gods or divine ancestors who created the world and the people, harmonized the pretemporal chaos, and ever since have returned cyclically to restore order in the visible world.[56]

After the Christianization of Bulgaria, the Christian leader can no longer be a king-god, but must be merely a king by God's grace and appointment. He is no longer the incarnation of a divinity but the lieutenant of the Lord, who is the unique source and possessor of every power. Looking for images and models to conceptualize their rulers in the context of the Holy Scriptures, the neophytes arrived at the kings of the children of Israel—the unique scriptural model of terrestrial power by the Lord's grace.

The way in which the Old Testament images are linked to the state and used to create the new identity of the people, the state, and its ruler is of great interest. In the Bulgarian case this affiliation takes place by the abovementioned integration of the mythological pagan text of the Bulgars into a universal Christian chronicle—the insertion of the khans in the list of the kings of Israel and Judah. Thus the sacred history of the Bulgars is equated with the biblical text, and the

---

53 Nicholas I Patriarch of Constantinople, *Letters*, ed. R. J. H. Jenkins and L. G. Westerink (Washington, DC, 1973), 176; Rashev, "Tsar Simeon: prorok," 66–67; idem, *Tsar Simeon: Shtrihi*, 60ff.

54 This identification already has a long history from the second half of the nineteenth century (the pioneer is W. Tomaschek). See the bibliographical review: A. Burmov, "Vŭprosi iz istorijata na prabŭlgarite," *Godishnik na Sofijskija universitet, Istoriko-filologicheski fakultet* 44, no. 2 (1948): 6–9.

55 Among the many articles about pagan Bulgarian rulers, we cite only the very suggestive and recently published article by Florin Curta that is not only rich in ideas but also presents a perfect review of the sources and historiography on the pagan royalty in early medieval Bulgaria: "Qagan, Khan, or King? Power in Early Medieval Bulgaria (Seventh to Ninth Century)," *Viator: Medieval and Renaissance Studies* 37 (2006): 1–31. The kingship of the early medieval southern Slavs is presented in idem, *The Making of the Slavs: History and Archaeology of the Lower Danube Region, c. 500–700* (Cambridge, 2001), 311–31.

56 I. Biliarsky, "L'histoire et l'identité," *RESEE* 41.1–4 (2003): 39ff.; idem, "Ot mifa k istorii" (n. 3 above), 15–18.

people of the great steppes enter the Hebrew-Christian history of the world, the history of the Testament and salvation, and the Bulgarian neophytes become a chosen people of God, a new Israel.

King David was another Old Testament model king for a Christian ruler. He provides an especially important pattern for Byzantine political theory and practice, and we have every reason to mark out its path from Constantinople to Bulgaria.[57] We find some clear traces of the image of this Old Testament king and prophet in the *Apocryphal Chronicle*, although David is not specifically mentioned by name. We would like, however, to focus on the part of the text dedicated to the so-called "King Izot," the son of Ispor. The name is confusing, but there are Byzantine and Old Testament parallels to it. The first derives from the text of *De thematibus* of the emperor Constantine VII Porphyrogenitus. He hellenized the Armenian name of Ashot as Ἀζῶτος,[58] which is quite similar to the name of our king Izot. This fact presents an opportunity for the identification of Izot as someone with special relevance. As we shall see below, it was probably during the reign of Ashot the Curopalate that the story of the Georgian and Armenian Bagrationi dynasty's descent from King David was created. This Davidic paradigm of power is further developed in the *Apocryphal Chronicle* in the presentation of Izot's glorious victories. We pass over here other parallels, such as those to a certain Azotios in the *Patria Constantinopoleos*, whom the emperor Constantine vanquished in Byzantion at the foundation of the city of Constantinople,[59] and those to the city of the Philistines called Ashdod (Ἀζώτειος/Ἄζωτος), which had a special place in their struggle with the Children of Israel (see for example Joshua 11:22, 13:3, 15:46–47; Judges 1:18; 1 Samuel 1:1, 5–6, 5:3, 6–7, 6:17 and so on).

These latter two parallels are not so relevant to the present topic as the *Apocryphal Chronicle*'s text about Izot's victory over certain enemies: he "made perish the king Ozia . . . and Goliath the Frank from Overseas."[60] King Ozia's name relates to the name of Uzziah, whom we meet thirty-four times in the Old Testament and twice in the New Testament in the more hellenized form

---

57 Dagron, *Emperor and Priest* (n. 43 above), 48–53, 114ff., 199ff., 267–76, 313–18; S. Tougher, *The Reign of Leo VI (886–912): Politics and People* (Leiden–New York–Cologne, 1997), 122–32; L. Brubaker, *Vision and Meaning in Ninth-Century Byzantium: Image as Exegesis in the Homilies of Gregory of Nazianzus* (Cambridge, 1999), 105, 147, 177–78, 185–93, 199–200.

58 Constantini Porphyrogeniti, *De thematibus (introduzione–testo critico–commento)*, ed. A. Pertusi (Vatican City, 1952), 75 n. 7.

59 G. Dagron, *Constantinople imaginaire: Étude sur le recueil des "Patria"* (Paris, 1984), 45–48.

60 Tapkova-Zaimova and Miltenova, *Istoriko-apokaliptichnata knizhnina* (n. 16 above), 196.

of Ozias.[61] Several persons with this name are cited in the Holy Scriptures, but the most relevant to our topic is Uzziah, king of Judah, son of King Amaziah and father of King Jotham (see 2 Chronicles 26). He was a righteous and strong king, but "his heart was exalted so as to be corrupt, and he did wrong against the Lord, his God, and entered into the Lord's shrine, to burn incense on the altar of incense" (2 Chronicles 26:16 NETS). God punished him and he was leprous to the end of his days.

Is there any relation between the biblical Uzziah, king of Judah, and the one mentioned in the *Apocryphal Chronicle*? The two names have the same Slavic spelling. Ozia is called in the apocryphal text the "king from the East," who was killed by King Izot and by his warriors. The importance of King Ozia's name in the *Apocryphal Chronicle* is not its historical accuracy, but its ideological significance. Both kings are negatively portrayed: Uzziah was a victim of his pride, transgressed the Law, and was punished by God; Ozia of the *Apocryphal Chronicle* was an enemy of a good king, Izot, who vanquished him.

The other name of interest here, which provides more possibilities of interpretation, is "Goliath the Frank from Overseas." We avoid any attempt to identify him with a historical person such as the emperor Louis the Pious, some other Frankish ruler, or Harold Hardrada—the Viking from Iceland, who was a mercenary in Byzantium and later became the king of Norway.[62] For our purposes, again, it is enough that he is known by the biblical name Goliath. He, too, was defeated by King Izot. The text does not suggest any real event of Bulgarian history, but it evokes the battle between the Prophet and King David and the Philistine champion (1 Samuel 17). Thus King Izot recalls the glory of David and his people and the glory of Israel in the battle with their foes. The suggestion of the Davidic paradigm in the figure of the ruler Izot is incontrovertible, for this is surely the paradigm of the anointed king of the chosen people.

A Comparative View with Other Oriental Christian States

Let us now extend the scope of this inquiry into the use of Old Testament types in Bulgaria by looking at parallel processes in other countries on the periphery

---

61 We find it twice in 2 Kings (4 Kingdoms LXX), twice in 1 Chronicles, eleven times in 2 Chronicles, once in Esdras, thirteen times in Judith, twice in Isaiah, and once each in Hosea, Amos, and Zechariah. It is cited twice in Matthew (1:8–9). This is the name of the king of Judah.
62 A. Miltenova and M. Kajmakamova, "The Uprising of Petâr Delyan (1040–1041) in a New Old Bulgarian Source," *BBulg* 8 (1986): 235–36; for more about him see the *ODB* 2:902.

of Eastern Christianity: Ethiopia, Russia, and the Christian states in the Caucasus.[63] Though differing from one another in many respects, the processes in these three regions are similar in their exploitation of Old Testament images and especially in their use of the heritage of the kings of Israel to argue for the ruler's identity and power in a new milieu.

The Russian case should be closer to that of early medieval Bulgaria, not only because of the similar influence of Constantinople on both states, but also because of the common Slavic culture, official language, and literature. Here we shall focus our attention on the cult of the first Russian prince-martyrs, who became models of the holiness of the ruling dynasty, and its interpretation in the Old Testament context.

B. A. Uspensky published his observations on the connection of Old Testament readings to the office of the first Russian saints—Princes Boris and Gleb (d. 1015).[64] The story of their martyrdom is sometimes inserted into the readings of the Vespers service as an alternative text, replacing the required Old Testament reading from the book of Genesis, which tells the story of the slaughter of Abel by his brother Cain (Genesis 4).[65] Thus, the martyrdom of SS. Boris and Gleb entered the ecclesiastical lections and replaced the story about Cain and Abel because it was conceived as *a concrete local realization of the same story*. Russian history, therefore, also acquired its scriptural paradigm and became a part of the history of humanity by linking itself to the history of the people of Israel. In accordance with Uspensky's thesis, the affiliation to Old Testament history was necessary for the recently converted state to sanctify its new Christian identity, which is the identity of new Israel, the new chosen people.

There is a typological unity between the cited Russian case and the Bulgarian one, presented by the *List*: the insertion of the history of a newly converted people into biblical history.[66] The ideological functions are quite analogous. In

---

63 We would like to repeat that in the Eastern Orthodox countries, despite the local specific traits that we can discover especially in Russia and in the Caucasus, these ideas were communicated largely through the Eastern Roman Empire. Even in Muslim political thought the influence of Byzantium is crucial: Dagron, *Emperor and Priest* (n. 43 above), 51–53.
64 B. A. Uspenskij, *Boris i Gleb: vosprijatie istorii v drevnej Rusi* (Moscow, 2000).
65 Ibid., 9ff., Prilozhenie 1:112–18.
66 The *Paroimiai* mentioned above are not the normative texts of the Old Testament but some excerpts, designated to be read primarily during the service of Vespers. Nevertheless, we must keep in mind that at this time the text of the whole Old Testament was not accessible in Slavonic; for some centuries later, it was available only via these Vespers readings. So, the insertion of any text into the latter should be conceived exactly as an insertion into the Old Testament: "С известным приближением можно сказать вообще, что Паремейник—это не что иное, как Ветхий Завет в его богослужебной версии, иными словами, собрание текстов Ветхого

the cited case of SS. Boris and Gleb, the parallelism drawn between the Old Testament text and the creation of prototypes for the dynasty's goals establishes the same theology of power, state, and people. The comparison is made not simply to point to the sacrifice of the innocent or to seek a pattern to explain the holiness of the victims, but to affiliate Russian history to the history of the children of Israel and to identify the neophytes with the chosen people and their state and the power of its ruler to the divinely anointed Old Testament kings from Saul, David, and Solomon onward.

The Russian people have a long history of messianic ideas and self-identification as the chosen people. This forms the basis of their concept of the third Rome, the seventeenth-century schism, and the eschatological visions of the Old Believers up to the twentieth century. The image of the innocent victim is well represented in this complex of ideas, but it is based mostly on New Testament paradigms. Of course, every martyr and every innocent victim is either a prefiguration of the Lord Jesus Christ or has him as the archetype, which points to a New Testament ideal at the base of every Old Testament image. This is the case with the martyrdom of Abel.[67] It is not our goal to develop the topic further in this direction, but it should be noted that some of the above mentioned paradigms are quite important in all of the cultures we have examined. In a Christian milieu the study of Old Testament patterns will usually have some connection with the New Testament.

In medieval Georgia and Armenia the paradigm of the Old Testament was filtered through the heritage of the royalty of the chosen people. A long tradition concerning Hebrew presence in the Caucasus strongly influenced Georgian and Armenian cultures and provides an explanation for many later developments. We wish to focus, however, upon God's presence among his new chosen people and the way the Bagrationi dynasty justified their royal power by citing King David as their ancestor. Of particular interest is the *History and Narration of the Bagrationis* by the eleventh-century author Sumbat Davitis-dze, which is the main source of this story.[68] Of course, the story appeared much earlier (see below), but it was codified by Sumbat. The Bagrationis took power

---

Завета, вошедших в церковную службу" ("We can say that the Prophetologion is not something else but the very text of the Old Testament in its liturgical version, so a collection of the Old Testament texts that entered the ecclesiastical divine service"; Uspenskij, *Boris i Gleb*, 7).
67   As we see it can be related to the martyrdom of St. Stephen, to St. Demetrius, and so on to the Lord Jesus Christ himself (ibid., 39).
68   I use the Russian translation of the work: Sumbat Davitis-dze, *Istorija i povestvovanie o Bagrationakh*, ed. M. D. Lordkipanidze, Pamjatniki gruzinskoj literatury 3 (Tbilisi, 1979).

as the leading dynasty in Georgia in the ninth century. Their first great representative was Ashot the Curopalate, but even before his rule they had already governed some local Caucasian principalities.[69] It was during this earlier period that the story of the ruling family coming from the seed of the king and prophet David and thus of the family's affiliation with the terrestrial parents of Lord Jesus Christ was created. The story appeared in both Georgian and Armenian milieus and became a common historical and ideological topos to claim the source of the power of the dynasty and its priority over other pretenders to the royal crown.[70]

The legend of the origin of the Bagrationis from the king and prophet David was first mentioned in Armenian literature in the work of John Draschanakerttsi at the beginning of the tenth century. In Georgian literature this legend is known from the *Vita* of Gregory Handzteli, written by George Merchulé in the middle of the tenth century. In this text St. Gregory addresses Ashot the Curopalate as "lord, called son of David the prophet and God's anointed."[71] Obviously, the story was quite popular and widely known because it even entered the text of the *De administrando imperio* of Constantine Porphyrogenitus. The emperor wrote that the Iberians believe that they are descendants of the wife of Uriah, with whom King David committed adultery, and therefore they place their origins in Jerusalem.[72] Constantine VII cites not the genealogical line of Joseph, the husband of the Virgin Mary, but that of the Mother of God herself, which somehow contradicts the legend as we know it from Sumbat's text. Finally, this genealogy comes down to two brothers—David and Skandiatis—who moved to the Caucasus.

So, we arrive at Sumbat's history of the Bagrationis, which is the core source that influenced all medieval Georgian historiography, entering the subsequent chronicles of the country.[73] It contains a genealogy from Adam to King and Prophet David, followed by a genealogy from David to Joseph, the husband of the Virgin Mary, and then from Joseph's brother Cleopa to a certain Solomon whose seven sons left the Holy Land and went to Armenia. It had already stated that the *Church History* of Eusebios of Caesarea is the source for Cleopa.[74]

---

69 See the introduction to Sumbat's history by M. Lordkipanidze (ibid., 14ff.).
70 Ibid., 17–18.
71 Ibid., 13–14.
72 Constantinus Porphyrogenitus, *De administrando imperio*, ed. G. Moravscik and R. J. H. Jenkins (Washington, DC, 1967), 204.
73 Sumbat Davitis-dze, *Istorija*, 27–28.
74 Ibid., 19.

The seven sons of that Solomon who went to Armenia were baptized by the local queen, an unknown Rachael. Three of them remained there and their descendants governed the country, but four went to Georgia, where one of the brothers—Guaram—was elected *eristavi* (the ruler) and founded the dynasty of the Georgian Bagrationis.

The final example of Old Testament paradigmatic justification for a ruler and state's supremacy comes from the Ethiopian tradition. We shall focus mostly on the book of *Kebra Nagast* (Glory of the Kings), which presents the origins of Solomon's dynasty and the story of the arrival of the Ark of the Covenant in the African country.[75] It centers on the visit of the queen of Sheba, called Makeda, to Jerusalem and her relations with King Solomon. Here we shall briefly present the results of our research on this holy book of Christian Ethiopia, which is a separate study.[76] It is obvious that the text presents the story of the origin of the royal dynasty directly from the king and prophet Solomon and so links itself to the tradition that also provides the Davidic origin of Caucasian Bagrationis and the Bulgar khans, who continue the line of the kings of the chosen people. Both of these events (as well as the visit of the Queen of Sheba to Jerusalem and the transfer of the Ark) receive a Christian interpretation that is based not only on the Old Testament but also on the New—see the Gospel of Matthew (12:42) and the Gospel of Luke (11:31).[77]

Of special interest is Origen's allegorical interpretation of the biblical text on the visit of the queen of Sheba to Jerusalem found in his commentary on the Song of Songs.[78] In his interpretation, the queen is a proto-image of the Church of the Gentiles and King Solomon is the embodiment of Wisdom, of

---

75 *Kebra Nagast* was originally published with a German translation: *Kebra Nagast: Die Herrlichkeit der Könige (Nach den Handschriften in Berlin, London, Oxford und Paris)*, ed. C. Bezold (Munich, 1905). For this study we used mostly the English edition (E. A. Wallis Budge, *The Queen of Sheba and Her Only Son Menyelek [I]* [Oxford–London, 1932]) and the recent French translation (G. Colin, *La Gloire des rois [Kebra Nagast]: Epopée nationale de l'Ethiopie* [Geneva, 2002]).
76 See I. Biliarsky, "The Birth of the Empire by the Divine Wisdom and the Ecumenical Church," in *The Biblical Models of Power and Law / Les modèles bibliques du pouvoir et du droit* (Frankfurt am Main, 2008), 23–43.
77 Matthew 12:42 (RSV), "The queen of the South will arise at the judgment with this generation and condemn it; for she came from the ends of the earth to hear the wisdom of Solomon, and behold, something greater than Solomon is here." Luke 11:31 (RSV), "The queen of the South will arise at the judgment with the men of this generation and condemn them; for she came from the ends of the earth to hear the wisdom of Solomon, and behold, something greater than Solomon is here."
78 Origen, *Commentaire sur le Cantique des cantiques*, vol. 1, *Texte de la version latine de Rufin*, ed. and trans. L. Brésard and H. Crouzel, SC 375 (Paris, 1991), 1.2.14–15:198–201.

the incarnated Logos, who is the Lord Jesus Christ. We recall that the *Kebra Nagast* also addresses the issue of God's presence among his chosen people, as it is presented through the story of the Ark of the Covenant, which is perceived as the "home" of God and so a proto-image of the Virgin and of the Church. Thus the universal history rests in the paradigm of the Kingdom, which is conceived as a result of the encounter of the Christ-Logos-Wisdom with the Church in the images of king and prophet Solomon and the queen of Sheba.

In the Bulgarian texts and mainly in the context of the *List of the Bulgar Princes* we understand that there is an attempt to include the state in the new Christian conception of the world and its history through the incorporation of the khans in the list of the kings of Israel and Judah. It must be emphasized, however, that this conception lies within the closed tribal framework of the relation between the ruler and the people; there is no strong suggestion of some universal character of power. After the conversion of the ruling group, the king is no longer an emanation of a pagan god or cultural hero, but he is not yet a universal ruler, successor of the Roman emperors. He must become a lieutenant of God, and the people conceive themselves in the biblical category of the new chosen people. The usual biblical images to promote such a political ideology are the People of Israel and their anointed kings. Thus a new chosen people appeared, a new Israel, bearing, however, some traits of the ancient, and thus conserving its ethnic definition. Clan and tribal links remain important, expressly so. Elsewhere we formulated the thesis that by writing themselves into biblical history the Bulgarians broke the narrow framework of their tribal identity and adopted the universal road toward salvation.[79] They adopted their Christian identity via the Old Testament tradition, which is more closely connected to the concept of the tribe and ethnos than to the universalism of the empire. This view is expressed in the sources by the ideological interpretation of and identification with the images of the Old Testament kings.

Formally, we see a similar tactic in the other cited traditions—those of the Caucasus and Ethiopia, as well as those of Russia. The general aim in all is to include the newly Christianized people and state in the history of the testament of humanity (or of the chosen people) with God. In the Ethiopian, Georgian, and Armenian cases, but not in the Bulgar state, we see also the goal to promote and to sanctify a dynasty through its affiliation by blood with the seed of the

---

79   I. Biliarsky, "Srednovekovna Bŭlgarija: Tsarstvoto i naroda," Πολυχρονια: *Sbornik v chest na prof. Ivan Bozhilov* (Sofia, 2002), 25–40.

king and prophet David. A more important difference between the Bulgar state and all these others is the interpreting of the Old Testament models in light of New Testaments ideas, which resulted in interpretations with more ecumenical features.

Instead of a Conclusion

The study of the *List of the Bulgar Princes* and of the *Apocryphal Chronicle* reveals some very important features of the ideology of early medieval Bulgaria based on Old Testament models. Both texts are confusing and extant only in small portions; moreover, they are prophetic narratives that cannot be used as documents of real historical events. We have tried to illustrate the scriptural conception about the land, the people and the ruler, which is essential for the creation of the image of the new chosen people, as reflected in these texts.[80]

Our analysis of the two texts provides some parameters of the ideological complex, created in early medieval Bulgaria in the transitional period between the ethnic pagan state of the Bulgars and the Christian empire. There is in it an image of unity between the land, the people and the ruler based on Old Testament models. In ninth- and tenth-century Bulgaria the state maintained some facets of paganism, but was concomitantly creating a new Christian identity. The interpretation of the state, however, was not yet based on a vision of itself as being as ecumenical as the Byzantine model purported to be. The purpose of our two texts was to promote for the neophyte state a special place within the schema of the Christian world and mankind's progress toward salvation.

---

80 Of course, the Bulgarian case is not at all exceptional. The idea of being a new chosen people was very popular during the Middle Ages and continues so in modern, even contemporary times. We find it among many peoples and especially among other Slavic nations: Serbs, Russian, and Poles. Here, though, we refer especially to the Bulgarians' neighbors to the west, because the Polish and the Russian cases are mostly in the modern epoch and in completely different circumstances. Serbian political messianic ideas were developed in the late Balkan Middle Ages and present very rich material for the study of political theology: see B. Bojović, *L'idéologie monarchique dans les hagio-biographies dynastiques du moyen âge serbe*, OCA 248 (Rome, 1995); idem, "Une monarchie hagiographique: La théologie du pouvoir dans la Serbie médiévale (XII–XV siècles)," in *L'empereur hagiographe: Culte des saints et monarchie Byzantine et post-byzantine*, ed. B. Flusin and P. Guran (Bucharest, 2001), 61–72; J. Erdeljan, "Beograd kao Novi Jerusalim: Razmišljanja o recepciji jednog topos u doba despota Stefana Lazarevića," *ZRVI* 43 (2006): 97–111. The Serbian use of the Old Testament in the creation of the identity and the political ideology is much later and quite different from the Bulgarian case: it is not a transitional idea after the conversion to Christianity but a claim for the special status of a Christian milieu facing the infidel foe, so its basis, its texts, and its expression are different.

In a brief historical period after the pagan epoch, Bulgaria was eager to perceive itself as the new Israel, identified with the children of Israel, the chosen people, against the disintegrating Roman Empire. Later, from the time of Tsar Symeon onward, Bulgaria became a state with imperial pretensions based on the Roman/Byzantine model. It sacrificed its ethnicity in order to aspire to the creation of a universal empire. Such aspirations always remained in pipe dreams, but they strongly marked the ideology of medieval Bulgarian culture.

Institute of History, Bulgarian Academy of Sciences

ELEVEN

Connecting Moses and Muḥammad

JANE DAMMEN MCAULIFFE

Sometime at the very end of the ninth century or the beginning of the tenth, the Persian-born, Baghdādī polymath Abū Jaʿfar b. Jarīr al-Ṭabarī (d. 923/310) was putting the finishing touches on his universal chronicle, *The History of Prophets and Kings*. This enormous Arabic work begins with creation, moves through the periods of biblical prophets and patriarchs up to the time of Jesus, speaks of the Byzantines and Sasanians, elaborates the life of Muḥammad, and then chronicles the caliphs whose reigns span the first three Islamic centuries. In al-Ṭabarī's "History" we find the following anecdote:

> Moses sent out twelve chiefs, [one] from each of the Israelite tribes, who set out to bring him an account of the giants. One of the giants, who was called Og [ʿŪj or ʿĀj], met them [see Fig. 1]. He seized the twelve and placed them in his waistband, while on his head was a load of firewood. He took them off to his wife and said to her, "Look at these people who claim that they want to fight us." He flung them down in front of her, saying, "Shouldn't I grind them under my foot?" But his wife said, "No, rather let them go, so they will tell their people what they have seen."[1]

---

1   Abū Jaʿfar Muḥammad b. Jarīr al-Ṭabarī, *Taʾrīkh al-rusul wa-l-mulūk*, ed. M. J. de Goeje et al. (Leiden, 1879–1901), i, 498–99; *The History of al-Ṭabarī*, vol. 3, *The Children of Israel*, trans. W. Brinner (Albany, NY, 1991), 80–81. ʿŪj or ʿĀj b. ʿAnaq or ʿAnāq was the Arabic name of the biblical ʿOg, the giant king of Bashan. According to Abū Isḥāq Aḥmad b. Muḥammad al-Thaʿlabī, as quoted by B. Heller, "ʿŪdj was 23,333 cubits high, drank from the clouds, could reach to the bottom of the sea and pull out a whale which he roasted on the sun. Noah drove him in front of the ark but the Flood only reached his knees. He lived for 3,000 years." B. Heller-[S. M. Wasserstrom], "Ūdj," *EI*² 10:777–78.

FIGURE 1 *The giant Og with Moses, Muḥammad, and Jesus.* The giant Uj and the prophets Moses, Jesus, and Muḥammad, Baghdad or Tabriz, 15th century, opaque watercolors and gold on paper, 38 × 24.4 cm (photo courtesy of the Khalili Collections, London)

As al-Ṭabarī continues with this story, one related to the biblical account in Numbers 21:33–35, he interweaves phrases taken from the Qurʾān (Q 5:20–26, the qurʾānic passage that Muslim commentators have linked to the giant Og) with many non-qurʾānic details. Finally, al-Ṭabarī reaches the end of this anecdote:

> Ibn Bashshār—related to us—Muʾammal—Sufyān—Abū Isḥāq—Nawf: The base of Og's head was eight hundred cubits high, while Moses' height was [only] ten cubits and his staff [another] ten cubits. Then he [Moses] jumped into the air ten cubits and struck Og, hitting his anklebone. Og fell down dead, becoming a bridge for the people to cross over.[2]

Why would a tenth-century Muslim historian tell a tale of Moses taking a Superman-style leap to whack a giant with his rod? Why, more generally, would he devote a significant segment of his universal history to the story of Moses? Did he see a far greater continuity between earlier scriptures and the Qurʾān, between Moses as prophet and Muḥammad as prophet, than has generally been conceded?

The story of Moses as recounted in the biblical books from Exodus to Deuteronomy offers a prophet's portrait that is unmatched in scope and detail until the Gospels' portrayal of Jesus. Although the qurʾānic depiction of Moses is far more elusive and episodic, it does constitute the most complete prophetic portrayal to be found in the Qurʾān. Here are the highlights: exposed at birth but rescued through his sister's intervention, Moses eventually finds succor at his own mother's breast. He is raised in Pharaoh's household, but then forced to flee Egypt after coming to the rescue of an Israelite and killing the man's Egyptian attacker. Escaping to Madyan, he eventually marries the daughter of a shaykh to whom he has dedicated almost a decade of service. In a theophany in the valley of Ṭuwā, Moses is commissioned by God with a message for Pharaoh and provided with the signs of his prophethood. The subsequent encounters with Pharaoh, and with his magicians, result in multiple miracles, most of them devastating to the Egyptians. Moses' reception of the tablets of the Law, his destruction of them when he sees the golden calf, Israel's forty years in the wilderness—all echo events that receive much more elaboration in the Hebrew Bible.

---

2 Ṭabarī, *Taʾrīkh*, i, 501; Brinner, *History*, iii, 83.

The Question of Sources

A deceptively simple question presents itself when we read the Moses material in the Qurʾān—how did it get there? The several answers to this question open up multiple modes of qurʾānic studies, the different ways in which the Qurʾān has been read and interpreted. Certainly the answer given by most Muslim scholars of the Qurʾān, the theological answer, is swift and straightforward: Muḥammad knew about Moses because God told him. In the main, Muslim scholarly literature makes a clear theological claim about the relationship of the Hebrew Bible, and of the New Testament, to the Qurʾān. That literature recognizes that the three scriptures share much material and that the names of Abraham and Joseph, of Moses and Jesus cross these canons. They regard the Qurʾān as sequentially positioned in—to use a Christian category—the "stream of revelation." From this perspective the Qurʾān offers a divine re-presentation of the same truth that informed such predecessors as the Torah (*Tawrāh*) and Gospel (*Injīl*). Just as God revealed his will to Moses and to Jesus, he has done the same for Muḥammad, speaking in "clear Arabic"[3] for the benefit of this recipient and his followers. Viewed theologically, replication is not a product of biblical borrowings or influence but of re-revelation.

But uncompromising theological assertions were not the only answer that Muslim tradition gave to the question "How did Muḥammad know about Moses?" Various passages in the Qurʾān recount the charges levied against Muḥammad by hostile members of his early audiences. These opponents ridiculed Muḥammad's insistence that he was the recipient of divine revelation. They dismissed his claim with statements like "What he's telling us is a forgery and a falsehood," or "He's just repeating ancient fables (or writings) that have been recited to him," or, yet again, "He's being taught all this by mere mortals" (Q 25:4–5; 26:195; 16:103; 41:14, 44). But who were these surreptitious teachers? From whom was Muḥammad securing his information? Some recent studies have sifted through the anecdotes that can be found in ancient exegetical literature about Muḥammad's so-called "informants."[4] The composite profile that emerges from these studies presents us with a group of low-born foreigners,

---

3 bi-lisānin ʿarabiyyin mubīnin (Q.26:195) and the numerous references to *qurʾānan ʿarabiyyan*.
4 See especially, C. Gilliot, "Les 'informateurs' juifs et chrétiens de Muḥammad: Reprise d'un problème traité par Aloys Sprenger et Theodore Nöldeke," *Jerusalem Studies in Arabic and Islam* 22 (1998): 84–126 and idem, "Informants," *Encyclopaedia of the Qurʾān*, ed. J. D. McAuliffe (Leiden, 2000–2006), 2:512–18.

frequently slaves, who were nevertheless literate and could read the Torah and/or Gospel and who, in the eyes of Muḥammad's opponents, were the real source of his "revelation." Occasionally, Muḥammad's wife Khadīja is viewed as a conduit. Narratives (*asbāb al-nuzūl*) connected to the interpretation of Q 16:103, the *locus classicus* for the exegetical treatment of this issue, recount stories of Khadīja being taught by a Christian slave and, in turn, teaching Muḥammad.[5]

Interestingly, the qurʾānic rebuttal of these accusations is philological, as the key verse itself demonstrates. Faced with the charge that "a mere mortal is teaching him," Q 16:103 responds "the speech of him [i.e., the informant] at whom they hint is barbarous; and this [i.e., the Qurʾān] is pure Arabic." The rebuttal provided by later commentators and apologists, however, flips the category from "informant" to "predictor" or "prognosticator." As depicted in the Muslim exegetical sources, these so-called informants do not compromise either the Prophet's integrity or the priority of his scriptural knowledge. Rather they foreground Muḥammad as already fully aware of all he has been accused of surreptitiously studying.[6] More importantly, some of these figures are presented as recognizing or validating his prophethood.

One such story, probably the most famous, concerns a Syrian monk whose name is usually given as Baḥīrā. As related in the most esteemed biography of the Prophet, the *Sīra* of Ibn Isḥāq (d. 767/150), Muḥammad's uncle and guardian took him on a commercial caravan journey to Syria. To quote from Ibn Hishām's (d. 833/218) redaction of Ibn Isḥāq's *Sīra*: "When the caravan reached Buṣrā in Syria, there was a monk there in his cell by the name of Baḥīrā, who was well-versed in the knowledge of the Christians. A monk had always occupied that cell. There he gained his knowledge from a book that was in the cell, so they allege, handed on from generation to generation."[7]

Because of a premonition that came to him in prayer, Baḥīrā invited the entire caravan to dinner. Initially, the elders left the young Muḥammad to guard the baggage (Fig. 2) but, at the monk's insistence, they finally brought him forward. When "Baḥīrā saw him he stared at him closely, looking at his body and finding traces of his description (in the Christian books)." He quizzed the boy

---

5   Abū Isḥāq Aḥmad b. Muḥammad al-Thaʿlabī, *Al-Kashf wa-l-bayān ʿan tafsīr al-Qurʾān* (Beirut, 2002) 6:43.
6   Muḥammad b. Isḥāq, *Sīrat rasūl Allāh* (recension of ʿAbd al-Malik b. Hishām), trans. A. Guillaume as *The Life of Muhammad* (London, 1955), 193. Ṭabarī, *Taʾrīkh*, 1:1123–27; *The History of al-Ṭabarī*, vol. 6, *Muḥammad at Mecca*, trans. W. Montgomery Watt (Albany, 1988), 44–46.
7   Ibn Isḥāq, *Sīrat* (Guillaume), 79.

about his condition and circumstances (Fig. 3) and then "looked at his back and saw the seal of prophethood between his shoulders in the very place described in his book." Baḥīrā cautioned Muḥammad's uncle, Abū Ṭālib, to guard the boy "because a great future lies before this nephew of yours."[8]

Continuing with the question, How did biblical material find its way to the Qurʾān, we come, of course, to the world of Western, that is, non-Muslim scholarship on the Qurʾān. Here one discovers another long and productive tradition of academic work, much of it dating from the seminal publication of Abraham Geiger's nineteenth-century doctoral thesis at the University of Marburg, *Was hat Mohammed aus dem Judenthume aufgenommen?* ("What did Muhammad borrow from Judaism?"), which was published in English under the less provocative title *Judaism and Islam*.[9] Following upon Geiger's work came titles like *The Origin of Islam in Its Christian Environment*, *The Jewish Foundations of Islam*, *The Biblical Narratives in the Qurʾān*, and "The Christian Influence on the Qurʾān."[10] (Parenthetically, I should note that by confining myself to the last one hundred seventy-five years of non-Muslim scholarship, I am leaping over the centuries of premodern, polemical reading of the Qurʾān, centuries populated with people like John of Damascus, Peter the Venerable, and Martin Luther.)

Some of the more interesting versions of this post-Geiger line of scholarly exploration move beyond the unidirectional notion of biblical (and extrabiblical) influence on the Qurʾān—and post-qurʾānic literature—to look at how "the rich reservoirs of traditional lore tapped and channeled by the Qurʾān and its expounders"[11] have reentered Jewish and Christian sources of the medieval period and beyond. A fascinating example of such analysis traces the Solomon and Sheba story from the biblical narrative (1 Kings [3 Kingdoms LXX] 10:1–3), through midrashic and targumic material and then connects those sources with the qurʾānic account in Q 27:15–44. From there, the literary detective work moves to a much-elaborated version of the story to be found in al-Thaʿlabī's (d. 1035/427) eleventh-century "tales of the prophets."[12] The later reintegration of

---

8   Ibid., 80–81.
9   Bonn, 1833, and New York, 1898 (repr. 1970), respectively.
10 R. Bell, *The Origin of Islam in Its Christian Environment* (London, 1926); C. C. Torrey, *The Jewish Foundations of Islam* (New York, 1933); H. Speyer, *Die biblischen Erzählungen im Qoran* (Hildesheim, 1961); and E. Gräf, "Zu den christlichen Einflüssen im Koran," in *Al-Bāhith: Festschrift Joseph Henninger zum 70. Geburtstag am 12 Mai 1976* (St. Augustin bei Bonn, 1976), 111–44.
11 J. C. Reeves, "Some Explorations of the Intertwining of Bible and Qurʾān," in *Bible and Qurʾān: Essays in Scriptural Intertextuality*, ed. J. C. Reeves (Atlanta, 2003), 43.
12 Abū Isḥāq Aḥmad b. Muḥammad al-Thaʿlabī, *Qiṣaṣ al-anbiyāʾ al-musammā bi-ʿArāʾis al-majālis* (Cairo, 1960).

FIGURE 2 *Muḥammad stays with the baggage.* Muḥammad's prophetic nature is recognized by a monk, fol. 148a of *Qiṣaṣ al-anbiyā'* of Isḥāq b. Ibrāhīm b. Manṣūr b. Khalaf al-Naysābūrī, copied 1577, 21.3 × 13 cm (photo courtesy of Topkapı Palace Museum, Istanbul)

FIGURE 3 *Baḥīrā speaking with Muḥammad*. Muḥammad's prophethood recognized by the monk Baḥīrā, page from a dispersed *Anbiyāʾ-nāma*, Rachel Milstein et al., *Stories of the Prophets: Illustrated Manuscripts of Qiṣaṣ al-Anbiyāʾ* (Costa Mesa, CA, 1999), pl. XLII (photo courtesy of Rachel Milstein and Mazda Publications)

this now-Islamized material into nineteenth-century Hebrew literature and folklore brings the process full circle.[13]

More recent work has recast the whole question of specific forms of Jewish or Christian influence on the Qurʾān by suggesting a more pervasive connection. Studies by both Gunther Lüling and Christoph Luxenberg (pseudonym) have attempted, in different ways, to discern a Christian underlay of the present text of the Qurʾān. Lüling sees a pre-Islamic Christian liturgical text as a primitive layer, a text whose meanings have been Islamized and to which Muslim additions have been made. Lüling's thesis posits and then elaborates several stages of textual revision taking place before, during, and after the life of Muḥammad.[14] At some points, Lüling argues that certain qurʾānic vocabulary should be understood with meanings that are closer to Hebrew or Aramaic cognates than to significations in classical Arabic. Luxenberg expands this insight to assert that the literary Arabic of the Qurʾān is a product of a Christianized Syro-Aramaic culture. Concentrating upon passages considered "difficult" by both Muslim and Western scholars, that is, those that have generated widely variant interpretations, Luxenberg either translates the Arabic into Aramaic or tries to find an Aramaic reading for the Arabic consonants stripped of their diacriticals (*rasm*). Both approaches, particularly that of Luxenberg, have been sensationalized in the media and greeted with scholarly skepticism.[15]

The Question of Literary Function

The "source" question, the question about how biblical and extrabiblical material found its way into the Qurʾān, is but one of the issues that has captured the attention of both Muslim and Western scholarship as it contemplates the relation of these two scriptural traditions. Equally important have been literary

---

13   J. Lassner, *Demonizing the Queen of Sheba: Boundaries of Gender and Culture in Postbiblical Judaism and Medieval Islam* (Chicago–London, 1993). Lassner points to a 1702 Yemenite account in Hebrew by a certain Saadiah Ben Joseph and to material found in the Israel Folklore Archives. For a more recent work of intertextual analysis, see S. L. Lowin, *The Making of a Forefather: Abraham in Islamic and Jewish Exegetical Narratives* (Leiden, 2006).

14   G. Lüling, *Über den Ur-Qurʾān: Ansätze zur Rekonstruktion vorislamischer christlicher Strophenlieder im Qurʾān* (Erlangen, 1974; 2nd ed. 1993). Translation and reworking published as *A Challenge to Islam for Reformation* (Delhi, 2003).

15   C. Luxenberg (pseudonym), *Die syro-aramäische Lesart des Koran* (Berlin, 2000), translated in English as *The Syro-Aramaic Reading of the Koran: A Contribution to the Decoding of the Language of the Koran* (Berlin 2007). For a rendering of both Lüling and Luxenberg see H. Motzki, "Alternative Accounts of the Qurʾān's Formation," in *The Cambridge Companion to the Qurʾān*, ed. J. D. McAuliffe (Cambridge, 2006), 59–75.

queries about how this material functions in the Qur'ān. Speaking very generally, one can think of the prophet stories in the Qur'ān as preoccupied with both punishment and prefiguration. As a genre, these narratives exhibit a repetitive literary structure: God sends a prophet to a particular people; the people deride or ignore the prophet's warnings and pronouncements; God punishes the recalcitrant people and vindicates the prophetic message. Qur'ānic passages that fit this structure are frequently construed by Muslim commentators as providing solace or encouragement to the prophet Muḥammad. But in some instances they are interpreted as doing more than this. They prefigure Muḥammad as God's final prophet, the "seal of the prophets," and nowhere is the topos of prefiguration more pronounced than with the character of Moses (Fig. 4).

Moses' name is mentioned 136 times in the Qur'ān, far more than any other prophet. Direct and indirect allusions to Moses can be found throughout the text, and careful scholarship has traced the biblical and extrabiblical connections.[16] Virtually every major element in Muḥammad's prophetic vocation finds its counterpart in the life of Moses: divine protection in infancy; a theophanic election and prophetic commissioning; the public denial and rejection of each prophet's "signs" or proofs; God's gift of a "book" or "scripture"; the patient endurance of persecution; eventual divine deliverance and destruction of the enemy; the final triumph of the prophet's faithful followers. Each topic has been the subject of extended commentary and scholarly analysis, but I restrict my attention to one that captured particular pictorial attention—one of two great signs of Moses' prophethood, his rod.[17]

This rod's miraculous nature was first revealed as God spoke from the fire and commanded Moses to cast it down. When the rod began to writhe like a snake,

---

16   Y. Moubarac, "Moïse dans le Coran," in *Moïse: L'homme de l'alliance*, ed. H. Cazelles et al. (Paris, 1955); M. Causse, "Théologie de rupture et théologie de la communauté: Étude sur la vocation prophétique de Moïse d'après le Coran," *Revue d'histoire et de philosophie religieuses* 44 (1964): 60–82; Eng. trans., "The Theology of Separation and the Theology of Community: A Study of the Prophetic Career of Moses According to the Qur'ān," in *The Qur'ān: Style and Contents*, ed. A. Rippin (Aldershot, 2001), 37–60; R. Tottoli, *Vita di Mosè secondo le tradizioni islamiche* (Palermo, 1992), 373–91.

17   R. Tottoli, "Il bastone di Mosè mutato in serpente nell'esegesi e nelle tradizioni islamiche," *Annali dell'Istituto Universitario Orientale di Napoli* 51 (1991): 225–43 and 383–94. Looking also at both Jewish and Christian exegesis of the biblical account of Moses' rod, Tottoli draws upon the writings of Irenaeus (c. 190), Origen (d. 254), and Cyril of Jerusalem (d. 386) and their typological explanation of the rod's transformation as a prefiguration of the Incarnation and of the Crucifixion. The rod is counted among the sacred treasures of the Topkapı Palace in Istanbul. For a photograph and description see H. Aydın, *The Sacred Trusts: Pavilion of the Sacred Relics, Topkapı Palace Museum, Istanbul* (Somserset, NJ, 2004), 144–45. On the rod see above, pp. 12, 168, 191.

FIGURE 4 *Gabriel between Moses and Muḥammad.* The Prophets Moses and Muḥammad Conversing with the Archangel Gabriel, Turkey, 16th century, Gouache on paper, 31 × 20.5 cm, Museum für Islamische Kunst, Staatliche Museen zu Berlin, Berlin, Germany (photo courtesy of Bildarchiv Preussischer Kulturbesitz/Art Resource, NY)

Moses fled in fear (Fig. 5).[18] In Q 2:60 (cf. 7:160) Moses strikes a rock and twelve streams gush forth to satisfy his thirsty followers. In Q 26:63 he parts the sea with it and it swallows Pharaoh's pursuing army.[19] Jewish and Muslim sources give this rod a prehistory that stretches back to Adam and reaches Moses through the Arab prophet Shuʿayb, who is presented as Moses' father-in-law.[20] Surely the

18   Q 27:10; 28:31; 20:17–21; 7:107/26:32.
19   In medieval Islamic magical literature, such as the *Shams al-maʿārif wa-laṭāʾif al-ʿawārif* and *Manbaʿ uṣūl al-ḥikma* of Abū al-ʿAbbās al-Būnī (d. 1225), the words inscribed on Moses' rod (of which there are various listings) are the true source of its power. A. Fodor, "The Rod of Moses in Arabic Magic," *Acta Orientalia Academiae Scientiarum Hungaricae* 32 (1978): 9. Article reprinted in *Magic and Divination in Early Islam*, ed. E. Savage-Smith (Aldershot, 2004), 103–23.
20   B. Wheeler, "Moses," in *The Blackwell Companion to the Qurʾān*, ed. A. Rippin (Oxford, 2006), 260. See also Wheeler's *Moses in the Quran and Islamic Exegesis* (London, 2002). John Reeves's examination of postbiblical and post-Qurʾānic sources persuades him of a strong eschatological connection, a prospective scenario in which "the future agent of deliverance,

FIGURE 5 *Moses' rod turns into a snake/dragon at Madyan*. The Legends of the Prophets, Iran, 1580, manuscript on paper, fol. 74, 17.9 × 13.6 cm (photo courtesy of the Spencer Collection, The New York Public Library, Astor, Lenox, and Tilden Foundations)

most popular story, however, pits Moses' magic rod against the machinations of Pharaoh's sorcerers (Q 7:117): "And we inspired Moses, saying "Throw your rod," and thereupon it swallowed up their [the sorcerers'] lying show" (Fig. 6).

It is worth noting that the topos of a triumphant Moses, of God's intervention against the oppressions of Pharaoh, did not end with the Qurʾān.[21] Al-Ṭabarī's account of the final battle against the last Umayyad caliph, Marwān b. Muḥammad, much of whose army drowned when a pontoon bridge was cut, recalls the destruction of Pharaoh's army in the Red Sea. The words of Q 2:47 are placed in the mouth of ʿAbdallāh b. ʿAlī, the victorious ʿAbbāsid commander: "And we divided the sea for you, and delivered you, and drowned Pharaoh's people while you were beholding."[22] A more contemporary example of this trope is the political propaganda found frequently in today's Muslim world that casts the government and/or its leaders in the role of Pharaoh while the opposition and reformist forces don the mantle of Moses.

The Question of the Bible's Continuing Validity

The final question by which I will attempt to capture lines of scholarship that connect the Bible and Qurʾān brings us to the realm of what I have sometimes called "Muslim biblical studies." Beyond the questions of source identification to which, in their different ways, both Muslim and non-Muslim scholars have addressed themselves, and beyond the literary analysis that looks at how biblical topoi function in the Qurʾān, there stands the question of validity or viability. If, from a Qurʾān-centered perspective, revelation is sequential and supercessionist, does the Bible have any continuing value? Muslim scholarship offers two different responses to this question, maintaining an uneasy tension between them.

---

mirroring his ancient Mosaic prototype, will come equipped with a wonder-working 'staff,' perhaps even the very effective one previously wielded by Moses." *Trajectories in Near Eastern Apocalyptic: A Postrabbinic Jewish Apocalypse Reader* (Atlanta, 2005), 199.

21 The Constantinian identification with Moses at the battle of the Milvian Bridge is noted in Gilbert Dagron's study of the priestly role of the Byzantine emperor, *Emperor and Priest: The Imperial Office in Byzantium*, trans. J. Birrell (Cambridge, 2003), 98. As an important Byzantine relic, the Rod of Moses was one of the signs of imperial power used in the investiture ceremony for the emperor; ibid., 84. For an earlier treatment of its ceremonial use, see A. Pertusi, "Insigne del potere sovrano e delegate a Bisanzio e nei paesi di influenze bizantina," in *Simboli e simbologia nell' alto medioevo: XXIII Settimana di Studio del Centro Italiano di Studi sull' Alto Medioevo (3–9 aprile 1975)* (Spoleto, 1976), 2:515–16.

22 Ṭabarī, *Taʾrikh* (n. 1 above), 3:41; *The History of al-Ṭabarī: Volume XXVII; The ʿAbbāsid Revolution*, trans. J. A. Williams (Albany, 1985), 164–65.

FIGURE 6 *Moses' rod/snake swallows Pharaoh's magicians.* Musa's rod swallowing the magicians of Egypt and their arts, Stories of the Prophets, Iran, 15th century, manuscript, pl. X, 15.6 × 12.6 cm (photo courtesy of the Spencer Collection, The New York Public Library, Astor, Lenox, and Tilden Foundations)

On one side stands the long polemic of textual derogation. Subsumed under the technical term *taḥrīf*, meaning "alteration," this tradition stresses the corrupted nature of existing versions of the Jewish and Christian scriptures.[23] Certain verses in the Qurʾān lodge various charges against the continuing reliability of earlier revelations. Exegetical discussions of these indictments generated a substantial and complex literature, but for purposes of simplification they can be classified under the three general categories of concealing, changing, and misinterpreting. Precisely who was responsible for each of these activities, and to what degree, as well as when such textual manipulation occurred, remain contested issues in the classical sources.

Modes of scriptural distortion were sometimes thought to be contemporaneous with Moses and sometimes with Muḥammad. Ordinarily, conscious complicity was charged, especially of Muḥammad's Jewish and Christian contemporaries, but occasionally errors of transmission, both oral and scribal, were implicated. Although the sources sometimes mention legal or financial motives for scriptural distortion, overwhelmingly they ascribe it to theological obstinacy: Jews and Christians willfully refused to recognize or acknowledge the clear descriptions of Muḥammad and of his eventual appearance that could be found in their own scriptures.

This brings us to the second response made by Muslim biblical scholars to the "continuing validity" question—the assertion that these earlier scriptures announce, predict, and attest to Muḥammad, his prophethood, and the victories of his community. On the basis of specific qurʾānic clues, these scholars were convinced of the predictive value of prior scriptures and began to search the texts for the precise references to which certain qurʾānic verses alluded. The degree to which such activity was prompted by the obvious example of the Christian use of Jewish scripture remains a contested question within Islamic studies. Unquestionably, however, the precedent of creating a sectarian self-identity through both adoption and rejection of a prior scripture had already been set. The ostensible and stated mandate, however, for the Muslim scriptural search were passages in the Qurʾān that became the proof texts upon which the enterprise of what I would call "affirmative" Muslim biblical studies was erected.

A number of verses are repeatedly cited as qurʾānic warrant for searching the Hebrew Bible and the New Testament. Q 7:157, for example, begins: "Those who

---

23 For an extended discussion of both *taḥrīf* and of the predictive use of biblical material, see J. D. McAuliffe, "The Qurʾānic Context of Muslim Biblical Scholarship," *Islam and Christian-Muslim Relations* 7 (1996): 141–58.

follow the Messenger, the unlettered (*ummī*) prophet whom they find written with them in the Tawrāh and the Injīl, he orders them to do right and forbids them from doing wrong. He makes good things lawful for them and makes foul things prohibited to them. He rids them of their burden and the fetters (*aghlāl*) which were on them. Those who believe in him and honor and help him and follow the light which is sent down with him, those are the fortunate (*mufliḥūn*)."

Several elements of this passage encouraged classical scholars to search the Bible or, at least, to accumulate information that was assumed to have a biblical basis. The commentators regularly gloss the phrase *whom they find written with them in the Tawrāh and the Injīl* as the description (*naʿt* or *ṣifa*) of Muḥammad that is to be found in those books. Some commentators cite specific biblical passages, while others convey a more general sense of searching Jewish memory by repeating an affirmation associated with Kaʿb al-Aḥbār (d. 652–53/32), purportedly one of the earliest Jewish converts to Islam and a stock conduit in the Muslim conveyance of Jewish lore.

What kind of biblical verses caught the eye of Muslim exegetes as they searched the scriptures for those promised passages? A catalogue of the citations most commonly culled from the Hebrew Bible and the New Testament can be extracted from books of qurʾānic exegesis and those that tell the "stories of the prophets" (*qiṣaṣ al-anbiyāʾ*), from polemical treatises, from heresiographical works, and from a genre of Islamic literature devoted to the proofs of Muḥammad's prophethood (*dalāʾil al-nubuwwa*). These works span the centuries from the initial stages of Islamic literature to the present day.

After the pattern set by the earliest works, the regularly cited biblical passages are, for the most part, simply copied from one source to another, with set texts regularly used in support of set subjects. Those subjects themselves repeat themes of prophetic annunciation and description, of religious restoration and renewal, and of community inauguration and conquest. Many passages present verses and themes that became standard in Christian-Jewish polemic. For example, virtually the entire messianic typology that Christians drew from the Jewish scriptures was easily transferred to Muḥammad.

For example, when searching the Hebrew Bible, Muslim sources frequently note Deuteronomy 18:18 (NETS), "I will raise up for them a prophet just like you [Moses] from among their brothers, and I will give my word in his mouth, and he shall speak to them whatever I command him." This is interpreted as a direct reference to the advent of Muḥammad. Similarly, Moses' blessing in Deuteronomy 33:2 (NETS modified), "The Lord has come from Sinai and appeared to us from Seir and hasted from Mount Pharan," provided Muslim biblical exegetes with an opportunity to adduce Christianity's abrogation of Judaism and then Islam's abrogation of both.

Previously I noted a tension in Muslim biblical scholarship between denying the reliability of earlier scriptures and probing them for predictive proof texts. What remains a significant backdrop to both of these conversations is the large shadow cast by the doctrine of abrogation (*naskh*). For Muslims, the revelation of the Qurʾān effectively relegates earlier scriptures such as the Hebrew Bible to the status of museum pieces, items of antiquarian interest. Unlike Christian use of the Hebrew Bible, no continuing liturgical function was served by these earlier books, which remain foreign to the daily experience of most Muslims. Their viability has been usurped by God's final disclosure, and their continuing vitality can be assured only if they are understood and interpreted within a qurʾānic perspective. The Qurʾān, of course, confirms and corroborates those portions of the Torah and Gospel that remain valid, even if superfluous (Fig. 7).

A related attitude addresses that vast store of narrative that can be drawn from other Jewish and Christian sources. Muslim writers were not slow to access this treasure trove, and countless medieval works, whether exegetical, literary, historical, mystical or devotional, include this material. There was a catholicity of vision and spirit in many of these writings, and the enrichment provided by *isrāʾīliyyāt*—the term eventually used for this Jewish and Christian lore—was but one element of this attitude.[24] Eventually, however, a more restrictive attitude prevailed and continues to predominate. Biblical and extrabiblical material that fell beyond the boundaries of the Qurʾān was ignored or dismissed, discouraging the further development of Muslim biblical scholarship—but perhaps not permanently.

A Concluding Comment on "Connecting"

Where will future intersections of biblical and qurʾānic scholarship, of connecting Moses and Muḥammad be found? Anyone attempting an answer must first take note of a new willingness in the academic study of religious texts to ask comparative questions and to raise intertextual investigation. During the second half of the twentieth century "comparative religion" and comparative studies generally became suspect. Such work was discouraged because it was deemed either superficial or so skewed to one side of the comparative equation that the

---

24 See J. D. McAuliffe, "Assessing the Isrāʾīliyyāt: An Exegetical Conundrum," in *Story-telling in the Framework of Nonfictional Arabic Literature*, ed. S. Leder (Wiesbaden, 1999), 345–69.

FIGURE 7 *Muḥammad leads Abraham, Moses, and Jesus in prayer.* Iran, manuscript (photo courtesy of Bibliothèque nationale de France, Paris)

results were inevitably unreliable. Particularly in fields that required substantial philological preparation, the command of several languages and their associated bodies of literature was not often found in a single scholar. There was also a methodological uneasiness at the prospect of imposing, inappropriately or inadequately, a set of categories or a vocabulary drawn from one tradition onto another. In some cases these efforts were roundly excoriated as imperialist or hegemonic. Even when viewed more benignly, such approaches struck many as veering too close to a missionary spirit that compares in order to contrast negatively.[25]

More recently, however, scholars of the Qurʾān and scholars of the Bible have begun to search for confluence and connection, particularly in the analysis of their respective exegetical histories. An inaugural conference that I hosted in 1997 in Toronto on comparative exegetical practice in Judaism, Christianity, and Islam has been followed by dedicated attention to this topic in two major professional societies, the American Academy of Religion and the Society of Biblical Literature. In the publications that these initiatives have generated, scholars have traced the hermeneutical similarities to be found in texts produced in very different times and places. They have noted commonalities of textual reception across a broad range of production and dissemination conventions. While conscious of the danger of false or facile comparison, scholars of comparative exegesis have focused on the parallel practices of glossing and periphrasis, of both inner-qurʾānic and inner-biblical interpretation. They have also attended to philological and historical intersections and to the ways in which interpretive actions create structures of authority and of restricted textual access.[26]

Concurrently, the efforts I have described to view the Qurʾān within a broader historical and geographical framework will continue to expand. In the last several decades the study of Islamic origins has increasingly situated itself within the larger arena of the world of late antiquity.[27] While such efforts were

---

25 An effort to resuscitate the comparative perspective within religious studies generally is presented in K. C. Patton and B. C. Ray, *A Magic Still Dwells: Comparative Religion in the Postmodern Age* (Berkeley, 2000).
26 Relevant publications include J. D. McAuliffe, B. D. Walfish, and J. W. Goering, eds., *With Reverence for the Word: Medieval Scriptural Exegesis in Judaism, Christianity, and Islam* (New York, 2002) and J. C. Reeves, ed., *Bible and Qurʾān: Essays in Scriptural Intertextuality* (Atlanta, 2003).
27 A helpful entry into this line of investigation is offered by R. G. Hoyland in his *Seeing Islam as Others Saw It: A Survey and Evaluation of Christian, Jewish, and Zoroastrian Writing on Early Islam* (Princeton, 1997). Very recent scholarship is presented in G. S. Reynolds, ed., *The Qurʾān in Its Historical Context* (London, 2008).

not absent from earlier generations of qur'ānic scholarship, they have assumed centrality in the last several decades. As sophisticated, source-critical perspectives have come to dominate the study of early Islamic history, blurring the demarcation between Muslim and non-Muslim sources, the interpretive value of extra-Islamic material is growing more widely recognized and more fully integrated. New readings and fresh assessments of Greek, Syriac, Hebrew, Coptic, Armenian, and Persian texts beckon those scholars who seek to enhance our understanding of the full historico-cultural context of the Qur'ān's genesis and of its relations to earlier sacred literatures.

Bryn Mawr College

ABBREVIATIONS

AB	*Analecta Bollandiana*
AbhGött, Philol.-hist.Kl.	Akademie der Wissenschaften, Göttingen, Philologisch-historische Klasse, Abhandlungen
ACO	*Acta conciliorum oecumenicorum*, ed. E. Schwartz and J. Straub (Berlin, 1914–)
AnnalesESC	*Annales: Économies, sociétés, civilisations*
AnzWien	Anzeiger der [Österreichischen] Akademie der Wissenschaften, Wien, Philosophisch-historische Klasse
AP	*Apophthegmata patrum*
ArtB	*Art Bulletin*
BBTT	Belfast Byzantine Texts and Translations
BBulg	*Byzantinobulgarica*
BHG	*Bibliotheca hagiographica graeca*, 3rd ed., ed. F. Halkin, SubsHag 47 (Brussels, 1957; repr. 1969)
BMFD	*Byzantine Monastic Foundation Documents: A Complete Translation of the Surviving Founders' "Typika" and Testaments*, ed. J. Thomas and A. C. Hero (Washington, DC, 2000)
BMGS	*Byzantine and Modern Greek Studies*
BollGrott	*Bollettino della Badia greca di Grottaferrata*
BZ	*Byzantinische Zeitschrift*
CahArch	*Cahiers archéologiques*
CCSG	Corpus christianorum, Series graeca
CFHB	Corpus fontium historiae byzantinae

CPG	*Clavis patrum graecorum*, ed. M. Geerard and F. Glorie (Turnhout, 1974–87)
CSEL	Corpus scriptorum ecclesiasticorum latinorum
CTh	*Theodosiani libri XVI cum constitutionibus Sirmondianis et leges novellae ad Theodosianum pertinentes*, ed. Th. Mommsen and P. M. Meyer (Berlin, 1905)
DOP	*Dumbarton Oaks Papers*
DOS	Dumbarton Oaks Studies
DSp	*Dictionnaire de spiritualité ascétique et mystique*
ΔXAE	*Δελτίον τῆς Χριστιανικῆς ἀρχαιολογικῆς ἑταιρείας*
EHR	*English Historical Review*
Ἐκκ.Φάρ.	*Ἐκκλησιαστικῆς Φάρος*
EI²	*Encyclopaedia of Islam*, 2nd ed. (Leiden–London, 1960–)
FM	*Fontes minores*
GBA	*Gazette des beaux-arts*
GCS	Die griechischen christlichen Schriftsteller der ersten [drei] Jahrhunderte
HTR	*Harvard Theological Review*
IM	*Istanbuler Mitteilungen*
JEChrSt	*Journal of Early Christian Studies*
JHS	*Journal of Hellenic Studies*
JÖB	*Jahrbuch der Österreichischen Byzantinistik* [note: before 1969, *JÖBG*]
JÖBG	*Jahrbuch der Österreichischen Byzantinischen Gesellschaft* [note: after 1968, *JÖB*]
JSAH	*Journal of the Society of Architectural Historians*
JTS	*Journal of Theological Studies*
JWarb	*Journal of the Warburg and Courtauld Institutes*
Lampe	G. W. H. Lampe, ed., *A Patristic Greek Lexicon* (Oxford, 1961)
LXX	Septuagint
Mansi	J. D. Mansi, *Sacrorum conciliorum nova et amplissima collectio* (Paris–Leipzig, 1901–27)
MedSt	*Mediaeval Studies*, Pontifical Institute of Mediaeval Studies
MGH, Auct. Ant.	Monumenta Germaniae historica, Auctores antiquissimi
MGH Poetae	Monumenta Germaniae historica, Poetae latini medii aevi
NachrGött	*Nachrichten von der Akademie [Gesellschaft] der Wissenschaften zu Göttingen*, Philologisch-historische Klasse
NETS	*A New English Translation of the Septuagint*

OCA	*Orientalia christiana analecta*
OCP	*Orientalia christiana periodica*
ODB	*The Oxford Dictionary of Byzantium*, ed. A. Kazhdan et al. (New York–Oxford, 1991)
OHBS	E. Jeffreys, J. Haldon, and R. Cormack, eds., *Oxford Handbook of Byzantine Studies* (Oxford, 2008)
PG	Patrologiae cursus completus, Series graeca, ed. J.-P. Migne (Paris, 1857–66)
PW	*Paulys Real-Encyclopädie der classischen Altertumswissenschaft*, ed. G. Wissowa (Leipzig, 1893–)
RAC	*Reallexikon für Antike und Christentum*
RBK	*Reallexikon zur byzantinischen Kunst*, ed. K. Wessel (Stuttgart, 1963–)
REB	*Revue des études byzantines*
RESEE	*Revue des études sud-est européennes*
RSBN	*Rivista di studi bizantini e neoellenici*
RSV	Revised Standard Version
SC	Sources chrétiennes
Settimane	*Settimane di studio del centro italiano di studi sull'alto medioevo*
StP	*Studia patristica*
SubsHag	Subsidia hagiographica
TLG	Thesaurus Linguae Graecae
TM	*Travaux et mémoires*
TU	Texte und Untersuchungen zur Geschichte der altchristlichen Literatur (Leipzig–Berlin, 1882–)
VChr	*Vigiliae christianae*
VizVrem	*Vizantiiskii vremennik*
WByzSt	Wiener byzantinistische Studien
ZhMNP	*Zhurnal Ministerstva Narodnogo Prosveshcheniia*
ZRVI	*Zbornik radova Vizantološkog instituta, Srpska akademija nauka*

ABOUT THE AUTHORS

IVAN BILIARSKY is Senior Fellow at the Institute of History, Bulgarian Academy of Sciences and Professor in Law History, University of Varna. He works on the history of law and its institutions, juridical and political terminology, and the religious basis of political ideology and of identity. Recent work includes *The Biblical Models of Power and Law / Les modèles bibliques du pouvoir et du droit* (edited with R. G. Păun, 2008) and *Juridical Terminology in Mediaeval Bulgaria* (forthcoming).

NICHOLAS DE LANGE is Professor of Hebrew and Jewish Studies at the University of Cambridge. He directed the research project "The Greek Bible in Byzantine Judaism," funded by the Arts and Humanities Research Council, and is coeditor of *Jewish Reception of Greek Bible Versions* (with Julia G. Krivoruchko and Cameron Boyd-Taylor, 2009).

ELIZABETH JEFFREYS is Bywater and Sotheby Professor of Byzantine and Modern Greek Language and Literature Emerita of Oxford University, and Emeritus Fellow of Exeter College, Oxford. Among her recent books are *The Age of the Dromon* (with John Pryor, 2006) and *Iacobi Monachi Epistulae* (with Michael Jeffreys, 2009).

DEREK KRUEGER, Professor of Religious Studies at the University of North Carolina at Greensboro, is the editor of *Byzantine Christianity* (2006). He has written on hagiography, the cult of saints, monasticism, and hymnography, and is currently investigating the liturgical formation of identity and the place of desire in monastic literature.

JOHN LOWDEN is Professor of History of Art at the Courtauld Institute of Art, University of London. His latest books include *Medieval Ivories and Works of Art* (with John Cherry, 2008) and *The Jaharis Gospel Lectionary* (2009).

PAUL MAGDALINO studied at Oxford and taught for most of his career at the University of St Andrews. He has also held appointments at Harvard and Koç University, Istanbul, and served on the board of Senior Fellows in Byzantine Studies at Dumbarton Oaks from 2001 to 2007. He has published extensively on many aspects of medieval Byzantine history.

JANE DAMMEN MCAULIFFE is President of Bryn Mawr College and formerly Dean of the College at Georgetown University. Her research focuses on the Qurʾān, early Islamic history and the interactions of Islam and Christianity. She has recently published the six-volume *Encyclopaedia of the Qurʾān* (2001–6) and is the editor of the *Cambridge Campanion to the Qurʾān* (2006).

JAMES MILLER, an independent scholar residing in Milwaukee, Wisconsin, studies the Old Testament, especially the Septuagint. His concern for the history of liturgy developed while studying in Orthodox seminaries. His dissertation on the Biblical Odes in the Codex Alexandrinus builds upon his research into Old Testament lectionaries and the Prophetologion.

ROBERT NELSON has long been interested in illuminated Greek religious manuscripts, their social uses as objects, as well as the interplay of text and image. He teaches Byzantine art at Yale University, where he is currently chair of Medieval Studies and of Renaissance Studies.

ROBERT OUSTERHOUT, a specialist in Byzantine architecture, is Professor in the History of Art Department at the University of Pennsylvania, where he also serves as Director of the Center for Ancient Studies. He writes frequently about the monuments of Constantinople, Jerusalem, and Cappadocia.

GEORGI R. PARPULOV studied history and art history at the universities of Sofia, Chicago, Illinois (Urbana-Champaign), and Vienna. He has worked at the Walters Art Museum in Baltimore, where he published "A Catalogue of the Greek Manuscripts of the Walters" (2004). At present he is lecturer in Byzantine art and archaeology at the University of Oxford.

CLAUDIA RAPP is a professor in the Department of History at the University of California, Los Angeles. Educated at the Freie Universität Berlin and Oxford University, she has taught at Cornell, Utrecht, and the Central European University (Budapest). Her publications have dealt with hagiography, literary culture, and the Church in late antiquity and Byzantium. She is now writing a monograph on ritual brotherhood (adelphopoiesis) in Byzantium.

INDEX

Page numbers in *italics* indicate illustrative material.

Aaron (OT patriarch), 125, 163, 193, 203, 208, 266
'Abdallāh b. 'Alī, 291
Abraham (OT patriarch)
  altar of, Jerusalem (no longer extant), 238–39
  in Byzantine dating structure, 163
  covenant with, 155
  in Eucharistic prefigurations, 155, 172
  in Islam, 282, 287n13, *296*
  as monastic model, 201–9 *passim*, 214, 215n59, 220
Acts of Peter, 157n15
Adam (OT figure)
  in Bagrationi genealogy, 273
  Byzantine dating structure and, 158, 163–65, 170
  Golgotha and Mount Moriah, association with, 239
  in monastic readings of OT, 215–16
  Rod of Moses and, 289
  as typology for Christ, 179, 216
Adam and Eve ivory and bone caskets
  Cleveland Museum of Art, 145–46
  Darmstadt, Landesmuseum, 145–46
  Milan, Museo delle arti decorative, Castello Sforzesco, 145–46
  New York, Metropolitan Museum of Art, 145–46, *149*
  St. Petersburg, Hermitage Museum, 145–46
Adler, William, 163
Adomnan (abbot of Iona), 238n52, 239
Africanus. *See* Julius Africanus
Ağaçlı Kilise, Güzelöz, 231–32
Agapetos, 192
Agathias (author), 185
Agesilaos of Sparta, 194
Ahab, as negative OT imperial model, 176, 187–88, 192
al-Aḥbār, Ka'b, 294
Akathistos hymn/service, 17, 93, 101
Akylas (Aquila; translator of OT into Greek), 4, 44–48, 50–53
Alculf (bishop and pilgrim to Jerusalem), 239
Alexander, Paul, 173
Alexander the Great, 164, 182, 194, 196
Alexandrinus codex (London, British Library, MS Royal I.D.v–viii), 108n4, 154, 218n72
Alexios I Komnenos (emperor), 111
allegorical readings of OT, 213–16

altar of Abraham (Jerusalem relic; no longer extant), 238–39
Ambrose of Milan, 181, 232
American Academy of Religion, 297
Amiatinus codex (Florence, Biblioteca Medicea-Laurenziana [Laur.], siglum A), 108–9
Amos (biblical book), 270n61
Amphilochia (Photios), 6n20, 169
amulets, Solomon depicted on, 74
Anastasios I (emperor), 171, 194, 245
Anastasios of Sinai, 18n66, 28n116, 169
Anastasis Church, Jerusalem, Enkainia of, 235, 251
Anderson, Jeffrey, 119
Andrew of Crete, 6, 18n66, 26
Andronikos II (emperor), 36, 38
Andronikos III (emperor), 38
Angelov, Dimiter, 196
Anicia Juliana, 14, 243–47
annus mundi (Byzantine dating structure), 157–58
Antioch
  Persian siege of, 14, 171–72
  stone sculpture from (Princeton, University Art Museum), 144–45, *146*
Antirrheticus (Evagrios Pontikos), 219–20
Antony the hermit (saint), 201, 202, 210
Aphraat (holy man), 185
Apocalypse of Daniel, 258
apocalyptic
  in Bulgarian use of OT models for the state, 264
  in chronicle of John Malalas, 160, 172
  Islam, Moses in, 289–91
  Jewish versus Christian, 5, 28–29
  in Russian use of OT models for the state, 272
  Temple, problem of representation of, 225
apocryphal and pseudepigraphical texts
  Bulgaria, OT models for the state in, 258, 261–62
  common roots of Judaism and Christianity visible in, 30
  history, Byzantine understanding of, 154, 156–57, 167, 169
  Octateuchs, camel-like serpent in, 143
  "The Temple of the Lord," use of, 10. *See also* names of specific texts
Apocryphal Chronicle, Bulgarian, 256, 258–59, 262–70, 276
Apophthegmata patrum, 200, 201–6, 208, 213, 217
Apuleius, 167
Aquila (Akylas; translator of OT into Greek), 4, 44–48, 50–53
Aramaic (language), 4, 40, 41, 50, 287
architecture, Byzantine. *See* sacred space in Byzantine architecture
Archival Chronicle (Chronograph), 259–60
Aref/Arethas (Bulgarian ruler mentioned in *Apocryphal Chronicle*), 259
Areobindos (husband of Anicia Juliana), 245
Arethas of Caesarea, 6n15, 22
Argive kings, 164
Arianism, 185, 187, 191–92
Aristeas, Letter of, 111–15, *112*, 154n1
Aristotle, 177
Ark, Noahide, 179, 224
Ark of the Covenant, 3, 22, 25, 74n53, 274–75
Armenia, OT models for the state in, 272–73, 275–76
Arsenios (abba), 208, 210
Artemios (saint), *Miracles* of, 89n50
Asan Palaiologos family, 114
asceticism. *See* monasticism and the OT in Byzantium
Ascetic Sermon (Ephraem the Syrian), 103n114
Ashot the Curopalate, 269, 273
Asparuch (Ispor; Bulgar khan), 266, 269
Assyrian empire, OT contribution to Byzantine understanding of, 155–56, 161, 170–72
Athanasia of Aegina, 91
Athanasios of Alexandria
  on canon, 59n7
  emperors, OT models for, 154, 163n43, 179n14, 191–92
  monasticism, OT models for, 191–92, 199, 209–10, 217–18
  on psalmody as part of personal devotions, 80–81, 83, 85n42
Athens, National Library of Greece MS 3, 89, *90*

MS 15, 84n39
Athos manuscripts
　MS Dionysiou 65, 96–97
　MS Iveron 22, 91n61
　MS Lavra Δ 45, 82n24
　MS Lavra Δ 70, 83n29
　MS Pantokratoros 43, 91n61
　MS Vatopedi 602. *See* Vatopedi Octateuch
　MS Vatopedi 625, 82n24
　MS Zographou slav. I.Δ.13 (Radomir Psalter), 92n63
Attila the Hun, 268
Augustine of Hippo (saint), 59n7
Augustus Caesar, 167n55, 177, 178, 194
Auxentios (abbot), 6n15
Avars, Persian alliance with, 15–19, 27, 173, 194–95
Avitochol (mythical Bulgar prince), 256, 268
Azotios (in *Patria Constantinopoleos*), 269
azymes, Byzantine accusations of judaizing based on Latin use of, 30

Babylonian empire, OT contribution to Byzantine understanding of, 155–56
Bačkovo, Monastery of the Mother of God Petritzonitissa at, 219
Bagrationi dynasty (Caucasus), 272–74
Baḥīrā (Syrian monk), 283–84, *285–86*
Baḥīrā speaking with Muḥammad, page from a dispersed *Anbiyā'-nāma*, 283–84, 286
baptism, 179, 214, 232
"barbarians"
　Avars, Persian alliance with, 15–19, 27, 173, 194–95
　Bulgarians as, 255, 268
　Vandals, Temple relics recovered from, 248
Barberini Euchologion (Vat. Barber. gr. 336), 190n55, 191
Barberini Psalter (Vat. Barber. gr. 372), 95n78
Bardill, Jonathan, 245–46
Bar Kochba coinage, Temple images on, 237
Barsanouphios and John, *Questions and Answers*, 78n4, 83n32, 84n36, 95n81, 214n56

Basil I (emperor), 6, 22, 29, 249
Basil II (emperor), 23
　Menologion of, 23, 24
　Psalter of (Venice, Biblioteca Marciana, MS gr. 17), 82–83, 114
Basil of Caesarea (saint), 6n15, 200, 210–12, 213, 219
Basil (metropolitan of Neopatras), 28n116
Basil the Younger (saint), 26–27
Basileios *kalligraphos*, 132
basilicas, 227
BAV (Rome, Biblioteca Apostolica Vaticana). *See* Vatican Library
Beatrice, Pier, 166
bema, 231–32, 252
Bernabò, Massimo, 109, 111, 143
Bernard the Monk, 238n52
Bessarion (Vat. Lib. MS Grottaferrata G.b.I), 190–91n55
Bible
　Byzantine lack of familiarity with, as a whole, 55–59
　Islam, validity in, 291–95
　manuscript record of whole Bibles/whole OTs, 57
　Slavonic, translations into, 64, 259–61
　spiritual exegesis and allegory, monastic, 213–16
　See also canon of Old Testament in Byzantium; Greek (language), translations of OT into; New Testament in Byzantium; Old Testament in Byzantium; *specific books, e.g.,* Genesis
Bibles moralisées, 34, 150–52
biblical realism, 208
Biliarsky, Ivan, 255, 303
bishops, OT models for emperors used by, 180–81, 188–92, 197
BL. *See* London, British Library (BL)
Blachernae, imperial palace at, 36
Blanche of Castile (queen of France), 151
Blues and Greens (charioteer teams, Constantinople), 178, 188
Bodleian Library. *See* Oxford, Bodleian Library
Bolman, Elizabeth, 231
Bologna, University Library, MS 3574, 47n18
Book of Ceremonies, 11–12, 188

Book of Iannes and Iambres, 157, 167–69
Book of the Prefect (Book of the Eparch), 10, 21
Boris and Gleb (Russian saints), 271–72
Bradshaw, Paul, 80
Branham, Joan, 229
Breviarium (Patriarch Nikephoros), 187
Breviarius (ca. 500), 238, 239
British Library. *See* London, British Library
Buchthal, Hugo, 24
Bulgaria, OT models for the state in, 8, 255–77
    Apocryphal Chronicle, 256, 258–59, 262–70, 276
    compared to other peripheral Christian states, 270–76
    judaizers, 257–58
    the king, 265–70
    knowledge of/familiarity with OT, 259–62
    List of the Names of Bulgar Princes (Khans), 256–58, 262, 263, 265, 268, 271, 275, 276
    new Israel, Bulgarian state and people as, 256–57, 262–65, 275, 276
    Nikephoros compared to Ahab/Pharaoh, 187
Burton-Christie, Douglas, 202–3
Byron, George Gordon, Lord, 170
Byzantine chronicle. *See* Christian world chronicle
Byzantine studies, 2–3
Byzantium, Old Testament in. *See* Old Testament in Byzantium

Cain and Abel (OT characters), 271–72
Cairo Genizah manuscripts, 40, 45–46, 47, 48, 49
Cambridge, MA, Houghton Library, MS gr. 3 (Harvard Psalter), 91n61, 95–96, 96n86
Cambridge, UK, Fitzwilliam Museum 364*, 49–50
Cambridge, UK, University Library
    MS T-S C6.117, 48n23
    MS T-S K24.14, 48n21
    MS T-S Misc. 28.74, 47n19
    MS T-S NS 309.9, 48n20

Cambridge, UK, Westminster College, Talmudica I.110, 48n23
Cameron, Averil, 196
canonical hours, 85, 101
canon law, 18, 19, 27
canon of Old Testament in Byzantium
    concept of, 59–60n7
    gradual development of, 154
    monasticism and, 200, 203, 205, 211, 220–21
    Prophetologion and, 59, 66n29, 67–68, 73, 74–76
    Testament of Solomon and, 74–75
    variations in different Christian traditions, 2, 154
    See also apocryphal and pseudepigraphical texts
canons, hymnographic, 85, 101
Canticles or Odes in psalters, 85, 100
Capitula admonitoria (Agapetus), 192
Cappadocia, painted templon or chancel barrier from, 231
Carolingian Francia, 9, 30
Cassiodorus, 108, 175n2
catenae
    captions derived from, 137
    Jewish midrash compared to, 42
    on lectionary, 55
    monastic, 218n72
    Octateuch catena manuscripts, 110n15, 114, 117, 119–20, 127, 131
    Octateuchs, marginal catenae in, 110, 120, 151
    psalters with, 82, 83
    See also commentaries; glosses and glossaries; scholia
Caucasus, OT models for states of, 272–74
Cave of Treasures, 143
Ceremonies, Book of, 11–12, 188
Chalcedon, Council of (451), 13, 188–89, 246
chalice of Solomon (Hagia Sophia, Constantinople; no longer extant), 249
Chapters on Love (Maximos the Confessor), 204
Chios, Nea Mone church, mosaic of the Anastasis, 248–50, *250*
Chora, Church of the, Constantinople

(Kariye Camii, Istanbul), 31, *33*, 36–38, *37*, 113, 231, *232*, 252
chosen people. *See* new Israel, identification of Christian Byzantium as
Chosroes (Persian ruler), 183
Christianization of Old Testament in Byzantium, 3–4, 8
Christian sources for Islamic portrayals of Moses, 282–87, 293
Christian Topography (attrib. Kosmas Indikopleustes), 14, 131, 133–41, 143, 169
Christian world chronicle
  defined, 157–58
  development of, 157–61
  OT sources, complex relationship to, 153–54
  See also John Malalas
Christmas, feast of, 64n25, 71
1 and 2 Chronicles (biblical books), 108n4, 224n5, 270
Chronicon Paschale, 153n, 158, 160, 163n39, 171n70, 186–87
Chronograph (Archival Chronicle), 259–60
church architecture. *See* sacred space in Byzantine architecture
Church History (Eusebios). *See* Eusebios of Caesarea
Cleopa (brother of Joseph the husband of the Virgin Mary), 273
Codex Alexandrinus (London, British Library, MS Royal I.D.v–viii), 108n4, 154, 218n72
Codex Amiatinus (Florence, Biblioteca Medicea-Laurenziana [Laur.], siglum A), 108–9
Codex Grandior (no longer extant), 108
Codex Sinaiticus (London, British Library, Add. MS 43725), 154
Codex Vaticanus (Vat. MS gr. 1209), 154
coins and coinage
  Bar Kochba coinage, Temple images on, 237
  Rex regnantium coins of Justinian II, 18, 29
Cometopouloi, 258, 266
commentaries
  Jewish, 42, 48–49

psalters with and without, 82–83
  of St. Basil on Isaiah, 6n15
  See also catenae; glosses and glossaries; scholia
comparatio or *synkresis*, OT models for emperors in mode of, 180, 194
comparative religion, future studies in, 295–98
Constantine I (emperor)
  Bulgarian use of OT models for the state and, 263–65, 267, 269
  OT models for emperors, 13, 176, 178, 182–83, 187–90 *passim*, 193, 267, 291n21
  sacred space in Byzantine architecture and, 226–27, 248
Constantine V (emperor), 19–20, 187
Constantine VII Porphyrogenitus (emperor), 11, 22–25, 173, 191n56, 269, 273
Constantine IX Monomachos (emperor), 249–50
Constantine-Cyril (saint), 6n15, 28n116, 45
Constantinople
  Blues and Greens (charioteer teams), 178, 188
  Chora, Church of the (Kariye Camii, Istanbul), 31, *33*, 36–38, *37*, 113, 231, *232*, 252
  Hagia Sophia (Great Church), 14, 229, 239–43, *240*, 247–52, 261
  Jerusalem, identification with, 16–17
  liturgical celebration of founding of, 68
  Nea Ekklesia, 22, 29, 249
  Persian/Avar attack on (626), failure of, 16–17
  Pharos Church, 29, 31
  St. Polyeuktos, 14, 243–47, *244*, 252
  SS. Sergios and Bacchos, 245–47
  as second Jerusalem, 14
  Sleepless Monks, Monastery of, 85n39
  Theotokos Evergetis, Monastery of the, 204
  Virgin Hodegetria icon (destroyed in Ottoman conquest), 38
  See also Great Palace, Constantinople
Constantius II (emperor), 191–92, 194
Contra Apionem (Josephus), 154n2, 164n44

Copenhagen, Royal Library, cod. GKS 6, 120
Coptic *Life of Makarios of Alexandria*, 208
Corippus (epic poet), 194, 242
Cotton Genesis (BL MS Cotton Otho B.VI), 8, 144
councils of the church
    Chalcedon (451), 13, 188–89, 246
    Quinisext Council (Council in Trullo; 692), 18, 19
Covenant, Ark of the, 3, 22, 25, 74n53, 274–75
Covenant history, Byzantine understanding of, 155
Croke, Brian, 246
Cross. *See* True Cross
Cyprus Plates (David Plates; New York, Metropolitan Museum of Art, and Nicosia, Cyprus, Museum of Antiquities), 17, 29, 181, 248n97
Cyril (saint and apostle to the Slavs), 259n21, 260–61, 265
Cyril of Jerusalem, 59n7, 154, 236–37, 288n17
Cyrus (Persian ruler), 156, 182, 194

Dagron, Gilbert, 173, 176, 226, 241, 247, 248, 249
Daniel (biblical book/prophet)
    apocalyptic interpretation of, 5
    emperors, as model for, 175
    as monastic model, 201, 207, 209, 211, 212
    monastic use of, 209, 212
    succession of world empires in, 14, 28
Daniel, Apocalypse of, 258
Daniélou, Jean, 179
Daniel the Stylite, 14n52
Danube associated with River Jordan, 263–64
Darius I (Persian ruler), 156
David (OT king)
    Bulgaria, OT models for the king in, 266, 269–70
    in Byzantine dating structure, 163
    Caucasus, OT models for the king in, 272–73, 275–76
    emperors identified with, 22–25, 29, 173, 176, 181–96 *passim*, 248
    horn of the anointing of, displayed at Hagia Sophia, Constantinople, 243, 249
    as monastic model, 201–6 *passim*, 210, 214, 217, 218, 220
    Pharos Chapel representation of, 31
    psalter portraits of, 93–95, *94*
    synchronism with Priam, 170
David of Thessalonike, *Life* of, 208
David Plates (Cyprus Plates; New York, Metropolitan Museum of Art, and Nicosia, Cyprus, Museum of Antiquities), 17, 29, 181, 248n97
De administrando imperio (Constantine VII Porphyrogenitus), 11n38, 24, 273
Deesis, 95
De fide orthodoxa (John of Damascus), 259
De Lange, Nicholas, 39, 303
De' Maffei, Fernanda, 125–26
Demetrius (saint), martyrdom of, 272n67
demons
    OT phrases used to combat, 219–20
    Solomon's control over and building of Temple, 238
Deuteronomy (biblical book)
    identification of Christian Byzantium with Israel described in, 13, 18
    illustrated Octateuchs, 124
    Islamic use of, 294–95
    monastic models drawn from, 205, 211
    as text in Octateuch and Pentateuch, 107
Dictys of Crete, 170n66, 171
Diegesis peri tes Hagias Sophias, 239, 241
Digenes Akrites, 23
Diocletian (emperor), 175, 181, 186
discipline, monastic, OT models for, 210–12
dish divination (lekanomancy), 169
doxai, rubrication of psalms by, 89
Ducas (historian), 38
Dura Europos synagogue paintings, 144, 237

Easter (Pascha), 63n19, 64n25, 66–67, 71–72, 160
Ecclesiastes (biblical book), 7, 47, 53
ecclesiastical architecture. *See* sacred space in Byzantine architecture
Ecclesiasticus (Sirach; biblical book), 156, 200

Ecloga of George Synkellos, 157n13, 158, 159, 160, 161n37, 164, 169
Ecloga of Leo III and Constantine V, 19–20, 21
Edict of Milan, 227
Egeria (pilgrim), 234–36, 238, 251
Eirenaios (Irenaeus of Lyons), 162, 288n17
Eisagoge (law code), 21
ekphonetic notation (neumes), 61
Elevation of the Cross, feast of, 250
Elias Ekdikos, 83n34, 100n98
Elias the Younger (saint), 10, 209
Eliezer, Rabbi, *Pirke* of, 143
Elijah (prophet)
    emperors identified with, 22, 29, 173, 195
    as monastic model, 199–16 *passim*
    robe of, displayed at Hagia Sophia, Constantinople, 243
Elisha (prophet), as monastic model, 206, 209, 214–15
emperors, OT models for, 7, 175–97
    bishops' use of, 180–81, 188–92, 197
    Bulgarian kings, 265–70
    comparatio or *synkresis*, 180, 194
    coronation ceremony, 190–91
    in direct addresses, 180–81, 188–92
    exemplum, Roman mode of, 177–81, 190, 192, 195, 197
    in historical narratives, 181–87
    identification of Christian Byzantium with new Israel, 12–19, 38, 175–76
    Macedonian emperors' use of OT models, 22–25, 38
    in Mirrors of Princes, 192–93
    Palaiologan preference for NT models, 38
    in panegyrics, 193–96
    Rod of Moses and Throne of Solomon, use of, 12–13, 22n87, 173, 191, 267
    sacred space in Byzantine architecture and, 248–50
    "The Temple of the Lord" as term, use of, 11–12
    typos/typology, Christian mode of, 179–81, 190, 192, 194, 195, 197
    See also specific OT figures, e.g., Moses, Pharaoh
Engberg, Sysse Gudrun, 62, 65, 72, 250–51
enkainia ceremony, 250–51

Enoch (OT figure), 161, 162, 216
Ephraem the Syrian, 77–78, 80, 83, 103n114
Epiphanios of Cyprus, 200, 217
Epiphanios of Salamis, 59n7, 154
Epiphany, feast of, 64n25, 71
Epitome of Traianos, 159
Erechtheus (Assyrian ruler named in John Malalas's chronicle), 167
Ernik (son of Attila the Hun), 268
Erotapokriseis (Anastasios of Sinai), 169
eschatology. *See* apocalyptic
Esdras (biblical books), 270n61
Ethical Discourses (Symeon the New Theologian), 215–16
Ethiopia, OT models for the state in, 274–76
Ethiopic (language), 108, 156, 186
Eucharist, 62n18, 72, 155, 172, 230–31
Eudokia (empress), 186
Euripides (classical playwright), 171
Eusebios of Caesarea
    on canon, 154n2
    Christian world chronicle and, 158, 159n24, 160, 164, 169
    on Cleopa, 273
    emperors identified with OT models by, 13, 176, 182–87 *passim*, 193, 267
    Holy Sepulchre, Jerusalem, description of, 233–34, 236–38
    Martyrs of Palestine, 175
    Tyre, dedicatory speech at cathedral of, 226–27, 229, 248
Eustathios of Epiphanaeia, 159, 166
Eustathios of Thessalonike, 9
Eustratios (biographer of patriarch Eutychios), 15
Euthymios (abbot; 11th century), 10
Euthymios the patriarch (saint), 205, 260
Eutychios (patriarch), 15
Evagrios Pontikos (monk), 219–20
Evagrios Scholastikos (ecclesiastical historian), 159, 185
Evergetinon or *Synagoge* (Paul Evergetinos), 204–5
Excerpta barbari, 164n45, 166, 167, 168, 171
exemplum, OT models for emperors in Roman mode of, 177–81, 190, 192, 195, 197

Exodus (biblical book)
  Book of Jubilees and, 157
  identification of Christian Byzantium with Israel described in, 13, 18, 19
  illustrations in Octateuchs, 125, 127, 130, 134, 136
  John Malalas, chronicle of, 161–63, 165–69
  monastic models drawn from, 211, 213, 215
  in Prophetologion, 69
  psalters, devotional images in, 100
  as text of Octateuch and Pentateuch, 107
  theological history, OT contribution to, 155
  Vatopedi Octateuch, Genesis and Exodus missing from, 125
Ezekiel (biblical book), 16–17, 49, 242
Ezekiel, Temple of, 224, *225*, 246
Ezra (biblical book), 224n5

familiarity with/knowledge of OT
  in Bulgaria, 259–62
  in Byzantium, 9–10, 26, 55–59, 73–76
Faust legend, 157
Flavius Josephus, 126, 154n2, 156, 157n13, 164n44, 224n5
Florence, Biblioteca Medicea-Laurenziana [Laur.]
  MS 9.28, 139, 141
  siglum A (Codex Amiatinus), 108–9
Florence Octateuch (Biblioteca Medicea-Laurenziana [Laur.] MS plut. 5.38), 109
  catenae, lack of, 114
  distinguished from other surviving illustrated Octateuchs, 109
  iconography of, 126, 127, *128*
  liturgical rubrics in, 114
florilegia, 200
forced conversions of Jews, imperial attempts at, 5, 6
Fourth Crusade, 25–26
France
  Bibles moralisées, 151
  Carolingian Francia, 9, 30
  Jewish glossaries from, 48
  OT narrative, representations of, 31–36, *32*
Frank, Georgia, 208
Freer Gallery of Art, vii

Gabriel between Moses and Muḥammad (Berlin, Museum für Islamische Kunst, Staatliche Museen), 288, *289*
Gabriel-Radomir (Bulgarian tsar), 258
Galerius (emperor), 175
Geiger, Abraham, 284
Gelasius of Cyzicus, 185
Gelzer, Heinrich, 158, 163
Genesis (biblical book)
  Book of Jubilees, 156–57
  cosmology of, 3, 7
  fifth century mss. of, 8
  illustrations in Octateuchs, 126–27, 130, 134n62, 141–42
  John Malalas, chronicle of, 161–63
  monastic models drawn from, 202, 215–16, 220
  in Prophetologion, 67, 70
  Russia, OT models for the state in, 271
  as text in Octateuch and Pentateuch, 107
  theological history, OT contribution to, 155
  Vatopedi Octateuch, Genesis and Exodus missing from, 125
  visual elements added to illustration of biblical story, 75–76n58
Genesis Rabbah, 143
George Merchulé, 273
George the Monk
  chronicle of, 10n31, 80n11, 158, 160, 169
  Continuator of, 80n11
George of Pisidia, 9n26, 17, 183, 195
George Synkellos, 157n13, 158, 159, 160, 161n37, 164, 169, 187
Georgia, OT models for the state in, 272–74, 275–76
Germanos I (patriarch), 187n43, 229
Germanos Maroules (saint), 80
The giant Og with Moses, Muḥammad, and Jesus (London, Khalili Collections), 279–81, *280*
glosses and glossaries
  Jewish, 46, 48–50, 51n27, 52, 53
  in psalters, 82–83
  See also catenae; commentaries; scholia
Glykas (Michael, chronicler), 169n63
Gog and Magog, 16–17

Goliath the Frank from Overseas, 269, 270
Gordon, Charles, Garden Tomb in Jerusalem discovered by, 223
Gospel Books, quire divisions in, 124. *See also* New Testament
government. *See* politics and the state
Grandior codex (no longer extant), 108
Great Church (Hagia Sophia), Constantinople, 14, 229, 239–43, *240*, 247–52, 261
Great Horologion, 79n6, 85n43, 85n45, 92n68, 93n71
Great Palace, Constantinople
   church of the Lord, 11–12
   hall of the Magnaura, Throne of Solomon in, 12, 22n87, 173, 191
   Nea Ekklesia on edge of, 22, 29, 249
   Pharos Church, 29, 31
   pillaging and destruction of, 36
Greek (language)
   Eusebios surviving in Latin translation from, 186
   Jewish use of, 4, 39, 40, 42–45, 50–51
Greek (language), translations of OT into
   Christian Bibles, influence of Jewish Greek OTs on, 52, 54
   Jewish. *See* Jews and Judaism
   Letter of Aristeas on, 111
   See also Septuagint
Gregory (annotator of Harvard Psalter), 96
Gregory (author of *Life* of St. Basil the Younger), 26–27
Gregory Antiochos, 25n104
Gregory Handzteli, *Vita* of (George Merchulé), 273
Gregory of Nazianzos (saint), 22, 59n7, 154, 192, 205, 213
Gregory Pakourianos, 219
Gregory the Presbyter, 260
Gregory of Sinai (saint), 79
Gunter, Ann, vii

Haggai (biblical book), 236
Hagia Sophia (Great Church), Constantinople, 14, 229, 239–43, *240*, 247–52, 261
hagiographical literature, comparisons to OT figures in, 175n2, 206–10
Harold Hardrada (king of Norway), 270
Harrison, Martin, 243–44, 246, 247–48

Harun ibn Yahya, 12n42, 249n104
Harvard Psalter (Cambridge, MA, Houghton Library, MS gr. 3), 95–96
Hebrew (language)
   Book of Jubilees or *Little Genesis*, 156
   Genesis Rabbah, 143
   Jewish use of and familiarity with, 4, 39, 40, 42–45, 50–51
   translation of OT into Greek from. *See* Greek (language), translations of OT into
Heidelberg, cod. Palat. Gr. 356, 196
Helena (saint and empress), 248, 264n41
Hellenic Chronicle, 256–57
Heraklios (emperor)
   forced conversion of Jews, attempt at, 5
   identification of Christian Byzantium with Israel under, 15–16, 173
   OT models for, 17, 29, 181–82, 194–96, 248n97
hermits. *See* monasticism and the OT in Byzantium
Hermogenes (classical rhetorician), 196n75
Herodotus (classical historian), 170, 185
Herod's Temple, Jerusalem, hypothetical reconstruction of, 224, *224*
Hesseling, D. C., 47, 50
Hesychios Illoustrios, 159
Hexapla (Origen), 53
Hexateuchs, 108n4, 108n6
Hezekiah (OT king), 14, 161, 163, 170, 172
Hilary of Poitiers, 59n7
Historical Palaea, 259, 261–62
history, OT and Byzantine understanding of, 7, 153–74
   apocryphal and pseudepigraphical texts, 154, 156–57, 167, 169
   chosen people, Byzantine self-identification as, 155, 156, 172–74
   chronicle versus history, debate regarding, 161n33
   dating structures, 157–58, 163–64, 172
   emperors, historical accounts of, 181–87
   non-theological history, contribution to, 155–56
   theological history, contribution to, 154–55

history, OT and Byzantine understanding of (*continued*)
   See also Christian world chronicle; John Malalas
History of the Monks of Egypt, 208
The History of the Prophets and Kings (al-Ṭabarī), 279–81, *280*
Høeg, Carsten, 61–64
Holy Cross. *See* True Cross
"Holy Land Experience" (Orlando, FL), 223, 225
Holy Sepulchre, Jerusalem, 14, 233–39, *235*, 250, 252
Homer, 170n66, 171, 184
horns of the anointing (Constantinople and Jerusalem; no longer extant), 238, 243, 249
Horologia, 85, 102n106, 102n108, 103n116. *See also* Great Horologion
Hosea (biblical book), 270n61
hours, liturgy/books of, 84–85

Iakobos (archbishop of Bulgaria), 26n105
Iannes and Iambres, Book of, 157, 167–69
Ibn Hishām, 283
Ibn Isḥāq, 283
iconoclastic controversy, 20–22, 169, 187
icons, 31, 38
Ignatios of Antioch, 233
Ignatios the Deacon, 9n26
imperial ideology. *See* emperors, OT models for
imperial palace. *See* Great Palace, Constantinople
Inachos of Argos, 164
Interpreted Palaea, 259, 261–62
Iphigeneia in Tauris (Euripides), 171
Iran. *See* Persia, Byzantine conflict with
Irenaeus of Lyons (Eirenaios), 162, 288n17
Irnik (mythical Bulgar prince), 256, 268
Isaak (monk and challenger of Valens), 187
Isaak Komnenos (younger brother of John II Komnenos), 111–14, *112*, 118, 205
Isaiah (biblical book/prophet)
   Bulgaria, OT models of the state in, 262–64, 266n45, 270n61
   Constantinople identified with Jerusalem in, 16, 17
   in Eustratios's life of patriarch Eutychios, 15
   Jewish versus Christian interpretations of, 6n15
   John Malalas on Sennacherib, 161, 170–72
   in Prophetologion, 67, 68, 69
Isaiah, Vision of, 258
Islam, Byzantine influence on, 271n63
Islam, Moses in, 8, 279–98
   future studies in confluence and connection, 295–98
   The History of the Prophets and Kings (al-Ṭabarī), 279–81, *280*
   literary function of, 287–91, *289–90*, *292*
   précis of qurʾānic depictions of Moses, 281
   prophet Moses and prophet Muḥammad, association between, 281, 288, *289*
   rod of Moses, 288–91, *290*, *292*
   sources for, 282–87, *285–86*
   validity of Bible in Islam, 291–95, *296*
Islamic conquests
   Bulgaria in 9th century and, 259
   Israel, identification of Christian Byzantium with, 17, 18, 25
   Jewish response to, 5–6
   Joshua, identification of Byzantine emperors with, 23
   manuscript tradition in Byzantium and, 65n28
   Palaeologan reversion to NT figures, 38
Isperich (Bulgarian prince), 263
Ispor (Asparuch; Bulgar khan), 266, 269
Israel, new. *See* new Israel, identification of Christian Byzantium as
Istanbul, Ecumenical Patriarchate, MS Kamariotissa 3, 82n24
Istanbul, Topkapı Sarayı
   MS gr. 8. *See* Topkapı Octateuch
   Muḥammad stays with the baggage, fol. 148a, *Qiṣaṣ al-anbiyāʾ*, manuscript, 283, *285*
   Rod of Moses (Byzantine relic), 13, 173, 191, 243, 267
Italian Giant Bibles of Romanesque period, 35–36
Izmir, Evangelical School, MS A.1. *See* Smyrna Octateuch
Izot (son of Ispor; Bulgar khan), 269, 270

Jacob (OT patriarch), 31, 155, 206, 208, 209
James, Protevangelium of, 10n31
James of Kokkinobaphos, 114
James of Nisibis, 206
Jeffreys, Elizabeth, 153, 303
Jeremiah (biblical book), 10, 155n4
Jerome (theologian and translator of Vulgate), 59n7, 156n10, 158, 186, 199
Jerusalem
    Anastasis Church, Enkainia of, 235, 251
    Constantinople identified with, 16–17
    Gordon's Garden Tomb, 223
    Holy Sepulchre, 14, 233–39, *235*, 250, 252
    Nea (basilica), 14, 247–48
    omphalos (navel of the world), 238
    OT relics, 238–39
    St. Sabas, Lavra of, 79
    Zacharias, altar with blood of, 238
    See also Temple, Jerusalem
Jerusalem, MS Taphou 53, 92n68
Jewish Antiquities (Josephus), 126, 156, 157n13
Jewish Wars (Josephus), 224n5
Jews and Judaism, 39–54
    Akylas (Aquila), Greek translation of OT by, 4, 44–48, 50–53
    biblical story illustrations, elements from Jewish lore added to, 75–76n58
    Cairo Genizah manuscripts, 40, 45–46, 47, 48, 49
    Christian Bibles, influence of Jewish Greek OTs on, 52, 54
    in Eustratios's life of patriarch Eutychios, 15
    forced conversions, imperial attempts at, 5, 6
    glosses and glossaries, 46, 48–50, 51n27, 52, 53
    haggadah, 75n56
    iconoclasm and, 20
    identification of Christian groups with Israel, 12–19
    Islamic portrayals of Moses, sources for, 282–87, 293
    Justinian's *Novel*, legislation regarding Jews in, 5n7, 43, 44, 46
    Karaites and Rabbanites, 40
    Khazars, conversion to Judaism of, 16, 28n116, 45
    languages used by, 40, 42–45, 50–51
    manuscripts produced by, 39–40, 45–50
    Masoretic text, 41, 46, 51
    memorization of Greek OT text, 51, 53
    midrash, 41–42, 44, 143, 284
    Mishnah, 41
    Octateuch illustrations, Weitzmann's theory of Jewish pre-Christian origins for, 142–50, *146–49*
    Persian and Islamic inroads, Jewish response to, 5–6, 15
    prophecy, interpretation of, 10n27
    relationship between Christian Byzantines and, 4–5, 40–41
    relationship of medieval Greek OT texts to ancient versions, 51, 53
    role of Bible in medieval Judaism, 40, 41–42
    scholarship and biblical study, 39, 41–42
    scholia and commentaries, 42, 48–49
    Septuagint, use of, 4, 44, 154
    Symmachos, Greek translation of OT by, 44
    Talmud, 40, 41, 44
    targum, 41, 50, 284
    Theodotion, Greek translation of OT by, 44
    Torah, role of, 41, 51, 107 (*See also* Torah)
    use of Greek translations by, 50–51, 52–53
Jezebel (OT queen), 185n35, 208
Job (biblical book/character), 7, 48, 211
Johannes Scotus Eriugena, 252n112
John II Komnenos (emperor), 111
John of Antioch, chronicle of, 159, 160–61
John the Baptist, Nativity of, 70
John Cassian, 81n16, 84n36, 89, 95n80
John Chrysostom (saint), 10n31, 23, 62n18, 163n43, 169
John of Damascus, 259, 284
John of Diolkos, 208
John Draschanakerttsi, 273
John the Exarch, 259
John of Gaza, 78, 83–84, 95n81, 214n56
John Geometres, 1
John Grammatikos (patriarch), 169
John the Lydian, 193
John Malalas
    dating structures used by, 163–64

John Malalas (*continued*)
  development of Christian world chronicle and, 158, 159, 160
  emperors, OT models for, 186, 187
  identification of Christian Byzantium with Israel, 14–15
  John of Antioch and, 159n19
  millennialism of, 160, 172
  Moses cited as source by, 161–62
  Pharaoh's *Magoi*, account of, 161, 165–69
  on Sennacherib, 161, 170–72
  sources for, 159–60n25, 165–66, 170–71
  Theosophy, 166, 168, 171
  use of OT narrative by, 161–65
John Moschos, 219
John of Nikiu, 169, 186–87
John the Persian (abba), 203
John Rufus, 207
John Tzetzes, 9
Johnson, M. A., 261
Jonah (biblical book), 46–47, 53, 187n43
Joseph (OT patriarch)
  Antioch, stone sculpture from (Princeton, University Art Museum), 144–45, *146*
  Cassiodorus on, 172n2
  in Islam, 282
  John Malalas on, 162
  as monastic model, 206, 209, 214
  in Octateuch illustrations, 127, 145, *146–48*
Joseph and Aseneth, 156
Josephus (Flavius Josephus), 126, 154n2, 156, 157n13, 164n44, 224n5
Joshua (biblical book/leader)
  Bulgaria, OT models of the state in, 263, 269
  imperial identification with, 23, 29, 196
  monastic identification with, 209
  Octateuch, as part of, 107
  trumpets used at Jericho, displayed at Hagia Sophia, Constantinople, 243
Joshua ivories (New York, Metropolitan Museum, and London, Victoria and Albert), 132–33, *135*, 144
Joshua Roll (Vat. Palat. gr. 431)
  earlier version of, 132–33, 142
  ideological significance of, 7

illustrated Octateuchs and, 118, 124, 131–33, *134–37*, 142
imperial identification with Joshua, 23
Joshua ivories and, 132–33, *135*, 144
Western mss. compared, 34
Josiah (OT king), as monastic model, 205–6
Jovian (emperor), 194
Jubilees, Book of, 156–57, 163, 166, 169
Judaism. *See* Jews and Judaism
judaizers and judaizing, 6, 18, 20, 27, 30, 257–58
Judges (biblical book), 70, 107, 269
Judith (biblical book), 154, 270n61
Julian the Apostate (emperor), 184–85, 192
Julian calendar, 66–67
Julian the Samaritan, 186
Julius Africanus (Sextus Julius Africanus)
  Christian world chronicle and, 158, 159, 160, 161n37, 163n39–40, 163n43, 164, 165n50
  George Synkellos on, 159n24
  Origen on Akylas to, 44
Justin I (emperor), 244, 245
Justin II (emperor), 194
Justinian I (emperor)
  as *exemplum*, 178
  Hagia Sophia, Constantinople, as rebuilt by, 14, 239–43, *240*, 247–51
  identification of Christian Byzantium with Israel, 14–15
  Novel, legislation regarding Jews in, 5n7, 43, 44, 46
Justinian II (emperor), 18–19, 25, 29

Kalavrezou, Ioli, 24
Karaites, 40
Kariye Camii, Istanbul (Church of the Chora, Constantinople), 31, 33, 36–38, *37*, 113, 231, *232*, 252
Karvuna, Land of, 263, 264
Kastor of Rhodes, 164, 167
kathismata, rubrication of psalms by, 89–92, *90*, 95
Kebra Nagast (Glory of the Kings), 274–75
Kedrenos, chronicle of, 126, 158, 169
Kekaumenos (advice writer), 11, 80
Khadīja (wife of Muḥammad), 283

Khazars, 6, 28n116, 45
1 and 2 Kings (3 and 4 Kingdoms in Byzantine OT)
   in 6-book division of OT, 108n4
   Bulgaria, OT models for the state in, 256, 257, 270n61
   Cairo Genizah palimpsests, 45
   Islam and, 284
   John Malalas on Sennacherib, 161, 170–72
   monastic models drawn from, 202, 206, 212, 215, 216
   in Prophetologion, 68n37, 69, 74n53
   Temple, descriptions of, 224n5
   Vat. gr. 333 containing 1-2 Samuel and, 120
kingship. *See* emperors, OT models for; politics and the state
Kinney, Dale, 227
knowledge of/familiarity with OT
   in Bulgaria, 259–62
   in Byzantium, 9–10, 26, 55–59, 73–76
Koder, Johannes, 226
Kokkinobaphos Master, 113–14, 115, 119
Kosmas Indikopleustes, *Christian Topography*, 14, 131, 133–41, 143, 169
Kosmosoteira Monastery (Theotokos Kosmosoteira), Thrace, 113, 205
Krautheimer, Richard, 227–29, 251, 252
Kresten, Otto, 133
Krueger, Derek, 199, 303

languages
   Aramaic, 4, 40, 41, 50, 287
   Ethiopic, 108, 156, 186
   Jews, languages used by, 4, 39, 40, 42–45, 50–51
   See also Greek; Hebrew; Slavonic
Latin West
   Apophthegmata Patrum, Latin translation of, 204
   azymes, Byzantine accusations of judaizing based on Latin use of, 30
   Bibles moralisées, 34, 150–52
   Fourth Crusade, 25–26
   Octateuchs in, 108–9
   OT models compared to Byzantium, 31–38, *32*
   See also France

law codes, Byzantine, influence of OT on, 19–21
lectionaries
   as counterpart to modern Bible, 55–56, 58
   in monastic liturgies, 216–17
   Octateuch functioning as, 114
   Prophetologion as, 60, 217
   See also Prophetologion, liturgical use of
lekanomancy (dish divination), 169
Lent
   Mass of the Presanctified Gifts during, 217
   Persian attack on Constantinople, commemoration of, 17
   Prophetologion, use of, 63n19, 65, 67, 69–72
Leo I (emperor), 189–90
Leo III (emperor), 6, 19–20, 29, 98n93, 187n43
Leo V (emperor), 11
Leo VI the Wise (emperor), 22, 249
Leo the Grammarian, 249
Leo of Ochrid, 30n127
Leo the Philosopher, 11n39
Leo Bible (Vat. Reg. gr. 1), 35, 95n78
Lesbos, Leimonos Monastery, MS 295, 84n39
Letter of Aristeas, 111–15, *112*, 154n1
Letter to Marcellinus (Athanasios of Alexandria), 217–18
Leviticus (biblical book), 107, 157n13
Licinius (emperor), 226–27
List of the Names of Bulgar Princes (Khans), 256–58, 262, 263, 265, 268, 271, 275, 276
literacy rates in Byzantium, 58, 72
Lithuania, Judaizing tradition of Grand Duchy of, 257
liturgy
   baptism, 179, 214, 232
   Bulgarian, 261
   Constantinople, founding of, 68
   enkainia ceremony, 250–51
   Eucharist, 62n18, 72, 155, 172, 230–31
   of hours, 84–85
   imperial coronation ceremony, 190–91
   Islam, no use of OT or NT in, 295
   Jewish use of Bible in, 41, 42

liturgy (*continued*)
   modeling of other celebrations after Pascha, 71–72
   monastic, 199, 209, 215, 216–20
   Octateuch containing rubrics for, 114
   OT material in, 66n31
   Psalms/psalters, use of, 41, 81–82
   Russian, 271
   two interlocking cycles of liturgical year, 66–67
   See also lectionaries; Prophetologion, liturgical use of; *specific feasts and liturgical periods, e.g.,* Lent
Lives. *See under specific person, e.g.,* Synkletike
London, British Library (BL)
   Add. MS 19,352 (Theodore Psalter), 30, 93
   Add. MS 43725 (Codex Sinaiticus), 154
   MS Cotton Otho B.VI (Cotton Genesis), 8, 144
   MS Or. 480, 108n8
   MS Royal I.D.v–viii (Codex Alexandrinus), 108n4, 154, 218n72
Louis II the Pious (king of the Franks), 270
Louis VIII (king of France), 151
Louis IX (St. Louis; king of France), 31, 34, 35, 36, 151
Louis IX, Psalter of (Paris, Bibliothèque nationale, MS lat. 10525), 34, 35
Lowden, John, 34, 107, 304
Ludwig, Claudia, 195
Luke Chrysoberges (patriarch), 85
Lüling, Gunther, 287
Luther, Martin, 284
Luxenberg, Christoph, 287
LXX. *See* Septuagint

Macarian homilies, 200, 213–14
Maccabees (biblical books), 154, 156
Macedonian emperors, use of OT models by, 22–25, 38. *See also specific Macedonian emperors*
Magdalino, Paul, 1, 304
Magnaura, hall of the, Great Palace, Constantinople, Throne of Solomon in, 12, 22n87, 173, 191
Magoi of Pharaoh, John Malalas's account of, 161, 165–69

Makarios of Alexandria, 200, 208, 213–14
Makarios of Corinth, 80n14
Makarios the Egyptian, 221
Malachi (biblical book), 48
Malalas. *See* John Malalas
Manasses, chronicle of, 158
Mandylion of Edessa, 23, 25
Manganeios Prodromos, 173n77
Manuel Holobolos, 26n105
manuscripts (specific)
   Athens, National Library of Greece, MS 3, 89, *90*
   Athens, National Library of Greece, MS 15, 84n39
   Athos. *See* Athos manuscripts
   Baḥīrā speaking with Muḥammad, page from a dispersed *Anbiyā'-nāma*, 283–84, *286*
   Barberini Euchologion (Vat. Lib. MS Barberini gr. 336), 190n55, 191
   Barberini Psalter (Vat. Barber. gr. 372), 95n78
   Basil II, Psalter of (Venice, Biblioteca Marciana, MS gr. 17), 82–83, 114
   BAV (Rome, Biblioteca Apostolica Vaticana). *See* Vatican Library
   Bessarion (Vat. Lib. MS Grottaferrata G.B.I), 190–91n55
   BL. *See* London, British Library
   Bodleian Library. *See* Oxford, Bodleian Library
   Bologna, University Library, MS 3574, 47n18
   British Library. *See* London, British Library
   Cairo Genizah manuscripts, 40, 45–46, 47, 48, 49
   Cambridge, MA and UK. *See entries at* Cambridge
   Codex Alexandrinus (London, British Library, MS Royal I.D.v–viii), 108n4, 154, 218n72
   Codex Grandior (no longer extant), 108
   Codex Sinaiticus (London, British Library, Add. MS 43725), 154
   Codex Vaticanus (Vat. MS gr. 1209), 154
   Copenhagen, Royal Library, cod. GKS 6, 120

Cotton Genesis (BL MS Cotton Otho B.VI), 8, 144
Florence. *See entries at* Florence, Biblioteca Medicea-Laurenziana
Harvard Psalter (Cambridge, MA, Houghton Library, MS gr. 3), 95–96
Heidelberg, cod. Palat. Gr. 356, 196
Istanbul. *See entries at* Istanbul
Izmir, Evangelical School, MS A.1. *See* Smyrna Octateuch
Jerusalem, MS Taphou 53, 92n68
Joshua Roll (Vat. Palat. gr. 431). *See* Joshua Roll
Leo Bible (Vat. Reg. gr. 1), 35, 95n78
Lesbos, Leimonos Monastery, MS 295, 84n39
London, British Library. *See* London, British Library
Louis IX, Psalter of (Paris, Bibliothèque nationale, MS lat. 10525), 34, 35
Milan, Biblioteca Ambrosiana, MS + 24 sup., 84, 85, *86*, 87
Milan, Biblioteca Ambrosiana, MS F, 52
Morgan Library. *See* New York, Morgan Library
Mt. Athos. *See* Athos manuscripts
Mt. Sinai. *See* Sinai, Monastery of St. Catherine
New York, Morgan Library, MS 350 (Morgan Picture Bible), 34
New York, Morgan Library, MS 638, 34, *35*, 36
NYPL. *See* New York Public Library
Ohrid, Naroden muzej, MS gr. 20, 103–5
Oxford. *See* Oxford, Bodleian Library
Paris. *See* Paris, Bibliothèque nationale
Paris Psalter (Paris Bibl. Nat. gr. 139). *See* Paris Psalter
Patmos. *See* Patmos manuscripts
Psalter of Basil II (Venice, Biblioteca Marciana, MS gr. 17), 82–83, 114
Psalterium aureum Turicense (Zürich, Zentralbibliothek, RP 1), 89
Psalter of St. Louis (Paris, Bibliothèque nationale, MS lat. 10525), 34, 35
Psalter Vienna (Österreichische Nationalbibliothek, MS theol. gr. 177), 84n35

Radomir Psalter, Athos, MS Zographou slav. I.Δ.13, 92n63
Rome, Biblioteca Apostolica Vaticana. *See* Vatican Library
St. Petersburg. *See entries at* St. Petersburg
Sinai. *See* Sinai, Monastery of St. Catherine
Smyrna Octateuch (Izmir, Evangelical School, MS A.1). *See* Smyrna Octateuch
Spencer Psalter (New York, NYPL, MS Spencer gr. 1), 100n97
Topkapı Octateuch (Istanbul, Topkapı Sarayı, MS gr. 8). *See* Topkapı Octateuch
Turin, Biblioteca Reale, cod. Var. 484, 98, 99
Turin, Biblioteca Universitaria, MS B.VII.30, 85n44
Uspensky Psalter (St. Petersburg, National Library of Russia, MS gr. 216), 80n15, 100
Vatican Library. *See* Vatican Library
Vatopedi Octateuch (Athos MS Vatopedi 602). *See* Vatopedi Octateuch
Venice. *See* Venice, Biblioteca Marciana
Washington DC, Dumbarton Oaks Museum, MS 3, 102–3
Zürich, Zentralbibliothek, RP 1 (*Psalterium aureum Turicense*), 89
manuscripts (types and characteristics)
   Bibles moralisées, 34, 150–52
   ekphonetic notation (neumes), 61
   florilegia, 200
   Hexateuchs, 108n4, 108n6
   hours, liturgy/books of, 84–85
   Italian Giant Bibles of Romanesque period, 35–36
   Menaion, 65, 82
   Menologion, 10, 23, 24
   Oktoechos, 82
   Parakletike, 82, 104n116
   Pentecostarion, 65
   quire divisions, 124
   Triodion, 65, 82
   See also catenae; commentaries; glosses and glossaries; lectionaries; Octateuchs; Pentateuch;

manuscripts (types and characteristics) (*continued*)
    Prophetologion; Psalms/psalters; scholia; Septuagint; Torah
Marcellinus, Letter to (Athanasios of Alexandria), 217–18
Marcian (emperor), 13, 189
Marcus Aurelius (emperor), 178
Mark Eugenikos, 77–78
martyrion, use of, 235, 236–37
Martyrs of Palestine, 175
Mary of Egypt, 98n93
Masoretic text, 41, 46, 51
Maurianos (*comes*), 167n55
Maurice (emperor), 178
Mavropous, (John), 173
Maxentius (rival of Constantine I), 182, 183, 187
Maximos the Confessor, (saint), 6, 204, 214–15
McAuliffe, Jane Dammen, 279, 304
Melchisedek (OT figure), imperial identification with, 29, 173, 193
Melito of Sardis, 59n7, 154
Menaion, 65, 82
Menologion, 10, 23, 24
Menologion of Basil II, 23, 24
Methodios (saint and apostle to the Slavs), 259–61
Michael VIII (emperor), 38
Michael Maleinos, 209
Michael Stoudites (abbot), 93
midrash, 41–42, 44, 143, 284
Milan, Biblioteca Ambrosiana
    MS + 24 sup., 84, 85, *86, 87*
    MS F, 52
Milan, Edict of, 227
millennialism. *See* apocalyptic
Miller, James, 55, 304
Milner, Christine 246
Milvian Bridge, battle of, 182, 183, 187, 291n21
Miracles of St. Demetrios, 19
Mirrors of Princes, 192–93
Mishnah, 41
monasticism and the OT in Byzantium, 7, 199–221
    belt or cincture, 212
    canonical texts, 200, 203, 205, 211, 220–21
    discipline, OT models for, 210–12
    foundational monastic writings, 200, 201–6
    hagiographical literature, 206–10
    liturgies, 199, 209, 215, 216–20
    psalmody as part of ascetic life, 77–81, 200, 217–19 (*See also* Psalms/psalters)
    singing psalms, monastic disapproval of, 84
    spiritual exegesis and allegory, 213–16
Monophysites, 18, 168
Morgan Library. *See* New York, Morgan Library
Moses (OT patriarch)
    Bulgaria, OT models for the king in, 266n48, 267–68
    in Byzantine dating structure, 163
    Covenant with, 155
    emperors associated with, 13, 173, 176, 182–84, 190, 195, 196
    John Malalas, cited as source by, 161–61
    as monastic model, 205, 206, 207, 208, 211, 213–15
    Plato's temporal relationship to, 164
    See also Islam, Moses in; rod of Moses
Mother of God Petritzonitissa, Monastery of, at Bačkovo, 219
Mt. Athos manuscripts. *See* Athos manuscripts
Mt. Nebo, Chapel of the Theotokos, *230*, 230–31
Mt. Sinai manuscripts. *See* Sinai, Monastery of St. Catherine
Muḥammad and Moses, as prophets, 281, 288, *289*. *See also* Islam, Moses in
Muḥammad b. Isḥāq, 283n6
Al-Mundhir, 171
Muslims. *See entries at* Islam

navel of the world (*omphalos*), 238
Nea (basilica, church of the Theotokos, Jerusalem), 14, 247–48
Nea Ekklesia, Constantinople, 22, 29, 249
Nea Mone, Chios, mosaic of the Anastasis, 248–50, *250*
Nebuchadnezzar (Babylonian ruler), 156, 192, 256

Nelson, Robert, 1, 304
neumes, 61
new Israel, identification of Christian Byzantium as, 3, 9, 25–30
   Armenian and Georgian adaptation of, 272–74
   Bulgarian adaptation of, 256–57, 262–65, 275, 276
   continuing popularity of concept, 276n80
   emperors, OT models for, 12–19, 38, 175–76
   general Christian self-identification as fulfillment of OT history, 155, 175
   history, OT contribution to Byzantine understanding of, 155, 156, 172–74
   icons, restoration of veneration of, 21–22
   Islamic conquests and, 17, 18, 25
   Louis IX and Capetian France, 34
   origins of, 173
   Persia, Byzantine conflict with, 14, 15, 173
   Russian adaptation of, 272
New Testament
   Book of Iannes and Iambres, references to, 167, 169
   Bulgarian reading of OT in light of, 276
   Ethiopia, royal dynasty of, 274
   Islam, Jesus in, *280*, 282
   monastic models drawn from, 203, 205, 206, 212
   OT as precursor to, 155
   quire divisions in Gospel Books, 124
   sacred space in Byzantine architecture and, 233
   Slavonic, translation into, 260
   typology in, 179
   ultimate subordination of OT imagery to, 29–31, 38
New York, Morgan Library
   MS 350 (Morgan Picture Bible), 34
   MS 638, 34, *35*, 36
New York Public Library (NYPL)
   The Legends of the Prophets, Iran, 1580 manuscript, Spencer Collection, 289, *290*
   MS Spencer gr. 1 (Spencer Psalter), 100n97
   Stories of the Prophets, Iran, 15th century manuscript, Spencer Collection, 291, *292*

Nicholas Mystikos (patriarch), 9n26, 267–68
Nicholas Stoudites, 10n27
Nikephoros II Phokas (emperor), 23, 80, 187
Nikephoros (patriarch), 9n26, 187
Nikephoros Basilakes, 9
Nikephoros Ouranos, 96–97
Niketas, Bible of, 2n3, 114, 120n39
Niketas Choniates, 9, 25n105, 187n39
Niketas the Paphlagonian, 22
Niketas Stethatos, 209
Nikodemos Hagiorites, 80n14, 96n86, 98n93, 103n113
Nisteros (abba), 201–2
Noah (OT patriarch)
   Byzantine conceptions of history, Noah's sons in, 165
   in Byzantine dating structure, 163
   Covenant with, 155
   emperors, OT models for, 195
   as monastic model, 214, 216
   Og the giant in Islamic folklore and, 279n1
   in typology, 179
Noah's Ark, 179, 224
Nomos georgikos (Farmer's Law), 21
Nomos Mosaikos, 20, 21
Nouthesia Gerontos (Admonition of the Elder), 20–21
Novel of Justinian I, legislation regarding Jews in, 5n7, 43, 44, 46
Novgorod, Judaizing tradition of, 257–58
Numbers (biblical book), 107, 130, 281
numismatics
   Bar Kochba coinage, Temple images on, 237
   Rex regnantium coins of Justinian II, 18, 29
Nunc dimittis, 15

Octateuchs, 107–52
   Bibles moralisées, relationship to, 150–52
   biblical books included in, 107
   catenae in, 110, 151
   catena manuscripts, 110n15, 114, 117, 119–20, 127, 131
   Christian Topography (attrib. Kosmas Indikopleustes) and, 131, 133–41, 143, 169

Octateuchs (*continued*)
  common models or sources, 131–41, 169
  defined, 107
  earlier manuscripts, continued use of, 117
  evidence from descendant manuscripts, 127–30
  Genesis cycle and, 141–42
  iconography of, 125–27, *128, 129,* 130
  innovation, use, number, and status of, 107–9
  Joshua ivories and, 132–33, *135,* 144
  Joshua Roll and, 131–33, *134–37,* 142
  Letter of Aristeas included in, 111–15, *112*
  Milan, Biblioteca Ambrosiana, MS F, 52
  Septuagint text and, 130–31, 137
  significance of illustrated Byzantine examples, 109–11
  texts of, 107 (*See also* Deuteronomy; Exodus; Genesis; Joshua; Judges; Leviticus; Numbers; Ruth)
  Weitzmann's Jewish pre-Christian theory regarding, 142–50, *146–49*
  working processes of artists and scribes, 119–25, *121–23*
  See also Florence Octateuch; Topkapı Octateuch; Vatican Library MS gr. 746; Vatican Library MS gr. 747; Vatopedi Octateuch
Odes or Canticles in psalters, 85, 100
Og the giant, Muslim story of Moses' fight with, 279–81, *280*
Ohrid, Naroden muzej, MS gr. 20, 103–5
Oktoechos, 82
Old Testament in Byzantium, 1–38
  architecture and, 7, 223–53 (*See also* sacred space in Byzantine architecture)
  Bulgaria, 8, 255–77 (*See also* Bulgaria, OT models for the state in)
  canon. *See* canon of Old Testament in Byzantium
  Christianization of, 3–4, 8
  extent of adoption of language and mentality of, 9–12
  history, understanding of, 7, 153–74 (*See also* history, OT and Byzantine understanding of)
  iconoclastic controversy, 20–22
  imperial ideology, 7, 175–97 (*See also* emperors, OT models for)
  importance of studying, 1–7
  Islam, 8, 279–98 (*See also* entries at Islam)
  Jews and, 39–54 (*See also* Jews and Judaism)
  knowledge of/familiarity with, 9–10, 26, 55–59, 73–76
  Latin West compared, 31–38, *32*
  law codes, influence of OT on, 19–21
  literal reading and imitation of OT, blockage of, 26–30
  manuscript record of whole Bibles/whole OTs, 57
  monasticism, 7, 199–221 (*See also* monasticism and the OT in Byzantium)
  new Israel, Byzantium as, 3, 9, 25–30 (*See also* new Israel, identification of Christian Byzantium as)
  NT, ultimate subordination to, 29–31, 38
  Octateuchs, 107–52 (*See also* Octateuchs)
  orthodoxy and theocracy, Byzantine sense of, 28–29
  Prophetologion, 55–76 (*See also* Prophetologion)
  psalter and private devotion, 7, 77–105 (*See also* Psalms/psalters)
  Septuagint. *See* Septuagint
  time period covered, 8
  translations. *See* translations of OT
  See also specific books, e.g., Genesis
Olybrios (son of Anicia Juliana), 244, 245
omphalos (navel of the world), 238
On the Eight Parts of Rhetorical Speech, 196
Oneirocriticon of Achmet, 11
On Magistracies (John the Lydian), 193
On Political Science, 192–93
oral, visual, and written tradition, nexus between, 75–76
oral recitation of psalms, 83–84
oral Torah, 40
Origen of Alexandria
  Akylas's translation of OT into Greek and, 44, 53
  on canon, 59n7, 154
  Ethiopia, royal dynasty of, 274
  Hexapla, 53
  on rod of Moses, 288n17
  on spiritual and moral exegesis, 213

Orpheus (as source for John Malalas), 162, 171
orthodoxy, Byzantine sense of, 28–29
Ousterhout, Robert, 223, 304
Oxford, Bodleian Library
 MS Auct. D.4.1, 92n67
 MS Auct. T.4.4, 79n7
 MS Barocci 15, 95
 MS Barocci 182, 161n34
 MS Holkham gr. 1, 92n66
 MS Laud. gr. 2, 92n66
 MS Opp. Add., 47n18
Oxford, David Cycle of mural (?) paintings in, 24
Ozia/Ozias/Uzziah (OT king), 269–70

Pachomios (monastic founder), 210
Palaea chronographica/Palaea interpretata, 259, 261–62
Palaia, 75n56, 157n13, 157n15, 169n64
Palaiologan emperors, preference for NT models, 38. See also specific Palaiologan emperors
Palestine, as Christian holy land, 13–14. See also Jerusalem
palimpsests, 45–46, 48, 53
Palladios, 84n36
Pambo (abba), 208
panegyrics, OT models for emperors in, 193–96
Panofsky, Erwin, 228
Pantinos (saint), 10
Parakletike, 82, 104n116
Parimijnik (Slavic Prophetologion), 64
Paris, Bibliothèque nationale
 MS Abbadie 22, 108n8
 MS éthiop. 3, 108n8
 MS gr. 13, 82n24
 MS gr. 139. *See* Paris Psalter
 MS gr. 164, 88n47
 MS gr. 169, 93, *94*
 MS gr. 331, 84n38, 91n61
 MS gr. 510 (homilies of Gregory of Nazianzos), 22
 MS lat. 10525 (Psalter of Louis IX), 34, 35
 Muḥammad leads Abraham, Moses, and Jesus in prayer, Iran, manuscript, 295, *296*

Paris, Ste. Chapelle, 31–34, *32*, 36
Parisian bibles of thirteenth century, 36
Paris Psalter (Paris Bibl. Nat. gr. 139)
 commentary in, 82
 emperors, OT models for, 23–24
 Exaltation of David (fol. 7v), 24, 35, *frontispiece*
 ideological significance of, 7
 ownership of, 114
Paroimiai, 259, 261, 271–72n66. *See also* Prophetologion
Parpulov, Georgi R., 77, 304
Pascha (Easter), 63n19, 64n25, 66–67, 71–72, 160
Patmos manuscripts
 hours, books of, 84–85
 MS Patm. 31, 28n116
 MS Patm. 65, 83n29
 MS Patm. 66, 83n29
 MS Patm. 159, 83n29
 psalters, 83
Patria Constantinopoleos, 269
Paul Evergetinos, 204–5, 208
Paul the Silentiary, 229, 239
Paulinus (author of *Vita Ambrosii*), 181n18
Paulinus (bishop of Tyre), 226, 229, 248
Pelagius and John (Latin translators of *Apophthegmata Patrum*), 204
Pentateuch
 Jewish manuscripts of, 45, 50, 53
 law codes, Byzantine, influence on, 21
 Octateuch, relationship to, 107
 texts of, 107
 See also Deuteronomy; Exodus; Genesis; Leviticus; Numbers; Torah
Pentecostarion, 65
periousios laos, as name for imperial army, 25, 29
Persia, Byzantine conflict with
 Antioch, siege of, 14, 171–72
 Avars, Persian alliance with, 15–19, 27, 173, 194–95
 Heraklios, use of OT models for, 194–95
 history of Persian empire, OT contribution to Byzantine understanding of, 155–56, 182
 identification of Christian Byzantium with Israel and, 14, 15, 173

Persia, Byzantine conflict with (*continued*)
   Jewish response to, 5
   John Malalas's account of Sennacherib as typology for, 171–72
Peter, Acts of, 157n15
Peter of Argos (saint), 25n102
Peter Damaskenos, 83, 89, 91n56, 100n96
Peter Deljan, 258
Peter the Iberian, *Life* of, 207
Peter the Venerable, 284
Petissonius (pharaoh named in John Malalas's chronicle), 167
Petritzonitissa Monastery, Bačkovo, 219
Phalek (OT patriarch), 161, 163, 164
Pharaoh (OT figure)
   imperial ideology, negative OT model for, 176, 182–88 *passim*, 192, 195
   Joseph in prison with Pharaoh's butler and baker, in Octateuch illustrations, 145, *146–48*
   Magoi of Pharaoh, John Malalas's account of, 161, 165–69
   Petissonius (pharaoh named in John Malalas's chronicle), 167
Pharos Church, Great Palace, Constantinople, 29, 31
Philemon (Egyptian abba), 80
Philip of Macedon, 164
Philokalia, 80n14, 83n33–34, 91n56, 91n58, 213
Philokrates, 111
Philo of Alexandria, 155n6, 179
Philotheos (author of ceremonial treatise), 10
Philotheos Kokkinos (patriarch), 79, 80, 85, 101
Phokas (emperor), 181
Photios (patriarch)
   Amphilochia of, 6n20, 169
   Bible as a whole, knowledge and use of, 56n2
   on Hesychios Illoustrios, 159n22
   identification of Christian Byzantium with Israel, 21–22
   on Jews, 6
   on language of Septuagint, 11n39
   Nomos Mosaikos, 20
   Octateuchs and, 107n1, 108n5, 141
   on Pharos Church paintings, 31

Piacenza Pilgrim, 239
Picus Zeus, 164, 165, 167n55
pignora imperii, 12–13, 173, 194, 267
Pilgrim of Bordeaux, 238
Pirke (Rabbi Eliezer), 143
piyyutim, 42
Plato, temporal relationship to Moses, 164
Platonism, *typos* in, 179
Pliny the Elder, 167
Plukhanova, Maria, 258
Poemen (abba), 204
Polish identification with new Israel, 276n80
politics and the state
   Caucasus, OT models for states of, 272–74
   Ethiopia, OT models for the state in, 274–76
   Mirrors of Princes, 192–93
   theocracy, Byzantine sense of, 28–29
   See also Bulgaria, OT models for the state in; emperors, OT models for
Prefect, Book of the, 10, 21
Presanctified Gifts, Mass of, 217
Presentation of the Virgin in the Temple, architectural setting for, 231–32, *232*
private devotion and the psalter. *See* Psalms/psalters
Procheiros nomos, 21
prokeimenon, 60n9, 69, 70
Prokopios of Gaza
   emperors, OT models for, 172, 179n13, 185, 194
   Octateuchs, 107, 110n15
   on sacred space in Byzantine architecture, 229, 239–41, 245, 248n94
prophecy, Jewish and Christian interpretation of, 10n27
prophet Moses and prophet Muḥammad, 281, 288, *289*. *See also* Islam, Moses in
Prophetologion, 55–76
   Bible and OT, entire, lack of, 55–59
   in Bulgaria, 259, 260, 261, 271–72n66
   canon of OT and, 59, 66n29, 67–68, 73
   contents of, 66, 72–73
   as counterpart to modern OT in Byzantium, 59–60, 72–76
   defined and described, 60

familiarity and accessibility of texts, 73–76
knowledge, oral, visual, and written mediation of, 73–76
manuscripts extant, 62–63
origins and history of manuscript tradition, 63–65
as OT lectionary, 60, 217
printed editions in Greek and Slavic, 64
scholarly research regarding, 60–65
Septuagint and, 60–61, 63, 64n23
transmigration of texts, 64–65
Prophetologion, liturgical use of, 60
cycles of liturgical year, role in, 66–72
evolution and devolution of, 62–65
familiarity with text resulting from, 73
as OT lectionary, 60, 217
Slavonic, 260, 261, 271–72n66
transmigration of texts, 64–65
Protoevangelium of James, 10n31
Proverbs (biblical book)
monasticism and, 200, 207, 220
in Prophetologion, 67, 70, 74n53
as wisdom literature, 7, 200
Psalms/psalters, 7, 77–105
ascetic/spiritual life, psalmody as part of, 77–81, 200, 217–19
Cairo Genizah palimpsests, 45
commentaries, with and without, 82–83
contents of, 85, 88, 92–93, 100–105
divinatory sentences for individual psalms, 88
doxai, rubrication by, 89
emotional poetry of, 3
entirety, recitation of psalms in, 88–91
hours, liturgy of, 84–85
illustrations, 93–100, *94*, *99*
imperial ideology and, 181, 189
kathismata, rubrication by, 89–92, *90*, 95
knowledge and use of, 9–10, 55
law codes, Byzantine, influence on, 21
liturgical use of, 41, 81–82
Odes or Canticles in, 85, 100
oral recitation, 83–84
poetic excerpts added to, 96–97
prayers added to, 91–93
printed versions, uniformity of, 92n65
public worship contrasted, 81–82

sacred space in Byzantine architecture and, 230, 241
singing psalms, monastic disapproval of, 84
Slavonic, translation into, 92, 260
specific thoughts, specific psalms as prescriptions for, 85–86, 219
standing to recite, 91
theological versus devotional prayer, 82–83
variety in format, 92, 100
Psalter of Basil II (Venice, Biblioteca Marciana, MS gr. 17), 82–83, 114
Psalterium aureum Turicense (Zürich, Zentralbibliothek, RP 1), 89
Psalter of St. Louis (Paris, Bibliothèque nationale, MS lat. 10525), 34, 35
Psalter Vienna (Österreichische Nationalbibliothek, MS theol. gr. 177), 84n35
pseudepigrapha. *See* apocryphal and pseudepigraphical texts
pseudo-Makarios the Egyptian, 221
pseudo-Symeon, chronicle of, 158, 160, 169

Quinisext Council (Council in Trullo; 692), 18, 19
Quintilian, 177
quire divisions in manuscripts, 124
Qumran scrolls, 156
Qur'ān, Torah and, 282, 283

Rabbanites, 40
Rabshakeh, in chronicle of John Malalas, 170
Radomir Psalter, Athos, MS Zographou slav. I.Δ.13, 92n63
Rahlfs, Alfred, 59n7, 60–61, 63n19, 71–72, 107n3
Rapp, Claudia, 175, 305
Rashev, Rado, 267
Ravenna, San Vitale, OT narrative mosaics of, 155n7
reader, office of, 73–74
relics
altar of Abraham (Jerusalem relic; no longer extant), 238–39
chalice of Solomon (Hagia Sophia, Constantinople; no longer extant), 249
in Hagia Sophia, Constantinople, 243, 249

relics (*continued*)
    horns of the anointing (Constantinople and Jerusalem; no longer extant), 238, 243, 249
    icons versus, 31
    pignora imperii, 12–13, 173, 194, 267
    ring of Solomon (Jerusalem; no longer extant), 238
    Rod of Moses (Istanbul, Topkapı Sarayı), 13, 173, 191, 243, 267
    Solomon, objects associated with, 12, 22n87, 173, 191, 238, 249
    Table of Solomon (Constantinople, Great Palace; no longer extant), 12n42, 249
    of Temple, recovered from Vandals, 248
    Throne of Solomon (Constantinople, hall of the Magnaura, Great Palace; no longer extant), 12, 22n87, 173, 191
    See also True Cross
Religious History (Theodoret of Cyrrhus), 206–7
Res gestae divi Augusti, 177
Rhetorica ad Herennium, 177
Rhetorica Marciana, 196n75
ring of Solomon (Jerusalem relic; no longer extant), 238
Robert of Clari, 243
Rod of Moses
    Byzantine relic (Istanbul, Topkapı Sarayı), 13, 173, 191, 243, 267
    in Islamic folklore, 288–91, *290, 292*
Romanos I (emperor), 6, 23
Romanos II (emperor), 11n38, 24
Romanos the Melode, 241–42
Rome, Biblioteca Apostolica Vaticana (BAV). *See* Vatican Library
Rosenthal, Marvin, 223
rubrication of psalms with *doxai* and *kathismata*, 89–92, *90*, 95
Russia
    Bulgaria compared, 271–72, 275
    Judaizing heresy in, 257–58
    new Israel, identification with, 272, 276n80
Ruth (biblical book), as part of Octateuch, 107

Saadiah Ben Joseph, 287n13
Sabas (monastic founder and saint), 210
Sabas (owner of Athos, MS Dionysiou 65), 96–97
Sabas (possibly archbishop of Serbia), 91–92
Sabinian (bishop), 189
Sackler Gallery of Art, vii
sacraments
    baptism, 179, 214, 232
    Eucharist, 62n18, 72, 155, 172, 230–31
sacred space in Byzantine architecture, 7, 223–53
    basilicas, 227
    Chora, Church of the, Constantinople (Kariye Camii, Istanbul), 31, *33*, 36–38, *37*, 113, 231, *232*, 252
    emperors, OT models for, 248–50
    Hagia Sophia, Constantinople, 14, 239–43, *240*, 247–52
    Holy Sepulchre, Jerusalem, 14, 233–39, *235*, 250
    martyrion, use of, 235, 236–37
    metaphorical relationship to Temple, 226–33, 251–53
    Nea Mone, Chios, mosaic of the Anastasis, 248–50, *250*
    Pharos Church, Great Palace, Constantinople, 29, 31
    physical relationship to Temple, lack of, 227, 231, 242, 251–52
    Presentation of the Virgin in the Temple, architectural setting for, 231–32, *232*
    representations of OT narratives, 30–34, *32, 33*
    Ste. Chapelle, Paris, compared, 31–34, *32*, 36
    San Marco, Venice, Cotton Genesis copied in mosaics of, 144
    San Vitale, Ravenna, OT narrative mosaics of, 155n7
    SS. Sergios and Bacchos, Constantinople, 245–47
    St. Polyeuktos, Constantinople, 14, 243–47, *244*, 252
    Temple of Jerusalem and, 7, 223–26, *230*, 230–32, *232* (*See also* Temple, Jerusalem)
    terminology of Temple applied, 225–26, 245

Theotokos, Chapel of the, Mt. Nebo, *230*, 230–31
Tyre, dedicatory speech of Eusebios at cathedral of, 226–27, 229
"Sailing to Byzantium" (W. B. Yeats), 253n114
St. Catherine, Monastery of, Sinai. *See* Sinai, Monastery of St. Catherine
Ste. Chapelle, Paris, 31–34, *32*, 36
St. John the Forerunner of Phoberos, Monastery of, 212
St. Neophytos, Monastery of, Cyprus, 205
St. Petersburg, National Library of Russia
    MS gr. 216 (Uspensky Psalter), 80n15, 100
    MS gr. 229, 82n24
    MS gr. 266, 92n68
    MS gr. 269, 35n137
St. Polyeuktos, Constantinople, 14, 243–47, *244*, 252
St. Sabas, Lavra of, Jerusalem, 79
SS. Sergios and Bacchos, Constantinople, 245–47
Saller, Sylvester, 230
Samuel (Bulgarian tsar), 258
1 and 2 Samuel (biblical books)
    in 6-book division of OT, 108n4
    Bulgaria, OT models for the state in, 256, 265, 266, 269, 270
    monastic models drawn from, 202, 204
    Vat. gr. 333 containing 1-2 Kings and, 120
San Marco, Venice, Cotton Genesis copied in mosaics of, 144
San Vitale, Ravenna, OT narrative mosaics of, 155n7
Schechter, Solomon, 40
Scheja, Georg, 242
scholia, 48–49, 53, 82. *See also* catenae; commentaries; glosses and glossaries
Scripture. *See* Bible
Selection, 20
Seleucia Pieria, near Antioch, stone sculpture from (Princeton, University Art Museum), 144–45, *146*
Sennacherib (Assyrian ruler), in chronicle of John Malalas, 161, 170–72
Septuagint (LXX)
    Byzantine familiarity with texts of, 9, 26
    catena manuscripts, copies of, 119–20
    critical editions of, 61
    Ecclesiastes text compared with Cairo Genizah fragment, 47
    Jewish community and, 4, 44, 154
    Octateuch illustrations, as underlying source for, 130–31, 137
    OT in Byzantium represented by, 154
    Prophetologion and, 60–61, 63, 64n23
    quire divisions in, 124
    Temple called *skene tou martyriou* in, 237
    "The Temple of the Lord" as term, use of, 10, 11
    Verzeichnis (Rahlfs) listing of extant mss., 57–58n3
Seraglio Octateuch. *See* Topkapı Octateuch
Serapion (abba) and the prostitute, 88
Serbian identification with new Israel, 276n80
Sergios the Deacon, 25–26n105
serpent in garden of Eden, Octateuch representations of, 125–26, *128*, *129*, 143
Severus of Antioch (patriarch), 160n28
Sextus Julius Africanus. *See* Julius Africanus
Shahîd, Irfan, 247–48
Sheba, Queen of, 274–75, 284
Shu'ayb (Arab prophet), 289
Simon Magus, 157, 167
Sinai, Monastery of St. Catherine
    MS gr. 30, 101–2
    MS gr. 40, 91n62
    MS gr. 550, 82n24
    MS gr. 869, 84n39
    MS gr. 1186, 139, 141
    MS gr. 2123, 93n69
    MS gr. 2132, 92n65
Sinaiticus codex (London, British Library, Add. MS 43725), 154
singing psalms, monastic disapproval of, 84
Sirach (Ecclesiasticus; biblical book), 156, 200
Sisyphos of Kos, 170n66, 171
Skoutariotes, chronicle of, 158
Slavonic (language)
    John Malalas's chronicle translated into, 169, 171n72
    Palaia, 157n13
    Parimijnik (Slavic Prophetologion), 64
    psalter translated into, 92, 260
    translations of Bible into, 64, 259–61

Sleepless Monks, Monastery of, Constantinople, 85n39
Smith, Jonathan Z., 234
Smyrna Octateuch (Izmir, Evangelical School, MS A.1; presumed destroyed in 1922)
  Bibles moralisées, relationship to, 150n85
  common model, evidence of, 127
  iconography of, 125–26
  Kokkinobaphos Master and, 115
  Kosmas manuscripts and, 137
  place in family of five Byzantine illustrated Octateuchs, 110
  prefatory gatherings missing from, 115
  repairs to, 117
  size of, 118
  Topkapı Octateuch and, 125
  Vat. gr. 746 and, 125
  working processes of artists and scribes, 119, 120, *121*, 123–25
Society of Biblical Literature, 297
Socrates (church historian), 183–84
sola scriptura, Karaite espousal of, 40
Solomon (OT king)
  Anicia Juliana compared to, 245
  in Byzantine dating structure, 163
  Byzantine familiarity with, 74–75
  Constantinopolitan statues of, 247, 249
  emperors identified with, 184, 186, 191, 193, 195, 248–50
  Ethiopia, OT models of the state in, 274–76
  as monastic model, 203
  Queen of Sheba and, 274–75, 284
  relics associated with, 12, 22n87, 173, 191, 238, 249
  Temple of, 5, 224, 242 (*See also* Temple, Jerusalem)
Soncino, Eliezer, 50
Song of Songs (biblical book), 3
Sophronios of Jerusalem (patriarch), 15–16, 18n66
Sozomen (church historian), 178, 181, 184
"speech-in-character" (rhetorical technique), 211
Spencer Psalter (New York, NYPL, MS Spencer gr. 1), 100n97

spiritual exegesis and allegory, monastic, 213–16
Spiritual Homilies (Makarios of Alexandria), 200, 213–14
The Spiritual Meadow (John Moschos), 219
staff of Moses. *See* Rod of Moses
the state. *See* politics and the state
Stephen (saint), martyrdom of, 272n67
Stoudios monastery, 63
Strategios (monk and chronicler), 15
Sumbat Davitisdze, 272, 273
Sylvester (saint), *Life* of, 248
Symeon (Bulgarian tsar), 255, 257, 260, 265n42, 267–68, 277
Symeon, canticle of, 15
Symeon the Logothete, 11
Symeon the Metaphrast, 96
Symeon the New Theologian, 91, 208–9, 215–16
Symeon the Stylite (saint), 206–7
Symmachos (translator of OT into Greek), 44
Synagoge or *Evergetinon* (Paul Evergetinos), 204–5
Synkellos. *See* George Synkellos; Theodore Synkellos
Synkletike, *Life* of, 207–8
synkresis or *comparatio*, OT models for emperors in mode of, 180, 194
syn (Greek) used to render *et* (Hebrew), 47
Syriac *Cave of Treasures*, 143
Syriac Life of Symeon the Stylite, 207
Syro-Aramaic culture, 287

al-Ṭabarī, Abū Jaʿfar b. Jarīr, 279–81, 283n6, 291
Table of Solomon (Constantinople, Great Palace; no longer extant), 12n42, 249
taḥrīf, 293
Talbot, Alice-Mary, vii–viii
Talmud, 40, 41, 44
targum, 41, 50, 284
Temple, Jerusalem
  Bar Kochba coinage, Temple images on, 237
  buildings replicating or superseding, 14
  Dura Europos synagogue paintings, 237
  as epitome of sacred space in Byzantium, 7, 223–26

330   INDEX

Ezekiel, Temple of, 224, *225*, 246
Hagia Sophia, Constantinople, and, 14, 229, 239–43, *240*, 247–52
Herod's Temple, hypothetical reconstruction of, 224, *224*
Holy Sepulchre and, 14, 233–39, *235*, 250, 252
hypothetical reconstructions of, 224, *224–25*
metaphorical relationship of Christian churches to, 226–33, 251–53
physical relationship of Christian churches to, lack of, 227, 231, 242, 251–52
Solomon's Temple, 5, 224, 242
specific architectural symbols associated with, *230*, 230–32, *232*
St. Polyeuktos, Constantinople, and, 14, 243–47, *244*, 252
"The Temple of the Lord" as term, Byzantine use of, 10–12
terminology of Temple applied to church buildings, 225–26
Vandals, recovery of relics from, 248
Zerubbabel, Temple of, 224, 226
Testament of Solomon, 10n31, 74–75
al-Thaʿlabī, Abū Isḥāq Aḥmad b. Muḥammad, 283n5, 284
Themistius (orator), 178, 194
theocracy, Byzantine sense of, 28–29
Theodora (empress), 208
Theodore Daphnopates, 9n26
Theodore Metochites, 36
Theodore Prodromos, 9, 10n27, 25n104, 113
Theodore Psalter (London, British Library, Add. ms 19,352), 30, 93
Theodore Stoudites, 6, 9n26, 10n27, 11, 210
Theodore Synkellos, 16–17, 27, 173, 181, 194
Theodoret of Cyrrhus, 108, 110n15, 169, 181, 184–85, 206–7
Theodosios Diakonos, 9n26
Theodosius I (emperor), 178, 181, 194, 247
Theodosius II (emperor), 183–84
Theodotion (Greek translator of OT), 44
theological history, OT contribution to, 154–55
Theophanes (author of *Chronographia*), 19, 187–88
Theophanes the Confessor, 158, 159n20

Theophanes Continuatus, 169
Theophany, 71
Theophilos (emperor), 11
Theophylaktos Simokattes, 178–79n13, 181n19, 185
Theosophy (John Malalas), 166, 168, 171
Theotokos, Chapel of the, Mt. Nebo, *230*, 230–31
Theotokos Evergetis, Monastery of the, Constantinople, 204
Theotokos Kosmosoteira monastery, Thrace, 113, 205
Thessalonike, massacre at, 181
Thrace, Theotokos Kosmosoteira monastery, 113, 205
Throne of Solomon (Constantinople, hall of the Magnaura, Great Palace; no longer extant), 12, 22n87, 173, 191
Thucydides (classical historian), 170, 185
Thurn, Johannes, 165, 166, 171n72
Tiglath-Pileser III (Assyrian ruler), 155–56
Timotheos (source for John Malalas), 166
Timothy Aelurus (patriarch), 189
Tobit (biblical book), 156
Topkapı Octateuch (Istanbul, Topkapı Sarayı, MS gr. 8)
  iconography of, 125–26, *129*
  Kokkinobaphos Master and, 113–14, 115, 119
  later use, no evidence for, 117
  Letter of Aristeas prefacing, 111–15, *112*
  ownership of, 111
  place in family of five Byzantine illustrated Octateuchs, 110
  sigla, 110n15
  size of, 118
  Smyrna Octateuch and, 125
  unfinished nature of, 118–19
  Vat. gr. 746 and, 125
  Vat. gr. 747 and, 119
  Weitzmann's theory of Jewish pre-Christian origins for illustrations, 145, *148*
  working processes of artists and scribes, 119, *122*, 125
Torah
  Letter of Aristeas on translation into Greek, 111

Torah (*continued*)
   monastic *typikon* functioning as, 206
   oral Torah, 40
   place in Christian jurisprudence, 19, 107
   Qur'ān and, 282, 283
   role in medieval Judaism, 41, 51, 107
   See also Pentateuch
Tougher, Shaun, 249
Traianos, *Epitome* of, 159
Trajan (emperor), 178
Transfiguration of Christ, feast of, 69
translations of OT
   Ethiopic, Octateuchs in, 108
   into Slavonic, 259–61
   See also Greek (language), translations of OT into
Treitinger, Otto, 173
Triodion, 65, 82
Trojan War, in chronicle of John Malalas, 170, 171, 172n75
troparia, 69, 70, 84, 91, 92n65, 96, 104n118
True Cross
   discovery of, 173, 263, 264
   Elevation of the Cross, feast of, 250
   recovery of, 15, 17, 195
   veneration of, 20, 29, 173, 238
Trullo, Council in (Qunisext Council; 692), 18, 19
Tübingen Theosophy, 166
Turin, Biblioteca Reale, cod. Var. 484, 98, 99
Turin, Biblioteca Universitaria, MS B.VII.30, 85n44
Turkic traditions, Bulgarian importation of, 255
typika, 100–101, 205–6, 219, 261
typology
   monastic use of, 216, 220
   OT models for emperors in Christian mode of, 179–81, 190, 192, 194, 195, 197
Tyre, dedicatory speech of Eusebios at cathedral of, 226–27, 229

Uriah the Hittite, 202, 273
Uspenskij, T., 111
Uspensky, B. A., 271
Uspensky Psalter (St. Petersburg, National Library of Russia, MS gr. 216), 80n15, 100
Uzziah/Ozia/Ozias (OT king), 269–70

Valens (emperor), 178, 185, 187, 194
Valentinian (emperor), 185, 189
Vandals, Temple relics recovered from, 248
Vatican Library, Rome
   MS Barberini gr. 336 (Barberini Euchologion), 190n55, 191
   MS Barberini gr. 372 (Barberini Psalter), 95n78
   MS Chisi. R.VIII.54, 119–20
   MS gr. 333, 120
   MS gr. 663, 79n7
   MS gr. 699, 139
   MS gr. 746. *See* Vatican Library MS gr. 746
   MS gr. 747. *See* Vatican Library MS gr. 747
   MS gr. 752, 25, 80n15
   MS gr. 1153–54, 120
   MS gr. 1209 (Codex Vaticanus), 154
   MS Grottaferrata G.B.I (Bessarion), 190–91n55
   MS Palat. gr. 356, 196
   MS Palat. gr. 381, 35n137
   MS Palat. gr. 431. *See* Joshua Roll
   MS Reg. gr. 1 (Leo Bible), 35, 95n78
Vatican Library MS gr. 746 (Octateuch)
   iconography of, 125–26
   Joshua Roll and, 132, 133, *139*, *141*
   Kosmas manuscripts and, 137
   place in family of five Byzantine illustrated Octateuchs, 110
   prefatory gatherings missing from, 115
   sigla, 110n15
   size of, 118
   Smyrna Octateuch and, 125
   Topkapı Octateuch and, 125
   Vat. gr. 747, relationship to, 123, 125
   Vatopedi Octateuch copied from, 115–19, *116*
   working processes of artists and scribes, 119, *123*, 123–25
Vatican Library MS gr. 747 (Octateuch)
   common model, evidence of, 127
   earlier manuscripts, continued use of, 117

iconography of, 125–26
Joshua Roll and, 132, 133, *138, 140*, 142
Kosmas manuscripts and, 139, 143
Letter of Aristeas prefacing, 115
lost Genesis model for, 142
place in family of five Byzantine illustrated Octateuchs, 110
script of, 114
sigla, 110n15
size of, 118
Smyrna Octateuch and, 125
Topkapı Octateuch and, 119, 125
Vat. gr. 746, relationship to, 123, 125
Weitzmann's pre-Christian Jewish theory and, 142, 143
working processes of artists and scribes, 119, 120, *121*, 123–25
Vaticanus codex (Vat. MS gr. 1209), 154
Vatopedi Octateuch (Athos MS Vatopedi 602)
Bibles moralisées compared, 151–52
Genesis and Exodus missing from, 125
Joshua Roll, illustration copied from, 118, 124, 131
ownership of, 114, 115
place in family of five Byzantine illustrated Octateuchs, 110
prefatory gatherings missing from, 115
sigla, 110n15
size of, 118
Vat. gr. 746, copied from, 115–19, *116*
Western mss. compared, 34–35
working processes of artists and scribes, 119, *123*, 124
Venice, Biblioteca Marciana
MS gr. 17 (Psalter of Basil II), 82–83, 114
MS gr. 44, 196n75
MS gr. II.113 (coll. 565), 97–98
Venice, San Marco, Cotton Genesis copied in mosaics of, 144
Verzeichnis (Rahlfs), listing of extant LXX mss. in, 57–58n3
Vienna, Österreichische Nationalbibliothek
MS 1179, 150n85

MS theol. gr. 11, 39, 120
MS theol. gr. 31 (Vienna Genesis), 8, 145, *147*
MS theol. gr. 177 (Psalter Vienna), 84n35
MS theol. gr. 336, 97–98
Virgin Hodegetria icon (Constantinople; destroyed in Ottoman conquest), 38
Vision of Isaiah, 258
visual arts. *See specific items and* Adam and Eve ivory and bone caskets; coins and coinage; manuscripts; Octateuchs; sacred space in Byzantine architecture
Vitae. See under specific person about whom Vita *is written, e.g.*, Gregory Handzteli

Warland, Rainer, 231
Washington DC, Dumbarton Oaks Museum, MS 3, 102–3
Weitzmann, Kurt, 109, 111, 142–50
Western empire. *See* Latin West
Whitby, Mary, 153n, 172n75
Wiedemann, Thomas, 177
Wilkinson, John, 226, 227, 235
William of Tyre, 250n107
wisdom literature, 7, 200, 207–8
world chronicle. *See* Christian World Chronicle
written, oral, and visual tradition, nexus between, 75–76

Yeats, W. B., "Sailing to Byzantium," 253n114

Zacharias, altar with blood of, 238
Zechariah (biblical book), 16, 270n61
Zeno (emperor), 167n55
Zephaniah (biblical book), 236–37
Zerubbabel, Temple of, 224, 226
Zonaras, chronicle of, 125–26, 158
Zuntz, Günther, 55–57, 61–64, 74
Zürich, Zentralbibliothek, RP 1 (*Psalterium aureum Turicense*), 89